Mary McGrory

Also by John Norris

Disaster Gypsies
Collision Course

Mary McGrory

The First Queen
of Journalism

John Norris

VIKING

VIKING
An imprint of Penguin Random House LLC
375 Hudson Street
New York, New York 10014
penguin.com

Portions of this book appeared in *Politico* magazine.

Excerpts from columns published in *The Washington Star* and *The Washington Post* © 2014, The Washington Post. Reprinted with permission.

Photographs appear courtesy of:

The Washingtoniana Collection, District of Columbia Library: pages 2 (bottom), 7 (bottom), 9 (top left), 14 (top)

© The Estate of Garry Winogrand, courtesy Fraenkel Gallery, San Francisco: page 8 (top)

Mary McGrory Papers/Library of Congress: pages 9 (bottom), 10 (center), 11 (center), 12 (top right), 13 (top, center), 15 (top)

Lyndon Baines Johnson Presidential Library: page 10 (top)

Copyright The Estate of Bill Eppridge: page 11 (bottom)

Richard Nixon Presidential Library: page 12 (bottom)

All other photographs: Courtesy of the McGrory / Beatty Families

ISBN 978-0-525-42971-5

Printed in the United States of America
1 3 5 7 9 10 8 6 4 2

Set in Garamond Premier Pro
Designed by Francesca Belanger

To my wife, Brenda,
and children, Ian, Eliza, and Phoebe
who make my heart brim with love, laughter, and joy

Contents

Mary McGrory

CHAPTER ONE

A Boston Girl from Out of the Blue

In April 1954, Newbold "Newby" Noyes, an editor at the *Washington Evening Star*, strode into the paper's book review department. He approached Mary McGrory's desk carrying two cold bottles of root beer. McGrory had been reviewing books at the *Star* for more than a decade and was known as a sparkling wit and one of the finest wordsmiths on the staff.

Noyes offered her a root beer as he pulled up a chair and opened with an unusually candid question in tones loud enough to be heard across the room. "Say, Mary, aren't you ever going to get married?"

Mary knew that he wasn't just making small talk. There were precious few women in the newspaper business, and editors often demanded that they quit if they wed. Some female reporters went so far as to hide their marriages to avoid being dismissed.

"Well, you know, I hope so," Mary responded, "but I don't know."

"Well, because if you're not going to get married," Noyes continued, "we want you to do something different. We just always figured that you would get married and have a baby and leave us, so we haven't tried to do a great deal. But we think you can do more."

McGrory asked Noyes what "doing more" might entail.

He put it simply: "We think you should add humor and color and charm and flair to the news pages."

Mary sipped her root beer and smiled coyly. "Oh, is that all?" Her response was glib, but she recognized the opportunity. Mary always embraced the advice she had once laughingly given an intimidated relative when he walked up to the buffet at a Washington gala: "Always approach the shrimp bowl like you own it."

"Yes," Noyes said. "We want you to start at the Army-McCarthy hearings."

The Army-McCarthy hearings marked a pivotal point not only for Senator Joseph McCarthy of Wisconsin, but for the nation. By early 1954, McCarthy had aggressively gone after alleged Communists in the State Department and the U.S. military on the basis of largely fabricated evidence, denigrated a number of senior officers appearing before his committee, and even taken on President Dwight Eisenhower, suggesting that the president wasn't fully committed to fighting Communism.

An enraged Eisenhower eventually adopted a more confrontational approach, and the administration argued that McCarthy's chief counsel, Roy Cohn, had sought special treatment for one of McCarthy's former staffers who had been drafted into the army.

The high-stakes Army-McCarthy hearings, charged with getting to the bottom of the matter, commenced on April 22, 1954, and were televised live to a spellbound nation.

Noyes offered Mary McGrory some basic advice as she went to cover the hearings: "Now, you must go every day, and you must watch everything, and you must take lots of notes."

McGrory entered the Senate hearings, she later said, "paralyzed with fear" and overwhelmed by the crush of reporters, staffers, Capitol Police officers, and spectators jammed into the room. Suddenly a friendly face materialized: Mike Dowd, the police inspector in charge of Senate security. He escorted McGrory to a front-row seat at a long press table. Dowd, an Irish immigrant whose daughter Maureen would go on to become McGrory's colleague and close friend, later said he had just wanted to help a nice Irish girl on her first big assignment.

As the vituperative anti-Communist crusader entered the hearing room amid a cascade of flashbulbs and shouted questions, McGrory felt a twinge of recognition. "I had seen his likes all my life, at wakes, at weddings, at the junior prom," McGrory observed of McCarthy. "He was an Irish bully boy."

McCarthy kept Roy Cohn close at hand as his legal counsel. Joseph Welch, a dignified six-foot-three, sixty-three-year-old trial lawyer from Boston, served as counsel for the army. McCarthy's objections during the proceedings were so frequent that his nasal "Point of order" refrain soon became a national catchphrase.

When Mary returned to the *Star* from her first day of hearings, she sat down to pull together her furiously scribbled notes. She struggled. Noyes's verdict on her first draft was blunt: "No. No. No. No, Mary." The column read like a wire service story. He wanted her to write like a drama critic covering a play. He wanted her to put readers in the room. "Write it like a letter to your favorite aunt."

After six hours of flustered rewrites, McGrory's first column appeared on April 23, 1954. She took Noyes's instruction almost literally, and the column began: "It's too early yet to tell about the plot, but they've certainly got a cast there. The star, Senator McCarthy, ploughs his high-shouldered way through the crowds amid small cheers." McGrory described Cohn as looking like a boy who had been reprimanded at school and "come back with his elders to get the thing straightened out." Secretary of the Army Robert Stevens looked "about as dangerous as an Eagle Scout."

Her voice was distinctly her own, no mimic of the established reporters of the day. It might have been her only shot at working in the newsroom, but she avoided playing it safe. McCarthy had destroyed the careers of scores of journalists, politicians, and government employees who had dared to oppose him as the Red Scare consumed the nation, yet Mary was willing to portray him as obnoxious and overbearing. The *Star* had always been conservative in its editorial line, but suddenly a fresh, impertinent voice was leaping off the page, covering the biggest story in town with a decidedly liberal bent.

With the first column under her belt, Mary returned for the second day of hearings still feeling somewhat overwhelmed. Noyes suggested that she feature army counsel Joseph Welch in a column, but Mary was hesitant.

Noyes, who was pleased with the eventual results of Mary's first column, prodded. "Well, what did you notice about Welch?"

Mary was struck by the contrast between Welch's calm and Senator McCarthy's lurid paranoia. Welch wore a vest and sported a pocket watch. He was polite and courtly. "He keeps telling you there is another world," Mary shared with Noyes. "He's always pulling out his watch and saying, 'Well, I can get the 5:15 train to Boston if we are going to adjourn at such and such an hour,' always bringing the normal, ordinary world into the room."

"Well, I think you better write him," coaxed Noyes. She did. "In the flood of the lighted jungle of the hearing room, Mr. Welch, who might have stepped out of the *Pickwick Papers*, does not appear entirely in his element," Mary wrote. "A tall man, he has a long face and owlish eyes. He beams rather than smiles, and sometimes when he is listening to a witness he puts the tips of his fingers together and looks as rapt as one might who was listening to the fine strains from the Boston Symphony Orchestra."

Mary had found a good guy in a story that badly needed one, and she and Welch would develop a lasting friendship.

But being on deadline was a new and unnerving experience for the former book reviewer. The newsroom clocks induced despair. While Mary wrote beautifully, she was a bleeder, sweating over every sentence. She chewed her pencils, chain-smoked, and nervously balled up scraps of newspaper in her fingers, which Chick Yarbrough, a fellow reporter, took to calling "anguishes." One morning, he playfully counted the wads of paper scattered across Mary's desk and left her a note. "There were 36 anguishes last night; you must have had a very bad time."

Mary's coverage of the hearings for the afternoon newspaper was unflinching. She described Welch staring at McCarthy as "a scientist might observe a new and unpredictable monster." Her columns quickly became the talk of the town. In just a few days of covering the McCarthy hearings, Mary received more mail than she had in thirteen years reviewing books, and she responded to all of it—as she would her entire career. As

Mary recalled, "All of a sudden people wanted to adopt me, marry me, poison me, run me out of town." "So you have joined the hate campaign against our good Senator McCarthy and Mr. Cohn," one reader complained. "Your article in Friday's *Star* is plainly the product of a person of low-class breeding and retarded mentality."

But others were kind. Readers asked Mary the color of her eyes, her favorite food, and whether she was single. A nurse in a local hospital wrote to Mary, telling her that the patients in the recovery room eagerly awaited her stories every night. A caller to the *Star*'s switchboard thanked Mary for having "more courage than most of the men" writing about McCarthy. A couple from Maryland, fearing for Mary's safety, wrote to ask if someone was protecting her. (Mary's all-time favorite piece of fan mail came from a reader who insisted, "I hope to make the name Mary McGregory a household word." The cartoonist Herbert Block henceforth insisted on calling Mary "McGregory" whenever they spoke.)

Not everyone at the *Star* was happy with Mary's sudden prominence. The paper's managing editor, Herbert Corn, disliked the informal tone of Mary's work and thought her approach was risky, even dangerous. He also took considerable grief from other editors for letting a woman cover politics. Newby Noyes kept Corn at bay.

Mary never described her coverage of McCarthy as courageous or innovative, but it was both. The writing was fluid and intimate. Her willingness to direct sarcasm at McCarthy was radical. Longtime CBS news anchor Roger Mudd commented, "It was the Eisenhower era, the McCarthy era; it was a time of intense conformity, and she didn't conform." She wrote about the foibles and hypocrisies of senators and presidents as comfortably—and as pointedly—as though she were sitting at the kitchen table gossiping about the neighbors. Her writing just felt different. Her powers of observation were superb. Howard Shuman, a longtime Hill staffer who saw Mary in action many times over the years, marveled, "Mary could look at the back of the neck of someone and tell you what their real personality was."

Slim, vivacious, and attractive, Mary was a fresh face among the almost exclusively male press corps. Radio newsman Walter Winchell and
columnist Walter Lippmann both went out of their way to say how much
they enjoyed her columns. Mary also became quite close to political columnist Doris Fleeson, who worked for the United Feature Syndicate.
Mary not only emulated Fleeson's strong belief in the merits of doing her
own legwork but was also a fan of her sartorial style, marveling that when
she visited Fleeson at her Georgetown townhouse, she "found the scourge
of statesmen sewing fresh white collar and cuffs on her dark blue dress."
As the buzz around Mary's Army-McCarthy columns grew to a roar, it
was Fleeson who observed, "She's been coiled up on her bookshelf all
these years just waiting to strike."

Throughout the hearings, McCarthy continually threatened his Senate colleagues, but in the hearing room and across the nation, the senator's
abrasive appeal was wearing thin.

It was obvious that Roy Cohn had sought special treatment for David
Schine, the unpaid McCarthy investigative aide serving as a private at
Fort Dix who had been granted extra leave and lighter duties because of
his ties to McCarthy and Cohn. (It was a poorly kept secret that Roy
Cohn was a closeted homosexual, and he seemed to have had unrecipro-
cated romantic feelings toward Schine.) The hearings degenerated into a
steady stream of mutual recriminations. As Mary wrote one day before
the hearing's most iconic moment, "No doctor is in attendance at the
McCarthy-Army hearings, because the only thing likely to be slain is a
man's good name, and there's no cure for that."

On June 9, 1954, Senator McCarthy, annoyed with Welch's line of
questioning, accused one of the attorneys at the Bostonian's firm of having Communist ties. Welch had kept the attorney in question, Fred
Fisher, away from the hearings because he knew that he was vulnerable;
Fisher had briefly belonged to a blacklisted group after law school. Welch
and Cohn had made a gentleman's agreement that Fisher's name would
not come up during the hearings. Mary set the scene: "During the six

stormy weeks of the hearings, Mr. Welch has borne Senator McCarthy's personal attacks on him with equanimity and grace, sometimes merely acknowledging them with an interested nod. But the senator's attack on Mr. Welch's friend brought an end to this silent toleration of McCarthyism. It also brought forth a display of eloquence and indignation that rocked the caucus room."

Welch's words were powerful as he made a plea to not assault the integrity of a man he knew well: "Until this moment, Senator, I think I never really gauged your cruelty or your recklessness." McCarthy disregarded Welch's protests until Welch finally reached his breaking point: "Let us not assassinate this lad further, Senator. You have done enough. Have you no sense of decency, sir, at long last? Have you left no sense of decency?" After a bit more sparring, Welch made clear he was done with the matter: "If there is a God in heaven, it will do neither you nor your cause any good. I will not discuss it further." The room burst into applause. McCarthy was heard muttering, "What did I do? What did I do?" after the exchange. Welch, too, was shaken by the back-and-forth. Mary wrote that he was "looking for once, every minute of his sixty-three years."

But Welch had broken McCarthy's thrall. The senator's popularity plummeted after the hearings. McCarthy was censured by his Senate colleagues before quickly descending deep into alcoholism. He was dead three short years later—a broken and disgraced figure, although still revered by his most die-hard partisans.

Mary produced a column from every single day of the hearings, thirty-six in total, and her career exploded onto the national stage. Her coverage of the Army-McCarthy hearings reached the final round of consideration for the Pulitzer Prize that year. Tom Oliphant, who was the *Boston Globe*'s Washington correspondent for many years, argued that Mary's work was "central to McCarthy's demise—in the same way Edward R. Murrow's work in the young medium of television at CBS was—because it was devastatingly accurate as opposed to self-indulgently accusatory."

What was it about Mary that felt so different, so revolutionary? It wasn't just being a woman in a man's town, though that might have helped. It wasn't just that she wrote beautifully, which she did. At the time, focusing on the personal side of politics and what made politicians tick seemed almost rebellious. What was new was television, and McGrory realized that with the advent of these instant images, print reporters needed to offer a more evocative take on the day's events if they hoped to compete with the evening news.

While Mary McGrory not only changed the notion of whom we were willing to accept as a journalist and fundamentally altered how we talk about politics, her career arc was unexpected. Mary's backstory was humble. She was born in the Roslindale neighborhood of Boston on August 22, 1918—two years before women were given the right to vote. Her father was a postal clerk, and her mother did part-time accounting work to help make ends meet.

Mary was fond of describing her first-generation upbringing as equal parts romantic and puritanical. Her father represented the romantic part of the equation, and indeed, Mary's reminiscences of her father are so glowing that they need to be taken with a grain of salt. According to Mary, her father, Edward McGrory, was a true Christian gentleman who taught her to cherish literature, long walks, and fresh raspberries. By Mary's own account, her father was the finest Latin scholar ever to attend South Weymouth High School and was awarded a coveted scholarship to Dartmouth that he was never able to take advantage of because his father died shortly before freshman year. He had to abandon his studies to support his seven younger siblings.

If Mary's father brought the light Irish romanticism to her upbringing, her mother, Mary Catherine McGrory, brought a steely puritanism. Deeply religious and a disciplinarian, Mary's mother had an exceedingly well concealed sense of humor. Everyone who knew Mary agreed that her own charm was intertwined with a rigid, even authoritarian, streak. "She was not a laughing Colleen," observed Mary's close friend and fellow Bostonian Mark Shields. "There was a sternness, an assertiveness, that one did not necessarily associate with Irish at that time." Mary's nieces and nephew talked about this side of Mary's personality, fairly or unfairly, as coming from her mother.

Mary idolized her father throughout her life, writing about him in her columns and sharing warm anecdotes about him. By contrast, Mary never wrote a word about her mother in a single column, never mentioned her mother to friends later in life, never talked about her in a single interview, and never discussed her impact on any facet of her upbringing. "I only heard her speak of her father with the utmost love, affection, respect, and admiration," recalled Elizabeth Shannon, who knew Mary for decades. "I literally never heard her say anything about her mother—good or bad." Mary was not estranged from her mother, but the relationship was chilly.

Identity was paramount in the Boston of Mary's youth. The city's Irish, Italian, Jewish, German, and other communities mixed either uneasily or not at all. Bigotry ran hot. Protestants disparaged Catholics as unwashed pawns of the pope. Irish Catholic priests threatened their flocks with excommunication for even participating in Protestant weddings. It was an atmosphere where your last name and church set your course. The Boston Irish maintained a fierce us-against-them mentality, even as they evolved from oppressed minority to a dominant majority in the city. As the Boston Irish increasingly controlled the city, they propelled the Protestant elite, or "Brahmins," out toward well-heeled suburbs.

Mary's parents represented an intermarriage of sorts. The McGrory half of her lineage was indeed Irish, emigrating from County Donegal in the 1860s, but her mother's maiden name was Jacobs, and her family had emigrated from Germany to Boston in the 1880s.

The German influence on Mary's upbringing was considerable. Her household was bilingual. Mary's favorite dish as a girl wasn't corned beef and cabbage; it was sauerbraten and spaetzle. Yet as an adult, Mary virtually never mentioned the German side of her heritage. Her friends and colleagues later in life had no idea that she was of anything other than purely Irish descent. All of them saw Mary's fundamental Irishness as central to her personality—which, although something of a contrivance, it was.

Perhaps this is not surprising. Mary grew up in a very Irish Catholic neighborhood in a very Irish Catholic town in a period bookended by two world wars fought against the Germans. She had a good Boston Irish name and a mother with little discernible accent, and nothing was to be gained in social settings, school, or the workplace by self-identifying as anything other than Boston Irish. Mary decided that her public face would be that of a McGrory rather than a Jacobs, and with the zeal of a convert she became more Irish than any Irishman. Like her mother, Mary's German heritage was simply written out of the story.

With her family deeply committed to her education, McGrory was accepted to the Girls' Latin School, in Boston, the finest public school for young women in the United States at the time. It was a stroke of good fortune, and it was at Girls' Latin that Mary developed a manner that convinced most who met her later in life that she must have come from a wealthy East Coast family.

The school, located on Huntington Avenue in Boston, was famously demanding. As seventh graders, the girls waded through Caesar's *Commentaries on the Gallic War* in Latin, and Mary likened the course work to service in the Marine Corps: "It was basically impossible."

Although only a ten-cent trolley-car ride away from her neighborhood, Girls' Latin thrust Mary into a different—and far more urbane—world. The school was a short walk from the wonders of Copley Square: the Museum of Fine Arts and its magnificent John Singer Sargent murals, the Romanesque spires of Trinity Church, and the beautiful arched reading rooms of the Boston Public Library, where Mary worked summers shelving books.

The years at Girls' Latin cemented Mary's love of the written word. As a voracious reader she gravitated to the melodrama and heaving bosoms of period pieces like *Wuthering Heights* and *Jane Eyre*. Mary's musings in her journal at the time were deeply bifurcated. One moment she would dream of a career as a reporter or a famous author, and the next she would resign herself to being a schoolteacher or being trapped in

Roslindale in perpetuity. She toyed with the idea of becoming a nun. She always attended Sunday Mass and was never one to get in trouble or be disrespectful. Yet underneath the surface she yearned for the adventures of a fictional heroine. Mary's buttoned-down manner concealed a streak of impetuousness, and her ambitions felt at odds with her prospects. It was as if the world of literature had allowed her to glimpse a new world of which she could not be part.

Mary went on to become the first in her family to graduate from university—Emmanuel College, in Boston. (Mary had her heart set on attending Radcliffe College, Harvard's all-women sister school, but her scholarship application was rejected because of her mediocre math and science scores.)

Mary graduated from Emmanuel with a bachelor of arts degree in English in June 1939, and by her twenty-first birthday she was enrolled at the Hickox Secretarial School, learning typing and shorthand. The restless optimism of the Girls' Latin years was gone. "With the passing of the years has come the realization that I shall not, as I have always fondly fancied, grow up to be a remarkable woman," Mary wrote at the time. Neither employment nor romance were anywhere in sight.

On September 8, 1939, after a bout of pneumonia, Edward McGrory passed away. He was fifty-nine years old. News of Europe descending into the horrors of World War II dominated the headlines. It was a dark time, and by January 1940 Mary was feeling theatrically sorry for herself, bemoaning that her best hope was to "find some nice congenial job in a nut and bolt factory, and settle down to a nice, even melancholy for the rest of my lonely days."

Her mood rebounded considerably in March 1940, when she landed a job cropping pictures for textbooks in the art department at the Houghton Mifflin Publishing Company, earning $16.50 a week. After about a year, and against her mother's advice, Mary left the relative security of her position for a brief, unhappy stint working on a local mayoral campaign in 1941.

Again out of work, Mary decided to pursue her dream of working at a newspaper. She had been attracted to journalism as a girl by reading about the comic strip adventures of Jane Arden, a prototypical spunky female reporter.

Thanks to a tip from one of her former Houghton Mifflin colleagues, Mary landed a position as an assistant to Alice Dixon Bond, the literary editor of the *Boston Herald Traveler*, in 1942. (The *Herald* and the *Traveler* were separate papers housed in the same building.) Mary and Bond had little in common. Bond was a Beacon Hill socialite inclined to floral prints and pearls who covered the literary scene in the fawning tones of a high-minded gossip columnist. The book review department was staid, but Mary loved the chaos of the nearby newsroom, with its pastepots, piles of newspapers cluttering the surfaces of cramped rows of wooden desks, and editors yelling to be heard over the din.

Mary started out in journalism with no connections and no credentials, at a time when the field was dominated by men, from publishers down to the lowliest copyboy—hardly a suitable profession for a nice Catholic girl from Roslindale. As author and media historian Eric Alterman joked, "Reporting was seen as a job for winos, perverts, and those without sufficient imagination to become gangsters."

Mary longed to work in the newsroom, but Alice Dixon Bond viewed Mary's ambitions as unlikely and improper. Frustrated, Mary appealed directly to George Minot, the *Herald Traveler*'s editor, for a chance to write color stories or features. Minot brushed her off, saying that she was too shy to make a good reporter.

In March 1946, Mary's editors grudgingly agreed to let her write a column about her dog. Her story about Mac, her unruly pet with the demeanor of the "MGM lion with a hangover," was a surprise hit with readers. In a stroke of luck that would irretrievably change her life, John Hutchens, the editor of the *New York Times Book Review*, read some of Mary's work and liked it. Hutchens asked Mary if she would be interested in writing occasional reviews for the *Times* while keeping her position at the *Herald Traveler*.

Mary's review of Richard Burke's *Reluctant Hussy* appeared in the *Times Book Review* in June 1946, with Mary declaring it to be "an unabashed bonbon of a novel." A review in the *Times* was a significant feat for any writer; it was almost unheard of for a twenty-eight-year-old woman in the 1940s. Arthur Gelb, the former managing editor of the *Times*, commented, "The *Book Review* was so sacrosanct, such an institution, it had such power, that getting your name in that *Book Review* became one of the great achievements." In 1946, the *Times* had only four women working as reporters or editors, all of whom were junior staffers relegated to a single row of desks.

In the spring of 1947, Hutchens informed Mary that the *Washington Star* was looking for an assistant book critic, and she made the leap, moving to the nation's capital in August to begin working at the *Star* for a salary of seventy dollars per week. Mary expected her mother to disapprove, but her aunt Kate came to the rescue, saying that she would look after Mary's mother. For Mary, her aunt Kate's willingness to assume these family responsibilities was a gift beyond measure. She finally had freedom to roam beyond Roslindale. Despite Mary's eagerness to escape Boston, she loved it all the more for having left it.

Arriving in a capital that had become a boomtown as a result of the growth of government during World War II, Mary was struck by a feeling of openness and mobility. Washington's avenues were broad and tree-lined, unlike Boston's cramped streets. More important, "in Boston, your name or your face froze you into place," she said. "In Washington, nobody knew exactly who anybody else was," allowing her to invent herself as the person she wanted to be. While her identity had been a source of persistent unease in Roslindale, her slightly airbrushed image as classically Boston Irish became a source of enduring pride in Washington.

The *Washington Star* was one of the most important and successful newspapers in America at the time. Founded in 1852, the paper was owned and run by three families: the Kauffmanns, Noyeses, and Adamses. The *Star* was moderately conservative in outlook, a pillar of the Republican establishment. Tradition meant a great deal at the paper, and legend had it that President Abraham Lincoln had personally handed Crosby S. Noyes a copy of his second inaugural address so it could be printed in the *Star*.

Afternoon newspapers like the *Star* were a daily marvel at a time when most people still settled down to read the news after getting home from work. The *Star* actually produced five different versions of the paper throughout the course of the day, from its first edition, at nine in the morning, to the final edition of the day, the "red streak," which had the closing numbers for Wall Street and was sold only at newsstands. All of its home deliveries were of afternoon editions, and deadlines for the *Star*'s reporters and columnists were all pinned to its identity as an afternoon paper.

It was a massively labor-intensive operation. Reporters called in stories to dictationists, who typed on mimeograph paper. The stories were physically cut and pasted together after being marked up by editors, manually set in type, and printed. The *Star* traditionally hired many of its press operators from the local school for the deaf, Gallaudet University, since they were unperturbed by the ceaseless noise from the huge presses. The relentless pressure to deliver created a great spirit at the *Star*, and the newsroom was loose, chaotic, boozy, and full of gifted, difficult souls. Getting the story meant everything. "It was heaven," Mary said. "Just a wonderful, kind, welcoming, funny place, full of eccentrics and desperate people trying to meet five deadlines a day."

Mary fit in easily at the *Star*. "Newsrooms are large places, full of messy desks and lippy people who hang around gossiping and making cheeky remarks about their betters," she later recounted, "until deadlines, when they become distraught, turn pale, or red, groan, bark, curse, kick wastebaskets, and behave in the other socially unacceptable ways common to people who must write in a hurry."

The freewheeling atmosphere of the newsroom was usually transported to the preferred neighborhood bar, the Chicken Hut, after hours. Mary sang, drank, and smoked along with the boys as reporters gabbed about stories, complained about editors, and lambasted one another's mistakes. For Mary, the *Star* was like Girls' Latin School leavened with sarcasm, alcohol, and nicotine. Thrilled with her new circumstances, Mary put romance on the back burner, leading one of her friends to complain that she was giving short shrift even to men with "all a gal could want."

Although Mary fit in with reporters, her Catholicism set her slightly apart from the rest of the breed. She didn't like it when reporters gambled, and she took the Church's dim view of things like premarital sex seriously. She also had an abiding belief in the importance of doing good works. Not long after settling in Washington, Mary visited the St. Ann's Infant and Maternity Home, a short walk away from where she was living, by Dupont Circle. St. Ann's was a refuge for unwed mothers and their children, and its clientele was mostly young Catholic girls who had gotten into trouble.

Mary introduced herself to the sisters who ran St. Ann's. Chatting over tea, she opined that many of the single women she met in Washington were alarmingly self-absorbed, and she wanted to volunteer at the orphanage. The sisters, never having had a volunteer, weren't sure what to make of this insistent young woman. As they tried to diplomatically say "No, thank you," one of the orphans wandered in from the playground and clambered into Mary's lap. With upturned eyes, he asked Mary if she was going to stay the night. St. Ann's had its first volunteer.

Mary became a fixture at St. Ann's. Since many of the children struggled with the rolling *r*'s of her last name, they took to calling her Mary Gloria. Mary loved the mispronunciation; it sounded exotic and Italian. For more than five decades, she spent hours each week reading with the children and trying to give them the small, unremarkable luxuries of a normal family life—someone to kiss a skinned elbow or teach them the alphabet song. "Mary could be wearing her nicest clothes, and be headed to a fancy embassy dinner party right after helping out at St. Ann's," Sister Mary Bader explained, "but she would never flinch as a muddy kid came right off the playground into her arms."

Mary was brazen in pressing others at the *Star* into her cause. It was Mary's insistence on enforced volunteerism that led columnist Maureen Dowd to describe her as "she who must be obeyed." Few of her fellow reporters dared say no when it came to helping with the field trips and picnics for the kids from St. Ann's. Every "volunteer" was given a clearly assigned role—from driving the van to making peanut-butter-and-mayonnaise sandwiches. Any volunteer who missed the "junior picnics" with the children was not allowed to attend the "senior picnics"—the alcohol-soaked dinners that followed.

Mary instituted an annual Christmas party for the orphans, usually held at the house of a coworker. She soon enlisted Tommy Noyes, the youngest of three Noyes brothers at the paper, to play Santa. The Christmas party evolved so that it was staged around the same careful ritual every year: Santa would pretend to be asleep on the couch when the orphans arrived, and the children would rouse him with a steadily rising chorus of "Jingle Bells." Santa would then provide gentle encouragement and admonitions to the children before gifts were opened. As the columnist Anthony Lewis observed, "I can't imagine any other journalist in Washington doing what she did with the children."

Back at the *Star*, Mary complained that "no one seemed to pay the slightest attention" to her book reviews, but her time in the book department helped shape her personality in important ways. She learned to deliver a tough critique and look an author in the eye afterwards. She came to appreciate that the most successful authors made themselves into their most interesting characters. She began to develop an eye for fashion, and she could hold her own in conversation with even the most jaded of reporters. But hers remained a small job in a much bigger world.

While still reviewing books, Mary prodded editor Newby Noyes for a chance to cover politics, and finally, in 1953, Newby suggested that she do a series of profiles on some of the more interesting politicians in town. These were the first stories to showcase classic Mary style and craftsmanship. She described Senator Alexander Wiley of Wisconsin as running on a platform of "preparedness, non-intervention, and cheese" in speeches that displayed "marvelous disregard for unity, coherence, and emphasis."

Mary's 1953 profile of Lyndon Baines Johnson, who had just become Senate minority leader, drew the most attention. Mary spent a good deal of time with Johnson as she prepared her story, and the senator already had a reputation for intimidating even the most battle-hardened journalists. But Mary was not cowed by the voluble LBJ, and she delivered a solid character study of the Texan.

Mary, as she would do many times in the years to come, got a quote out of Johnson that was a little more quotable than he would have liked. Johnson told Mary that while many people in Washington thought he was too conservative, his constituents back home tended to think he was too liberal. "I'm a Communist in Texas," drawled LBJ, "and a Dixiecrat in Washington." Johnson liked the quote until it started appearing in Texas newspapers and he was forced to downplay it. After the piece ran, Johnson wrote to Mary in buttery tones, saying how glad he was that Mary had enjoyed her visit and how pleasurable it had been "to cooperate with such an acute and perceptive writer."

It was Mary's political profiles that gave Newby Noyes the confidence to send her to cover the Army-McCarthy hearings in 1954. After languishing as a book reviewer for thirteen years, with her heart in politics the entire time, opportunities suddenly unfurled before McGrory.

Soon after the hearings, Mary was moved to the national desk, an almost unheard-of step at the *Star* for a reporter who had not first served a shift at the city desk. "Some old hands took a dim view of having a woman on the national staff, particularly one with such wispy credentials and provocative views," Mary reflected. "But ancient cub as I was, I was launched at last."

By August 1954, James "Scotty" Reston, the powerhouse Washington bureau chief and columnist for the *New York Times*, had begun aggressively courting Mary to jump to his paper. Reston had earned a reputation as the quintessential Washington insider, a reporter who was a leader of the very establishment he covered. Reston approached Mary suggesting that he didn't really have a slot open but was interested in fitting her into his talented team.

But the negotiations with Reston took a dramatic turn for the worse, spawning a piece of journalistic lore in Washington in the process. He told Mary that he would love to have her working at the *Times*, but she would also need to "handle the switchboard in the morning." A near Pulitzer winner, Mary was being asked to answer the phones in addition to her other duties. "It was such a gross insult there was nowhere to begin," Mary said, "because it showed a mind-set that there was no getting around. I was so embarrassed for him that I didn't really tell anyone at the time."

Anthony Lewis, who worked under Reston in the Washington bureau around the same time, saw Mary as a cultural challenge for Reston and the *Times*. "The paper was very antsy about reporters having a point of view," he said. Arthur Gelb concurred: "In those days, the *Times* was very restrictive in terms of giving writers license, and I don't know if Mary would have been happy at a paper like the *Times*."

The United Press also offered Mary a position as a columnist but made clear that she would first have to serve a stint as a wire service reporter. "What's the point of that?" she said. "That's like a dog walking on its hind legs. It's quite remarkable that he can do it, but what does it prove?"

The *Star*'s increasingly successful crosstown rival, the *Washington Post*, also took a run at Mary around 1958. Phil and Katharine Graham invited Mary to dinner, which Mary described as one of "those fabled, dazzling affairs where I sat next to notables whom I had no other chance of meeting, especially if I had written rude things about them." When Phil Graham put together a lucrative bid for Mary's services, she wrote to Newby Noyes, who was vacationing at his family home in Sorrento, Maine. Newby's reply was prompt: "Don't you move a goddamn inch." He gave her a raise and showered her with acclaim. Mary stayed put.

With her newfound success, Mary was able to also begin exploring the world, and she began what became an annual vacation pilgrimage to Italy.

On her trips, she would sit on the Spanish Steps, try on dresses at Fontana's, and eat lasagna verde on the Piazza del Popolo. She luxuriated. She sipped Campari and sodas at the bar of the Plaza Hotel, where she stayed and where she became something of an icon: Maria Gloria, *la giornalista americana.* The staff effusively encouraged her halting efforts to speak Italian. Mary sometimes traveled with friends to Italy but often went by herself. "It didn't matter where in Italy, she was ready to accept any of it, and love all of it," remembered her friend Gerry Kirby.

Mary's friends back in Roslindale recognized that she was becoming cosmopolitan in ways that seemed difficult to fathom. Visiting her apartment in Washington felt like an introduction into a foreign land, a whirlwind of politics, cocktail parties, and world events. But there was also a lingering sense among her friends and family in Boston that maybe Mary should put aside the foolishness of the newspaper business, come home, get married, and have children. Indeed, when she had a chance to watch Mary work anxiously on deadline during a visit to Washington, her mother commented, "You should have taken the job with the phone company."

In 1955, Mary visited the picturesque town of Positano, Italy, with its colorful houses rising sharply up from the coast like a disheveled wedding cake. A local festival was scheduled to begin the next day, and Mary watched frantic preparations on the beach as volunteers built and decorated a bandstand. There were sack races, and local boys tried to scale a greased flagpole. Around noon, some of the revelers climbed under the bandstand to sleep before an afternoon parade.

As Mary stood on the terrace watching the fireworks that completed the day, an Italian man, Vito Rispoli, caught her eye. "I didn't like him," recalled Mary, "or so I thought." The next day, Mary traveled by boat to the island of Capri. While Capri was lovely, a discouraged Mary thought it was so romantic that it should be declared off-limits to all but honeymooners. After dinner back at the hotel, Mary again bumped into Vito, and she was charmed. They talked about Positano and the chaotic state of Italian politics. Vito made her laugh.

Vito appeared at the hotel the next evening as well. When an English-woman knocked a table over and onto Mary's foot, Vito leapt up. He joked that the foot might have to be cut off as he ordered the waitstaff to bring ice and bandages. Mary turned scarlet as a crowd of cooks, bellboys, and fellow guests gathered around, but she was beguiled by Vito's lavish attention.

After an evening out with a fellow traveler, Vito and Mary ended up in Positano's deserted piazza. He put his head in her lap as they talked of travel and philosophy; he called her pet names.

The next day, Mary went off for some solo sightseeing, but her mind was on her Italian squire. That night she wore her best brown-and-blue dress. Mary and Vito walked through the steep streets and then sat on the pier, looking out at the Mediterranean. He asked her questions about relationships and sex. She blushed. The two went back to Vito's room, and he tried every form of persuasion to get her to spend the night. She was torn but retreated to her hotel. Mary, despite having had a number of boyfriends, was in her thirties and still single, at a time when most young women were married in their twenties.

Mary extended her stay. After a day at the beach, she and Vito went up to the piazza in the afternoon to watch the Sunday crowds heading for the cinema. He offered running commentary on the passersby. Mary again went to Vito's room. The sound of an accordion in the distance added to her longing.

Vito asked Mary to explain why she was so reluctant to make love. She was unable to provide an explanation that seemed rational by his standards. Mary walked back to her room, thinking she would never see Vito again.

But he appeared at the hotel for dinner again that night. Mary thought it gallant. It was not long before the two were again engrossed in conversation on the stone steps by the town's lion statues. "He was so amusing and perceptive, in that setting especially, so much a man," Mary wrote.

After several brandies, Vito tried one more time. He argued that cigarettes were to be smoked, food to be eaten, women to be loved. He said

Mary was like the sea itself: slow to warm but likely to hold its warmth for a long time. He said she was a strange woman. "And considering how I felt about him, I had to agree," Mary confided to her journal. "This has been an argument with him and others for many years." Mary could not bring herself to sleep with him. In all likelihood, she was still a virgin. She confessed that she was not always sure why: "I trust God knows the answer, for I do not." With considerable remorse, Mary passionately kissed Vito goodbye.

CHAPTER TWO

Arrived

In August 1956, Newby Noyes dispatched his new political reporter to cover the presidential campaign pitting the enormously popular President Eisenhower against the Democratic standard-bearer, Illinois governor Adlai Stevenson. Mary was initially assigned to cover Stevenson's running mate, Senator Estes Kefauver of Tennessee.

"There's just one question we want answered in our stories about campaigns," Newby told Mary as he sent her out on the trail: "How is he doing?" Joining a small corps of largely young and untested reporters that included Tom Winship of the *Boston Globe* and Blair Clark of CBS News, Mary immersed herself in an odyssey of small towns, second-rate hotels, and county fairs. It was exhausting, exhilarating, and slightly ridiculous in the way that only campaigns can be. The reporters on the Kefauver campaign were tight-knit, spending their days banging out stories on planes and buses and their nights drinking and dissecting the day's events.

Kefauver was the kind of politician that reporters loved: a loquacious, progressive southerner who drank too much and had an eye for the ladies. The senator was candid over drinks on the campaign plane, confident that his comments were off the record when he wanted them to be. He was also a relentless campaigner. "Unlike Mr. Stevenson, who persists in regarding the campaign speech as an art form," Mary penned, "Senator Kefauver obviously still believes that the road to the White House is paved with pressed palms."

For a former corporate lawyer and Yale Law School grad, Kefauver had an earthy style. He mangled the names of local candidates and told corny jokes, all of which Mary found more endearing than off-putting. At a rally in Worthington, Minnesota, a local party bigwig presented

Kefauver with a prizewinning live turkey, which promptly defecated on the stage as the vice presidential candidate held it aloft.

The 1956 campaign marked the birth of Mary's "bearers"—the affectionate term given to the legion of male reporters she politely dragooned into carrying her typewriter and luggage. There has never been any journalist before or since who had so many eventual Pulitzer Prize winners serve as their bellhop. Mary explained, "This was back in the Dark Ages when there were at the most two women on a trip, and we were treated like white goddesses on safari. Yes, dear sisters, we may have been oppressed, but we were spoiled too." Mary was proud that she never carried anything heavier than her notebook on the road. Mary's cousin Brian McGrory joked that when Mary's colleagues weren't carrying her bags on the campaign trail, the candidates were.

Mary once observed, "To be a woman reporter in the man's world of Washington in the 1940s and 1950s was to be patronized or excluded or both," but she also used her sex to her advantage when possible.

She was often given nicer hotel rooms than the men were or offered a ride in the candidate's car rather than on the bus. Mary acknowledged that many feminists might have viewed her approach as treasonous, yet as a pioneer in her field, she was never uncomfortable making the most of what she called the "enjoyable side of inequality." Instead of seeing herself as an oppressed minority, Mary viewed herself as an elite.

Former CBS anchor Dan Rather described the environment. "She was traveling, by and large, with proverbial whiskey-breathed, nicotine-stained, stubble-bearded, experienced reporters. Not a gentle world, and not genteel." Rather noted that on the press bus there was an unspoken but clearly established hierarchy, with the old pros sitting on the outside right behind the driver. "The fact is that Mary pretty much sat where she damned well pleased, with the exception of a few old bulls."

Reflecting her Girls' Latin training, Mary spoke with the perfect diction of Katharine Hepburn and often addressed her bearers in almost regal tones: "Dear boy, would you be so kind to give me a hand with this?" "The best part of being a newspaperwoman is newspapermen," she observed. "I cannot speak too well of them. They are always communicative and sometimes witty; approached non-competitively they are capable of chivalry." The *Washington Post*'s David Broder noted that Mary "demanded—not asked, but demanded—all of the courtesies that the 19th century gentleman would have been expected to provide for a woman."

Not everyone approved of Mary's neo-Victorian style. Reporter Jack Germond took umbrage with her demands and noted with pride that he never carried Mary's bags. "It seemed to me that she got more and more imperious," he said, "but she was an awfully complicated person."

One of Mary's favorite bearers and drinking buddies, whom she first met on the Kefauver campaign, was Blair Clark of CBS News. Tall and handsome, Clark grew up in East Hampton, New York, as part of a well-to-do family that had made its fortune as founders of the Coats and Clark Thread Company. Clark had attended all the right schools, going to prep school at St. Mark's before attending Harvard as a classmate of John Kennedy.

Clark had also served a stint at the CBS Paris bureau in the early 1950s, where he became friends and drinking buddies with Crosby Noyes, the middle of the three Noyes brothers at the *Star* and a foreign correspondent at the time.

Some of the Western Union cables from Mary and Clark back to Crosby Noyes in Washington illustrate how much Mary enjoyed life on the trail.

Mary and Clark first wired Noyes from the Hotel Fort Des Moines, in Iowa (which bragged that it had just undertaken "the largest mass installation of TV sets in Iowa"), with fake outrage that Noyes had failed to inform them that they shared the same birthday. "Sir, it has come to our attention," they teased, "that you may have committed a breach of human kindness so gratuitous, gross, and graceless that if facts bear it out, neither of us wishes to have anything to do with you ever, ever again." Noting that Noyes had helped celebrate Clark's birthday in Brussels just two years earlier, and claiming that the demoralized Clark had been reduced to spending his birthday crying quietly in his hotel room, the two demanded that Noyes explain without delay.

Noyes responded as the Kefauver party was checking in to the Hotel Eugene, in Oregon: "Accepting the fact that in our profession we have little control over the people with whom we are forced to associate, a special word of cautionary advice is clearly called for under the present circumstances. Mr. Blair Clark of the Columbia Broadcasting System has an international reputation for conduct so spectacularly outrageous that few respectable members of society care to invite him to birthday parties. Much as we deplore the discussion of personalities, we feel it our solemn duty to advise you that his version of the events of August twenty-second last amounts to the purest fabrication, concocted no doubt for some sinister motive of his own."

After visiting Sidney, Montana, the Kefauver entourage switched to a smaller DC-3 aircraft so that they could land in Kalispell, where Kefauver was scheduled to give a speech at the Flathead County High School. Mid-flight, the sleek silver prop plane encountered violent thunderstorms. As lightning flashed outside, the plane dipped and yawed wildly. A loose mimeograph machine tumbled down the aisle. Mary, who was not a fan of small planes, sat next to reporter Al Spivak, clutching his arm in terror. Kefauver, the would-be vice president, sprawled in a Scotch-induced slumber and wearing a silk eyeshade, seemed oblivious.

As the campaign moved on to Rock Springs, Wyoming, things veered further into the absurd. The DC-3 was able to land at the airport, but the airport didn't have any stairs tall enough to reach its door. With no other alternative, Kefauver and the reporters deployed the plane's emergency shoot and slid down. Mary might have had men carry her typewriter, but she was game for adventure. The reporters soon dubbed themselves the Kalispell Choral Society and the Wyoming Sliding Chute Federation and worked up a late-night drinking song: "Slide, Estes, Slide."

It was with great sadness that Mary learned that she was being dispatched to cover Adlai Stevenson. It was a more important assignment, but Mary knew that it would not be nearly as fun as barnstorming across the West with Kefauver and his group of half-mad reporters. The group held a rollicking going-away party, and Mary cried when she left.

The next day, a hungover Mary arrived at the Denver airport for her connecting flight to take her on to the Stevenson campaign. She called the Western Union office to see if the *Star*'s editors had wired updated instructions. There were twelve collect telegrams waiting for her. As Mary had the telegrams read to her over the phone, she broke into an irrepressible grin. They were all mock missives from reporters on the Kefauver campaign. A telegram from "Vice President Nixon" congratulated Mary on leaving the low-flying Kefauver plane. A faux message from union chief George Meany took Mary to task for her labor policies, suggesting that she "either hire personal bearer or pay union scale." The final wire, from Blair Clark, noted that the campaign plane had turned off its motor for three minutes over Kalispell in tribute.

As Mary got off the telephone, she turned and bumped into a friend, young Senator Jack Kennedy, who was passing through the airport on his way to make a campaign appearance on behalf of the Stevenson ticket.

Mary had first laid eyes on JFK, "thin as a match and still yellow from malaria," when he returned to a hero's welcome in Boston after World War II, at a 1946 celebration at the Parker House Hotel. Kennedy's exploits as a highly decorated captain of a torpedo boat in the Pacific were widely known in the city, thanks to the substantial favorable publicity purchased in the local newspapers by his father, Joe Kennedy. JFK made a largely forgettable speech about Ireland, but Mary always remembered the radiance of his smile.

A few short months later, Kennedy declared a bid for Congress from the same spot. Many of the local political pros were initially disdainful, dismissing JFK as a spoiled dilettante and dubbing him "Harvard Irish." Although Mary thought Kennedy was unpolished, she recognized his raw political skills and his rare ability to convince people that he was somehow a more perfect version of themselves.

Mary befriended a number of his staffers during the campaign, a mix of Boston Irish pols and young intellectuals who had connected with Kennedy at Harvard and in the military. Mary recalled that Kennedy's aides were always trying to get him to wear a hat, hoping that it would make him look older. "At the last minute going out the door, he'd reach in the closet for any hat that was there," Mary remembered. "He'd put it on, and sometimes it wouldn't go down over his hair, sometimes it fell down over his ears." There was a great deal of excitement around Kennedy. He was young, good-looking, and a war hero. Kennedy's refined charm and intelligence were a striking change from the rough-hewn ways of most Boston Irish politicians. Kennedy won the congressional seat comfortably.

After they both moved to Washington, Kennedy, then single and a freshman member of Congress, asked McGrory out on a date—but he did so through an intermediary, as was sometimes his style. Mary was offended. She made clear that it was not how she expected to be approached. JFK then asked her out in person, and they had dinner together in February 1948.

Mary was always tight-lipped about the encounter, but she told a friend that Kennedy simply had to do something about his unkempt hair. Seeing how animated Mary became when she discussed current affairs, Kennedy told her that she should write about politics. She agreed, sharing her frustrations that the editors at the *Star* had not yet let her do so. Some of Mary's relatives speculate that Mary had a love affair with JFK, but it was clear that if there was romance, it did not go very far. Mary was well enough attuned to Boston's ingrained class distinctions to know that Kennedys were happy to consort with commoners but did not marry them, and she was not one for empty assignations.

Mary and Kennedy did become friends. Several years later, she bumped into him near his office. JFK said that he was contemplating a 1952 run for the Massachusetts seat in the U.S. Senate against incumbent Henry Cabot Lodge. Mary discouraged him, pointing out that Lodge was popular and came from the state's most important Republican family, and that 1952 was shaping up as a good year for Republicans as President Truman's poll numbers sagged. Kennedy made his position clearer: he was going to enter the race. Mary kept at Kennedy. "But why?" she asked. "What's the choice between you and Henry Cabot Lodge?" As Mary later recounted with a smile, "I have no reason to think he enjoyed the conversation, and he certainly didn't take the advice."

During the campaign, Mary went to Boston to watch a debate between Kennedy and Lodge at Waltham High School. Mary was impressed by Kennedy. She noted with satisfaction that his chestnut-colored hair was carefully brushed. "Always a man for direct confrontation, he was delighted to have a debate with the incumbent," Mary wrote. "He came on, composed as a prince of the blood." During the debate, a local sitting next to Mary leaned over and whispered, "He's a thoroughbred." Although some graded the debate a draw, Mary knew a winning style when she saw one. "Here was this handsome, graceful, articulate creature, and I think everybody was inclined to give him exactly what he wanted, which was a seat in the senate." Couple this with his rich father's willingness to spend amply on his behalf and the Kennedy campaign machine was in full swing.

JFK was the kind of Boston Irish politician for which Mary's late father had always yearned: serious, well-read, and eminently presentable. It is no wonder Massachusetts governor Paul Dever dubbed JFK "the first Irish Brahmin." Although Dwight D. Eisenhower swept Massachusetts by more than 200,000 votes in winning the presidency in 1952, Kennedy snuck past Lodge in the Senate race as his political career continued its meteoric and carefully engineered rise. But Mary was still skeptical about JFK's ultimate potential. Kennedy seemed too young and untested, and Mary wondered how the family's enormous wealth and sometimes lawless sense of privilege would play on the national stage. Asked later if she thought she was dealing with the future president of the United States during their early encounters, Mary replied, "I certainly didn't."

As Mary chatted amiably with JFK at the Denver airport that day in 1956, Kennedy noticed that she was carrying a small stack of funny hats that she had collected on the campaign trail. JFK began trying the hats on one by one as they talked, goofing around and striking exaggerated poses.

As the two parted, Mary could not help but marvel at how much things had changed since her days in the book review department.

Mary carried a lingering sadness with her as she left the Kefauver campaign. During the late nights and while bouncing across the countryside in the campaign bus, something most unexpected had happened. Mary had fallen in love. Her heart was drawn not to the dashing Kennedy but to her fellow reporter Blair Clark.

Mary never talked about her romantic life; she was concerned that any whiff of impropriety could derail her career. Love was still a firing offense for a woman in the newspaper business, and this romance had a great deal going against it. Blair was not only a fellow journalist, but a married man. Mary was overcome with intertwined feelings of attraction and despair. Debonair and witty, Blair was everything that Mary dreamed of in a man.

Although they often worked together in close quarters, Mary and Clark were remarkably discreet about their feelings. Even their closest friends had no inkling of their romance or the steady stream of correspondence between them. Both went out of their way to avoid being seen together after hours or in social settings, for fear of arousing suspicion.

About the only person Mary confided in was Sister Editha, the head of St. Ann's orphanage at the time. Sitting on the floor at St. Ann's one afternoon, Mary told Sister Editha of her love for Clark, with immense sadness etched on her face. Mary had written Blair telling him that she was afraid to see him because it felt like playing with fire.

Sister Editha tried to assure Mary that she was doing the right thing. Mary was not so sure. Clark had told Mary that his marriage was in considerable trouble, but Mary was uncomfortable with an affair. She craved Blair in a way that she had never craved anyone before. Unsettled, Mary reluctantly left Blair and joined the Stevenson campaign.

Adlai Stevenson's press corps was much larger than Kefauver's, with some ninety reporters in total, two of them women. Mary described the sharp contrast between the Kefauver and Stevenson operations: "One has the atmosphere of a schoolyard at recess time; the other, of a classroom just before midyears." Where Kefauver delivered a standard stump speech at every stop, reporters covering Stevenson were bombarded with rewrites and new speeches almost by the hour.

Stevenson was a gifted speaker but an obtuse politician, the kind of man to be irritated by applause during his speeches. After reading a sympathetic Mary column about him, Stevenson signaled for her to approach the stage at a Democratic Party event. Several reporters gave Mary a boost so she could get within earshot. "My dear," Stevenson said, "I read your stories and found them absolutely bewitching." It was the first and last time that Mary would ever recall a politician describing her work as such, and she did seem to be falling under his spell.

Reporter Al Spivak, who also covered Stevenson around this time, noted of Mary, "It was fascinating to watch her. She was totally absorbed with Stevenson. For want of a better term, I would say that she was in love with Stevenson, but I do not mean that in a romantic way; idyllically."

Mary was not shy in expressing her support. Herb Klein, Richard Nixon's longtime press aide, recalled first seeing Mary on Vice President Nixon's press bus in 1956. "We were in a motorcade where the crowds were enthusiastic, waving Eisenhower-Nixon signs at the press. Mary couldn't hold herself in. She periodically shouted back at them cries of 'Yea, Stevenson.'" She was not exactly a model of journalistic impartiality. Mary saw Nixon as a white-collar version of Joe McCarthy, his career largely propelled by impugning opponents as Communist sympathizers.

Stevenson lost the election badly, with Eisenhower sweeping forty-one of the forty-eight states. America liked Ike. It was a disheartening and lopsided loss, and Mary wept on Election Night.

While presidents and presidential campaigns were a lifelong mainstay of Mary's work, covering Congress was an equally important beat, onto which she slipped naturally in the 1950s. Congress—what Mary often referred to as the federal entertainment center—was a far more florid institution then than it is today. Congressmen slurped down bourbon, conducted tawdry affairs, and exchanged cash for votes with startling brazenness.

Mary could pierce even the mundane nonsense of everyday life in Washington with her tart prose. A pair of members debated on the floor of Congress "like two elderly polar bears negotiating the pas de deux from 'Swan Lake.'" Efforts by a politician to restrain a freelancing underling were akin to "a small man trying to take a large dog for a walk." "Did you see Mary's story this morning?" became a common refrain among the press corps.

Mary's writing was unusually erudite. She often sprinkled classical references into her stories—even at the risk of losing a few readers along the way. One editor joked that only Mary could get Pericles on the front page of the *Star*. When editors complained about sophisticated word choices, Mary handed them a dictionary. Her writing on politics bore little resemblance to her earlier book reviews. There was a nimbleness and an easy, spiky humor, which breathed life into her political coverage that had been largely absent from her reviews. It was as if the rough-and-tumble of the newsroom had finally allowed Mary to be at ease.

Journalist and author Russell Baker recalled that when he started out as a reporter, in the mid-fifties, Mary was already a legend of sorts at the Capitol. A number of congressional graybeards pointed Mary out to Baker as "the very model of what I, as a congressional correspondent, *should never be* if I wanted to succeed covering the Hill." Mary's mortal sin: she had printed, verbatim, the harshly anti-immigrant views of a Pennsylvania congressman. "No reporter had ever before done him that discourtesy," Baker recalled, explaining that most reporters in those days thought it unfair to accurately quote congressmen.

The great key to Mary's success on the Hill was her dedication to spending long hours roaming the halls, talking to members and their staffs, and sitting through lengthy press conferences and hearings. "She was absolutely loyal to that proposition that if you didn't see it yourself and ask questions about it yourself, you had no right to sit down and write about it," Roger Mudd observed.

Mary would sit patiently on the leather benches below the old oil portraits of politicians in the Speaker's Lobby, off the floor of the House of Representatives, lying in wait for members of Congress. That patience was usually rewarded. "Men naturally like to explain things to women," Mary

observed, "and I have given them exceptional opportunities in that regard." Mary was flirtatious and persistent, and her soothing voice reeled
politicians in. She beguiled.

Mary complained halfheartedly that she often played the role of ther-
apist to politicians looking to unburden themselves about wayward children and unhappy wives. But Mary's were crocodile tears; she enjoyed the
socializing as much as the politics. Many Republicans in Congress, accus-
tomed to reading Mary's sharp words, were pleasantly surprised to find
Mary gracious in person. "The fact that I don't raise my voice," Mary remarked dryly, "seems to impress them favorably."

Increasingly, Mary carved out her own world in Washington, regularly
hosting parties that became local legend as senators, Supreme Court justices, and journalistic heavyweights commingled with interns, copyboys,
relatives, and church volunteers. At the parties she threw in her corner
apartment on Macomb Street, perched above Rock Creek Park, everyone
was expected to pitch in. According to Mary's spirit of militant volunteerism, the most senior of senators had to tend bar, and the most important of
journalists had to bring a dish to share. You could not only meet the great
and the good at Mary's soirees; you could also see them humbly pass hors
d'oeuvres and take drink orders. (One accomplished professional woman in
Washington remembered being reduced to tears when Mary told her she
was "not a good helper" when she was taking a break from her duties.) Mary
frowned upon guests arriving late or leaving early, and the lions of Washington's establishment quailed at the thought of telling Mary that they
would be unable to attend one of her parties.

The cocktails flowed freely, and almost every party eventually turned
to slightly drunken song. Congressman Eugene McCarthy would recite
verses of Yeats and sing Irish ballads. Mary would dance in stocking feet
and deliver renditions of ditties from *My Fair Lady*. Bobby Kennedy insisted on singing his old camp song at one of Mary's parties. He left soon
after, only to burst into the room again fifteen minutes later because he had
remembered the second verse of what Mary called "Camp Wianagoni"

and felt the need to share it. Supreme Court Justice Arthur Goldberg and his wife wrote to Mary after another party, apologizing that they were not better prepared with a song list. One congressman performed a Russian dance. Reporter Tom Winship remembered a colleague turning to him in wonderment during the middle of one of Mary's raucous gatherings and asking in bewilderment, "What in heaven's name is this all about? Is the *Star* really like this all the time?"

McGrory took to calling her regular guests the Lower Macomb Street Choral Society. It was no wonder that Adlai Stevenson cheerily told her, as he departed from one of her parties, "Let me know when the club meets again. I would like to be a member."

Mary's cooking was notable, but not for the right reasons. Mary often served canned asparagus spears wrapped in white buttered bread, convinced it was both delicious and elegant. "Her Jell-O Surprise was frightening," said Maureen Dowd, "and her meatloaf worse." Mark Shields appeared to be only half-joking when he spoke in passing of a lasagna that sent seven people to nearby Sibley Hospital.

As Don Graham, the *Washington Post*'s publisher after Kay Graham retired, observed, "Obviously the center of Mary entertaining was Mary. It was a performance of sorts. She loved music and she loved poetry and she loved people, with something of an emphasis on Irish people." As she sat in her favorite chair, the parties were a chance for Mary to bask in good company, drink, talk politics, and laugh.

Hosting also allowed Mary to avoid the awkward scenes that often greeted her at stodgy Washington gatherings in the fifties, when her hosts didn't know whether to treat her as a reporter or as a woman—those were definitely different categories. The men would retire to one room after dinner to talk politics, smoke cigars, and drink Scotch, while women went to another to discuss more refined topics. Where would Mary go? (Most often with the men, but uncomfortably so for her hosts.) At her own parties, no one wondered if she had one drink too many or whispered about the man who had given her a ride home.

But while Mary was able to hold parties the way she liked, other Washington institutions were more resistant to change, none more so than the National Press Club, an important local venue for politicians and other prominent public figures to deliver speeches and make news. The club had a strict no-women policy.

When journalist Sarah McClendon applied for membership to the National Press Club in 1955, she was never given the courtesy of a response. A year later, a deal was negotiated whereby women reporters were allowed to sit in the balcony during lunch speeches if they would be escorted up the fire exit before the lunch and whisked from the premises immediately after the speaker had concluded. They could not ask questions or be served a meal, and they were wedged into the eaves next to the bulky, blazing-hot television lights. It was a deliberate humiliation, what author Nan Robertson called "one of the ugliest symbols of discrimination against women to be found in the world of journalism." Reporter Haynes Johnson concurred, saying that it was an outrage that "Mary McGrory and Doris Fleeson had to sit in the goddamn balcony" while "kids like me were down on the floor."

Mary bitterly resented it, and years later she still brimmed with anger as she described looking down on "some fat lobbyist lighting his cigar and having his second cup of coffee." It wasn't until 1959 that the situation began to change, when President Eisenhower invited Soviet leader Nikita Khrushchev to visit Washington. The State Department wanted to hold Khrushchev's speech at the press club, and Khrushchev insisted women be included. The leaders of the press club reluctantly and bizarrely agreed to allow 1.4 female reporters to cover the event for every 10 male reporters in attendance. It would still be more than a decade before women were allowed to become members of the press club.

When women were finally allowed on the main floor to eat lunch during special occasions, Mary was asked how she liked it. "The food was better in the balcony," she harrumphed.

But despite the many degradations, Mary's writing was only becoming more popular. In September 1957, George Minot, her former editor at the

Boston Herald Traveler, who had insisted that she was too shy to make a good reporter, wrote Mary asking if his paper could carry several of her columns a month. Not long after, the managing editor of the *Boston Globe* asked if his paper could carry some of her work. This led Newby Noyes to suggest that Mary syndicate her column. But while Mary was enthusiastic about the idea of her column appearing in Boston, she was wary of syndication.

A handful of men—and they were all men—stood at the intellectual apogee of journalism and dominated the opinion and editorial pages of the major dailies at the time. It is difficult to overstate the influence of these pundits in an era before opinion was democratized and the Internet made it so that everyone could contribute to the cacophony of commentary. These self-appointed sages, like Walter Lippmann and Joe Alsop at the *New York Herald Tribune* and Scotty Reston at the *New York Times*, appeared in hundreds of papers across the country. They adroitly trafficked in their roles as consummate insiders. They were journalists in name, members of the ruling elite in practice. They dined with presidents and saw it as their duty to guide their hand. These pundits told the country what to think and could sway public opinion to a degree that is almost unfathomable today.

Mary viewed most columnists (with the exception of Walter Lippmann) as thumb-suckers rather than reporters. She did not believe her writing befitted the traditional "wise man" approach of most opinion writers of the day. She didn't want to pontificate about grand national ideas, demurring to Noyes that traditional columnists were different from "people like me who only know what they see and a little poetry." Mary wanted to cover politics from the front lines, and she was worried that syndication would force her to become something she was not.

But she was about to become more popular than she had ever imagined, and it would only lend momentum to the notion that Mary was indeed the new face of opinion writing. In November 1958, *Time* ran a major profile of Mary. She made such an impression on Tommy Weber, the photographer sent to take her picture, that he wrote a colleague, "If I put down all my thoughts, Boyd would make me send Time Inc. a check for the privilege of covering the babe. This gal has everything—manners of a lad—a wonderful voice—attractive as hell to look at—and a touch of come-on that gives guys noises in the head. Why don't we hire her?"

Dubbing Mary the "Queen of the Corps," *Time* observed, "Her technique is all her own. Pert and comely, she sits quietly in meetings and hearing rooms, watching gestures, listening to sounds, painting mental pictures. She writes swiftly and well, turns out some of the most perceptive, pungent copy in Washington, D.C." Not only did United Press's Washington bureau chief call Mary's writing the best he had ever seen, but *Time* also quoted Scotty Reston of the *New York Times* as saying that she had the "poet's gift of analogy."

The article noted that Mary lived simply on her $160-a-week salary and was a regular volunteer at St. Ann's. When the *Time* reporter asked Mary why she was still single, she responded with both humor and rue: "I guess the men think the best thing about me is my writing."

The *Time* article led to a rush of letters and calls to Mary from friends, family, and former colleagues. Joseph Welch wrote to Mary of his joy in reading the piece and how it had triggered fond memories of getting to know her during the Army-McCarthy hearings, recalling her as "eager, inquiring, and damned pretty." Welch continued, "I have not forgotten what you did for me. I never will." Welch seemed to have a crush on Mary, and a short time later he sent her a note playfully cut and pasted from the letters of magazine headlines, as in a ransom note. "Joseph N. Welch Hopelessly Confused by Mary McGrory," it read. "What to do about the torrid but tender American Woman. She must be exotic. The world is yours."

In the wake of the *Time* article, new opportunities appeared in bunches. On a single day—November 7, 1958—Mary received letters from editors at Doubleday, Charles Scribner's Sons, Alfred A. Knopf, and McGraw-Hill asking if she was interested in writing a book. Columnist Stewart Alsop wrote to Mary: "When are you going to write a piece for the *Saturday Evening Post*? I've always said you're the best feature writer in the business, and now I see *Time* is saying the same thing."

The level of interest was striking, and testament to an important fact: Publishers weren't reaching out to Mary simply because they thought it would be good to hear a woman's view on politics. Instead, the acclaim surrounding her column spoke to an obvious commercial appeal. Mary wrote beautifully, she was attractive, and a woman in the halls of power felt sexy and modern.

Perhaps the only thing more striking than the torrent of book offers was Mary's response: a polite "No, thank you" to almost all. Mary joked to one of the publishers that her work looked good in the newspaper only because she was competing with reporters "dictating from gas stations during riots on deadline." Mary could have had her pick of book or magazine deals, but she just wanted to be a reporter. The closest she ever came to writing a book was contributing single chapters to three different political volumes, in 1959, 1961, and 1966.

The attention kept coming. In January 1959, *Editor & Publisher* ran another profile of Mary, with some of her colleagues calling her the finest reporter since legendary World War II correspondent Ernie Pyle. *Newsweek* ran its own story on Mary in 1960, dubbing her a "round-faced, leprechaun-turned-reporter" with "the brightest eyes in the Washington press corps."

In February 1960, Mary surrendered, and her column went into syndication. She was given a flexible writing schedule, and she guaranteed other newspapers at least two columns a week—which was not difficult, since she averaged a column every other day for the *Star*. The *Globe* was one of the first papers to pick up her column, calling her "Boston's gift to the national press."

Notably, Mary's columns in the *Star* were printed on the first or third page, not on the opinion-and-editorial pages. Mary felt strongly about her placement. As Newby Noyes observed, "The amusing thing about her attitude was that even if all she did was comment, she still didn't want to be regarded as a commentator or a columnist."

The commingling of reporting and commentary on the news pages occasioned complaints from some readers. Wrote one, "You probably have some good reasons for violating the basic concept of journalism which states that opinion should be confined to the editorial pages and not passed off as 'reporting.' May we know what it is?" In response, the *Star* ran a note from Noyes: "We use Miss McGrory's articles in the news columns because the news of what she reports is made more newsworthy by her own perceptive style of reporting it." It wasn't a very satisfying answer.

Mary, for good and bad, was one of the important forerunners in the trend of newspapers blurring the line between hard reporting and commentary. It would become increasingly difficult for editors and readers all across the industry to discern when a reporter's thumb was on the scale.

Russell Baker was impressed that Mary maintained her blue-collar approach to legwork after being syndicated. "Mary did something remarkable: She went to work. Once I got a column I took it as a license to never go back to the Hill again." Within a year of syndication, she had appeared in some forty newspapers across the country and, as Haynes Johnson argued, "Mary became the premium political columnist in the country."

As Mary's syndication negotiations played out during 1958 and 1959, she had become quite close to Allen Drury, a fellow journalist who covered Capitol Hill and an aspiring novelist. "It seemed to me once that Mary was fond of Allen Drury, who was a colleague on the *Star*," Baker recalled. "Allen switched to the *Times* about the same time I did." Baker, his wife, Drury, and Mary ate out occasionally. "My wife and I thought of them as—what?—not lovers, certainly, but a couple who dated," Baker said. "People still dated back then. They just seemed comfortable well together."

It was around this time that Drury published his first novel, *Advise and Consent*, about a contentious political battle between a fictional president and Congress. Both Mary and Baker provided nice blurbs for the back cover of the book, and Mary's review in the *Star* was gushing.

The book was a sensation, and it leapt onto the *New York Times* bestseller list, where it remained for 102 weeks. Baker described the sudden success. "Allen had a million dollars right away, and quit the *Times*. A million was real money in those days." With his newfound wealth, Drury booked passage on a transatlantic liner for a luxury cruise, and he decided to take a very special female guest: his mother.

This was not the news for which Mary had hoped. "Mary was flabbergasted," Baker explained. "I can still hear the incredulity with which she spoke the words 'With his *mother*!'" Mary's dreams of a romantic getaway were dashed. However, there was more to the story. "I've since thought that she suspected, or even realized for the first time," said Baker, "that Allen was gay—which he was, of course, though he was deeply closeted, in the 1950s style. I have often speculated on what his trip to Europe with his mother did to Mary's thinking about her own life."

While Mary was attracted to Drury, she still carried a torch for Blair Clark, and her heart raced when she learned that Clark and his wife, Holly, were divorcing at around this time.

Mary made sure she had frequent reasons to visit Blair in New York City, and the two remained in regular contact despite her concerns about the intensity of her own feelings. But Mary always remained so discreet in her interactions with Blair that not a whisper of gossip about the two circulated in the newsroom.

The biggest political story of 1959 was the wide-open 1960 presidential race. Vice President Nixon was the presumptive favorite on the Republican side, and a host of Democratic contenders actively explored their chances. The country was still in a glow from the Eisenhower years, with *Look* magazine describing Americans at the time as "relaxed, unadventurous, comfortably satisfied with their life, and blandly optimistic about the future." Cars, television sets, and all the consumerism made possible during the 1950s were a powerful tonic.

In April 1959, Mary joined JFK as he made an early West Coast swing to consult party leaders in California and build support for entering the presidential race. Party bosses were unconvinced, and they remained wary of Kennedy's Catholicism, Ivy League education, and youth. Senators Hubert Humphrey and Lyndon Johnson were safer alternatives, and there was still talk of Adlai Stevenson being drafted at the convention.

"The sun-tanned senator with the wind-blown haircut looks very much at home in casual California," Mary wrote of Kennedy, "and many here are charmed, finding his lean and graceful form a welcome change from the paunchy politicos they are usually called upon to follow." Mary added a comment from an observer in San Francisco who, upon seeing Kennedy for the first time, blurted out, "Why, he's just a boy."

After spending about a week traveling together, Mary, JFK, and Kennedy's confidant Steve Smith shared a flight back to Washington. Mary asked Kennedy bluntly, "Why do you want to be president?" Kennedy carefully ticked through the likely Democratic candidates, assessing their respective strengths and weaknesses at length. As Mary put it, Kennedy's message was clear: "Why not me?" In May 1959, she still thought it preposterous that Kennedy could win the presidency.

Reporter Edward Morgan attended a small dinner party with Mary at Kennedy's elegant, narrow, three-story Federal home on N Street in Georgetown in 1959, recalling that she "had him on the griddle most of the evening about his campaign for the White House. He loved it." Morgan thought Mary had a unique ability to needle someone like Kennedy with humor and affection. Years later, when she was asked when she'd first conceived of a Kennedy presidency, Mary laughed and said, "At his inauguration."

By the time Kennedy announced he was running, in early January 1960, with a brief statement from the marble confines of the Senate Caucus Room, Mary was very supportive. "The young Massachusetts Democrat not only sounded like a man who knows where he is going, but acted and was treated like a man who was already there." She argued that JFK's deft fielding of questions from reporters at the press conference helped Kennedy quickly achieve the "priceless intangible" of looking presidential.

But behind the scenes, Mary still preferred Stevenson, and she said that the Kennedy clan was "incensed that I favored Adlai." The Kennedys thought that Mary should be for them at all times, because she was Catholic and from Boston.

As the 1960 politicking began in earnest, Mary was dispatched to cover Nixon. Up to that point in her career, she had written little about him, and her pieces did not demonstrate any particular animus toward the vice president. With a challenge from New York governor Nelson Rockefeller failing to gain traction, Mary observed, "The way it is now, all that Vice President Nixon needs to do in order to be nominated and elected is to follow the advice a Boston politician once gave an ambitious junior: just wear a clean shirt every day and show up at the office." The more time Mary spent with Nixon, the less she liked him. She thought he was awkward and addressed crowds as if "speaking to a not very bright child."

The campaign also thrust Mary and Blair Clark back together again, on the heels of his divorce and at a time when Clark's star was rapidly rising at CBS News. Mary wrote to Clark frequently, and Blair responded with equally flirtatious, if less frequent, letters. Mary and Blair were together on the Kennedy campaign plane, the *Caroline*, in February 1960 when staffers announced that the plane was making an impromptu visit to Las Vegas to stay overnight at the Sands Hotel. The Rat Pack—Frank Sinatra, Dean Martin, and Sammy Davis Jr.—had established the Sands as the most happening spot on the Strip, a desert retreat where hot days in the sun gave way to long nights filled with gambling, showgirls, swizzle sticks, and an intoxicating atmosphere of anything goes. As Clark said of Las Vegas, "There was no goddamn reason for stopping there except fun and games."

JFK, some of his campaign team, and several reporters went to see Sinatra perform that night at the Copa Room, where Ol' Blue Eyes went out of his way to introduce Kennedy as the next president of the United States. Sinatra and Dean Martin kidded with the candidate, with Martin pretending to have forgotten his last name in an alcoholic fog. The stage patter was boozy and off-color, and the audience in the smoke-filled room roared. Clark remembered "bimbos and showgirls" congregating around Kennedy's table, and he and Mary were taken aback when they received a call from Sinatra not long after his performance inviting them to join him and Kennedy for drinks in his suite.

When they went up to Sinatra's suite, two women were also having drinks there along with Jack Kennedy and his younger brother Teddy. One of them was a striking, dark-haired beauty, Judith Campbell, who ultimately became Kennedy's most notorious paramour because of her ties to mob boss Sam Giancana. Mary and Blair excused themselves after a few drinks. "We sensed that Jack and Frank and a couple of the girls were about to have a party," Clark recalled.

In March 1960, Mary went to Wisconsin to cover the spirited primary battle between Kennedy and Humphrey. She described Wisconsin as "a portly, Teutonic old lady, full of beer and cheese. She is kindly and stolid and has a weakness for wild men and underdogs in politics." Mary's editors, delighted with her story, wired her at the Hotel Kaiser Knickerbocker: "Recommending beer and cheese for entire staff in hopes of fermenting copy superb as yours."

Mary trailed the candidates through beer halls, bowling alleys, factories, fish fries, shopping malls, and potluck suppers. She described the well-financed Kennedy operation as "crisp, lordly and perfectly organized," while Senator Humphrey's was "sketchy, frantic and largely do-it-yourself." Like a glossy ad for the latest cigarette brand, the Kennedy campaign felt luxe. Yet despite his charisma, JFK conveyed a certain remoteness, and Mary noticed that his reaction to the adoring crowds was to extend his arm forward with the hand upraised, as if subconsciously trying to hold them at bay.

After JFK made an appearance at a local television studio in Wisconsin, he and Mary walked back to their hotel. She would later recall:

> I had been with Hubert Humphrey, as he knew. We were walking down the corridor, and he took my arm simply because he was so tired. I think he really needed someone to lean on momentarily. He wanted to know what Humphrey was saying and what he was doing; what his crowds were like. I had a rundown of the counties that Humphrey

thought he was going to take, so I ran those all by him, and he said where Humphrey was wrong, and what he would take, and what he wouldn't take, and so forth. And then, suddenly, I think I was just supposed to disappear because I had made my little report on the Humphrey camp, and he had something else to do, and that was the end of it.

Mary did not think Kennedy unkind, just focused. "He was terribly economical with his time, I think. Either you informed him or you amused him. Once you ceased doing either or both, you were really supposed to disappear."

Kennedy combined his background in Boston ward politics with the modern tools of the trade, like polling. He berated his staff with language befitting a longshoreman and inspired what Mary called an almost "feudal loyalty" from his inner circle. A large part of Kennedy's appeal to voters was his appearance, which Mary said suggested "to the suggestible that he is lost, stolen, or strayed, a prince in exile perhaps, or a very wealthy orphan. Whatever it is, it is pure gold."

As primary day approached in Wisconsin, Mary reflected on the two weary candidates:

They have withstood gnawing winds at plant gates. They have walked up and down streets in towns with unpronounceable Indian names, approaching strangers and asking favors of them. They have dispatched their wives and sisters to far-away places to drink gallons of coffee, suffer curious stares, and answer personal questions. They have eaten villainous meals in obscure cafes, interrupted by autograph seekers and well-wishers, been expected to be kindly, virtuous, amiable, all-knowing, sincere, promising, great, and folksy. They have done things, in short, that no man but a politician seeking the power and the glow of the White House would do for love or money.

Kennedy won Wisconsin narrowly, stoking fears that his popularity with Protestants was limited. Humphrey was reinvigorated as he headed toward the next primary battle with Kennedy, in West Virginia.

. . . . .

On the campaign trail, Mary encountered fierce anti-Catholic sentiment that fueled doubts that JFK could win the presidency. One voter complained to her that Kennedy would take his marching orders from the pope. Mary wrote back to her friend Liz Acosta, "There is a wounded rhinoceros trapped in the plumbing of this hotel, but from what I've seen we're damn lucky it's inside, so we say nothing. Jack K. is in fine form, makes a good underdog. I like this ever-better than Wisconsin, even though some of the anti-Catholic stuff is hair-raising." The Kennedy family poured money into the West Virginia race, both aboveboard and underneath the table.

The Kennedy forces were too much for Humphrey, and Mary reported from the "confused desolation" of the Humphrey headquarters on primary night as the results came in. Making her way past "a couple of sad secretaries, staring blankly at the blackboards," she went up to Humphrey's hotel suite, where the disappointed candidate and his staff were drafting a concession speech. Bobby Kennedy pushed his way into the room.

"Hiya, Bobby," said Humphrey in greeting. RFK and Humphrey shook hands, and Bobby gently kissed Senator Humphrey's wife, Muriel, on the cheek. Speaking to a dejected crowd well after midnight, the Minnesota senator announced that he was suspending his candidacy. Mary watched as a misty-eyed Bobby Kennedy walked over and put his arm around Humphrey. JFK was gathering momentum.

Knowing that he was more popular with rank-and-file Democrats than with party leaders, Kennedy competed in numerous primaries, and he rattled off a series of wins in doing so. By May, this strategy had left Kennedy running hard, but because it was still a time when nominees were determined more by backroom deals at the convention than by the actual results of primaries, he was aware that his real opposition wouldn't emerge until delegates gathered in Los Angeles. Mary traveled with Kennedy as he stumped in Oregon and California, with Humphrey still on the ballot in Oregon. "I remember one night, very late, in a hotel corridor," Mary said about a conversation with Kennedy. "Oh, we'd had a dreadful day." Kennedy turned to Mary and said, "I hate this. This is a waste of time. Hubert can't win. He can't win. I don't mind campaigning, but I don't like this."

Mary was a constant presence behind the scenes, and she was allowed remarkable access to planning and strategy discussions. Because Mary wrote color stories, seemed discreet, and was a woman, candidates wanted to impress and flatter her. They enjoyed her company, even when they took exception to her columns. Mary developed an almost unrivaled ability to interact with candidates when they were out of the public eye. This also meant that she had a great deal of inside information that she never used. Mary was more interested in capturing the character of politicians on the page than trading her access for exclusives.

As Mary's colleague Duncan Spencer observed, Mary did not write "tips, scoops, rumors." She wrote "what she sees, what she hears, sometimes what people tell her, she writes what is on their faces, what their clothes or pace show—knowing with the sureness of good nerves what clues are given by the surface." Access was vital for Mary, and as she said, "I have to see, I have to hear. I'm primitive."

Mary's ability to move behind the scenes during campaigns had much in common with Theodore H. White, the noted chronicler of U.S. presidential campaigns. White wrote his first in-depth campaign portrait in 1960, and his book *The Making of the President 1960* subsequently became a bestseller. Mary and White were good friends and shared Boston roots, with White having attended the Boys' Latin School. While they both practiced personality-driven, observational journalism, Mary thought that White was far too reluctant to offer criticism. Both White and Mary changed how Americans talked about campaigns and how journalists wrote about them, as they painted their stories in intimately personal terms. They illuminated the fact that the most important parts of campaigns usually happened far away from the podium.

Senator Lyndon Baines Johnson still hoped to derail Kennedy at the convention, as did Adlai Stevenson. Yet even as Kennedy rolled to multiple primary wins, LBJ remained coy about his own intentions. Johnson finally announced his candidacy just six days before the convention, while JFK had spent two years organizing and planning for the race. It was a major miscalculation on Johnson's part.

Both Johnson and Stevenson hoped their late bids for the nomination would succeed, but Kennedy was greeted like an idol at the Democratic convention in Los Angeles. Mary was taken aback by the fervor. "Some 3,500 placard-waving enthusiasts mobbed him on the airfield. They clawed at each other in their enthusiasm to get to him. They all but tore his arm out of the socket to shake his hand. They screamed 'we want Kennedy' even though he was right there." Stevenson's arrival was comparably airless and low-key as he told his supporters, "I am not here to promote my candidacy."

In a bold yet seemingly quixotic move at the convention, Mary's friend Senator Eugene McCarthy made an impassioned, lectern-thumping speech from the podium in support of Adlai Stevenson shortly before the delegates were scheduled to vote. McCarthy was no fan of the Kennedys and had once argued privately that he thought he was better suited to be president because he was "twice as liberal as Humphrey; twice as Catholic as Kennedy."

Mary had gotten to know McCarthy during the 1950s, and they had a great deal in common. Hailing from the small town of Watkins, Minnesota, McCarthy, like Mary, was of half-German descent yet always identified himself as thoroughly Irish Catholic. Both were known for their wit and a great love of the classics, particularly the poetry of Yeats. Deeply religious, McCarthy had studied to become a Benedictine monk before his career veered into teaching and Minnesota politics. Throughout his life, McCarthy remained a student of religious philosophy, always eager to engage in theological debate. Both Mary and Gene considered themselves *Commonweal* Catholics, after the name of a popular Catholic publication that placed considerable emphasis on social justice and intellectualism while frowning on the increasingly harsh anti-Communist excesses of the early 1950s.

McCarthy's speech at the convention was brilliant. He lit up the massive L.A. Memorial Coliseum as he pleaded with delegates to support Stevenson: "Do not reject this man who made us all proud to be called Democrats. Do not leave the prophet without honor in his own party." McCarthy's passion and eloquence poured out in probably the best speech he ever delivered. The crowd responded with a cascading roar as exhilarated delegates leapt to their feet. Mary was stirred, and surprised that McCarthy, "a sedate mumbler in the Senate," had been so forceful. McCarthy had gotten people more excited about Stevenson than Stevenson ever had, and Mary admired his reckless fire.

"I was in Stevenson's suite in Los Angeles the night he knew for once and for all, he would never be president," Mary would recall. Stevenson had watched Senator McCarthy's speech on television and then turned to Mary and remarked in approval, "Magnificent." On the floor of the convention, Wyoming pushed Kennedy over the top for the nomination. Mary saw Stevenson and his trusted adviser George Ball headed to another room to draft a concession statement. "Now for some purple prose," he said lightly to Mary. She could not tell whether he was resigned or relieved. "Thus ended a tentative and diffident thrust that was doomed from the start," wrote Mary of Stevenson's last presidential bid, "but which had moments of crazy elation and brought the one note of simple fervor to a pre-packaged convention."

Mary, like most, was surprised by Kennedy's choice of Lyndon Johnson as a running mate. It appears that Kennedy offered Johnson the nomination largely as a means of assuaging Johnson's ego, hoping that he would turn down the position. Bobby Kennedy, who had been sent to the convention as an emissary to Johnson, was shocked when LBJ indicated that he wanted the nomination, and his efforts to get his brother to dump Johnson from the ticket were fruitless. Bobby and LBJ were both notoriously prickly personalities, and their relationship would come to be defined by bitterness and distrust.

After Adlai Stevenson introduced Kennedy for his acceptance speech, which drew the convention to a boisterous close, Stevenson spotted Mary in the crush and offered her a ride back to town in his Cadillac. As the two were ushered into the limousine, JFK joined them in the backseat. It was a remarkable moment. Mary departed the convention sandwiched between the Democratic Party's past and future.

The conversation was strained.

"You look wonderfully well, Jack," Stevenson commented. "So tan."

Kennedy, still crackling with adrenaline, explained that it came from sitting in the back of convertibles during the campaign.

Stevenson grimaced and shook his head. "I never would do that. It's awful, the sun in your eyes, the dust, you can't see for hours afterwards."

Although neither said anything, Kennedy and Mary must have shared the same thought at that moment: this was why Kennedy was the nominee and Stevenson was not. Politics was a contact sport, and Stevenson never had the heart for it.

At the Republican convention in Chicago, the nomination of Nixon was a foregone conclusion, and the spectacle felt hollow to Mary, even more so because of the scene she had just left. "Two weeks ago at this time, the Democrats were boiling through the halls of the Biltmore in Los Angeles, singing and shouting," she wrote. "There was snake-dancing in the lobby whenever anybody had the room, and at three o'clock in the morning, they were singing 'My Wild Irish Rose' in the bar." The delegates, although they supported Nixon, had a hard time hiding their disappointment that President Eisenhower was departing the national stage.

After the conventions, there was a brief period in 1960 when both Senator Kennedy and Vice President Nixon, who would periodically preside over the Senate, could be found attending to their routine duties on the floor of Congress, wishing they were out on the campaign trail. Mary described them from her perch in the Senate press gallery: "When Mr. Nixon presides over the Senate, which he has done infrequently, he engages in rather lonely conversation with the Senate parliamentarian," while just twenty feet away, "his rival, Senator Kennedy of Massachusetts, has transformed the back row of the Democratic side into a reasonable facsimile of his porch at Hyannis Port. He receives a constant stream of fellow senators from all parts of the country."

As August ended, the two tickets began a mad dash that would not end until Election Day, and Mary was along for every step of the ride, including a tour of the South with Lyndon Johnson. She described Johnson playing to his strengths: "The Senator's accent, as he pushes deeper into the South on his whistle-stop tour, subjecting himself, as he says 'to the wisdom of the people,' sounds as though every syllable has been individually fried in fatback," Mary penned. "Senator Johnson has transformed the South in the last few days from a political or even geographical area into an amorphous emotional entity where everyone is either a friend or a relation."

Mary's volume of writing during the 1960 race was prodigious, with columns often appearing daily. Nixon was frequently in her sights. The insincere self-deprecations that filled his speeches were like fingernails on a blackboard to Mary. In the hands of a more nimble politician, the constant references to his roots would have been endearing rather than cloying. "He was an unhappy man, and he was a man just eaten alive by resentment and envy," she said of Nixon. "A sense of grievance is not a good paramount quality in a president."

Nixon bent over backwards during the 1960 campaign trying to soften his image. That strategy appeared to backfire when Kennedy and Nixon famously met in their first televised debate. Nixon, who was under the weather, was pallid and halting, while the telegenic Kennedy came across as urbane and in command. His own partisans feared that Nixon had gone soft.

Their first debate is frequently cited as marking the onset of television's dominance of American politics, and certainly Kennedy benefited from the medium. The impact of television was a shock to print reporters. "The thing about being a reporter was that you were one of the select few that had a place at great events and were in fact ordered to go there," Mary commented. "And the camera goes everywhere. It goes to Egypt to the depths of the temple, it goes on bombing runs. It goes to the darkest heart of a riot, and it goes to Buckingham Palace, and interviews at 10 Downing

Street. There is so much immediacy, and we come lumbering up in the rear a day later. It is very hard to hold your ground."

Mary couldn't help but notice how the day after the Nixon-Kennedy debate, people came up to both men and said admiringly, "I saw you on television," as if that mattered more than anything they said.

While she disliked Nixon, Mary thought he won the second debate decisively, saying he had the look "of a man who wishes to become President of the United States and is apparently ready to fight for it."

Mary continued to marvel at the intensity of the crowds pouring out to greet JFK. "Every time the Senator passes down a main street or before an airport barrier, the sounds are of a Sunday afternoon at the beach, with shrieks of pleasure going up as each new wave comes in. But the Senator has learned to take it with a grin. . . . He talks to them and they talk back." Mary was delighted to see Kennedy lifted by a measure of genuine joy as he sprinted through seventeen states in the final days of the campaign.

On the eve of the election, Kennedy and his team were optimistic, but Kennedy's Catholicism continued to create an undercurrent of apprehension. With the polls tight, no one knew how great a liability his religion would be in the privacy of a voting booth.

Mary returned to Boston with JFK for Election Day. She watched as Kennedy and his very pregnant wife, Jackie, voted at 8:40 in the morning at the old West End branch of the Boston Public Library. Mary might have been dismissive of Kennedy's prospects when he first explored a candidacy, but she was overjoyed that a Boston Irishman stood a whisper away from the highest office in the land.

Kennedy and a large entourage then made the short flight to Hyannis Port. During the flight, the last press "pool" of the campaign—the handful of reporters given closest access to the candidate for the day—was announced. Mary was not selected. She was furious.

"It was the last straw," Mary said. "When we landed at the airport, Mrs. Kennedy was there, and said something pleasant about something I had written, and this stirred up my emotions all over again." Mary stalked over to JFK and lit into him. "What do you have to do to become a pool reporter in this cavalcade? I have followed you for four years," Mary demanded, "and I have never so much as ridden in the pool car." (This coming from a woman who had shared a limousine ride from the convention with Kennedy and Stevenson.)

Teddy White used the ensuing exchange for the opening for his book, *The Making of the President*.

> As he arrived in Hyannis Port, accompanied by more than a hundred correspondents, and more than 80 staff members from the other planes, the tensions broke ridiculously for a moment. Many of this group had followed him now for some 44,000 miles of campaigning since Labor Day, and one of the reporters, strained, caught him, insisting she was being prevented from observing him closely, deprived of her proper rotation in the "pool" choice of reporters who are closest to him. Gravely, and because he was fond of her and knew her to be devoted to him, and because, moreover, this is a man who never forgets either friend or enemy, he turned and said, "You and I will never be apart, Mary." And yet he knew, and everyone knew, that if his hope, which she shared, came true, he would be apart, unreachably, from these people who had been his friends.

The election results were some of the closest in American history. Early returns for Kennedy in the industrial Northeast were solid, but Nixon showed surprising strength in the Midwest and the West as he steadily narrowed the gap. At three in the morning, Nixon spoke from California—not conceding, but acknowledging that Kennedy might have won the election. After little more than an hour's sleep, Mary was back at work by five in the morning. Kennedy's press secretary, Pierre Salinger, informed reporters that there would be one final press pool that would go to the Kennedy compound and await the final results. When he called out Mary's name as part of that group, a small cheer erupted among the assembled press corps.

With some satisfaction, Mary noted that the last pool "was the best of the campaign." On the manicured lawn that swept down toward the sea,

JFK's father, Joseph Kennedy, gruffly ordered that extra chairs be retrieved from the house for a group photo. Mary greeted JFK in the yard as he carried his daughter, Caroline, piggyback on his shoulders. With some amusement, Mary watched a "bewildering succession" of Kennedy family members head out for brisk walks along the beach that fronted the six-acre compound. Nixon conceded that afternoon. Out of 68 million votes cast, only 113,000 separated the two men.

Kennedy made a brief speech claiming victory at the bunting-draped Hyannis Port armory. He assured his pregnant wife, "Not much longer, Jackie," as she stood by his side. Kennedy's closest aides stood around the foot of the platform, overcome with emotion. Mary described the scene in a letter to Teddy White. "Hard-hearted Jack with tears in his eyes and his voice," she wrote, "the very first time I have seen the slightest display of emotion in the candidate and his team." JFK had won.

CHAPTER THREE

He Would Have Liked It

A thick, wet blanket of snow arrived on the eve of John F. Kennedy's inauguration in January 1961, tying Washington in knots. Thousands of cars were abandoned by commuters. With temperatures hovering in the low twenties on Inauguration Day, army snowplows helped clear the streets. The trees along Pennsylvania Avenue glistened in icy sheaths. Mary recalled the scene as Kennedy prepared to take the oath of office: "The sky was cloudless, the sun dazzling. A sharp wind knifed across the Capitol, stiffening the fingers of us reporters who sat at trestle tables in the plaza, stomping our frozen feet."

The official program for the inauguration featured short essays from a number of reporters, including one from Mary in which she described JFK on the campaign trail: "Poor men in West Virginia heard a man from Boston say he needed their help, and they gave it. In the alien corn of Nebraska, with a familiar chopping motion of his right hand, he explained that America can be 'great-ah,' and the farmers knew what he meant."

His words echoing across the Capitol, Kennedy declared, "The torch has been passed to a new generation of Americans—born in this century, tempered by war, disciplined by a cold and bitter peace, proud of our ancient heritage—and unwilling to witness or permit the slow undoing of those human rights to which this Nation has always been committed, and to which we are committed today." Mary described Kennedy at that moment as akin to "the captain on the bridge of a ship, outward bound."

Not long after the inauguration, Mary was at the White House after hours interviewing Kennedy's appointments secretary, Kenny O'Donnell, whose office was just outside the president's. Mary and O'Donnell had just begun talking when a restless President Kennedy burst into the room.

Spotting Mary, he enthusiastically invited her into the Oval Office. She stammered in agreement, although she would describe the next twenty minutes as the most miserable of her life. "I was never so unhappy. I called him Mr. President every other word so he'd be sure to understand that I was not going to presume old acquaintances in any possible shape or way." After all, not many people have their old dates become president, and she acted respectfully as if JFK, the same man she had happily given grief on innumerable occasions, had been transformed into a new person.

There was an awkward silence. Kennedy finally solicited, "How's everything going?"

Mary was suddenly hit with what she called a "terrible impulse" to unburden her troubles on the new president. She thought about telling Kennedy that her apartment was too noisy and that she had been arguing with her landlord. Given that Mary was increasingly consumed by her unresolved relationship with Blair Clark, one suspects that she also wanted to ask Kennedy about Clark, who had been his close friend and classmate at Harvard. Clark had just been promoted to general manager at CBS News, in no small part because of his close ties to Kennedy. Although he had finally left his wife, Mary's relationship with him had stalled.

But now she was sitting with the leader of the free world—how could she talk to him about her frustrating love life and paper-thin apartment walls? Mary was uncharacteristically dumbstruck. She started to get up at least four times, and Kennedy eyed her back down to her chair. "I was just absolutely quivering. Nothing would come," she recalled.

The two discussed Kennedy's young children. The president asked her what she thought of Caroline, and Mary said that she thought she was doing wonderfully. Kennedy expressed concern that his son was "not very good looking," which was ironic, given that JFK Jr. would one day be dubbed the sexiest man in America. Mary reassured the president. "Oh, in a year, he'll be running around. He'll be putting on funny hats," Mary said, remembering the Denver airport, "and you'll be laughing at him."

So ended Mary's first meeting with Kennedy as sitting president.

JFK nurtured close but carefully circumscribed relationships with reporters around his age, like Mary, Ben Bradlee, Russell Baker, Hugh Sidey, and Blair Clark. All of these reporters were well educated and were attracted to Kennedy's charm and easy intelligence. For reporters in the inner circle, their closeness with the new president was heady. Kennedy made them confidants and drinking buddies. He invited them to state dinners, and male reporters, like fraternity brothers, joined him for nude late-night swims off the back of the presidential yacht. Although Kennedy once famously said of the press, after he'd become president, "Well, I'm reading more and enjoying it less," he liked reporters, and he once speculated that he would have been a journalist if it weren't for politics.

Mary was taken with JFK. As John Seigenthaler, a journalist and an assistant to Robert Kennedy when he served as attorney general, observed, "If she could have painted a picture and brought it to life of the Irish Catholic President she wanted to see, that would be Jack." He added, "There was something of the Irish mother in the way she looked at him; something of the Irish sister. She loved him, and he knew he had her."

This was dangerous stuff for any reporter, and even more so for Mary, given her penchant for blending commentary and hard reporting.

Kennedy used his personal relationships with reporters to avert hard questions about his misbehavior. His extramarital exploits were brazen, and he knew full well that they could cost him dearly. "I was aware of a good deal of snickering and winking about Jack Kennedy's interest in, and prowess with, women," Mary observed. "It was understandable. He was the most charming man of his generation, and the most attractive. He had hazel eyes and hair to match, superlative cheekbones, and a smile that reduced women to pulp. But that was while he was a senator, and a bachelor, which made it of less political consequence. When he was in the White House, I heard tales, but had no way of verifying them."

When, years after Kennedy's death, Seymour Hersh wrote the controversial book *The Dark Side of Camelot*, which cataloged many of JFK's private misdeeds, Mary confided to a friend, "I found it painful to write about President Kennedy's private life. It was not admirable. We knew that before Sy Hersh told us." But Mary also understood Boston and the

Kennedy family. "As his father before him," Mary commented, JFK felt "that rules were for other people."

The bright optimism that Kennedy brought to his first term soon collided with the harsh realities of the Cold War. In April 1961, the administration botched the Bay of Pigs invasion when a group of CIA-trained Cuban exiles met with embarrassing defeat on the shores of Fidel Castro's Cuba. Shortly after the debacle, Mary spoke with Adlai Stevenson, who had been appointed by Kennedy as ambassador to the United Nations. As a frustrated Stevenson emerged from the White House, he vented to Mary, "That young man, he never says please and he never says I'm sorry."

Although Mary only periodically covered international affairs, she described the impact of the Bay of Pigs on Kennedy. "He seemed preoccupied to the point of melancholy," she wrote. "He constantly rearranged the papers on the lectern before him. It was as if, discouraged about the untidy world, he wanted at least to make order in his immediate vicinity."

But Kennedy would only gain further proof of how hard it would be to bend the world to his will in late May and early June of 1961, when Mary and fifty other reporters accompanied Kennedy on his first overseas trip as president, journeying to France, Austria, and the United Kingdom.

In Paris, JFK was greeted by French president Charles de Gaulle at the airport as the Marine Band played "La Marseillaise" and "The Star-Spangled Banner." "Making his way across the field, he spotted the familiar faces of the White House press corps," Mary remembered. "He waved to us, a low surreptitious, under-handed wave which somehow conveyed his whole situation."

The glamorous American president and equally glamorous first lady were a sensation in France. Parisian women bowed and giggled in front of photographs of JFK in shop windows. Parisians gathered in knots around Mary and other reporters just so they could register their approval of their American guest. Mary was assigned to the press pool covering Kennedy's evening visit to the palace at Versailles. The Kennedys and the de Gaulles were joined by 150 guests in the opulent Hall of Mirrors, with its gilded statuary and vaulted ceilings, for a six-course meal. Following the dinner, de Gaulle led Kennedy through the lengthy corridors to the Royal Opera hall for a special performance by the Paris Opera Ballet.

At intermission, Mary, who had stood for the first half of the performance in the small but exquisitely proportioned theater, cast about for a new perch. She noticed that the two presidents had disappeared into a small room behind the king's box. Taking a deep breath, Mary pushed through the mirrored door and was startled to find herself in a small chamber with Kennedy, de Gaulle, and a handful of the most privileged guests, sipping champagne. Mary had no business being there, but she realized that a sudden exit would have been as embarrassing as her uninvited entrance.

Kennedy glanced quizzically at Mary, bemused by her trespass. He approached, and they could not suppress their laughter.

"Well, it makes you think, doesn't it?" said the president, shaking his head. "Pretty impressive." He added, "This is a little different than Fred Waring and Lawrence Welk at the White House. We've got to start doing something different. I don't know just what, but we've got to do something."

Mary was surprised—and relieved—by Kennedy's attention. "The president did seem very happy to see me, and immediately clued into a conversation. He couldn't have been more friendly and approachable and casual and gay—the way he always was."

Mary asked Kennedy how he was getting along with de Gaulle. Kennedy raised his eyebrows and shrugged. "Have you met him?" he asked.

Mary said that she had not.

"Do you want to?"

"Yes, that would be nice."

Kennedy, not even bothering to try his French, introduced Mary to de Gaulle.

"General, I'd like you to meet a friend of mine, one of our journalists. This is Mary McGrory from the *Washington Star.*"

De Gaulle reacted with studied indifference, looking over Mary's shoulder. Kennedy chatted on amiably in English. Mary was struck by the fact that in a room full of French speakers, Kennedy gravitated toward her because she was safe and familiar. Behind all of Kennedy's manners and grace was a lasting shyness. "He preferred people to come to him," Mary said, because it gave him a sense of control.

Things took a far more serious turn as Kennedy headed to Vienna for his first meeting with Soviet leader Nikita Khrushchev. Many of Kennedy's key foreign policy advisers had argued against holding a summit with the Soviets so early in the term. Khrushchev was eager to intimidate Kennedy, and the discussions between the two were grim. Khrushchev berated and bullied the president to an embarrassing degree. He was particularly bellicose about Berlin, and an exasperated Kennedy finally made clear that Soviet adventurism could push the two nations into war. Recognizing that the talks had been a disaster, Kennedy told journalist Scotty Reston after the meetings, "I've got a terrible problem if he thinks I'm inexperienced and have no guts."

Not long after the Europe trip, Mary's relationship with Blair Clark came to a head. Irritated by Clark's continued indecision and upset that he had not been in contact with her when they had both been in Vienna, Mary wrote to Clark demanding that they sever all ties. If they were not going to be a couple, Mary wanted to stop tormenting herself. Maintaining a casual facade was simply too painful.

Clark responded at some length in a letter. "Dearest Mary bird, I have thought, hesitated, turned this way and that and—yes—suffered over how to respond to your letter of dismissal." Calling himself her "grand-ambivalent friend," he ruminated on what it would have been like if they'd sat down and truly discussed their mutual feelings.

How fierce I think we would have been, how merciless—especially you, sparing me (a little), but not yourself. I think we would have laughed, though, and found it hard to be solemn. (Indeed, I've never seen you that way.) All you want you say, is not to see me, and that is the simplest favor to grant, in my current obsessive state when I really see no one. If I tell you there is no way we can avoid each other given all the real and accidental links, I seem to be taking you too seriously in the farewell, or not enough. I see us meeting on the red carpet to the stairs of the Waldorf's Grand Ballroom at some Hibernian B'nai Brith dinner and being unable to carry off the estrangement, or laughing at the same thing—perhaps each other. Mary bird, it won't work. . . . I'm asking for a retraction, for another lease on a life we've never lived, for more charity. I love you Mary, and you know it. It's just that I won't do (much of anything.) Please spare me and forgive me.

The letter perfectly encapsulated all that Mary found equally maddening and appealing about Clark: the charm, irreverence, elusiveness, and unwillingness to commit. But his letter carried the day, and Mary was not strong enough to cut off contact.

Why did Mary continue to carry a torch for him? She always had a soft spot for lost causes—perhaps because it felt very Irish. Perhaps a relationship doomed to failure was purer and more romantic. The witty and pointed letters back and forth felt like the diary of a great love affair waiting to be saved by some miracle—Mary's own Jane Austen moment. Clark was a first-class flirt, and he offered Mary a sense of real intimacy, with the safety of distance. Because it was more a romantic than a sexual entanglement, her career wasn't at risk. Mary had achieved a love befitting a classic novel, but in many ways it was just as remote.

She also got to know the president's brother Bobby better during this period. Their relationship was complex. The attorney general was more confrontational, less literary, and more devout than the president. His reputation as the ill-tempered political enforcer of the Kennedy clan was well earned, and his appointment to the cabinet had been one of family loyalty over qualification.

Mary was uneasy about Bobby's sharp edges, and she described him like a British weather report: "Cloudy, with bright intervals." But despite some differences, Mary and Bobby forged a close bond. (As she also did with Bobby's wife, Ethel, who was a deeply observant Catholic and a great fan of Mary's work.)

Bobby's former press secretary, John Seigenthaler, noted that Bobby was wary of Mary as a reporter, and the younger Kennedy also knew that in Mary's eyes, he was always wanting in comparison with his brother. Haynes Johnson, a close friend of Bobby's, observed: "Jack was like a Boston Brahmin or an English lord and Bobby was a parish priest—tough as nails and would fight like hell."

Mary traveled to the Kennedy family compound at Hyannis Port as a guest. "Bobby tried to teach me to water ski," she remembered. "It was one of his few failures as a coach." As Mary confided to a fellow visitor, Oklahoma senator Fred Harris, the only way to get along with the Kennedys was to preemptively admit that you were an underachiever so that you could get enough space to sit and read a book rather than joining a touch football game.

Mary was invited to a number of the salons hosted by Bobby and Ethel at Hickory Hill, their sprawling Civil War–era white-brick home in McLean, Virginia. The gatherings became emblematic of the new administration, with artists, politicians, intellectuals, and others gathering to discuss great ideas of the day.

Mary also recalled a winter day when she emerged from the Justice Department after an interview. A black limousine pulled up next to her. It was Bobby and Ethel. Bobby rolled down the window and called out to her, "Are you coming to my party? We're having a reception for foreign students."

Mary replied that she had to get back to her office, and she started walking down 10th Street. A few seconds later, she heard pounding footsteps. Bobby was running after her. Reaching Mary, he leaned over, scooped her up, and threw her over his shoulder.

"You *are* coming to my party," said Bobby, roaring with laughter. Racing back down the street, he carried Mary up the stairs to the entrance of the Justice Department.

Not long after her trip to Europe with JFK, Mary traveled with Bobby,

Ethel, and a small congressional delegation to Rome for a private audience with Pope John XXIII at Castel Gandolfo. The pope, smiling, entered the high-ceilinged chamber wearing red shoes and a white cassock. The Americans dropped to their knees. The pope easily shifted from a gesture of benediction to motioning his visitors to rise. He invited all of the Catholics to receive his personal blessing while pointing out that "it wouldn't hurt" the non-Catholics to do so as well. Mary was particularly enthusiastic about Pope John's reforms, later codified in Vatican II, which, among other things, allowed Catholic masses to be held in local languages rather than Latin. She saw him as a much-needed breath of fresh air in the Church.

Mary had come far: she was a syndicated columnist, President Kennedy had personally introduced her to Charles de Gaulle, her niece and nephew had met JFK in the Oval Office, and now she was being invited to a private audience with the pope at the Vatican. Her life was almost inconceivable to her friends and family back in Roslindale.

In late July 1961, Kennedy announced from Washington that he was dramatically expanding the U.S. military in response to Nikita Khrushchev's threats. Mary described the president as he addressed the nation on the Berlin crisis: "Inside his stuffy, crowded office, the president was tense. Outside it was a perfect summer night, an almost full moon riding high, the trees black against the sky. The president looked hot and preoccupied." It struck Mary that Kennedy was trying to reason with the American public rather than rouse them. "We intend to have a wider choice than humiliation or all-out nuclear action," he said.

As the Soviets attempted to isolate West Berlin by erecting the Berlin Wall, in August 1961, Kennedy called for the active-duty military to be expanded by more than 210,000 men. Fears of a war between the two superpowers intensified. The wall's completion, which stopped the rush of immigration into West Berlin and trapped East Germans behind the Iron Curtain, ushered in an uneasy standoff that would endure for decades. The Cold War had its most physical embodiment: an ugly concrete scar running through the heart of Germany.

With Kennedy approaching the end of his first year in office and his tenure having been marked by the harsh realities of the Cold War, the editors at the *Star* assigned Mary an "anniversary" story in January 1962. She requested an interview with JFK through the White House press office at a time when numerous other reporters were working on similar pieces. Mary stewed when no response was forthcoming.

She called up Kenny O'Donnell to complain, touching his most sensitive nerve: clan loyalty.

"Kenny," Mary sighed, "I did not see Roscoe Drummond"—the head of the *Christian Science Monitor*'s Washington bureau, who had been granted a presidential interview—"in Wisconsin, and I did not ride any buses with Roscoe Drummond in West Virginia. I was there. Have you forgotten all your old friends?"

Mary was miffed, and O'Donnell knew it.

"Mary, Mary," he said, trying to calm her, "what do you want?"

"I want to see the president," Mary said.

"Do you want to come in this afternoon?"

"No, tomorrow morning will be all right."

So the next morning at 10:30, a grinning Kenny O'Donnell ushered Mary into the Oval Office with great flourish.

President Kennedy strode forward, rubbing his hands together. He gently placed a hand on Mary's arm. "There she is. I was wondering where you had been. I was just saying to Kenny the other day, 'We never see Mary anymore.'"

Kennedy wore a gray suit, and he looked tired, but not depressed. He noted in even tones that his first year had brought its share of disappointments. Mary was struck by his lack of swagger. She simply could not stay angry with him.

As the two drank their coffee, Kennedy said, "I see you're writing about Goldwater."

Senator Barry Goldwater, the conservative firebrand from Arizona, was widely expected to be Kennedy's Republican challenger in 1964, although the outspoken Goldwater had yet to formally announce his plans.

Mary nodded.

"I didn't read it," declared Kennedy. It came across as more of a rebuke than intended.

"Oh, you didn't," Mary responded, taken aback.

"No," Kennedy said. "Any story that starts out that a man would rather be right than president, I never finish." For the intensely pragmatic Kennedy, Goldwater's emphasis on ideology over electability was baffling.

"Except that in his case," retorted Mary, "don't you see that it's literally true?"

Kennedy pondered Goldwater's stance almost as a curiosity. "Oh, yes. I never thought of that."

Mary described the session with Kennedy in her column the next day. She omitted the exchange about Goldwater and wrote that Kennedy "stood on the eve of his first anniversary in power, attempting as always to convince with facts and figures rather than a show of feeling, making no great claims, aware of his problems, conscious of his responsibilities and, on Monday anyway, hopeful."

As the interview drew to a close, Kennedy suddenly proffered Mary an invitation to a White House congressional dinner that was scheduled a few days later. "Why don't you come? Why don't you come?" Kennedy gave a halfhearted explanation for why she hadn't gotten the peace offering of an invitation sooner.

At the dinner, JFK and Jackie made a grand entrance as the band played "Hail to the Chief." Mary was pleasantly surprised when Congressman Charles Halleck, the Republican House minority leader, called down the table during the meal to tell Mary how much he enjoyed her columns.

As the evening wound down, Mary and Kennedy chatted at some length in the hall. Both were enjoying themselves. She shared her surprise that Congressman Halleck was a regular reader.

Kennedy smiled. "He reads those stories, does he?" said the president. Then, referring back to their conversation in the Oval Office, he added, "And when he reads that you've said that a man would rather be right than president, he reads all the way through, does he?" Mary smiled.

The 1962 California governor's race gave Mary a chance to again cover the politician she loved to loathe: Richard Nixon. (She had once written to a friend about Nixon, "If he were a horse, I should not buy him.") Nixon hoped that a win in California would help rehabilitate his image and provide a springboard to the presidency. He regularly accused Governor Pat Brown of being soft on subversives, casting himself as the country's fiercest anti-Communist. "Just why Californians should be so obsessed with the subject of domestic communism is puzzling," pondered Mary. "Everyone here, including Richard M. Nixon, who brought it up, insists that communism is not a major issue in Mr. Nixon's campaign against Governor Edmund (Pat) Brown. It is merely the one that sets audiences on fire."

Mary knew the race would be tight, and as the contest neared its climax, the Cuban missile crisis erupted, in October 1962. With the United States and the Soviet Union on the brink of nuclear confrontation, the world held its collective breath. Although fears of a nuclear war were not new, the entire situation was enormously unsettling. It was not long before *Popular Mechanics* was selling do-it-yourself home fallout-shelter kits.

Mary was at the Beverly Hilton hotel with the Nixon campaign on Election Night. At one in the morning, Governor Brown, with a lead of 100,000 votes, claimed victory. Mary described the scene at the Nixon camp. "At 1:50, the atmosphere on the seventh floor was snappish. An aide stood on the barricades and threatened to call the fire marshal if the television cameras did not go back. A heated exchange followed and the cameras retreated a foot. Post-mortems were quietly being conducted between lesser staff aides and reporters." Campaign aide Caspar Weinberger, then the Republican state chairman, went down to the ballroom to tell bedraggled partisans that there would be no statement from Nixon.

The next morning when Herb Klein, Nixon's press secretary, told

Nixon that the press was waiting for a traditional concession speech, he replied simply, "Screw them." Klein went down to address the press in the Hilton's Cadoro Room, announcing that Nixon had conceded but would not appear. Klein was surprised as everyone else when Nixon, against his better judgment, decided to come down from his suite and take the podium. He was exhausted, unshaven, and surrounded by red-eyed assistants. The results made for one of Mary's most famous columns. It began, "For Richard M. Nixon, it was exit snarling. He bowed off the political stage, turning on friends and enemies alike, protesting all the while he had 'no hard feelings against anybody.'"

Mary could not have imagined better material, and she took Nixon apart in magisterial fashion.

> Mr. Nixon carried on for 17 minutes in a finale of intemperance and incoherence unmatched in American political annals. He pulled the havoc down around his ears, while his staff looked on aghast. His principal target was the press. But he was like a kamikaze pilot who keeps apologizing for the attack. Every time he scorched the Fourth Estate, his voice curling with rage and scorn, he insisted that he had no complaint. Throughout, he was obviously having a furious inner argument with himself. The schooled politician who came within an ace of the White House kept telling him not to do it. But the sore loser told him to keep going. Three times he said, "one last thing." But the rancor that had propelled him to confront his persecutors, whom he said at one point he has always respected, would not let him quit.

Nixon then uttered some of his most famous words: "You won't have Nixon to kick around anymore, because, gentlemen, this is my last press conference, and it will be one in which I have welcomed the opportunity to test wits with you."

Mary's column concluded, "No questions had been asked except by Mr. Nixon of himself. None actually remained, the former vice president having disposed of everything, including possibly his reputation, in his epic tirade."

Her column provoked intense reactions. One *Star* reader telegrammed the editors: "McGrory's column concerning Vice President Richard M. Nixon meanest, lowest, dirtiest diatribe yet written, your rag has reached a new low. Cancel my subscription and remove your yellow box from my property no later than today." Another wrote, "I know it's typical of the Irish to kick a man when he's down, but even the Irish are human beings who must have somewhere in their hearts a faint shred of compassion."

The vitriol was such that the *Washington Post*'s White House correspondent, Edward Folliard, felt compelled to write to the *Star* in Mary's defense: "I have been a reader of the *Evening Star* since I was in short pants. Never in all that time—and it has been an awfully long time—have I seen such meanness of spirit and such uncontrolled and unjustified rage as was poured into your letter to the editor department by those who wrote in to denounce Mary McGrory's story."

The response from other quarters was kinder. Ben Bradlee and humorist Art Buchwald cabled Mary: "Now that you don't have Nixon to kick around, you'll never write a better story." Mary also received a gracious note from W. P. Hobby of the *Houston Post*, a juror for the Pulitzer Prize that year: "Four of us read 78 entries in two days—some of them pretty grim. There was no question as to which of the 78 entries made the most enjoyable reading. . . . The Pulitzer group on national affairs seemed to be afflicted with the idea that everything has to be cosmic, so your entry didn't get recommended for the award, but it did make the day considerably brighter." Mary's style remained too unconventional for the Pulitzer's arbiters of taste.

When Eleanor Roosevelt passed away, on November 7, 1962, Mary flew to the funeral on Air Force One with JFK and a number of other senior officials and reporters. The president came to the front of the plane and saw Mary. His mood was light. The Cuban missile crisis had been successfully resolved through adroit backroom diplomacy that left Kennedy looking like he had stared down the Soviets.

"Say Mary, that was a nice story you wrote about Nixon." Grinning, he added, "I must remember to smile when I get defeated."

Kennedy sat down next to Chief Justice Earl Warren, who had earlier served as California's governor and who also disliked Nixon. Recently appointed justice Arthur Goldberg appeared, and Kennedy asked Warren, "Is Arthur being any help to you up there, Chief?"

Chief Justice Warren chuckled.

The president and Warren then huddled over a series of press clippings from Nixon's defeat in California. "It would have been hard to say, watching their faces," Mary commented, "who had enjoyed the downfall more, the Chief Justice or the President of the United States. They had their heads together over the clippings and were laughing like schoolboys."

Perhaps Mary's only regret from her "exit snarling" column was her absolute conviction that Nixon was finished as a politician, a view that she later called a huge mistake.

Despite her often grueling schedule, Mary remained committed to helping out with the orphans from St. Ann's. Instead of using the many demands on her time as an excuse to bow out of volunteering, Mary used her success to pull in high-profile supporters to her cause. Mary enlisted the Kennedys to help out at St. Ann's, and in 1961 she arranged for the kids' annual Christmas party to be held at the White House. Enthusiastic three- and four-year-olds ate ice cream and admired the largest Christmas tree they had ever seen. Carefully wrapped presents greeted the children, and a number of the Kennedy children joined the almost sixty kids from St. Ann's in the East Room. Sister Frances led the kids in "Joy to the World," and Bobby Kennedy sternly directed his own kids to wait their turn on Santa's lap. At the end of the party, a White House butler dutifully held a balloon for one of the orphans as he wrestled on his coat.

The event made a lasting impression on Bobby. He decreed that Mary must bring the children to swim at his house. Every Wednesday afternoon during the summer, Justice Department vans picked up Mary and the kids and trundled them out to Hickory Hill. Bobby attended a number of times, happily embracing soggy kids as they emerged from the pool, soaking his white dress shirt.

In 1962, Bobby again joined in the orphans' annual Christmas party, held at the home of one of Mary's coworkers. He had been asked to attend by one of the orphans, Rita, at a pool party. Although the festivities got off to a shaky start when one of the kids saw Santa emerging from a taxi, Saint Nick, thinking fast, explained that a minor sled accident had forced him into alternative transport.

The attorney general sat happily with the small, dark-eyed Rita in his lap. Mary had gotten Rita and several other girls small patent leather purses. They beamed. Unfortunately, as the kids dug into their ice cream and cake, Rita misplaced her bag. She accused one of the other girls of stealing it. As Rita fought back tears, Mary explained that some of the bags looked alike.

Bobby took charge. Mary laughingly wondered if he would bring in the police, or perhaps the FBI. "I'll handle the investigation myself," Bobby insisted. After finding Rita's bag under the coffee table, he held it aloft and exclaimed, "I broke the case. I broke the case."

"It was total immersion," Mary observed of Bobby's interactions with the kids. "Kennedy needed children as much as they needed him."

The year 1963 began sleepily. JFK had survived and thrived after his early foreign policy missteps. His successful handling of the Cuban missile crisis was widely viewed as a triumph. At the *Star*, Newby Noyes was promoted to executive editor, even as circulation slipped behind the *Washington Post*'s. Mary's mother and her aunt Kate moved out of their house on Kittredge Street in Roslindale, taking up residence in a nearby apartment. Mary continued her regular pilgrimages home and to Aunt Kate's place in Antrim, New Hampshire. As a girl, she had regularly traveled up to Antrim, where her Aunt Kate owned a small cottage on Gregg Lake. The entire family soon fell in love with Antrim and the lake—none more so than Mary. The log cottage, down a rough dirt road lined by a lush carpet of ferns, had a large fieldstone fireplace and white birch railings. Mary swam in the bracing lake water and took day hikes up nearby Holt Hill. Antrim was one of a handful of places that had a special hold on Mary.

In the spring of 1963, with Pope John XXIII lying critically ill, the *Star*'s editors dispatched Mary to Rome, and she was in St. Peter's Square when the fateful news arrived that the pope had died. "Death came to Pope John XXIII at the twilight of a glorious spring day," she wrote. "The last golden light of Rome filled the sky and a three-quarter moon was rising over the colonnade of St. Peter's Square when word came that he had finally begun that journey for which he had so often said he was ready."

Back at the White House, members of the cabinet debated whether Kennedy should cancel a planned trip to Italy. Daniel Patrick Moynihan, who was then Kennedy's assistant secretary of labor, wrote to Mary in Rome in late June 1963: "It is just as we feared—you won't ever come back to us. I was about to write you last week to say how absolutely startlingly marvelous everything you have written has been." Mary and Moynihan had become good friends, and she had deep affection for the cerebral New Yorker. In his letter, Moynihan described the debate at the White House regarding Kennedy's trip. When someone suggested that Kennedy should cancel the visit, the president declared, "Out of the question, I have to go to Rome in order to bring Mary back."

Returning from Rome, Mary covered JFK's Oval Office address on the night of July 26, 1963, when he announced his support for the Nuclear Test Ban Treaty.

Kennedy stopped to chat with Mary after the speech and asked how she was doing.

"I'm happy," said Mary. "I think this was a great moment. I think I'm even happier than you are."

Kennedy said, "Well, I'm happy."

Mary gently pushed back, "Well, you didn't sound that way."

Jabbing his left arm forward, Kennedy changed the subject. "What I want to know is why didn't the *Star* consider your credentials good enough to come to Ireland with us?" He was referring to a trip to Ireland the month before.

"Oh, I think it was something to do with immigration quotas," joked Mary, and the two laughed. But Mary also saw a message in Kennedy's inquiry. "It was interesting that he didn't want to waste any time discussing nuclear policy, when he did want to address a very specific inquiry indicating he knew who was where at all times."

But if international issues dominated the early part of Kennedy's term, domestic problems were never far beneath the surface, and the growing civil rights struggle was increasingly becoming a focus of Mary's writing. She pushed for a chance to do more reporting from the South, but her editors were concerned for her safety.

Martin Luther King Jr. delivered his "I Have a Dream" speech before a massive crowd in Washington on August 28, 1963. Mary attended the speech with Peter Lisagor of the *Chicago Daily News* and Kennedy pollster Lou Harris. She met Harris and Lisagor on the Capitol steps. The days before the speech had been incredibly tense, and Washington was on high alert, expecting violence. Large numbers of police and national guardsmen were positioned all over the city, and most Washingtonians stayed home from their jobs, fearing clashes in the streets. Mary's assessment of the threat was quite different; she brought a picnic basket of hard-boiled eggs, which she, Lisagor, and Harris ate as they stood at the Lincoln Memorial. They were just twenty feet away from King as he delivered his speech.

On September 15, 1963, in a savage rejoinder to Dr. King, the Ku Klux Klan bombed the 16th Street Church, in Birmingham, Alabama. The senseless attack wounded more than twenty and killed four young girls attending Sunday services. The attack on the church was so galling, and the March on Washington so orderly and respectful, that the national tide began to make a decisive shift in favor of civil rights.

Mary attended the memorial service for the children, in a crowded black church in Birmingham, and her series of columns from Alabama brimmed with outrage. Indeed, it is hard to imagine anything more appalling to Mary than an attack on innocent children in a church. "Dynamite has become a principal means of political expression in this strange, sick city," she wrote.

Mary ardently supported the role of faith leaders in promoting civil rights, and she delighted in seeing student protestors and nuns standing side by side under a common banner. On a plane ride back from Selma, Alabama, Mary insisted on helping a group of interfaith leaders write their public statement. It was an admirable sentiment, but the moment also underscored Mary's increasing willingness to write her own rules as a reporter.

Mary did not consider herself bound by normal standards of journalistic impartiality. "It is not my responsibility," she argued. "If I wanted to be fair and objective, I wouldn't be writing." Mary thought of herself not as a columnist but as a reporter who had been given license to deliver her opinion. If the Kennedys, as Mary argued, saw themselves as above the rules of society, Mary saw herself as outside the usual standards of journalism. As one letter to the *Star*'s editor during the 1960s complained, "This is not an account of events but an opinion, a loaded opinion—skillful, subtly, and dangerously loaded."

Haynes Johnson observed that Mary had "no qualms at all" crossing the lines that other reporters were reluctant to breach. "Her role was to influence events and to influence the world through her writings. If she could do it by personal importuning and pressure, she would do that."

By September and October of 1963, Mary was happily previewing the likely Republican presidential contenders. Although both Nelson Rockefeller and George Romney hoped to win the nomination, Rockefeller's divorce and remarriage had badly damaged him in the eyes of Republican voters, and Romney simply never caught fire. Former senator Henry Cabot Lodge, the U.S. ambassador to Vietnam, also hinted that he might run. But Barry Goldwater was the darling of the right, and his impolitic rhetoric thrilled conservatives. Kennedy relished the idea of running against Goldwater. Mary wrote that when Goldwater's name came up in press conferences, the president looked "like a child who wants to save his candy so he can savor it better later."

In mid-November, Mary received an invitation to a White House lunch scheduled for December 6, 1963. She noted with satisfaction that the invitation had arrived well in advance.

On November 14, Mary covered the president's press conference at the State Department Auditorium. At one point, a reporter invited Kennedy to criticize Congress for its failure to pass several key spending bills. But as Mary observed, "This most rational man refused. It was not his style. Instead, he quoted from the poet Arthur Hugh Clough: 'But westward, look, the land is bright.'"

It was the last time Mary would see John Fitzgerald Kennedy alive.

Just after 1:30 P.M. Eastern Standard Time on November 22, 1963, dazed reporters rushed into the *Star*. A weeping Mary was among them. JFK had been assassinated in Dallas.

At the center of the maelstrom was one of the *Star*'s editors, John Cassady. Cassady was well liked among the staff, and known for his unusually even temperament. Calm and deliberate, he was what one former colleague described as "an old style gentleman." Cassady was particularly influential on Mary, always able to coax columns out of her as deadlines approached.

Mary was dispatched to Andrews Air Force Base to meet Air Force One as President Lyndon Johnson and Jackie Kennedy arrived from Dallas with JFK's body. Several hundred people had gathered by the fence in the harsh artificial light of the landing strip. Bobby Kennedy waited restlessly, as did other members of the cabinet. Mary described the scene: "Secretary of Defense McNamara was by himself, looking off into the distance. McGeorge Bundy, the President's foreign policy adviser, was carrying a dispatch case under his arm. Theodore Sorensen, the President's young special counsel, looking white-faced and stricken, was unseeing and unhearing in the nightmarish light and noise."

A U.S. Navy hearse waited for the late president's body. "And a few minutes after six, United States Air Force One, all white and blue, landed amid a deafening roar," Mary penned. "The back door was flung open. But this time there was no familiar graceful figure, fingering a button of his jacket, waiting to smile, wanting to wave. Instead the light fell on the gleam of a bronze casket."

Kennedy's aides, who had loved him like a brother, were all there: Dave Powers, Larry O'Brien, and Kenny O'Donnell, among others.

"The men picked up their inexpressible burden and placed it on top of the platform, and it was lowered into the hearse. Then in the frame stood his wife, Jacqueline, in a rose-colored suit with black facings. By her side was his favorite brother, Robert, the Attorney General, who had somehow gotten onto the plane although he had never left Washington. He was holding Mrs. Kennedy by the hand. She was lifted from the platform and opened the door of the gray hearse and climbed in the back. Bobby followed her. Several minutes later, the new President walked slowly down the ramp with his wife. With tears on their faces, the leaderless men of the New Frontier went up to greet him."

After leaving Andrews Air Force Base, Mary had a cup of coffee in Bethesda and then went to the White House. In the lobby, she found Bob Healy, a reporter for the *Boston Globe*, looking like a wounded animal. The two retreated to the historic Hay-Adams Hotel for several Scotches. It was tempting to drink more, but both had work to do. They headed back to their respective offices.

Mary was asked to write both a news story about the scene at Andrews and an editorial. Mary went to her desk in the back of the *Star* newsroom and perched before her typewriter. Her heart felt like it was breaking.

Burt Hoffman, the editor on the national desk, came by her desk. "Newby's looking for you."

"I know."

"What are you going to do?" asked Hoffman.

"I'm going to write for the news side first," Mary said, "and then I'll do his editorial."

Newby emerged from his office not long after. He started circling Mary's desk, edging closer as he consulted his watch.

"I'm going to finish the news story," Mary told Newby, "and then take care of you."

Newby never forgot the scene. As he stood over her shoulder waiting for the copy, Mary typed away, tears streaming down her face.

The news story came quickly, and she churned out the editorial in about forty-five minutes.

There are no better examples of Mary's work than what she produced in the days following Dallas. Consider this excerpt from her editorial: "He brought gaiety, glamour, and grace to the American political scene in a measure never known before. That lightsome tread, that debonair touch, that shock of chestnut hair, that beguiling grin, that shattering understatement—these are what we shall remember."

"She wrote that column off the top of her head," recalled her colleague Lance Gay. "She said that was one of her easier columns to write. She came in and wrote. It was something she believed."

"That evening a group of us who lived on Macomb Street, out Connecticut Avenue, drifted over to Mary McGrory's," Patrick Moynihan recalled. Moynihan told the others, among them Mary, how he had been in the White House that afternoon, just down the hall from the Oval Office, when he heard the news. The staff was replacing the rug in the president's office, and the furniture had been out in the hall, with JFK's rocking chair sitting atop his desk, "as if new people were moving in."

After a long, uncomfortable pause, Mary declared, "We'll never laugh again."

"Heavens, Mary," Moynihan replied with a start. "We'll laugh again. It's just that we will never be young again."

As Moynihan would say later, "I don't think there's any point in being Irish if you don't know that the world is going to break your heart eventually. I guess that we thought we had a little more time."

On Saturday, the day after the assassination, Mary attended the wake in the East Room of the White House. As she entered, Kenny O'Donnell approached her. Mary had observed in her column that morning that O'Donnell would have been willing to die for Jack Kennedy. Wrapping his arms around her, he said, "I will love you forever for what you wrote about me."

Mary was dismissive. "Well, Kenny, everybody knows that's true." They went in.

A Catholic Mass was held as part of the ceremony, the first time a Mass had ever been conducted in the White House.

Like most newspapers, the *Star* printed extra copies for what it expected to be heavy public demand. The staff was shocked to see many of those extra copies come back unsold. People were home, glued to their televisions, and did not go out to buy the newspaper.

Mary was supposed to write a reminiscence of Kennedy for the next day's paper. She brought a draft to the desk of editor Bill Hill, who had a prickly relationship with many reporters.

Hill read the draft and said that it should be in the first person.

Burt Hoffman, who was watching the scene, began to protest. He was worried that Mary was on the edge of a breakdown.

Mary waved off Hoffman. "Burt, it's okay. He's right."

She went back to her desk and labored over the rewrite. She managed to produce a remembrance that was deeply personal without being self-aggrandizing. "When he came to the White House, suddenly everyone saw what the New Frontier was going to mean," Mary wrote. "It meant a poet at the inauguration; it meant swooping around Washington, dropping in on delighted and flustered old friends; it meant going to the airport in zero weather without an overcoat; it meant a rocking chair and having the Hickory Hill seminar at the White House when Bobby and Ethel were out of town; it meant fun at presidential press conferences."

On Sunday, November 24, Kennedy's body lay in state under the Capitol Rotunda. Mary worked through the crowd of hundreds of thousands of people waiting outside in near-freezing temperatures to pay their respects.

Back at the *Star*, she turned her attention to Kennedy's widow, Jackie. "From the moment she arrived back in Washington, erect and composed, wearing the blood-stained clothes of the infamous day in Dallas, she has imparted meaning and order to the chaos around her. She would not want anything to be lost to the world. She brought her two children to the Capitol yesterday. If she wanted them to see, however imperfectly, what their father meant, she also dramatized to the world and the evil people in it that a young father had been slain as well as a president."

As Mary completed her column that evening, she again spoke with her editor, John Cassady. "I'll go to the funeral," Mary said in low tones.

"You're not too tired?" Cassady inquired.

"No, I can do it."

On Monday, November 25, a million people turned out in the streets of Washington to watch Kennedy's final funeral procession as it traveled from the Capitol past the White House to St. Matthew's Cathedral, and on to Kennedy's final resting place at Arlington National Cemetery. During the ceremony at St. Matthew's, Mary whispered, "Goodnight, sweet prince," as Kennedy lay in his coffin.

After the funeral, Mary walked with William Walton, an old Kennedy family friend. The day was cold, and the two went to the Hay-Adams Hotel, just across Lafayette Square from the White House, for a glass of brandy. They reminisced, and for a moment, just a moment, in the overstuffed comfort of the cozy bar, it felt as though maybe Kennedy was not dead. They both knew better.

After some time, Mary stood up. "But Bill, now I have to go and write his funeral story."

Walton understood. He added a parting comment: "Do one thing for him. No crap."

"Okay," Mary said, "I'll do that. I'll try to do that."

Mary took a taxi back to the *Star*. John Cassady was on the desk. Mary settled in to write. It might have been the fatigue, the brandy, or the grief, but nothing came. "I had a total, complete block," Mary would recall. It was not long before she was surrounded by small piles of crumpled paper with abandoned leads.

Mary wrote long, ponderous sentences that hung like "Victorian crepe." Her prose felt leaden. The minutes turned to hours, and three hours stretched to four, and then five. All the emotion and exhaustion welled up within her, but her feelings were unwilling to escape to the page.

At around eleven, John Cassady approached gingerly.

"Are you sure you can do it, Mary?"

Mary sighed. "Yes, I know I can."

Cassady retreated.

Mary stopped and took a deep breath. She thought back to Girls'

Latin School and diagramming sentence after sentence. She thought about Kennedy the man, and traveling with him on the campaign trail.

And at that moment, Mary came to a fundamental conviction: in the presence of great grief and emotion, write short sentences.

She started to slash the long, soggy phrases in half. The writing began to move. Mary's column on Kennedy's funeral remains one of her finest. Here it is in its entirety:

Of John Fitzgerald Kennedy's funeral it can be said he would have liked it.

It had that decorum and dash that were in his special style. It was both splendid and spontaneous. It was full of children and princes, of gardeners and governors.

Everyone measured up to New Frontier standards.

A million people lined up every inch of his last journey. Enough heads of state filed into St. Matthew's Cathedral to change the shape of the world.

The weather was superb, as crisp and clear as one of his own instructions.

His wife's gallantry became a legend. His two children behaved like Kennedys. His 3-year-old son saluted his coffin. His 6-year-old daughter comforted her mother. Looking up and seeing tears, she reached over and gave her mother's hand a consoling squeeze.

The procession from the White House would have delighted him. It was a marvelous eye-filling jumble of the mighty and obscure, all walking behind his wife and his two brothers.

There was no cadence or order, but the presence of Gen. de Gaulle alone in the ragged line of march was enough to give it grandeur. He stalked splendidly up Connecticut Avenue, more or less beside Queen Frederika of Greece and King Baudouin of Belgium.

The sounds of the day were smashingly appropriate. The tolling of the bells gave way to the skirling of the Black Watch Pipers whose lament blended with the organ music inside the cathedral.

At the graveside, there was the thunder of jets overhead, a 21-gun salute, taps, and finally the strains of the Navy hymn, "Eternal Father Strong to Save."

He would have seen every politician he ever knew, two ex-Presidents, Truman and Eisenhower, and a foe or two. Gov. Wallace of Alabama had trouble finding a place to sit in the Cathedral.

His old friend, Cardinal Cushing of Boston, who married him, baptized his children and prayed over him in the icy air of his inaugural, said a Low Mass. At the final prayers, after the last blessing, he suddenly added, "Dear Jack."

There was no eulogy. Instead, Bishop Philip M. Hannan mounted the pulpit and read passages from the President's speeches and evoked him so vividly that tears splashed on the red carpets and the benches of the Cathedral. Nobody cried out, nobody broke down.

And the Bishop read a passage the President had often noted in the Scriptures: "There is a time to be born and a time to die." He made no reference to the fact that no one had thought last Friday was a time for John Fitzgerald Kennedy to die—a martyr's death—in Dallas. The President himself had spent no time in trying to express the inexpressible. Excess was alien to his nature.

The funeral cortege stretched for miles. An old campaigner would have loved the crowd. Children sat on the curbstones. Old ladies wrapped their furs around them.

The site of the grave, at the top of one slope, commands all of Washington. Prince Philip used his sword as a walking stick to navigate the incline.

His brother, Robert, his face a study in desolation, stood beside the President's widow. The children of the fabulous family were all around.

Jacqueline Kennedy received the flag from his coffin, bent over and with a torch lit a flame that is to burn forever on his grave—against the day that anyone might forget that her husband had been a President and a martyr.

It was a day of such endless fitness, with so much pathos and panoply, so much grief nobly born that it may extinguish that unseemly hour in Dallas, where all that was alien to him—savagery, violence, irrationality—struck down the 35th President of the United States.

Under the weight of tragedy, Mary produced a remarkable series of pitch-perfect columns—moving but not maudlin, graceful and understated. Haynes Johnson called them "the best thing I have ever seen in American journalism." Many of Mary's fellow journalists described it as criminal that she did not win a Pulitzer Prize for her work in 1963.

Jackie Kennedy wrote to Mary that her column on the funeral "will always be the best of all. It makes him so alive that I can't bear to read it too often."

But Mary was not entirely a stargazer when it came to Kennedy. She acknowledged his personal shortcomings and the problems during his term. "He invaded Cuba—and never relented in his hostility to Fidel Castro. He was slow on civil rights. He sent 17,000 Americans to Vietnam. . . . Those who did not know him or live through his death may find it difficult to understand the continuing bereavement of those who did. What was lost on that black day in Dallas was the irreplaceable sense of 'glad confident morning' that John Kennedy brought to the whole world."

On Thanksgiving Day, less than a week after the president's murder, Mary was invited, along with about twenty other guests, to Hickory Hill to have brunch with Bobby and Ethel Kennedy. The Kennedys struggled to put on a brave face as they served Bloody Marys to their guests. Mary entered, weeping, and threw her arms around Bobby. He did his best to brighten the mood, but the terrible strain was apparent on Bobby's face.

Mary coaxed Bobby into attending the annual Christmas party for the St. Ann's orphans. She let the children know that Bobby Kennedy would be coming and told them to be on their best behavior. She was particularly fond of one of the boys from St. Ann's, Michael Doyle, describing him as "the kind of child who melts you."

Author Peter Maas recalled the moment when Bobby entered the room: "All these little children—screaming and playing—there was just suddenly silence." Michael Doyle ran up to Bobby, stopped in front of him, and exclaimed, "Your brother's dead. Your brother's dead."

The adults were stunned into silence, and Bobby winced as if he had been struck. Michael Doyle burst into tears.

Bobby stepped forward and scooped up the boy, holding him close.

"That's all right," Bobby whispered to Michael. "I have another brother."

CHAPTER FOUR

Picking Up the Pieces

D rained, Mary took a short holiday in January 1964. Jackie, Bobby, and Ethel Kennedy telegrammed her as she departed from New York: "Miss Mary McGrory, passenger Oslofjord, care Norwegian American Lines, West Tenth Street, Sailing 8pm, New York. All the Kennedys send their love. Come back quickly."

Not long after Mary departed, the Beatles arrived in New York to screaming crowds of fans. Two days later, their appearance on *The Ed Sullivan Show* was watched by some seventy-three million Americans. Signs of protest against the conformity of the 1950s were beginning to ripple across the country.

Mary was discomfited by the idea of Lyndon Johnson having assumed the presidency. She thought LBJ was gargantuan in both his abilities and his shortcomings, a master political tactician defined by coarseness and insecurity. Johnson was painfully aware that many, like Mary, saw him as a step down from Kennedy. As he told a biographer, the circumstances of coming into the presidency were almost unbearable. "For millions of Americans, I was still illegitimate, a naked man with no presidential covering, a pretender to the throne." America was angry with Texas and Texans; the Dallas Cowboys football team was booed for coming from the town that killed Kennedy.

Mary attended LBJ's first major press conference, in March 1964. "The moment that would provide the most vivid contrast between him and his predecessor, President Kennedy, could not be put off forever. It is easy to understand why President Johnson wanted to." Mary even commented disapprovingly on the venue, calling the International Conference Room at the State Department "a depressing chamber, with a low ceiling that looks like an enormous ice-cube tray."

After Mary's comments, President Johnson grumbled to the head of the Associated Press, "When I sat down, they said I ought to stand up. When I stood up, they said I ought to sit down. When I had it in the State Department, Mary McGrory said the room was too dark. When I had it in the East Room, they said it was too light. And I don't give a damn. Just so it is comfortable for them." Johnson also complained to his aide Joseph Califano, "Mary McGrory is the best writer in Washington, and she keeps getting better and better at my expense."

Oval Office recordings made clear that Mary's columns troubled Johnson, and tapes from March 1964 captured the president telling Larry O'Brien, "Now you've got to get me straightened out with Mary. She's had three mean columns on me in the last ten days." O'Brien assured Johnson he would talk with Mary. "Just tell her that she can be in love with me, too, that I love her," LBJ said, "and I think she is the best writer in town."

When Mary started questioning the administration's strategy to pass civil rights legislation, President Johnson personally phoned Senate Majority Leader Mike Mansfield and insisted that he talk with Mary and "tell her that it is going very well and you're very happy with it." Johnson warned that Mary had "awfully good" sources in the Justice Department—Bobby Kennedy—and that she was intent on being a "troublemaker."

Mary met with Johnson in the Oval Office on March 24 for a full hour, as part of his effort to win her over. Johnson believed a personal approach to reporters was essential, as he described to biographer Doris Kearns Goodwin: "You learn that Stewart Alsop cares a lot about appearing to be an intellectual and a historian, so whenever you talk to him, play down the gold cufflinks which you play up with *Time* Magazine, and to him, emphasize your relationship with F.D.R. and your roots in Texas. You learn that Mary McGrory likes dominant personalities and Doris Fleeson cares only about issues, so with McGrory, you come on strong and with Fleeson you make yourself sound like some impractical red-hot liberal." Johnson's strategy of coming on strong with Mary was badly flawed. As Mary told Blair Clark, "I think he has done mighty well, but I'm afraid he lacks charm to an almost disastrous degree."

After the discussion at the White House, Mary's columns were more positive for a time, largely because it was obvious that Johnson was in an exceptionally good position heading into the fall election, with high poll numbers and rapid progress on an ambitious legislative agenda.

If Johnson was adjusting after an uneasy start, the same could not be said for Bobby Kennedy. With a bracing chill in the air, Bobby and Jackie Kennedy visited JFK's resting place at Arlington National Cemetery on the first Saint Patrick's Day after his death. The Irish ambassador placed a shamrock and a small clump of Irish sod on Kennedy's grave.

Mary and Bobby called on Jackie Kennedy at her temporary residence later that day. Mary and Bobby had talked a great deal after JFK had been killed, and he hoped that Mary could help cheer Jackie. As the three chatted, John Kennedy Jr., not yet four years old, rambled into the room. Jackie offered her son a small glass of ginger ale. The young Kennedy said that he wanted Coke instead. He kept after his mother until she relented, and Jackie finally gave her son what Mary described as a "thimbleful" of Coke. Mary told John Jr. that she lived near the zoo and asked if he might like to visit sometime, see the animals, and come by her apartment for a cup of tea. "Oh," interjected John Jr., "I'll have Coke."

Despite the light moment with John Jr., the conversation with Jackie and Bobby was excruciating. Jackie had been a pillar of strength and poise during the funeral. But with the television lights off and the motorcades gone, she had sunk into depression. Bobby, too, was smothered in grief, spending long hours staring out the window of his office at the Justice Department, unsure of where to turn. "He deserved pity because he had a broken heart," Mary recalled of Bobby. "He had found his greatest fulfillment in being his brother's keeper. Little mattered after that." As Mary prepared to leave, she tried to console Bobby, assuring him that brighter days were ahead. He sobbed in response.

That night, Bobby delivered a powerful Saint Patrick's Day speech in Scranton, Pennsylvania, on the legacy of being Irish and fighting for freedom. It was his first major address since his brother's death. He made a compelling case to the white, largely Irish American audience that they needed to care about issues like civil rights. Bobby closed his remarks with a poem his brother had read at a Saint Patrick's Day event several years earlier, an ode to the Irish patriot Owen O'Neill. He choked back tears as he read the poem's final lines: "Why did you leave us, Owen? Why did you die?" Mary knew that many angry, grieving Irish Americans were pushing for LBJ to nominate Bobby as vice president, although they knew it was unlikely.

The bad blood between President Johnson and Bobby was shaping the political landscape in important ways. For Democrats, a unified LBJ-RFK ticket in 1964 would have been an act of healing, but the rift between the two men was too profound for either to offer, or accept, an olive branch. It grated on Bobby that in order to keep his brother's agenda alive as a potential vice president, he needed to curry favor with Johnson. For his part, LBJ remained obsessed with Bobby, viewing him as an existential threat to his presidency.

Mary headed out on the presidential campaign trail, covering Barry Goldwater in New Hampshire. Goldwater was challenged in the Republican primary by Nelson Rockefeller and Henry Cabot Lodge, who, as U.S. ambassador to Vietnam, sent rather murky signals about the seriousness of his bid.

It was the first year that Mary had stayed at the Wayfarer Inn, just outside Manchester, New Hampshire. The inn soon became famous as the journalistic epicenter of New Hampshire presidential politics. Nothing in life made Mary happier than sitting at the Wayfarer's bar swapping rumors and stories with her fellow political junkies. The Wayfarer also offered her a seemingly endless pool of potential bearers, and as columnist Jules Witcover described it, the Wayfarer was where Mary "made her own wishes yours."

Mary liked the gentlemanly Goldwater on a personal level, and her affection came through in her columns. "The Senator, handsome and square-jawed, photographs beautifully. His voice is pleasant. He never shouts or pounds the podium." Mary sounded almost apologetic when she described his hawkishness, which she did frequently: "The Senator is not a blood-thirsty man. But he is a major general in the air force reserve and he cannot resist military shop-talk. . . . Thus when the Senator remarks off-handedly on coast-to-coast television on the possibility of blasting the leaves off the trees in the jungles of South Vietnam with nuclear devices, and people fairly jump out of their skins, he is genuinely puzzled." With Goldwater stumbling, President Johnson was content to mount a Rose Garden strategy, using the White House and its trappings to appear above the political fray.

Goldwater's most effective tactic in his somewhat hapless campaign was to capitalize on the growing wave of discontent among southern whites with the civil rights bill now nearing final passage. The South had long been the strongest of Democratic strongholds, but the civil rights bill, coupled with naked appeals from Republicans to disaffected whites, was realigning the American electoral map. Although Richard Nixon is usually described as the father of the Republican Party's racially divisive "southern strategy," the roots of this approach were very much evident in the 1964 presidential campaign.

In July 1964, Mary traveled to San Francisco for the Republican convention. The entire event was an enthusiastic calamity, an unchecked wave of backlash politics directed at long-haired kids, civil rights protestors, and a changing American moral landscape. Republicans seemed oblivious to the image they were projecting into America's living rooms. The convention was made famous by Goldwater's acceptance speech, in which he declared, "Extremism in the defense of liberty is no vice." The crowd loved Goldwater's take-no-prisoners approach, but the rest of America would not.

By contrast, the Democratic convention promised only one major piece of drama: LBJ's selection of a running mate. Mary hoped that either Gene

McCarthy or Bobby Kennedy would get the nod. She described McCarthy as a "relaxed, handsome, 47-year-old intellectual" and a Church layman "identified with the progressive elements in the church." It was not hard to understand the bond between Mary and Gene McCarthy. Both were tart-tongued, forward-thinking Catholics who loved the letters.

Mary and McCarthy had grown close over the years, and the two talked a number of times in the wake of Kennedy's assassination. McCarthy and JFK had never liked each other, and McCarthy had once bragged, "Any way you measure it, I'm a better man than John Kennedy." The Kennedy family still fumed over McCarthy's strong push for Stevenson at the 1960 convention. Bobby once grumbled, "Gene McCarthy felt he should have been the first Catholic president just because he knew more St. Thomas Aquinas than my brother." Bobby also jeered to a reporter—Martin Nolan of the *Boston Globe*—that McCarthy was not pure Irish, saying, "Gene's mother was German. That's why he's so mean." This led Nolan to retort, "What's your excuse?" Bobby's harsh words also help put in context Mary's decision to downplay her own German heritage.

"Gene really felt terrible about Jack Kennedy being killed," Mary said. "I think he was very jealous of him and resentful of him, but I can remember him calling me up and saying, 'Nothing's fun anymore.'" Mary urged McCarthy to visit Bobby and offer his condolences.

"But he might misunderstand," replied McCarthy.

"I don't think he would," Mary said. "He's heartbroken."

McCarthy did not go.

McCarthy just could not bring himself to be civil to JFK when he was alive. He shunned any rapprochement with Bobby after the president's death, even though he expressed worries to Mary that his long-running rift with the Kennedys would hurt his chances to be selected vice president. Mary took matters into her own hands and invited both Gene and Bobby to a party at her house, hoping to broker a peace. Gene arrived fifteen minutes after Bobby had departed.

On July 30, 1964, President Johnson and his aide Bill Moyers discussed potential vice presidential choices at the White House. Mary had spoken with Moyers a short time before, relaying to him some of Bobby's concerns. Mary said that Bobby was "very, very upset about the possibility" of Gene McCarthy being offered the vice presidential slot. Johnson asked Moyers why, and Moyers replied that Bobby had told Mary, "If he wants a Catholic, he ought to take the number one Catholic in the country."

"Well, who in the hell gives him the right to appoint himself number one Catholic?" the president complained. "This guy has never done anything but cause all this backlash. That's the only thing he's got to his credit." Moyers said that Mary was very opposed to the idea of excluding Bobby from consideration. "She was almost in tears," he said. This led LBJ to grumble, "I don't know why the younger generation can't come to me."

The next day, Johnson announced that he would not pick any current cabinet member as vice president—thereby eliminating Bobby, who was still attorney general, from consideration. Not long after, Bobby announced that he was leaving the administration to run for a Senate seat in New York.

If the vice presidential hunt was agonizing for Bobby, it was only marginally less so for McCarthy and Hubert Humphrey, LBJ's two finalists for the job. As Democrats headed to Atlantic City for their convention, Johnson put both Humphrey and McCarthy through a humiliating ordeal. In Mary's words, the president behaved like an "implacable Oriental potentate, demanding always one more test of strength, one more proof of loyalty before he chose."

Johnson ultimately settled on Humphrey, the least worst choice for Kennedy loyalists, given the repeated slights of Bobby. The choice balanced the ticket between North and South, conservative and liberal. Gene McCarthy, an assiduous nurturer of grudges even in the best of times, was infuriated by Johnson's very public degradation, privately calling Johnson "a sadistic son of a bitch."

In what was a bitter irony for President Johnson, Bobby Kennedy provided the convention's most memorable moment. Johnson had made sure that Kennedy would not speak until after the nomination, and he would be the last major speaker of the convention. LBJ's plan only ensured that Bobby had the last word. As Kennedy came to the podium to deliver his remarks, the delegates erupted in thunderous, cathartic applause that deafened the hall for almost a quarter of an hour. Bobby quoted Shakespeare in remembering his late brother: "When he shall die, take him and cut him out in little stars, and he will make the face of heaven so fine, that all the world will be in love with night, and pay no worship to the garish sun."

When Mary wrote, "A convention totally dominated by Lyndon B. Johnson had been captured by a Kennedy," President Johnson, at the White House, complained of Bobby, "You know, he's got all these Irish Catholic girls writing for him." It was a clear reference to Mary.

Shortly after the convention, Mary wrote to Blair Clark. Clark was winding up what had proved to be a brief stint as general manager and vice president of CBS News. While he had a knack for identifying on-air talent, his colleagues complained about his lack of managerial skills and a level of indecisiveness that was virtually debilitating (an opinion Mary surely shared). After being passed over to become president of the news division, Clark left CBS in 1964.

He then became the associate publisher of the *New York Post*, a paper owned by Dorothy Schiff, a slightly eccentric figure from a wealthy banking family. Schiff and Clark shared a passion for Democratic politics, and Schiff was drawn to Clark. Clark saw the move to the *Post* as a stepping-stone to ultimately buying the paper. The two worked out an informal agreement: Clark would purchase a one-quarter share of the paper over a six-month trial period.

Mary told Blair that he had not missed much at the convention, calling it a "heavy-handed, badly arranged drag." She thought Bobby's speech was the only redeeming moment: "When he quoted from 'Romeo and Juliet' (Do they teach Shakespeare at Harvard at all?) it was absolutely stabbing." Mary noted that she was disappointed for her "dear, distinguished friend" Gene McCarthy, but observed, "Now that I see how Lyndon treats Hubert like a copy-boy, I am reconciled."

Mary offered Clark some tongue-in-cheek career advice: "I would say how nice it would be if you went back to broadcasting. Then I would know where you were and what you are doing," she wrote. "We might even work out a code whereby you could send messages about your health and what you call your immortal soul by which I think you mean your heart, although I am never quite sure."

Mary, who was now in her forties, was still very attractive. "She always downplayed herself as a sexy woman," columnist Anthony Lewis commented, "but she was." Her wardrobe was simple but elegant, and many of her female friends coveted her Chanel suits. She moved easily in circles of power, and her persona was that of a successful modern woman as comfortable discussing the poetry of Yeats as she was the primary returns from New York. Men wanted to light her cigarette or refill her tumbler of Scotch, and she was happy to oblige. Mary had a good number of romantic choices, but she was still smitten with Clark and thrilled that they remained engaged in an extended, secretive, and somewhat lopsided pas de deux.

Mary noted in her letter that Walter Cronkite and several other reporters had held a birthday party for her at the convention, and one of her fellow journalists had even given her a ton of gravel for her garden. In what was clearly commentary on their relationship, Mary declared, "In horticulture, as in love, I am clumsy and doomed, but I blunder on."

Covering Goldwater in the Deep South was jarring for Mary. The Goldwater crowds were fevered, and the press itself was increasingly a focus of their anger. Crowds often booed the press bus, and Mary remembered older women coming up, pounding on the press bus windows, and shouting, "Tell the truth for a change."

LBJ had a tricky needle to thread in the South as he delivered a major address on civil rights at the Jung Hotel, in New Orleans, on October 9, 1964. Mary called it "the most moving speech of his campaign" as he made the case for civil rights from a southern perspective: "Robert E. Lee, a great son of the South, a great leader of the South—and I assume no modern day leader would question him or challenge him . . . told us to cast off our animosities, and raise our sons to be Americans."

The next day, Johnson, at his ranch in Texas, spoke with his press secretary, George Reedy, about the reaction to his speech.

Johnson was pleased: "Kay Graham told me that it is the greatest speech she's ever heard in her life. Mary McGrory told me about the same thing."

"It was, sir," said Reedy.

"Is Mary McGrory there?" asked Johnson.

Reedy was unsure. "I don't know that she went back or not last night."

President Johnson had something in mind. "If it doesn't get me in trouble, I wouldn't mind flirting with her out here [at the ranch]. . . . If she didn't mind having a date with me, I wouldn't mind her coming out here and resting with me. It wouldn't make her mad with Mrs. Johnson out here, would it?"

"I don't think so," said Reedy, "just as long as she doesn't get anything on the record."

"See if she's there," the president urged, "and tell her that . . . Lady Bird and I are out here and Liz is going to be out here." (Liz Carpenter was Mrs. Johnson's press secretary and staff director.) "I would just like to philosophize with her a bit. Just visit with her. If she doesn't have anything else to do, I'll have her come out in a helicopter."

Mary did not make the trip out to the ranch that week, but she took President Johnson up on the offer several weeks later when Johnson renewed the invitation. It was not out of the ordinary for Johnson to entertain a reporter, even a female one, at his ranch, and the fact that the original invitation was proffered when Lady Bird was also there with him suggests that licentiousness was not foremost upon his mind. But Johnson also had a fascination with Mary that stretched beyond her role as a columnist.

One afternoon in 1964, LBJ gave Mary a two-and-a-half-hour tour of the White House living quarters. When Johnson had to answer a phone call during the tour, he said he was "flirtin with Mareh McGrorah, she's right here beside me." Not long after, LBJ plucked Mary out of a White House reception for a private chat. One White House staffer called it "the most widely observed abduction in history." Mary said that the experience left her feeling like a "French peasant girl who wandered into the court of Louis XIV." But Mary saw clear limits to LBJ's charm. As she confided to Blair Clark, "He's an extraordinary man, the only one I ever met who thought that poll charts (he's at 79 percent in Massachusetts) are seductive."

But LBJ's courtship of Mary was not confined to the grounds of the White House. Mary's friend Elizabeth Shannon finally shared the story for the record. ("I was vowed to secrecy," she said, "but I suppose that now everybody is gone, it is not a secret anymore.") One quiet evening around this period, Mary's phone rang. The caller identified himself as a Secret Service agent and said that President Johnson wanted to stop by her apartment in fifteen minutes. "Oh, really," McGrory replied drolly, sure that the caller was a fellow reporter pulling her leg, but the man on the line insisted he was serious.

She went out into the hallway of her apartment building and found several Secret Service agents standing near the elevator. Realizing that the leader of the free world was indeed on his way, she ran back inside and frantically tidied up. Several minutes later, the president appeared at her door.

Mary was no stranger to power, but the impromptu nature of Johnson's visit was unnerving.

She invited the president in and offered him a drink. They engaged in some friendly small talk until Johnson, tumbler of Scotch in his large hand, finally put his cards on the table. "Mary, I am crazy about you," he confessed. He wanted to sleep with her.

Then, in what has to be one of the most awkward and unromantic propositions in presidential history, Johnson tried to make the case that since Mary had always admired Kennedy, she should now transfer her affections to him. Maureen Dowd, who heard about the encounter from Mary and attributed it to LBJ's perpetual rivalry with the Kennedys, said, "He wanted to have a reporter who had been their favorite reporter." She added, "It wasn't so much him pouncing on her as him competing with JFK." In LBJ's mind, sleeping with Mary, like raising the height of the toilets in the White House, was just another way to one-up the late president.

As Mary's friend Phil Gailey put it, "He assumed, I guess, that the only reason she loved the Kennedys was because they had power. What a klutz. He had about as big a chance of scoring with Mary as Richard Nixon did." Listening to Johnson's declaration, Mary later told her friends, she felt flattered, startled, and mortified at the same time. She took a deep breath and said, "I admire you, Mr. President, and I always will. And I think you are doing a terrific job, and that is where it stops—right there."

President Johnson finished his drink and said, "I just wanted you to know."

"Now I know," she replied. "Thank you." And with that, the president and his Secret Service detail departed. Perhaps it was no coincidence that Mary wrote, "as the campaign unfolded, it seemed the president did not wish merely to be elected; he wished to be loved."

But Lyndon Johnson was hardly the first powerful man to be intrigued with Mary, and she was uniquely bewitching to the day's alpha males. She was slim and attractive and yet could drink and smoke with the old bulls. She was funny and sharp, able to talk politics like a ward captain, and there was a twinkle in her eyes that suggested a certain mischief. Perhaps more than any other journalist in American history, she pushed her editors (and they were invariably men) to come to terms with the fact that women had something worthwhile to say.

But as much as Mary was willing to flirt to her journalistic advantage, she always kept these powerful men at an arm's length. And it was this aura of ultimate unattainability that was so intoxicating to powerful men used to getting their way.

Ultimately, Mary was never particularly at ease with sex or sexuality.

(Watergate co-conspirator John Ehrlichman would say many years later that Mary "would have been a Jesuit priest if only she'd been a boy.") But Mary also recognized that consummating a relationship with someone like LBJ would end badly for her and could place her entire career at risk.

President Johnson crushed Goldwater in the election, taking more than 60 percent of the vote and sweeping all but six states. Mary spent Election Day in New York with Bobby Kennedy, who won his Senate seat comfortably. The day was a blur. A victory party was assembled at the Fifth Avenue apartment of Kennedy's sister Jean Smith. Jackie Kennedy, the British ambassador, and Sammy Davis Jr. all attended. The victory celebration relocated to the famed steak-and-seafood house Delmonico's. Then Bobby kept going, visiting the Fulton Fish Market, near the foot of the Brooklyn Bridge—where he had begun his campaign eight weeks earlier—at four in the morning. The new senator laughed and said, "It smells better here than it did two months ago." As the workers jostled Bobby, one of them barked out, "For God's sake, don't kill him now, we need him."

Not long after the election, the *Star*'s publishers invited President Johnson for an "owners' lunch." As Tommy Noyes recalled, the sessions were usually built around an "ambassador, a Cabinet member, a new Redskins coach—some lion of the moment" who would participate in an off-the-record conversation attended by the paper's directors, editors, and key reporters. President Johnson initially declined the offer, but he invited the editorial staff and key political writers at the *Star*, including Mary, to a discussion at the White House. Mary sat in the chair normally reserved for the secretary of state in cabinet meetings, just at the president's elbow.

As she glanced around, looking for those small details that she could use in her column, Mary noticed four buttons directly in front of the president's chair. As Noyes recalled, Mary thought they must be "THE buttons, those legendary objects that, with the push of a presidential finger, would send the missiles on their way." Mary leaned in to get a closer look. Thinking that she might see DEFCON 1 and DEFCON 2, or MOSCOW and PEKING, she instead read the carefully typed labels: COCA-COLA, 7-UP, DIET PEPSI, and COFFEE.

Despite such light moments, the *Star* was headed in the wrong direction as it rapidly lost ground to the rival *Washington Post*. In 1959, the *Star* relocated from offices on Pennsylvania Avenue to a new building in a blighted neighborhood near the Capitol in an effort to make it easier for *Star* trucks to avoid afternoon traffic jams. However, circulation remained a problem, as did management in general. At one point, there were some forty-three relatives from the *Star*'s owning families on the payroll, several of whom were content to sit at their desks all day drinking. The paper's failure to compete meaningfully in the increasingly lucrative morning market was a slow suicide.

Still, the *Star* continued to attract good people, and many of the top names in journalism today cut their teeth working as junior staffers in the dictation bank at the paper during the 1960s. The *Star* remained a hothouse for eccentric talent, a freewheeling environment that bred intense loyalty.

Mary was more than just a high-profile columnist at the paper. She vacationed with the *Star*'s owners on a yacht in the Greek Islands, and served as a key bridge in employee-management relations. "Many of the younger reporters would take their cue from Mary," Newby Noyes explained. "She was in a position of leadership, and not always the easiest person to work with." Indeed, Mary once bragged that when it came to the internal machinations at the *Star*, "there wasn't a leaf that fell that I wasn't informed about."

As the *Star* lost market share, the *Post* and other rivals were able to lure away some of the paper's best reporters, and Ben Bradlee, who became the *Post*'s managing editor around this time and would become executive editor in 1968, was aggressive in trying to steal talent from the *Star*.

Haynes Johnson went to the *Washington Post* in the late sixties. After his departure, he attended a small dinner party hosted by Pat Moynihan and his wife. Mary, who could be quite caustic when she had been drinking, lit into him. "How could you have left the *Star*?" Johnson and the others were embarrassed, and a hush fell over the room. Johnson remained a close friend, but it was never quite the same. "She held grudges," he said. "That was just who Mary was."

The mid-1960s marked a series of sad passages for Mary—Kennedy's assassination, the death of the pope, and the stroke of her friend and fellow reporter Doris Fleeson. The period also marked the beginning of one of her great struggles: a very public campaign against the Vietnam War.

Vietnam struck a nerve, and Mary took it personally when several young men from her old neighborhood died in the conflict. In 1965 she was writing about the increasingly hostile reception administration officials were receiving on college campuses all across the country. By 1966 she embraced early Vietnam protests and noted that the administration's sunny version of events could not mask the fact that the conflict was "a running sore."

For years, Mary's columns had focused more on people than on issues as she wrote about the political scene. Yet once she started writing about Vietnam, it became a fixation, converting her from an observer into an activist. Some readers resented Mary's steady drumbeat of columns against the war. "I used to like to read you, you used to be funny, but now you're just so bitter and nagging," wrote one.

Mary was uniquely well positioned to launch an extended campaign against the war. While there was no shortage of Americans willing to question authority during the mid-1960s, Mary was a most presentable rebel. There was no mistaking her for a hippie. She didn't think much of Allen Ginsberg's poetry or Mick Jagger's on-stage antics. It wasn't like boxer Cassius Clay changing his name to Muhammad Ali and refusing to fight in Vietnam. Mary was impeccably mannered and attired. She wrote for a paper that was a pillar of the Washington establishment. She helped make objecting to the war respectable.

Both Bobby Kennedy and Gene McCarthy edged toward stronger positions against the war in 1966, and McCarthy in particular, who was still raw with anger because of his treatment during the vice presidential selection process, came to harden implacably against Vietnam. For his part, President Johnson was frustrated that his successful domestic reforms were increasingly being overshadowed by a conflict half a world away. Mary dubbed Vietnam "the specter at the feast of the Great Society."

By mid-1966 Mary was advocating for Bobby Kennedy to run for president in 1968 or 1972, describing him as the bright spark on an otherwise dreary political landscape. In October 1966, she traveled with Bobby on an eight-state western tour, keenly watching for any sign that he intended to run in 1968. Although RFK's public opposition to Vietnam had been deliberately vague, the hope that he might take a more adamant position led to an almost delirious welcome on college campuses as restless youth looked for someone to champion their cause. BOBBY IN '68 signs started appearing in the crowds.

Kennedy talked passionately about civil rights, the white backlash, and poverty. Mary felt as though the shroud that had enveloped Bobby since his brother's death was finally parting as he plunged into the enthusiastic crowds. As the entourage arrived at the Portland, Oregon, airport, Mary noticed that the BOBBY IN '68 signs had been supplanted by a starker directive on placards: BOBBY NOW! For Mary, the intense public reaction made the question of a presidential run by Bobby a matter of when, not if.

At Berkeley, always a hotbed of liberal politics, a one-hundred-piece band and a roaring crowd greeted Bobby. The American left, which had long viewed Bobby with suspicion, was eager to embrace him if he was willing to come out against the war. "In the end, though," Mary observed, "what was most significant about the trip was Kennedy's assessment of it. He concluded, despite the hysterical reception, that he could not take on Lyndon Johnson."

In New York, Blair Clark's dream of buying the *New York Post* with-ered on the vine: publisher Dorothy Schiff was reluctant to sell, and Clark had made little headway in raising the outside money he needed to make a serious bid. Schiff was gauzy in discussing Clark's reasons for leaving his job as associate publisher. Clark was more direct in his recollection. After they had dined together one night and gone back to Schiff's apartment, a tipsy Schiff made, in Clark's words, "what I can only call a pass, however ladylike." He stammered an excuse about why he needed to leave. As a Schiff biographer reported of Clark, "He left the apartment knowing that his career at the *Post* was over."

Although Clark managed to move from high-profile position to high-profile position with seeming ease, not all were impressed. Pollster Lou Harris argued that Clark was a "rich boy dilettante. He got himself into all kinds of enviable jobs, partly because he knew everybody, and because he was so affable and rich."

Clark and Mary spent a great deal of time together during 1966 and '67. Mary's niece Polly McGrory was one of just a handful of people to whom Mary confided her strong feelings for Blair, although she, too, re-mained puzzled with her aunt's reluctance to discuss matters of the heart. "If she was having an affair with Blair," Polly argued, "why not tell us about it? I don't understand what the secrecy was all about."

When it came to Mary's love life, the vast majority of friends and fam-ily never asked, and they were never told. No one dared press her on the subject. It said a lot about Mary, and her upbringing, that one of the very few people with whom she was at least partially candid about her feelings toward Blair was Sister Editha, the nun who ran St. Ann's for many years. Mary was eager for the world to see her opinion on the printed page four days a week, but she was appalled by the thought of telling friends and family about fond glances or stolen kisses.

Mary's intense privacy led to a spate of theories about her love life and sexuality among colleagues, friends, and family. Some thought that her admiration for politicians like President Kennedy and Adlai Stevenson made it hard for other men to achieve equal measure. Some wondered if she was gay. In many ways, both the St. Ann's orphanage and the *Star* served as substitute families for Mary.

Ben Bradlee suggested that Mary's fierce privacy led to a reputation as something of an old maid. "I didn't think she was a very sexual animal," he said. "She was careful, and she was old fashioned." Mary worried that her romantic life would adversely affect her career. "I think for a woman of her age to have a fulfilling career that was really demanding, and to want to make it to the top, which she did, it was very hard to be married," Cokie Roberts explained. "Men are scared of women like that," Roberts said, "and still are."

The choice between the front page and domestic life was stark. Mary felt that she could be a successful reporter or she could be happily married—not both—even as the 1960s tumultuously shuffled the American social order, opening doors for women and minorities that had long been closed.

By 1967, if there had been a physical relationship between Mary and Clark, it was a thing of the past. Their repartee remained flirtatious, and with Clark leaving the *New York Post*, Mary clung, against her better judgment, to the possibility of a lasting relationship or perhaps even marriage. When several dates between Clark's son Tim and Mary's niece Polly sputtered, Mary wondered to Clark, in April 1967, "Are we McGrorys too exacting, or are you Clarks too cavalier?"

Mary and Clark celebrated their mutual birthday together in New York in August 1967. He dropped her a note afterwards: "Sweet Mary, we had such fun on our birthday didn't we? And you were a darling to come up and co-celebrate it (or is that sacrilegious?) Love to you, dear. Blair."

But then, in September 1967, Clark wrote her again with devastating news. "By now you will have guessed my secret—what I couldn't bring myself to tell you on the phone Saturday. . . . I'm going abroad to meet a girl about whom I'm most serious; who I expect to marry." The woman, twenty-nine-year-old Joanna Rostropowicz, was a Polish sociologist and a divorced mother. The letter closed, "The fact is that I have inhibitions about telling you this central fact of my life. What that means about me and about you, I don't know, really. I tell it to you now, asking you to forgive my clumsiness, as you have so often. And I send you, dearest Mary, very much love. Blair."

Clark had told his fiancée about Mary and about Mary's strong feelings for him, but he insisted that the relationship had never been consummated. Joanna was unconcerned, acknowledging with some whimsy that Clark had been a ladies' man. (Mary and Joanna would meet only once in person after Joanna permanently relocated to the United States, at a party for John Lennon. Joanna was thrilled when she got a chance to dance with the former Beatle, but she also observed that Mary was "quite upset" and left the party early.)

Mary was shattered by the news that Clark was going to remarry and turned to Sister Editha for solace. Sister Editha, who was also friends with Clark, sent him a series of angry, reproachful letters. Although Mary was stunned by his declaration of love for another woman, she did not break off communication with him. She still hoped, seemingly against all reason, for his hand. Mary blamed herself to a degree, fretting that her unwillingness to step away from her work had made her unavailable. "Don't let your career get in the way of your personal life," she would confide to a young woman years later. "Sometimes you might have regrets that you should have married someone, but you let your career get in your way like I did."

Hiding her pain, Mary turned to a series of profiles of the likely 1968 Republican presidential contenders. The GOP contest lacked the Shakespearean drama of the confrontation between Bobby and LBJ, but the reports of Richard Nixon's permanent political demise had been premature. Nixon emerged from the debacle of the 1964 Goldwater presidential campaign in good shape. He spent much of 1966 stumping and fundraising for other Republican candidates, leaving any number of politicians in his debt.

Nixon faced surprisingly soft competition in the primary, including George Romney and the newly elected governor of California, Ronald Reagan. But Romney was virtually disqualified after saying he had been "brainwashed" by the generals and Johnson administration officials into buying an overly rosy vision of the war, and Reagan's views at the time were so extreme that they only boosted Nixon's popularity with moderate Republicans. Just five years after the debacle of the "exit snarling" speech, Nixon enjoyed a virtually unopposed path to the Republican nomination.

But for Mary, the Republicans were irrelevant to the great political question of 1967: What Democrat would demand an end to the Vietnam War? Mary entered a period in her career in which the lines between her personal and professional life were not just blurred but obliterated.

During the first half of 1967, Bobby Kennedy remained torn about how best to express his position on Vietnam, worried that a public split with LBJ on the war would only divide the party and ensure a Republican in the White House. At the same time, liberals and many of his closest advisers were clamoring for him to speak out on the issue.

If Bobby was initially reluctant to criticize LBJ on Vietnam, Gene McCarthy relished his own emerging role as a bomb thrower for the cause of peace. In August 1967, McCarthy accused President Johnson of imposing a "foreign policy dictatorship" and began seriously contemplating a White House run. No one, including Mary, gave McCarthy a snowball's chance in hell of succeeding. That October, Mary spoke with a reporter who was convinced that McCarthy was going to challenge Johnson. She insisted that it was simply "too preposterous" to consider.

Mary interviewed Bobby on November 16, 1967, in the New Senate Office Building. The intense and uncomfortable discussion was remarkable for its candor and for Mary's willingness to push Bobby in a way that no neutral journalist ever would. The two of them agreed that the Vietnam conflict had reached one of its last, best opportunities for negotiation. Mary goaded Bobby, saying that it was heartening McCarthy was going to run for president.

Bobby was annoyed. He asked if a McCarthy campaign would have any impact beyond making Mary feel better. How did she think McCarthy would campaign? Bobby answered his own question, observing that he thought McCarthy was lazy and indicating that he had gotten negative reports about McCarthy from his political networks in Detroit, Chicago, and Boston.

Kennedy thought McCarthy would have to "work his tail off" to make any impression at all on the public. Bobby had heard McCarthy in the Senate and thought he was a talented speaker, but he warned Mary that McCarthy's penchant for offhand remarks could prove costly. "Does he realize how different it is running for president?"

Mary said that it was plain that neither McCarthy nor anyone on his staff had a clue how to run a presidential campaign. By this point she was one of a select few serving as a kitchen cabinet for McCarthy as he developed his plans. She had told McCarthy that she thought it did not make sense for him to compete in the upcoming New Hampshire primary.

Bobby disagreed with Mary's assessment. He thought McCarthy *should* compete in New Hampshire but argued that he would need to avoid running a single-issue campaign. It was not enough to be against Vietnam; McCarthy had to present an alternative to Johnson's entire approach.

Kennedy thought LBJ was vulnerable in New Hampshire. Governor John King was weak; the state party chairman, Bill Dunfey, was not overly fond of LBJ; and the Democratic organization in the state was "next to nothing." Bobby thought McCarthy should stay away from university towns and disgruntled youth and focus more on small towns and more traditional Democratic constituencies. He thought that a policy based on a unilateral withdrawal from Vietnam would be a disaster and said that McCarthy should say that he would consult the military but "not take their words as coming from the last anointed."

Bobby's own opinion of the war was pointed: "The administration keeps claiming we are winning, but it is obvious we are not." He claimed that the war was fundamentally eroding America's international prestige, with President Johnson unable to travel to Europe or most of Latin

America for fear of widespread protests. Mary echoed the sentiment, observing that when she'd come back from her summer vacation in Italy, it
was apparent that the president was limiting his domestic travel to military installations. "Do you realize our president can't go anywhere except
under armed guard?" Mary complained. "It is like South America or something."

Kennedy maintained that McCarthy should "tell the people in the
small towns of New Hampshire that he is worried about the cities, about
the education of our children, about immorality, about violence." Suddenly it sounded as though Bobby was no longer offering McCarthy advice but thinking of the campaign *he* could wage.

Mary told Bobby point-blank that he should run for president—that
he must run for president. She warned him that his followers were disillu-
sioned with his unwillingness to challenge Johnson on Vietnam, and said
that traditional Kennedy voters would gravitate toward McCarthy "because he has the guts to take on the issue." It is hard to imagine a sterner
challenge to the ever-combative Bobby. Mary felt not only comfortable,
but compelled, to give Bobby campaign advice in much stronger terms
than she would have ever offered to his late brother.

Bobby insisted that he could not run and again expressed his fears that
it would split the Democratic Party. "I can't do it. I can't do it."

"Well," Mary snorted, "I never thought the Kennedys thought that
much for the party. You have your own party."

"I couldn't beat him," insisted Bobby.

Mary was incredulous. "Are you telling me that people would vote for
Lyndon Johnson instead of you?"

Bobby did not answer directly. "If you want to know, my mother and
my sisters agree with you," he said. Mary pointed out that even Gene Mc-
Carthy still hoped that Bobby would run. The majority of his friends
wanted him to get in; the campaign professionals around him thought it
unwise.

Kennedy fretted that the public would think he was running for president simply because he hated Johnson. But even as he resisted Mary's

continued entreaties, she could see the agony on his face. Finally, a frustrated Mary scribbled in her notebook, "Bobby is immobilized."

"We had a difficult conversation about it," Mary recalled. "I wish he had not hesitated. I think it all would have been different if he stood up earlier."

Mary's column the next day spelled out Bobby's predicament. "The sudden, startling emergence of Senator Eugene McCarthy of Minnesota as an alternative candidate to President Johnson has made life difficult for Senator Robert F. Kennedy of New York. . . . In the face of repeated and almost frantic pleas from his advisers, Kennedy is holding firm to his contention that any defiance of the president on his part would be laid entirely to personal ambition." Mary quoted Tennyson's poem "Ulysses" to make her case: "How dull it is to pause, to make an end, / to rust unburnish'd, not shine in use." Small wonder that Bobby once said of her, "Mary is so gentle—until she gets behind a typewriter."

John Seigenthaler remembered coming to Washington in 1967 for the annual Gridiron Club dinner. He chatted with Mary over drinks at the Jefferson Hotel. Seigenthaler, one of Bobby's key political confidants, was one of those counseling against a presidential run. As soon as he sat down, Mary was all over him.

"Why is that you think he shouldn't do this?" Mary demanded.

"Mary, it is crazy for him to do it."

Mary's voice rose with anger. "This war is a moral disgrace."

Seigenthaler tried to lighten the mood, joking that Mary sounded like Peter Edelman, one of Bobby's liberal antiwar friends.

Mary seethed. "Don't you understand?"

Seigenthaler knew that he had crossed a line. "She would not be teased about this," he said. "She knew where she was. She knew where the country was, and she knew Vietnam was a disaster."

Mary asked Seigenthaler why he was not telling Bobby "what he needs to hear about the war, instead of telling him what you think he needs to hear about politics." At a time when Bobby was struggling with the moral and political implications of a presidential run, Seigenthaler described Mary as being "like a little Irish mosquito buzzing around occasionally giving him a little nip, and it itches and he feels a little pain, and he was getting a lot of that from a lot of different places."

Mary covered Gene McCarthy's emergence as a presidential candidate with humor, skepticism, and a sense of relief that someone—anyone— was taking up the antiwar banner. Some of her columns on the candidate sounded shamelessly promotional, including when she wrote that the "handsome rebel's" antiwar rhetoric had "fallen like thunder on the ears of the protestors." Her description of McCarthy as "gentle, literate, and witty" left other reporters and political hands wondering if Mary was hopelessly in the tank for him. Nevertheless, with McCarthy's political chances almost universally deemed to lie somewhere between slim and none, most seemed willing to forgive Mary such excesses.

In the days before McCarthy made his formal announcement, Mary made the rounds with some key political players. She had a long conversation with Bill Dunfey, the New Hampshire state Democratic chairman. Dunfey felt that Johnson, although he had the state party machinery behind him, had made a key strategic error. Johnson was not on the primary ballot but was pushing for a strong write-in. Dunfey noted that JFK had gotten 43,000 write-in votes in 1960, and LBJ had managed only 29,000 in 1964—just four months after Kennedy's assassination. Anything below that 29,000-vote level would be seen as a disappointment for LBJ. Dunfey's bottom line for McCarthy in New Hampshire: "He hasn't got a damned thing to lose." Mary was encouraged but pressured Dunfey to do everything he could to get Bobby to jump in the race.

Several days later, Mary spoke with her friend Kenny O'Donnell, a longtime Kennedy loyalist. O'Donnell said that he had always been on friendly terms with McCarthy but would not serve as his campaign manager. Mary was trying to find seasoned political hands who might rally to the McCarthy cause while she was still trying to push Bobby into the race. O'Donnell said he thought McCarthy "had a lot of guts" and could potentially do well in New Hampshire, but he did not want to look like yet another former Kennedy hand attacking President Johnson. O'Donnell had a bleak view of the prospects for victory in Vietnam and said that, outside of the military, he could not think of anyone in government who supported the war. Mary's conversations led her to conclude that Bobby was simultaneously pleased that McCarthy was willing to take on Johnson and convinced that he would be "ground to powder" by the president's machine.

On November 30, 1967, Eugene McCarthy formally announced his presidential candidacy in the Senate Caucus Room, saying that President Johnson had set no limits on the price that he would pay for military victory in Vietnam. McCarthy admitted that his odds were sufficiently long, that it was difficult for many people to support him by light of day. When a reporter asked if he believed that the United States should stop communism, he replied tartly: "Yes, I do. And South Vietnam is the worst possible place to try."

When a journalist asked when he'd decided to run for president, McCarthy replied, "Well, it was nothing like St. Paul being knocked off his horse, I can tell you that. . . . I waited a decent period of time for someone else to do it." Mary's column the next day noted that most Democratic politicians were "breaking all track records in their flight" from McCarthy. "His skilled and spirited debut may not cause any tremors at the White House, where Robert Kennedy is viewed as the real enemy," Mary wrote. "But if the country is susceptible to wit and style reminiscent of Adlai Stevenson and John F. Kennedy, McCarthy may have to be taken more seriously than anyone—including McCarthy himself—takes him now."

In a sign of exactly how lightly McCarthy was taking his campaign, he declared to Mary and several other friends over drinks that if he won the nomination, he would choose Tommy Noyes from the *Star* as his running mate. Both McCarthy and Noyes agreed the essential role for a vice president was to do absolutely nothing.

In December 1967, Richard Nixon came to an owners' lunch at the *Star*. It was a small gathering, and Haynes Johnson attended, along with Mary. Nixon had not formally announced that he was running, but it was obvious that he was. Nixon picked at his food and then pushed it away. "I'm in training," he said with a tight smile. "Mary would ask these little, barbed questions, but they were reporters' questions," remembered Johnson, as Mary and Nixon continued to build a reservoir of mutual animosity. Johnson said the lunch meeting was "memorable beyond belief" in illuminating Nixon's personality: "He was going to do anything he could to get Mary if he had the power to do it, because Mary, and the Marys of the world, were a threat."

Mary tried as much as anyone to make Gene McCarthy's campaign credible. She was particularly eager to enlist Blair Clark to the cause, and Clark later acknowledged that Mary was "instrumental" in bringing him aboard the McCarthy campaign. Clark had gotten to know McCarthy casually in 1967, because they were mutual friends with the poet Robert Lowell, and McCarthy had long been a slightly frustrated poet himself. Shortly before McCarthy announced his bid, and after prodding by Mary, Clark wrote to McCarthy from London, saying that he hoped he would run and offering his services if he did.

Clark heard back from McCarthy shortly before he returned to the States in early December. Upon arriving in New York, he got hold of Teddy White, another old friend, who informed him that McCarthy was headed to Chicago for a press conference and speech. Clark decided to accompany White to Chicago. He and Mary met up almost immediately upon his arrival. Despite his still pending remarriage, it felt a bit like old times for the two.

Clark again offered his services to McCarthy, who asked him to travel to Massachusetts to get a handle on the primary in that state. Clark did, and reported back, unsurprisingly, that most of the party leadership remained beholden to the Kennedys.

McCarthy asked Blair Clark to become his campaign chairman.

Clark said he was not much of a chairman type.

"Fine," McCarthy responded. "Call yourself whatever you want."

Clark suggested that McCarthy might be better served by having someone who had actually run a national campaign in such a role, but he offered to fill in until McCarthy could find a more seasoned hand. With that, McCarthy made Clark his presidential campaign manager—the first of many signs that McCarthy didn't care much about titles, experience, or conventional wisdom when it came to running for president.

Clark quickly learned that McCarthy cared little for veteran political operatives, saying he "never even looked for one; didn't want one."

Blair Clark would lead Eugene McCarthy's charge against President Johnson and the Vietnam War. Mary was delighted. She would be by their side.

CHAPTER FIVE

Splendid, Doomed Lives

Much has rightly been made of the role of young people in 1968 as they took to the streets. This was the beginning of campus sit-ins, the protest anthems of Bob Dylan and Joan Baez, and the rising militancy of groups like the Black Panthers. But what is more easily overlooked is the revolution that took place within the establishment against Vietnam. People like Mary McGrory, Blair Clark, and Gene McCarthy, were not wild-eyed radicals. They were card-carrying members of the East Coast elite. All rejected the imperial folly of Vietnam, and all were willing to challenge the traditional political order in doing so.

By any measure of journalistic objectivity, Mary should have recused herself from covering the 1968 campaign. She had lobbied Bobby Kennedy to get into the race. She and Gene McCarthy were close friends and drinking buddies. She'd recruited a man she was in love with, Blair Clark, to sign on as McCarthy's campaign manager. These were not garden-variety conflicts of interest.

By early January 1968, Gene McCarthy had announced that he intended to compete in the New Hampshire Democratic primary, and Mary had tough words in her column for Bobby Kennedy as he remained on the sidelines: "The stormer of rapids and mountains, the bold invader of hostile states and continents, has been cast in the role of Hamlet, not daring to do what he most wants to do."

The situation between Mary and Bobby came to a head at the end of January 1968. At a routine breakfast with reporters, Bobby declared that he would not run against LBJ "under any foreseeable circumstances." Yet at almost that exact moment, nine thousand miles away, the Vietcong launched a massive, coordinated attack coinciding with the lunar new year: the Tet Offensive. In Saigon, Vietcong assaulted the airport and the presidential palace and occupied the U.S. embassy grounds for eight hours before being repulsed.

The scale and ambition of the Tet Offensive shocked the American public. Just two months before, American commander General William Westmoreland had declared that the North Vietnamese were "unable to mount a major offensive" and that the end of the war was in view.

Although the U.S. military soon turned back the attack, Bobby's pronouncement could not have been more ill-timed. Because he hadn't seen the news of the Tet Offensive come across the wires, the stories that came out after his press briefing made it sound as though Bobby was making his declaration to stay out of the race *despite* the Tet Offensive.

Mary was enraged when she saw Bobby's statement, seeing it as a profound betrayal of the antiwar cause. She sent Bobby a devastatingly blunt telegram: "St. Patrick did not drive all the snakes out of Ireland." Few male reporters in America had the nerve to challenge Bobby so directly. "She was just furious," recalled Bobby's confidant Peter Edelman, "and what a way to say it."

Journalist Rowland Evans remembered speaking with Bobby after he received the telegram, and he marveled at how harshly Mary seemed to have turned on Bobby. Bobby patiently explained to Evans that this was an Irish feud; the two would work it out; an outsider could not understand.

With the situation increasingly unsettled, Mary headed to her favorite presidential proving ground: New Hampshire.

On February 2, Richard Nixon officially announced his candidacy at the Manchester Holiday Inn, joking, "Gentlemen, this is not my last press conference." Nixon never liked reporters, but he did understand the media. He ran a shrewd, if cynical, press operation in 1968 and after by increasingly cutting the national press out of events and directing his message through the relative safety of scripted question-and-answer sessions filmed in studios. He was able to project an aura of openness with none of its perils. Little more than two weeks later, George Romney officially bowed out of the Republican race, leaving Nixon with only token resistance in the primary from Reagan and Rockefeller. Nixon made his position on Vietnam gauzy enough to keep both hawks and doves convinced he was on their side.

While Mary never relented in her suspicion of Nixon, she credited him with mounting a remarkable comeback and described his campaign operation in New Hampshire as "a model of organizational smoothness and cordiality."

If Nixon's campaign was orderly and buttoned down, Gene McCarthy's was anything but. Richard Goodwin, who had been a speechwriter for both JFK and LBJ, described the scene when he joined the McCarthy campaign: "There wasn't a single reporter, no speechwriter, no secretaries, not even a typewriter." Yet in the wake of the Tet Offensive, the McCarthy campaign began to snowball.

Mary remembered first arriving at McCarthy headquarters, in Concord, a short time later: "It was in the back of the building. I went in and it was total, one thousand percent activity. I hadn't seen so many people in a political headquarters since I could remember. It was just so immense you figured it had to make a difference."

Young people from all over the country poured into New Hampshire to get behind the McCarthy campaign, attracting a remarkable array of talented young organizers and activists. As Mary said, it was as if McCarthy had "pressed the button on an alarm bell and the entire college population of the United States rose up to help him." Mary helped the "kids" out with spending money and kidded that McCarthy's was the first campaign in history where haircuts were a legitimate campaign expense.

Blair Clark argued that it was Mary "who put these young campaigners on the front pages of the nation." She wrote charming columns about Ph.D.s from Harvard and MIT translating news releases into French for the French Canadians, respectfully debating the complexities of the war with puzzled housewives, and subsisting on peanut butter and jelly sandwiches as they slept on the floors of church basements.

Mary seemed to recognize that she had strayed into dangerous territory.

"Readers complained about a lack of objectivity," she would observe. "They were probably right. It's a little hard to keep your head with 21-year-old press aides who tell you that you're their substitute mother figure. Mass solicitude from a generation that hasn't been speaking to anyone over 30 can be pretty undoing."

In an oral history, Mary acknowledged that she probably hadn't applied the same standards to McCarthy she would have applied to anyone else. Certainly, the lines on any campaign are blurrier than either reporters or candidates would like to admit, and this sort of insider political trading is far from a hanging offense in Washington journalism. Genuine objectivity is often all but unrecognizable in the stew of Washington politics and personal relationships.

At other times, Mary was notably defensive about her behind-the-scenes role on the McCarthy campaign. Richard Stout of *Newsweek*, while working on a book about the campaign several years later, shared with Mary a draft chapter detailing McCarthy's messy management style: "McGrory, as a friend of Clark and McCarthy, found herself in the unavoidable position of listener and sometimes adviser who, to many on the staff, seemed as much a campaign manager as anyone else."

Mary took exception. "Nothing, dear Dick, could be further off the mark," she wrote. "Like every reporter I have ever met, I have the campaign manager streak in me, but early on, I was disqualified as a strategist in the McCarthy camp. When I was first informed the senator would make the run, I was not only disbelieving, but embarrassed. Almost immediately, I distinguished myself further by expressing the absolute certainty that entrance into the New Hampshire primary would be fatal." Mary noted that she had written critical stories about the campaign, and she closed with something of a plea: "I hope you will find some support for my contention that while personally involved to the extent of being a friend of the principals, I managed some professional objectivity."

Stout was unconvinced, and Mary was less than candid when it came to the extent of her involvement. If there is any doubt about Mary's influence with McCarthy, Blair Clark recalled a day when Marty Peretz, one of the campaign's leading donors, complained about his lack of access to the candidate and Clark responded, "You've seen Gene a lot; you know that nobody has access to Gene. Possibly Mary McGrory as an old friend and fellow Catholic. You and I aren't Catholics."

The dynamism of the McCarthy campaign in New Hampshire was all the more remarkable given McCarthy's diffidence as a candidate. His speeches tended to be scholarly ruminations rather than rousing calls to action, he did not like being on the stump, hated raising money or dealing with local politicians, and, as Blair Clark soon realized, "He didn't want a campaign." Once, in the middle of shaking hands in a crowd, McCarthy blurted out, "This is sort of a strange ritual."

Traveling back and forth to Washington, Mary attended cocktail parties where politicians lectured her that the young people flooding into New Hampshire were alienating good, stolid, traditional New Hampshire voters. Flying back up to New Hampshire, Mary sat down with Bill Dunfey, eager to see what he thought.

"Mary, old people like young people," Dunfey replied, "and they like having them come to their door."

Mary took umbrage that McCarthy's campaign was still being treated as a lark by most Washington journalists, many of whom shared Bobby's opinion that McCarthy lacked money, fire, and enough foreign policy expertise to be credible. She lamented to McCarthy that his challenge to Johnson had become "the biggest political joke in the country." The candidate was unperturbed. He reassured Mary in the language of his early years as an amateur boxer: "You fight from a low crouch. You wait for events. You let it come to you."

In her columns, Mary continued to draw the distinction between McCarthy and Bobby in bright lines. "McCarthy, one of the senate's thinkers, who merely wants to legitimize dissent, is tramping through the provinces making trouble for Lyndon Johnson. Kennedy, one of the world's doers, is sitting morosely on the sidelines," she wrote. "Both men are suffering excoriating criticism: McCarthy for doing the right thing badly and Kennedy for doing nothing."

Yet events continued to break against President Lyndon Johnson. In an unusually personal aside at the end of the *CBS Evening News* broadcast on February 27, 1968, Walter Cronkite announced to America his view that "the bloody experience of Vietnam" would almost certainly end in a stalemate. At the White House, Johnson reacted: "That's it. If I've lost Cronkite, I've lost middle America."

On the Sunday before the primary in early March, Mary came out of the Wayfarer and grabbed a copy of the morning paper. The headline announced that General Westmoreland was requesting another 210,000 American troops for Vietnam. The news only further galvanized the McCarthy forces. On the final weekend of the race, the campaign turned away 2,500 new volunteers because it was inundated with help.

The day of the primary, Mary spoke again with Bill Dunfey. "I have seen something I never saw before," he shared. "I drove across the state, and at every crossroads, I saw young people standing with literature outside polling places, holding the flag." Most pollsters thought McCarthy wouldn't capture more than 10 percent of the vote, but Dunfey thought he would do better than expected, potentially pulling up to a third of Democrats.

Mary watched the returns come in at McCarthy's cottage at the Wayfarer Inn, along with Abigail McCarthy, Blair Clark, and several others. McCarthy did not win the primary, but he shocked the world by capturing 42 percent of the vote, to Johnson's 49 percent. At campaign headquarters, college students chanted, "On to Wisconsin," the next primary. "I think I can get the nomination," declared McCarthy. For Mary, New Hampshire was his finest hour, a moment when the senator "knocked the establishment right out of the saddle."

When a reporter asked McCarthy if he had spoken with Bobby Kennedy after the results, he said no but added that he had enjoyed a fine discussion with the poet Robert Lowell.

The morning after the primary, McCarthy called the *Washington Star* offices. He demanded to speak with Tommy Noyes, having him pulled out of an editorial meeting. McCarthy then reiterated his strict instructions to

Noyes that when he occupied the White House, with Noyes as his vice president, Noyes was "to put his feet on the desk and never be heard from again."

Mary's column on the New Hampshire fallout cited Yeats: "All is changed; changed utterly." McCarthy was a sudden, unexpected political star. For Mary, New Hampshire in 1968 always stood as a brief, exemplary moment when youth, energy, and faith had changed American politics. She could never have imagined the horrors to follow.

Less than ten hours after McCarthy's breakthrough in New Hampshire, Bobby indicated to reporters that he was going to jump into the race, and an official announcement came several days later. McCarthy loyalists were livid, particularly after Kennedy's Shermanesque statement that he wouldn't run. Mary seethed, feeling that McCarthy had taken all the risks to soften the race for Kennedy's entry, and her resulting column was scalding. "Kennedy thinks that American youth belongs to him, perhaps as the bequest of his brother. Seeing the romance flower between them and McCarthy, he moved with the ruthlessness of a Victorian father whose daughter has fallen in love with a dustman to break it up." She described the Kennedy family as believing it possessed the right of eminent domain in American politics.

John Seigenthaler put it in plain terms: "She was pissed off at Bob," and she lashed into Bobby in ways that she never would have with JFK. But like all good Irish feuds, the anger flowed in both directions, and the Kennedy clan was angered that Mary was so full-throated in her support for McCarthy, given his obvious flaws. Mary's relationship with the Kennedys was often rockier than it was perceived by the outside world, where she was often viewed as reflexively pro-Kennedy. Interestingly, Ethel Kennedy, who was known to lash out at her husband's critics, maintained a good relationship with Mary despite the trying circumstances.

Ted Sorensen, Jack Kennedy's speechwriter, nicely framed Mary's dilemma with Bobby now in the race: "Poor Mary. Two Irish Catholics seeking the Democratic nomination."

Mary understood that the unconventional McCarthy campaign was largely unintelligible to the highly organized Kennedy camp. And as close as Mary was to McCarthy, she was honest about his deficiencies as a politician: "Detail bores him. He has a minute staff, and his tactics, apart from the issue, seem based largely on the lapses of the other side, which have been numerous." Mary described McCarthy as possessing only two advantages: "He has been smarter and braver."

But she only hinted in her writing at a personal relationship that was also unfolding. After one campaign stop in March 1968, Mary carefully filed away a tourist certificate she had collected with McCarthy. It declared that McCarthy was an "Admiral of Lake Superior" for having completed the drive around the Great Lake on "the most scenic highway in America." On the back, McCarthy had scrawled a poem for Mary:

> There in the savage orange of autumn tamarack,
> its rusted spikes reeling the slanted last of the northern day,
> down into dark root waters,
> among the least trees in the least land,
> In the darkening death camp of the tribe of trees,
> I saw you,
> green-gold willow arched and graced among spines and angled limbs,
> captive,
> queen,
> all lost light out of the smothering swamps,
> you beam back,
> redeemed.

Mary's column the next day made no mention of captive queens or green-gold willows, but she hinted at a bit of magic, describing his day of campaigning as one that made "politics seem like an innocent and beguiling business." She also noted, without mentioning the poem, that McCarthy "spoke of the tamarack tree, his current favorite political symbol," as he made his way through the northern forests.

There has long been speculation that Mary and the unhappily married McCarthy were romantically involved. The vehemence with which several of Mary's closest friends decline to discuss the issue gives further credence to the claim. Dominic Sandbrook, who wrote a well-regarded biography of McCarthy, noted, "I think it's very plausible that they had a romantic relationship—I'm guessing sometime between 1967 and 1969. She was certainly smitten with him for a time." Gwen Gibson, a female reporter who had traveled with Mary, maintained that a McGrory-McCarthy affair "was pretty much accepted as fact around Washington in those days."

Ben Bradlee concurred. "I think she did love Gene McCarthy, whether it was physical love or not." But Bradlee did not think much of the object of Mary's crush. "He was such a pain in the ass. McCarthy, he was hard to stay in love with."

The rumors of liaisons between Mary and McCarthy floated around the campaign as well. Student leader David Mixner, who would become a close friend of Mary's, said, "I don't know if there was ever a physical relationship, but it was a love story. She adored him, and he adored her." Like others, Mary's friend Phil Gailey had heard word of a Mary-Gene romance through the grapevine. "But what the hell, they were two adults, who had clearly had one thing in common: they hated the war in Vietnam and wanted the war to stop."

McCarthy's affections were not reserved for Mary, and Blair Clark was forced to clean up the mess from the candidate's increasingly brazen dalliances during the campaign. "It got to be known during the campaign that Gene had a girlfriend," Clark said, referring to Marya McLaughlin, who had worked for Clark at CBS and was the network's first on-screen female reporter. In February 1968, Clark flew to Boston in the middle of the night to tell McCarthy that rumors of the affair were all over Washington, including at the *Washington Post*, after he'd been seen emerging from McLaughlin's apartment at three in the morning. McCarthy's relationship with his wife was collapsing, and the two would split by the end of the year, although they would remain married—and living apart—for the rest of their lives.

The 1968 campaign was a time of enormous emotional turmoil for

Mary. She still yearned to be with Blair Clark, and one suspects that her romance with McCarthy was motivated in part by a desire to spite Clark. Mary's niece Polly was skeptical that Mary's romance with McCarthy ever amounted to more than a fling, because "she was still in love with Blair."

Torn between the two men and caught up in a quixotic effort to end the agony of the Vietnam War, Mary was wound tight. Both Clark and McCarthy were dashing, charming when they wanted to be, and immensely self-absorbed. One suspects that Mary was attracted to them in part because she knew the relationships would never work—and a relationship that couldn't work was no threat to her career or to the world she had created for herself. She seemed intent on softly sabotaging her chances for lasting love.

But if Mary's emotional state was volatile in 1968, the political landscape was even more so.

On March 31, 1968, President Lyndon Johnson dropped a political bombshell when he announced, "I shall not seek, and I will not accept, the nomination of my party for another term as your president."

Mary was in a college auditorium with the McCarthy campaign in Waukesha, Wisconsin, when the news came. In three months, McCarthy had gone from a laughingstock to essentially unseating a sitting president. Haynes Johnson remembered chatting with Mary in her hotel room later that evening as she sat with her covers pulled up to her chin, saying, "Dear boy, come let's talk about it." The traditional political order was unraveling before their very eyes.

Many reporters, including Mary, softened their judgment of President Johnson in the wake of his decision not to run for reelection. The ever media-sensitive LBJ was quick to notice, and he joked at the White House Correspondents' Dinner that the president of the Correspondents' Association should consider retiring to promote greater unity in the press corps. "And you'll find out that once you step aside," he said, "things start happening: Mary McGrory may even call you a statesman."

Johnson's withdrawal made McCarthy's April 2 primary victory in

Wisconsin anticlimactic. Bobby had entered the race too late to be on the ballot, and Johnson was no longer a candidate. But the shock waves continued.

On April 4, Mary was at a Democratic Party function in Washington when word arrived that Reverend Martin Luther King had been gunned down on the second-floor balcony of the Lorraine Motel, in Memphis, Tennessee. Mary was appalled by some of the reactions. "Of course, I'm from the South and I'm glad," one lobbyist told her.

Riots erupted in Washington and other major cities. Scores of homes and businesses were torched in Washington's traditionally middle-class black neighborhoods as gray smoke choked the U Street corridor. The National Guard was deployed to halt the advance of the furious crowds.

"I can remember riding down Connecticut Avenue the morning after the riots," said Mary, "and seeing a jeep and two young soldiers with machine guns. Connecticut Avenue early in the morning! What has happened?" It seemed as if the country was slipping toward madness.

Mary attended King's funeral at a packed church in Atlanta, where she squeezed into a pew next to Richard Nixon. As the service began, the two shared a hymnal—the only time the two ever sang from the same page in their long careers. "In the church, he was his mother's genteel son, making sure I was ready when he turned the pages," Mary recalled. "He sang the old hymns—'Softly and Tenderly,' 'In the Garden'—in his pleasant baritone."

The King assassination provided an uncomfortable window into Gene McCarthy's psyche and underscored why his campaign stumbled soon after its giddy turn in New Hampshire. Clark and McCarthy were in San Francisco when they learned that King had been shot. Walking down the hall with Clark afterwards, McCarthy remarked, "You know, he kind of brought it on himself. He shouldn't have gone to Memphis." Many of those who knew McCarthy best came to sour on him because of such moments. As reporter Jack Germond observed of Mary, "She had the notion that Gene McCarthy was going to be another Adlai Stevenson, and he wasn't. He was the most cynical man I ever met." McCarthy's behavior after the assassination stood in sharp contrast with Kennedy's, given that Bobby calmed an angry black crowd in Indianapolis with a heartfelt speech the night of the shooting.

McCarthy was increasingly counterproductive on the campaign trail. Asked on *The Tonight Show* if he would make a good president, the senator replied, "Yes, I think I would be adequate." As Blair Clark complained, "He was contemptuous about most other politicians...even Caesar could kiss the ass of somebody who would be useful to his cause, but not Gene." Bobby Kennedy was simply a stronger politician. McCarthy's chances of winning the nomination plummeted when Bobby entered the race, leaving McCarthy deeply embittered in a year when rancor was an overabundant commodity.

The Democratic contest took another sharp turn when Vice President Hubert Humphrey announced his presidential bid in late April. Humphrey chose not to compete directly with Kennedy and McCarthy in the primaries, instead relying heavily on delegates from states that were not holding primaries. Humphrey was in a difficult position and was initially unwilling to challenge Johnson's position on the war in order to maintain his support. As Mary lamented, "When people are voting for the president, good or bad, they at least want to believe that he is his own man."

For Mary, the great drama of 1968 had become "Robert Kennedy against himself." She was struck by the fact that even as Bobby tried to appear more presentable—trimming his hair, speaking in more modulated tones, and acknowledging some of the faults of his late brother's administration—the public response to him was increasingly manic. Bobby's preferred mode of communication was no longer speeches, but a visceral connection with crowds. Mary wrote, "Kennedy has spent most of his time on the back of an open car surrounded by people who come to touch him. He is not content with pulling them onto the streets. He wants them, it seems, to come at him. They respond with a kind of mass hysteria that is both frightening and dangerous." To Mary, Bobby launching into a crowd looked like a swimmer cleaving a heavy surf.

Kennedy prevailed in the Indiana primary in early May, but the margin was close. With Humphrey in the race and McCarthy proving to be more difficult to dispatch than planned, Bobby threw himself into campaigning with renewed fervor.

Bobby was a man on fire, and Mary, who knew him so well, could still discern his inner shadows despite the spotlight's glare: "Seen from afar, Kennedy is a compelling, summoning figure. Lean as a whip, dark blond hair falling over sunburned face, he is literally bent double by the clutching hands reaching up to touch him as if he were magic. Seen up close, Kennedy is a different man. Gray flints at his temples. His face is lined and gaunt. His blue eyes are blank and hunted."

McCarthy and Kennedy continued to jockey to see who would challenge Humphrey at the convention. Kennedy won Nebraska convincingly, while McCarthy carried Oregon—the first time a member of the Kennedy family had ever met defeat at the polls. The stage was set for a showdown in California, a must-win for both men. Bobby was infuriated that McCarthy remained in the race. "He just didn't think McCarthy was on the same plane as him politically," Peter Edelman explained. "He could not stand the idea of treating McCarthy as an equal."

After much taunting from McCarthy, Bobby agreed to a debate just days before the California primary. Blair Clark, Mary, and Robert Lowell gathered as McCarthy prepared for the debate. An aide with a lengthy set of issue papers hovered nervously outside the room. Clark tried to get McCarthy to break off the friendly chat with Mary and Lowell to prepare. The senator said he did not need to.

Most commentators scored the debate a draw. But some important measure of healing had occurred between Mary and Bobby by this point. She was steadily becoming more enthusiastic about a Kennedy nomination, and her relations with the Kennedy inner circle had never truly ruptured. Gene McCarthy had been so disappointing to Mary on so many levels and she might have decided that Bobby was simply the better man all along.

The California primary was held on June 4, 1968. After a busy day of campaigning, both Kennedy and McCarthy watched the returns in their hotels in Los Angeles. Bobby squeaked out a narrow 46–42 percent win. The sun-kissed Bobby took the stage at the Ambassador Hotel at around midnight and addressed a delirious crowd of eighteen hundred supporters. His wife, Ethel, pregnant with their eleventh child, stood by his side. Bobby yelled to be heard above the din, "Now it's on to Chicago," the site of the Democratic convention, "and let's win there." As Kennedy exited through the hotel's kitchen, a crazed gunman shot him repeatedly. Robert Francis Kennedy died twenty-six hours later.

Mary was in McCarthy's suite at the Beverly Hilton hotel. During the day, there had been a great deal of discussion among McCarthy's team about whether he should throw his support to Bobby if he lost California. McCarthy loyalists knew this was the best way to prevent Humphrey from securing the nomination, but they also doubted that McCarthy would be so selfless. In the suite, McCarthy, Clark, and two staffers worked on a congratulatory telegram to Bobby.

"I think that we could say 'fine' instead of 'splendid,'" McCarthy told the pair, "because I don't think the percentage will go that high."

There was a knock on the door. David Schumacher, a CBS reporter, came into the room. "Senator Kennedy has been shot." Everyone was stunned. Mary remembered someone exclaiming, "You're kidding." Schumacher assured them he was not and disappeared to get more information. Abigail McCarthy and Gene's two daughters emerged from an adjoining room. Schumacher returned to say that Kennedy had been shot in the head.

McCarthy slumped in a chair and put his hands over his eyes. "Maybe we should do it in a different way," he said. "Maybe we should have the English system of having the cabinet choose the president."

A group of police appeared at the hotel room door to guard McCarthy.

"It was the ghastly finale to a campaign that had brought two men into increasingly bitter conflict for a prize that neither could attain without the other's help," wrote Mary.

After learning the news, McCarthy half-turned to Clark and said, "You know, he kind of brought it on himself"—exactly the same words he had used after Martin Luther King's assassination. David Mixner, who remained active on the McCarthy campaign, summed up Gene's lasting animus toward the Kennedy family as "sad and tragic." He called McCarthy a man who enjoyed a phenomenal moment in the sun only to become "bitter that it was a cloudy day again."

On June 7, Mary received a Western Union telegram: "You are invited to attend a requiem Mass in memory of Robert Francis Kennedy at St. Patrick's Cathedral in New York City on Saturday, June 8, 1968, at 10:00 a.m."

Less than five years after burying Jack, the Kennedy clan gathered in New York to memorialize Bobby. Mary wondered if the country had entered "an era when the lunatics, not the leaders, are writing the history," and her remembrances of Bobby were shaded in bittersweet hues:

> Bobby was a Celt—"unassimilated," Robert Lowell once called him—warm-hearted, vindictive, humorous, moody, intuitive. He loved and hated, and was, in turn, loved and hated. He could never be unkind to anyone who had been kind to his brother, or kind to anyone who had been unkind. He was a natural organizer. He tried pathetically to be like his brother, to read the same books, cultivate the same people, and consult the same advisers. He was torn between what he felt and what he thought. . . . At the end, he was a forlorn figure, caught between the past and the future, motorcading between miles of people who rushed to touch him and reassure him. His tragedy was not only that he had not achieved his full potential, but that uncertainties and pressures had prevented him from seeing what it was.

Leonard Bernstein played a Mahler symphony at the Mass, and Andy Williams sang "The Battle Hymn of the Republic." Ted Kennedy delivered the eulogy for his older brother: "My brother need not be idealized, or enlarged in death beyond what he was in life; to be remembered simply as a good and decent man, who saw wrong and tried to right it, saw suffering and tried to heal it, saw war and tried to stop it." A line of mourners more than twenty-five blocks long waited to pass by the body.

Mary was torn with grief, writing of Bobby that "he attracted the adulation and the rage which his clan, with their splendid, doomed lives, aroused in a nation that had never seen such a compelling collection of human beings, so beautiful, so armored, and so vulnerable." Her parting words for Bobby sounded like those of a proud, wounded sibling: "He was, at the very least, a magnificent boy, who always did his best." *Time* magazine declared that Mary had delivered one of Bobby's most elegant remembrances despite having been one of his severest critics.

A special twenty-one-car funeral train carried Bobby's body from New York to Washington, where he would be laid to rest at Arlington Cemetery, by his brother's side. Hundreds of thousands of people lined the tracks as the train worked its way south toward Union Station: young people, old people, weeping housewives, poor black men wearing dark funeral suits, veterans holding Americans flags, policemen, Boy Scouts, and firemen all standing stiff at attention as the train rumbled by. A country stood vigil for a fallen son.

John Seigenthaler remembered seeing Mary on the train: "She just exploded in tears, not a word, just an explosion of tears. And she had cried fifteen times before that." The two embraced. On the train, there was discussion of whether thirty-six-year-old Teddy Kennedy should jump into the presidential race or join the Humphrey ticket as vice president.

Mary was riven by a sense of guilt after Bobby's death, and Bobby's press secretary, Frank Mankiewicz, tried to put the situation in perspective. "Maybe Bobby had gone too far with some things," he said. "Mary may have worried that she was not in a state of grace with Bobby when he died." Mary naturally reflected on how tough she had been on Bobby. Yet her remorse did not push her toward revisionism or hero worship. "You would have been hard put the day after Bobby had been killed to find a person on the McCarthy campaign who hadn't wished they had supported him," David Mixner said. "That was the climate. I don't think Mary regretted her words, but we all examined our relationship at that moment."

A year that began with bright promise had spiraled out of control. The very idea of politics, and the very idea of America, seemed threatened.

By early July Gene McCarthy felt revived, even though Hubert Humphrey had a significant delegate lead heading into the Chicago convention. Mary's notes from a private July 2 discussion with McCarthy paint the picture of a bold but badly out-of-touch candidate: "Thinks he will now get it. It seems ordained." McCarthy likened himself to a toreador poised to skewer the unsuspecting Humphrey. Mary's faith in him had waned, and she scrawled in her notebook that McCarthy had "lost his constituency with the kids." The Minnesota senator remained stubbornly unwilling to speak kindly about Bobby even after his death.

In early August, Mary traveled to the Republican convention, in Miami. Seeing the continuing tumult all across the land, the lack of drama around Nixon looked like a winning formula to most Republicans. People might have viewed Nixon as square, but he did not seem sinister or unpredictable, and his earlier image as a cruel partisan had largely been papered over. Richard Nixon had obvious appeal for the large segments of the country that longed for a return to calmer days. The only discordant moment at the convention was Nixon's rather bizarre choice of Spiro Agnew, the pugnacious governor of Maryland, as his running mate. Mary's takeaway from the week: "The Republican convention was a dull and lifeless affair, devoid of suspense or stars, fight, or fun. The Republicans thought it was wonderful."

Even before the Democratic convention, there were widespread fears that it would be a disaster. Adding further to the aura of unrest and unease, Soviet forces invaded Czechoslovakia just days before the convention, crushing a democratic uprising. The convention was also the last one where Democratic Party bosses retained an overwhelming say in choosing the nominee. Between them, Gene McCarthy and Bobby Kennedy had claimed nearly 70 percent of primary votes, while Humphrey took only about 2 percent, yet Humphrey was well ahead in the delegate count.

Antiwar-protesting yippies planned large demonstrations outside the convention, in what they dubbed a "Festival of Life." Chicago mayor Richard J. Daley vowed that no outsiders would take over his streets, his convention, or his city, and he mobilized a massive police and National Guard presence eager for confrontation.

As Mary arrived at the Conrad Hilton Hotel, which served as head-quarters for the candidates and the press, the atmosphere was menacing. There were policemen posted in force by the elevator banks, and many of them were smoking, since Mayor Daley had given them special dispensation to do so during the convention.

Mary wandered out into the streets with reporter Eric Sevareid. They saw a young protestor spread-eagled across the hood of a car as four policemen beat him with batons. The police knew that Mary and Sevareid were reporters—their press credentials were prominently displayed. "The cops wanted us to see them," she would recall. "They were making a statement." For Mary, the police weren't just attacking college kids—they were launching an assault on the counterculture, on music they didn't understand, and on young people who spoke out in ways they never had.

The scene inside the convention was raw. Although Mayor Daley and convention organizers tried to marginalize those state delegations supporting a peace plank, cameras captured them chanting and shouting in protest. Scores of delegates were arrested or expelled from the hall for opposing Vietnam. The Chicago police and National Guard antagonized unruly protestors, and the situation quickly descended into chaos.

As delegates watched scenes of police clubbing protestors in the streets, Senator Abe Ribicoff of Connecticut took to the podium to nominate Senator George McGovern of South Dakota. Ribicoff declared, "With George McGovern we wouldn't have Gestapo tactics out on the streets of Chicago." Mayor Daley screamed at Ribicoff in return, "Fuck you, you Jew son of a bitch."

Mary had described the New Hampshire primary as "one of the head-iest, most romantic chapters in American political history." But just seven months later the landscape was gushing poison and rage. Even years later, she remembered the convention with anguish and clarity: "You would see friends you knew coming in from the McCarthy campaign, coming in all bloody, because they had an encounter where they were in the wrong place at the wrong time according to the Chicago police. There just wasn't a right place for them to be. I remember getting up at 6 o'clock in the morn-ing; nobody slept. It was an atmosphere of riot."

Mary joined McCarthy in his hotel suite. The two discussed whether or not he should endorse Humphrey while McCarthy casually tossed an orange around the room, fondly remembering his days as an amateur baseball player in the Great Sioux League. Poet Robert Lowell, somewhat bored, sniffed that discussions of baseball were as boring as those about politics.

With darkness falling, the situation deteriorated further as the Na-tional Guard massed on a bridge to prevent demonstrators from moving across. "I ought to go down there," McCarthy declared. "Those are my people. I ought to speak to them." Musician Mary Travers, of the Peter, Paul and Mary trio, was also in the suite, and she offered to accompany McCarthy, before the Secret Service vetoed the plan.

A stream of supporters appeared in the hotel room, wiping tear gas from their eyes. The McCarthy campaign had set up a room on the fif-teenth floor of the hotel to provide first aid to bloodied protestors, and McCarthy, Mary, and several others went there to assess the situation. They met a young medical student who had been trying to help with the wounded but had been beaten by police for his efforts. His white smock was blood-spattered, his head bandaged.

"I'm pleased to meet you, sir," the med student said as McCarthy and Mary entered. "Welcome to the Democratic Party of Chicago."

McCarthy and Mary returned to the suite on the twenty-third floor.

Humphrey's eventual acceptance speech was impossible. He had to acknowledge the violence raging all around without further antagonizing either the police or the demonstrators. He had to thank President Johnson for his support while simultaneously appealing to Kennedy and McCarthy loyalists. He had to pay tribute to Martin Luther King and Bobby Kennedy while sounding optimistic. He could neither fully defend nor denounce a war in Southeast Asia that was tearing apart the country.

Much of Humphrey's speech was greeted with derisive jeers at the McCarthy headquarters. Many of the young volunteers donned black armbands. The end of any losing campaign is difficult, but this was calamitous. Mary described the convention as "a total, complete, utter nightmare."

With the nomination settled, young McCarthy staffers played bridge on the fifteenth floor. A group of police burst into the room, shouting that the students were being evicted from the hotel for throwing debris down on the national guardsmen, which they had not done. When one of the young staffers tried to retrieve his possessions, a policeman lunged and fractured his skull with a nightstick. The frightened and bloody students were herded into the elevator. By this point McCarthy and Mary had been told what was taking place, and they appeared in the lobby.

It was half past five in the morning. McCarthy quietly asked the policemen who was in charge. No one was willing to come forward. He instructed his volunteers to return to their rooms. The Chicago convention was over.

Mary's reporting from the convention touched off a firestorm at the *Star*. When editors reviewed Mary's report of McCarthy's volunteers being assaulted, they fiercely debated the prominence they should give the story. One of them, Burt Hoffman, resigned in disgust as other editors tried to bury the story. He was asked to return after tempers cooled.

Star readers had every right to be confused by the paper's coverage from Chicago. In one of her columns, Mary argued that a Boy Scout troop could have handled the protestors. Yet almost side by side with her accounts of police brutality was a story by Betty Beale regaling readers with accounts of rampaging yippies. A column by James J. Kilpatrick waxed poetic about the heroic patience of the Chicago police. As a *Star* reader complained, "One wonders if they were in the same city."

The focus shifted to the race between Humphrey and Nixon. Al Spivak, who had covered the Kefauver campaign with Mary and considered her a friend, turned in his press pass to become Humphrey's public affairs director. Mary had been highly critical of Humphrey, and Spivak arranged a lunch with her at Sans Souci, one of Washington's most fashionable restaurants at the time, in an effort to sway her opinion.

At lunch in the airy green-and-gold dining room, Spivak argued that no matter how negligent Mary might have felt Humphrey had been in not opposing LBJ on the war, Nixon was a far worse alternative. To Spivak's considerable frustration, Mary kept repeating the same phrase: "It is the war, dear boy. It is the war." The two finished lunch, and Spivak did not bother trying to contact Mary again. Their relationship was one more casualty of 1968.

Humphrey, who lagged behind Nixon in the polls, was unable to gain traction until late October, when he finally distanced himself from Johnson's Vietnam policy. A deeply embittered Gene McCarthy finally offered what passed for an endorsement, and many Humphrey partisans blamed McCarthy for their difficulties in bringing home Democratic votes. President Johnson announced a bombing pause, and Humphrey began to rise in the polls.

In the end, it was not enough. Nixon won the presidency, in a race that was surprisingly close, given Chicago, the war, and the vituperative Democratic infighting.

"Many Democrats feel remorse when they look back to 1968 and realize that by their fury with Humphrey over the Vietnam War, they let Richard Nixon come to office," Mary wrote years later, likely including herself in that group.

Mary was deeply disappointed that young people had not turned out to vote in larger numbers. "They quit in the most meaningful way," Mary disparaged. "I hate that word, but it is the only one that comes to mind."

Yet it was unfair to blame the youth for lacking enthusiasm about choosing between Hubert Humphrey and Richard Nixon.

No figure was more of a disappointment than Gene McCarthy. Mary wrote that many Americans viewed him as "a self-righteous spoiler who would not make the difference in politics, either for himself or, when the time came, for the vice president." McCarthy subsequently ran for president in 1972, as a Democrat, and in 1976, as an independent. Neither effort was particularly serious, and Mary found the bids embarrassing.

Mary wrote to a friend, "Someday someone will figure out why Gene dropped out so completely after the New Hampshire triumph and turned sour on the kids. I think it was his Kennedy fixation, but I'm not sure. I run into him now and again. He lives in the country and recites a lot of Yeats. He could have done so much more." Whatever sense of romance she had shared with McCarthy was dead—although she would always cherish the days of the New Hampshire insurrection.

Disenchanted with McCarthy, Mary's heart bent back toward Blair Clark, as futile as that may have been. Clark spent a great deal of time with Mary, perhaps in part because he knew how McCarthy had wounded her. Sister Editha sharply disapproved of Mary's lingering feelings for Blair, writing to her, "I cannot understand Blair, he is indeed aggravating—I think he is spoiled, and I think you have done a lot of it." Every time Mary and Clark pulled closer, Clark again retreated.

Sister Editha wrote to Clark on Christmas Eve 1968: "You are not helping Mary and Mary cannot help you—so I wish you would not phone her, write her, or see her. God put you here to do a certain work for him—find out what it is and do it." Editha sent Mary a copy of the letter, along with a short note: "I will always remember him in my prayers, but that is all—he needs them. I tell you, I had no idea he was so selfish, conceited, unkind, so insincere, and ungrateful. He is no martyr. How he could treat you as he has is beyond me."

Mary and Clark settled into an uneasy détente. He married his second wife, and he and Mary saw each other from time to time.

Mary retreated substantially from romance. Chagrined and hurt, she buried herself in her work, helping at St. Ann's, and entertaining. More than ever before, the *Star* served as Mary's substitute family and lover. As she said of the *Star*, "I breathe better there. I like the air, and the gossip, and the irreverence." She added, "I would have loved to be a housewife, but it just never happened that way. I want to drop dead in the newsroom."

When Mary was asked by interviewers, always in very delicate terms, about her romantic life, she insisted that she had not made a conscious decision to avoid marriage, saying, "The right man never asked." For Mary, that man was Blair Clark. Her friend Phil Gailey put it all in perspective. "She had a great life. She had interesting friends, and she did interesting things. She had fun every day. Hell, I don't think she missed anything. I don't think she would have traded it for marriage and a cottage and a white picket fence. What she had was incredible, and she knew it."

CHAPTER SIX

Nixon

O n an overcast Monday in January 1969, Richard Milhous Nixon was sworn in as the 37th president of the United States. His speech was deliberately subdued and largely free of soaring rhetoric as he talked of "small, splendid efforts" that improved neighborhoods.

Shortly after the inauguration, Mary used her column to plead with the new president to do something about the wave of crime that had descended on Washington and other major cities. She urged him to walk around the city after dark and even proffered a personal invitation: "Please come by my place any time. I think you will find the men of Precinct Eight speak well of my cheesecake, having sampled it in the course of investigations following four break-ins."

Mary's cheesecake recipe made an unexpected star turn during Nixon's first press conference. He explained that the Secret Service had warned him about crime when he had suggested going for a walk just the day before. "I had read Mary McGrory's column and wanted to try her cheesecake," Nixon added. "But I find, of course, that taking a walk here in the District of Columbia, and particularly in the evening hours, is now a very serious problem, as it is in some other major cities."

The *Star* made the most of Nixon's cheesecake mention, suggesting that "Mary McGrory's cheesecake has taken over the title as 'World's Most Famous'" and reprinting her recipe. Mary bemoaned the sudden attention, writing to a friend, "After a blameless life, I have become a straight man for Richard Nixon. What a fate!"

Mary hoped that the press and Nixon might achieve a lasting ceasefire, but it was not to be. Nixon quickly embraced a strategy calculated to paint the media as part of the problem. Vice President Spiro Agnew enthusiastically took to the offensive in 1969, lambasting "the effete corps of impudent snobs who characterize themselves as intellectuals" as he argued that reporters were inherently biased.

Nixon's emphasis on law and order, coupled with his attacks on the press, fit nicely with his broader narrative that a "silent majority" of Americans supported him on Vietnam and other issues. It was also an easy way for Nixon to implicitly make the case that someone like Mary, a reporter who was vehemently opposed to Vietnam, was somehow un-American. For the first time since the Joe McCarthy era, Mary began receiving heavy-breathing phone calls at two in the morning and anonymous messages that she was "mentally sick and should leave the country." With her column appearing in more than fifty papers around the country, Mary's national exposure translated into volumes of hate mail.

It's no surprise that her columns took on a sharper edge after 1968. She was incredibly frustrated with Vietnam, still mourning the losses of the previous year, and saddened by her personal life. Nixon, 1968, Vietnam, student unrest, failed romances with Blair Clark and Eugene McCarthy—all were corrosive. The poetry was not lost from Mary's style, but a certain gentleness was.

In March 1969, Mary waded into the Vietnam debate in an unusually direct way, brokering a parley between a handful of young war protestors and Nixon's chief of staff, John Ehrlichman. Ehrlichman later complained that Mary was a reporter who believed it was her karmic duty to "change the course of events by becoming personally involved."

Ehrlichman and Mary had discussed the antiwar demonstrations, and she'd suggested that he might benefit from meeting some of the young antiwar organizers she had gotten to know from the McCarthy campaign. To her surprise, Ehrlichman agreed, and Mary arranged a lunch for him at her apartment along with prominent young activists Sam Brown, David Mixner, and John O'Sullivan.

When Mixner, Brown, and O'Sullivan walked through Mary's door that Saturday afternoon, dressed in their best suits, there was an immediate problem. Mary took a look at Brown's long, shaggy hair and declared, "No, no, no, this won't do."

Thinking Mary was kidding, Brown laughed. Then, shooting his friends a panicked look as he realized she was not, he insisted that his hair was fine.

"Sam, this meeting is about the war, not your hair," Mary insisted. "I won't have it become an issue."

Mary led Brown into her bedroom, removed his jacket, draped a towel over his shoulders, and started cutting his hair. "Sam looked stricken," Mixner recalled. "The only reason he was saved from a crew cut was the ringing doorbell."

Impressions of the meeting differed sharply. Although the conversation over meatloaf and cheesecake began politely, the mood soured when the discussion of Vietnam began in earnest. Ehrlichman thought Mary behaved as if she were a teacher and the activists were her star pupils. He bridled at the young men's insistence that the administration's stubbornness on Vietnam left them no alternative but to "make foreign policy in the streets." He was also struck by how little respect the young men and Mary had for Gene McCarthy, despite having championed his campaign.

Sam Brown argued that campus unrest would continue until Nixon shifted his position on the war. Ehrlichman countered that the administration would not be intimidated by long-haired troublemakers and would take all necessary measures to prevent civil disturbances.

"Sir," David Mixner interjected, "there are thousands of us ready to be arrested because we will not serve in this war."

Leaning forward, Ehrlichman pronounced, "You will go!"

John O'Sullivan responded, "Never!"

Anger rising, Ehrlichman replied, "Then we will put you all in jail for a long time."

"There aren't enough jails to hold us all," Brown shouted back.

Then, in a moment that bordered on the surreal, Ehrlichman pointed his finger at each of the three young men in turn and feigned a German accent: "Then we will build the walls of our stockades higher and higher."

Mary was alarmed. "John, you can't mean that," she said to Ehrlichman. "That is uncalled for in this home. These are substantive people who believe deeply in peace. I will not have my guests threatened with prison."

The lunch discussion broke up not long after. After Mary closed the door behind Ehrlichman, Brown looked at her and raised his palms. "And for that I cut my hair?"

While the nation marveled at Neil Armstrong becoming the first man to walk on the moon in July 1969 and was slightly stunned by the enormous Woodstock music festival just a month later, Mary continued to focus her columns on the growing Vietnam protests. She treated the massive Moratorium to End the War in Vietnam march on Washington, in mid-November 1969—organized by Brown, Mixner, and others—as a cause célèbre. More than half a million people clogged the streets of D.C. on a brisk, clear day. The scruffy rebels whom Mary had welcomed into her living room had pulled off the largest antiwar protest in American history.

Mary appeared at the organizers' headquarters on the day of the moratorium carrying a picnic basket. She had brought David Mixner's favorite meatloaf. "I just brought food for my boys," she purred as she tried to work her way past a staffer barring journalists from entering. The other reporters shouted, "Don't let her in," but Mary was granted entrée. As she chatted with Mixner and others, the moratorium's press officer, Marylouise Oates, interrupted. "David, may I see you for a minute?"

Oates lit into Mixner as soon as they were in the hall: "Just what in the hell am I supposed to tell the other reporters now that you've let Mary inside? They're furious and I have to deal with them."

"But she brought us lunch," Mixner said in halfhearted defense.

"Lunch, hell!" Oates said. "She just got an exclusive. Now I have to go in there and get her and I'll be the bad apple in her eyes."

Oates asked Mary to leave, and Mary never forgave her for the transgression.

Mary always made it hard for people to draw clear lines. "She was the Irish mother," Mixner explained. "She would come show up with baskets of food. Sometimes they were baskets of food taking care of 'her kids,' as she called them, and other times it was a great way to get by other reporters and get good stories. Sometimes it was hard to tell the difference."

In any case, the young people loved Mary because of her vocal opposition to the war, and her affection for youth was genuine. She always believed that youthful idealism could change the world—even after the sharp disappointments of the previous year. For Mary, the success of the moratorium was restorative. "They had no idea what they had wrought," she wrote of the moratorium participants. "What they carried home from the bone-chilling day was a memory of community, of a single purpose, not spoken, but sung, from the platform."

In late 1969, Mary attended a party in Boston whose guests included a number of Harvard professors. Much of her cocktail chatter focused on National Security Adviser Henry Kissinger, who had previously taught at Harvard. The faculty she spoke with were still supportive of Kissinger, although skeptical of his private assurances that Nixon knew he had to end the war. The next day, Mary wrote a column that was probably tougher on Kissinger than her discussions at the party warranted: "Back in Cambridge, Henry Kissinger's performance gets low marks. His old colleagues at Harvard and MIT, whom he values and visits whenever he can, feel he has done little to change the course of the war and that he defends it with increasing offensiveness."

Mary had requested interviews with Kissinger in the past, but he had always declined. Yet by the time she arrived at the *Star* offices the day the column ran, one of Kissinger's military aides had already arranged a time for Kissinger to meet with Mary.

She interviewed Kissinger in his basement office at the White House. Mary argued that Vice President Agnew's harsh condemnation of the press and the administration's tough language toward protestors were making people feel unwelcome in their own country. She pointed out that she was close friends with many young people who opposed the war.

"Ah, the young people," Kissinger sighed.

"He gave me a big song and dance about how he missed young people," Mary said, "and how his relationship with the students had been so wonderful." Kissinger told her that he would love to meet the young leaders of the peace movement. Could Mary arrange it? Despite the earlier disaster with Ehrlichman, Mary was amenable. Kissinger made clear that the meeting would have to be small and secret. Mary agreed.

The group met at Mary's apartment around Christmas 1969.

Mary had invited David Hawk, David Mixner, and Sam Brown to the discussion. Hawk was facing an indictment for dodging the draft, but he was far from the stereotypical hippie. A swimming champion at Cornell, he was handsome and clean-cut. Mary believed, with something approaching certitude, that if anyone met and seriously talked to young men like Hawk, Mixner, and Brown, they would see the light on the war.

Kissinger appeared at Mary's apartment right on time. "He was charming," said Mary.

The five of them sat down for drinks. All three young men described their passionate, resolute opposition to Vietnam. "He listened with genuine interest, total attention," Mary said. "He heard them out, never interrupting, contradicting, arguing, or scolding."

"There is only one answer to this madness, and that is to bring the troops home now," Brown urged. "Not next year, but now."

"Sam, you know that is not possible," Kissinger replied. He argued that the protestors needed to demonstrate restraint: "This administration will not tolerate domestic violence or disruption because of the war. I warn you that there are elements in the White House who would welcome the opportunity to take reprisals against any of you if you were to provide them the excuse."

Kissinger "seemed struck by Hawk," Mary recalled, "a dark, direct, smiling young man, whose mind was wonderfully focused by the notion of going to jail for his convictions." After dinner, Kissinger continued to make the case that Vietnamization—the process of training South Vietnamese soldiers to take on greater and greater responsibilities—was working.

"Dr. Kissinger," Hawk asked, "what if Vietnamization fails?"

Kissinger insisted that the process was going well and that despite the tenacity of the Vietcong, the South Vietnamese were pulling together. "Well, we think we have a hope of success."

Hawk was not so easily dissuaded. "Dr. Kissinger, what if it doesn't work?"

Kissinger said that it would be obvious if they failed. He added that he was sending General Alexander Haig, "my best man," to the field so he could give him "the frankest of reports."

"What if it doesn't work?" queried Hawk for a third time.

"Then we will have another strategy," the national security adviser replied.

"And what is that?" Hawk asked.

Mary recalled the moment. Kissinger, "with the wise look that had disarmed so many," said simply, "That I cannot tell you." David Hawk left the meeting convinced that the administration would never end the war without outside pressure. After the meeting, Kissinger jettisoned his vow of secrecy as soon as it was convenient to do so, puffing himself up in the process by telling others that he was in "constant contact" with the peace movement.

"It was a mistake and I shouldn't have done it," Mary said in retrospect. She knew that many of her peers viewed her friendship with the peace movement leaders as a curiosity, but, as she maintained, "Had it been left to the World War II generation, we would have been in Vietnam forever."

By 1970 it had become clear to Mary that Nixon's plan to end the war in Vietnam was a cruel illusion. Nixon and his team increasingly made the case that the real problem wasn't the war, but the people protesting the war. In April 1970, President Nixon expanded and escalated the conflict by launching a major bombing campaign in Cambodia. Mary was outraged. Kissinger's Plan B was massive air attacks.

About a year after the meeting at her apartment, Mary sat next to Kissinger at a party hosted by the president of the Washington, D.C., city council. Kissinger had arrived late and joined the head table for dessert. In his deep, rumbling voice, he tried to charm Mary, asking when she might invite him to dinner. Mary, who had downed a number of cocktails by this point, snapped, "When you have the last American out of Vietnam."

She was deeply at odds with the *Star*'s editorial line on Vietnam during this period. "Mary was very upset that the paper wouldn't support her views," Newby Noyes said. "Sometimes she wouldn't even talk to me." Mary helped galvanize a staff protest in response to the U.S. invasion of Cambodia, offering to resign. Newby replied to her in writing: "I don't care what you write; just keep writing it for us."

Mary insisted that her inability to shift the *Star*'s editorial position on Vietnam was a sign of her limited influence as a columnist. "If those people on the *Star*, who are paid to read me are so totally unmoved, I can't imagine how the public is," she vented. "I have written anti-war articles practically four times a week and yet our paper has endorsed every step of the war, and I constantly get hate mail calling me a communist."

While Vietnam mightily frustrated Mary, she did not truly believe she lacked influence. Her columns were carefully dissected at the White House and in Congress. When she wrote columns complaining about surly treatment at her local post office, no less than the postmaster general attempted to mollify her. ("How can I call you Mary if you call me General?" wrote America's chief postal official in response.) Her humility was tactical. It allowed her to maintain the useful fiction that she was a helpless naïf.

Mary was a challenge for her editors to manage. "I think it was always understood that if they changed anything, I would go out the door, never to return again," Mary said. "Total freedom of expression is what I require." Reporter Edward Morgan recalled a lunch with Noyes during which Mary's name came up. Newby shook his head and clapped his hand to his brow. "I love her but she is constantly causing me headaches."

Mary repeatedly complained to Newby that the paper ran too many letters critical of her work. "Many of the letters I get about you are answered by a firm statement from me that the *Star* is proud to have you in the paper," he reassured her. "But when we get a flood of protest over something we do—whether it is an editorial, a news story, or a Miss Mc-Grory comment—I think we should give the dissenters a chance to blow off steam."

It was around this time that Liz Acosta was officially assigned as Mary's full-time assistant. Mary was the only columnist at the *Star* to be given both an office and a secretary. When Maureen Dowd first started at the *Star*, she noticed that Mary's small office was always the center of activity. "All the cute guy reporters at the paper—Phil Gailey, Fred Barnes, Walter Taylor, Lance Gay—were always clustered around her tiny little office, dancing attendance, fetching, serving, doting, like Las Vegas chorus boys," Dowd observed. "Naturally, I immediately decided I wanted to be a columnist." Acosta and another friend, Gertrude Cleary, were a constant presence at Mary's parties and social gatherings.

Mary lost two important women in her life in 1970 with the death of Doris Fleeson, in August, and her mother, in October. Gene McCarthy delivered the eulogy for Fleeson at the Navy Chapel, in Washington, celebrating her toughness by saying that she considered it her calling "to tell this world what was wrong with it, and who was wrong, and to suggest in terms that no one could misunderstand what she thought ought to be done." On October 3, Mary's mother died, at age eighty-one, after suffering a heart attack at Deaconess Hospital, in Boston. After a service at the Holy Name Church, in West Roxbury, she was buried in Roslindale's Old Calvary Cemetery.

Mary developed an even stronger bond with her aunt Kate after her mother's death. Kate would often stay with Mary in Washington for months at a time, and they were always together with other family members in Boston and Antrim during the holidays. Mary's friends were taken with Kate's decidedly no-nonsense worldview. "You know all they talk about is politics down there," Kate complained of Washington. "They never talk about the weather." When Aunt Kate sold her cabin in New Hampshire, Mary continued to travel up to Antrim every year at the end of the summer and often for Thanksgiving, with the Maplehurst Inn becoming her new home away from home in New Hampshire.

Mary's relationship with her surviving family, primarily her nieces and nephew, was enduring but sometimes—like all her relationships—complicated. Her nephew Ted McGrory and niece Anne Beatty and husband Tom effectively served as Mary's immediate family, welcoming her into their homes for holidays and family gatherings. Mary was generous and well loved by her surviving family, and she often brought unexpected delights into their lives: Ted Kennedy dropping her off at their front door; a chance to meet the president on visits to Washington; the thrill of mingling with Walter Cronkite at a party in Mary's apartment; a round of golf with Ethel Kennedy as Mary trailed behind in a cart; and playing touch football at the family compound in Hyannis Port.

But Mary was not always easy on those close to her. She could be demanding and critical. Her niece Polly, with whom she had a very close, but later strained, relationship, remembers feeling as if she couldn't do anything right when, before one of Mary's parties, Mary criticized her makeup and clothes. "That looks cheap," she said. Yet once the gathering began, Mary introduced Polly as her darling, talented niece. But it wasn't just family members who were judged. Maureen Dowd remembers Mary lecturing her at a restaurant in Rome because her bra strap was showing. Another friend was scolded because her skirt was too short. Mary approved and she disapproved, and there was no in-between—a trait that served her well as a columnist but was challenging on a personal level.

Family and friends sometimes struggled to escape their pigeonholed identities. Mary's niece Anne was designated as a campfire wood gatherer on the beach in Antrim when she was five. Mary, satisfied with her performance, assigned her the same role every year in perpetuity. "It was really hard to change categories," said Mary's nephew, Ted. "There was a no-trade clause."

"She did have a temper," Phil Gailey commented. "She did lash out sometimes, and usually the people who got the worst end of her tongue lashings were the people she cared about the most." By and large, people around Mary accepted that sudden storms came with her personality.

For someone with such a nimble mind, Mary viewed the world in largely binary terms: moral or immoral; good guy versus bad guy. Because she loved Antrim, everything about Antrim was brilliant. The locals were descendants of Revolutionary War heroes. The local production of *Oliver!* was "Broadway caliber," and Wayno's Grocery was "the finest in the country."

If everything about Antrim was good, everything about Richard Nixon was bad, and the two clashed in a most unexpected way in a July 1970 incident that only underscored how entrenched sexism still was in the newsroom.

Newby Noyes had invited Nixon to an owners' lunch. The president's press secretary, Ron Ziegler, called to say that Nixon would accept upon one condition: the lunch had to be stag; no women were to be included. Noyes suggested, half-joking, that the White House wanted to make the event stag because of Mary. Ziegler laughed off the question.

Word of Mary's exclusion quickly spread. Thirteen female *Star* employees complained to Newby and John Kauffmann, president of the *Star*. They also sent a telegram to Nixon, calling the move "an affront to all women staffers." The local Newspaper Guild telegrammed protests to Nixon, Ziegler, communications director Herb Klein, and the *Star*'s management, arguing that it was already hard enough for women in journalism without having sexism promoted at the "highest level." Several women staffers at the *Star* asked what the reaction would have been if the White House had asked for a "whites only" lunch. Kauffmann replied, "Of course, we would have immediately reacted and said no. But somehow when someone suggests you have something stag, you just don't react."

Mary did not lend her name to the protests, and she remained mum, as did most of the men on the staff of the *Star*.

On July 23, 1970, President Nixon was served shrimp cocktail and filet mignon in the *Star*'s boardroom. Mary, still the only woman on the *Star*'s national staff, ate an egg salad sandwich at her desk.

After his lunch, President Nixon toured the newsroom. Newby Noyes pointed out Mary's office, and Nixon stepped in to say hello. The small gray office wasn't much. The window was chipped, two telephones sat on the desk, and a large Italian traffic poster that warned FACILITATE PASSING . . . IF YOU WISH TO ARRIVE adorned one wall, surely leaving Nixon to ponder how so much torment could flow from such undistinguished quarters.

Nixon and Mary made awkward small talk.

Nixon observed that Mary had an orderly desk, "the neatest in the newsroom."

"Is that where you keep the cheesecake?" the president asked Mary, a reference to her column on crime.

She asked Nixon if he'd enjoyed lunch. The president noted that he didn't like to eat while talking. There was not much else to say, and Nixon departed.

Women were increasingly willing to challenge having the playing field of journalism tilted against them. One of the great symbols of sexism in journalism during the 1970s remained the annual Gridiron Club dinner. The event was a nearly century-old tradition featuring skits and musical numbers, and every president since Grover Cleveland had appeared at the ceremonies at least once. The dinners were a chance for Washington's senior journalists to mingle with politicians in an atmosphere of slightly drunken, and sometimes feigned, informality.

Women were not allowed to be Gridiron members. Mary and others decided to picket the dinner in 1970, and Mary did so because she objected to being kept away from a place where news was being made. "The question arises why any sensible woman would wish to attend such a fete," Mary wrote. "The answer is she doesn't. She just wishes to be asked."

For four years running, Mary and others picketed dinner guests. One policeman wondered at the fuss, telling the women that the attendees looked "like a bunch of old fogies anyway." The first woman, Helen Thomas, was finally admitted in 1975, and Mary was granted membership in 1976.

But Mary remained a reluctant warrior on the front lines of feminism. In 1971, Bella Abzug, the firebrand congresswoman from New York, contacted Mary. Abzug, along with Betty Friedan, Shirley Chisholm, and others, planned to launch a National Women's Political Caucus to promote gender equality, and Abzug was hoping for Mary's support. "Hundreds of women are coming, the feminist movement is on its way."

Mary was enthusiastic. "Oh, that's wonderful, Bella. That's marvelous," she said. "Now you're going to take a stand on the war."

Abzug hesitated. "Well, a lot of the women are Republicans," she explained, "and they would find it difficult to oppose Nixon on the war."

"Well, then, Bella, what's the point?" Mary asserted, "If they're just going to be like men, why bother?"

But despite the rhetoric and the real push of the women's movement, women applying for jobs at papers in the 1960s were told that they would be considered only for positions as mail clerks or researchers. Writing jobs were for men.

Mary obviously believed women to be every bit as capable as men, if not more so, but she was no knee-jerk feminist. As a self-made woman in a man's world, she expected other women to do the same. Reporter Lesley Stahl remembered sitting next to Mary at a congressional hearing when Mary told her that she resented the young women who had gotten their jobs through affirmative action. Stahl, who had gotten her job at CBS as a direct result of affirmative action, squirmed.

Mary did not hide her ambivalent feelings for the vocal feminism of the early 1970s. "I found its early advocates a bit strident," she explained. "They emphasized abortion and gung-ho careerism too much for me. I couldn't go along with the nursing mother who insisted on being a firefighter, and I didn't think that unisex restrooms were quite the thing. I was glad, however, to see that the 'either-or' syndrome which crushed so many women of my generation—marriage or a career—was being dissipated." Doris Fleeson's daughter wrote to Mary to complain, "Could you please stop being so 'diligently' anti-feminist?"

"She definitely fit in better with the men than the women," said her friend Phil Gailey. "She would send the women out to the kitchen to do the dishes and she would sit in the living room and talk with the men. For a woman who had broken such huge gender barriers in her day, I never understood why she cared so little about it." As Jack Germond observed, "Mary was not of the women's movement in any way, and she did not like being identified with it," adding, "She always treated women with, as we say, minimum high regard."

Elizabeth Shannon remembers getting to know Mary when she arrived in Washington in the early sixties, after graduating from college in Texas. Shannon had landed a position with the *Star*'s reporter training program. The trainees, who all sat in a common bullpen in the middle of the newsroom, covered decidedly unglamorous assignments like missing animal reports and the obituaries. Not long after coming to Washington, Elizabeth met her future husband, William Shannon, a political reporter for the *New York Times*.

William Shannon told Elizabeth that she should introduce herself to Mary, since Mary was an old friend.

"Oh, God," Elizabeth said. "She is such a star. I am a lowly reporter trainee. I am not sure I should do that."

A few days later, Mary stopped by the reporter trainees' table.

"Which one of you is Elizabeth?" she asked, somewhat menacingly.

"That's me," replied Shannon.

"I hear you are engaged to Bill Shannon," Mary said.

"Yes," she said brightly, "I am."

"How long have you been in Washington?"

"About four months," Shannon replied.

"Well, it didn't take you long to get what you came for, did it?" Mary walked away without another word. The four trainees stared at one another, stunned by the exchange. One of them was Carl Bernstein. "We are not going to let her get away with that," Bernstein declared.

Mary had to pass by the desk to get to her office, and Bernstein began surreptitiously flinging wads of paper in her direction whenever she appeared. Mary finally came over to the desk and said, "This has to stop." It did.

When Elizabeth shared the story with William Shannon, he roared with laughter. The three went out to dinner not long after, and Elizabeth and Mary became close friends.

Journalist Marjorie Williams noted that while Mary certainly "had a queenly expectation of deference," there was "something so gorgeous, in this irretrievably masculine town, about a woman who knew her due." Williams argued that Mary had made it acceptable for women to be more genuine in the workplace. "To be a woman in a man's town you had to be more careful, make yet a paler impression, than the Brooks Brothers suits all around you," she said. "Mary showed that you could be not only forgiven, but rewarded, for shedding that dreary disguise. Talent, Mary taught us, was the ultimate get-out-of-jail-free card."

When Williams had first started working with Mary, Mary sent her a personal note telling her to largely ignore the men in the newsroom—they were all bark and no bite. Mary would send nice handwritten notes when she liked one of Williams's pieces, something the male stars of the newsroom almost never did. Williams also received a three-word piece of advice from Mary when she began penning an op-ed column at the *Post*: "Subtlety is overrated."

"Mentoring, in today's parlance, wasn't her thing," reporter Gloria Borger explained. "Hard work was. It wasn't about complaining that you were taken less seriously than the men, or that you earned less, or that you got crummy assignments. It was about diligence, about doing your work well—and getting noticed for the right reasons." Mary was more a mother superior than a mentor.

Cokie Roberts argued that even though Mary was a notably reluctant feminist, her contributions were significant. "Mary was very much a trail-blazer for the women coming after her. We could not have done what we did if she had not done what she did, and kept doing it."

By 1971, President Nixon seemed to have emerged triumphant. His approval ratings were strong, the tumult of the late 1960s had died down to a very large degree, and the dishonors of his earlier campaign losses were an increasingly distant memory. He was in an enviable position heading into the 1972 presidential race. But in June 1971, the Nixon administration became embroiled in a high-profile showdown with the *New York Times* and the *Washington Post* after the leak of the Pentagon Papers, a classified Pentagon history of the Vietnam War. When the Supreme Court eventually ruled that the papers could publish the documents, it was an important reminder that there were limits to even the most imperial presidency.

Yet within the halls of the White House, the president and his inner circle were not going to accept such a rebuke easily, and they relentlessly plotted how to bring the full weight of the government to bear against their opponents. Surprisingly prominent among these enemies: Mary McGrory. Three years after sharing a hymnal with Nixon at Martin Luther King's funeral, Mary was in the crosshairs.

In September 1971, Charles Colson, Nixon's special counsel, drew up the infamous "enemies list," detailing twenty of Nixon's most hated opponents and political enemies. Mary's name was among them.

On September 18, Nixon and his chief of staff, H. R. Haldeman, met in the Oval Office to discuss their "tax list." Haldeman pointed out that the IRS had been instructed to go after some of Nixon's least favorite reporters. "They're going after a couple of media people. They are going after Dan Schorr, Mary McGrory," said Haldeman.

"Good," Nixon replied.

"They just want to harass them, just get them in a little trouble," Haldeman elaborated after a further exchange, "just give them a little trouble."

"Exactly," Nixon declared. "Pound these people."

"Just give them a little trouble," Haldeman repeated.

Nixon chortled before preemptively exonerating himself: "It's routine."

In separate conversations with Haldeman and John Ehrlichman, Nixon made clear what he expected of the next IRS commissioner: "I want to be sure he is a ruthless son of a bitch, that he will do what he's told, that every income tax return I want to see, that he will go after our enemies and not go after our friends."

"It isn't a matter of doing anything against the law," Haldeman responded. "It's a matter of using the law to its full—to our benefit rather than someone else's."

Mary's name came up frequently in the White House tapes, and denouncing her was a sure way to curry favor with the president. During one Oval Office meeting, press secretary Ron Ziegler complained about Mary McGrory and "her sick little world," before adding, "We shouldn't judge anything by her. Never have, never should." Henry Kissinger discussed possibly meeting with Gene McCarthy as part of his continued campaign to mute antiwar criticism but then complained, "If I have lunch with him, he'll leak to Mary McGrory."

William Safire, who was working as a White House speechwriter, remembered inviting Mary to a dinner party at his home. The next day, he was rebuked by Haldeman: "There is not a chance that you can ever persuade McGrory to ever be fair about anything to do with Nixon, and to invite 'them' into your homes is hopeless."

Mary was audited by the IRS in 1971. "She was in a dither," recalled her colleague Lance Gay. "It was a top-to-bottom audit and they wanted justification for everything." The audit quickly focused on Mary's charitable giving as an area of concern, particularly a "miscellaneous contribution" of cash to St. Ann's to help Sister Editha buy Christmas presents for the kids.

Mary's case was reviewed by the IRS district director, and Sister Editha eventually produced a receipt. The IRS informed Mary that it was willing to accept the receipt as legitimate but insisted that other charitable contributions were not properly documented and that Mary owed an additional thousand dollars in taxes and penalties.

She scrambled to produce additional documentation. Ironically, Mary eventually received a tax *credit* of $194.88 after the IRS audit was completed—she had actually failed to fully take her charitable deductions.

Mary was audited multiple years in a row during the Nixon era. There is probably no better indictment of Nixon's abuse of power than his use of the IRS to hound Mary for buying Christmas gifts for orphans. Frank Mankiewicz put it in perspective: "Intellectually, Nixon saw her as sort of like him, but totally an enemy. Of all the people on the enemies list, she was probably most the enemy."

For the Democratic Party, the 1972 presidential campaign only continued the suffering that had begun in 1968.

Ted Kennedy decided to sit on the sidelines after the fatal accident at Chappaquiddick, and the list of Democratic contenders was long, but not formidable. Continuing to describe politics as theater, Mary wrote from Manchester, "The New Hampshire primary is badly in need of a play doctor. After six months on the boards, it is dying on its feet. The cast is enormous, there is no end of jugglers and tumblers, but no plot has developed, no villain or hero has come down from the lovely hills."

Senator Ed Muskie of Maine was the front-runner, but in one of the Nixon campaign's dirty-tricks operations, operatives for the president spread the rumor that Muskie had derisively referred to French Canadians as "Canucks"—which would be an obvious problem, given New Hampshire's sizable French Canadian population. Standing on the back of a flatbed truck, denouncing both the Canucks accusation and charges in the *Manchester Union Leader* that his wife drank heavily, Muskie broke down in tears. Mary noted in her column that the conservative *Union Leader* had drawn blood from many a politician, "but until that moment never made one cry." The incident only became more infamous when Muskie subsequently insisted that the tears had been "melting snowflakes."

South Dakota senator George McGovern emerged as the alternative, bolstered by youth and antiwar voters. Yet McGovern was not the most convincing candidate to wage a general election. He came from a small state with little in the way of electoral clout, and his fiercely liberal positions were easily caricatured. Columnist Robert Novak cited an anonymous senator saying that if McGovern got the nomination, the general election would be all about his positions on "amnesty, abortion, and acid."

McGovern claimed the nomination at the July 1972 Democratic convention, in Miami. It was far more peaceful than Chicago, but it was still a train wreck. The Democrats had substantially changed their convention rules after 1968 in an effort to prevent party bigwigs from overruling the rank and file in selecting a nominee. But the pendulum swung too far, and the convention verged on ungoverned. "The spirit of the occasion," Mary wrote, "is aptly conveyed by a streamer that floats behind a plane that patrols the rain clouds overhead. It reads: 'McGovern is a disaster.'"

As the convention played out like a ragged circus on television, the party pros were telling Mary that McGovern could cost the party "every office from the courthouse to the White House." The convention was so badly stage-managed that McGovern accepted the nomination at three in the morning. Most Americans had turned off their televisions.

McGovern's most notable blunder at the convention was his selection of Senator Thomas Eagleton of Missouri as his vice presidential candidate. It quickly leaked that Eagleton was under medication for depression and had undergone shock therapy, but he resisted being removed from the ticket. Democrats were outraged that McGovern had failed to defuse the situation by either defending Eagleton or replacing him. As Mary jested, McGovern had become the only politician in history to be labeled "a spineless brute."

When Senator Eagleton read that Mary had described him as an eager "cocker spaniel," he shook his head and, referring to President Nixon's famous speech invoking his dog Checkers, said, "Instead of giving a Checkers speech, I've become Checkers."

As the Democrats imploded, two enterprising and largely unknown *Washington Post* reporters labored over a story that would change Washington. On June 17, 1972, a break-in occurred at Democratic headquarters, in the Watergate building. The *Post* assigned Bob Woodward and Carl Bernstein to the story, and the two dug relentlessly. This was the same scruffy Bernstein with whom Mary had clashed when he was a reporter trainee at the *Star*. Mary had later counseled him against leaving the *Star* for the *Post*.

Woodward and Bernstein soon reported that Attorney General John Mitchell controlled a secret fund linked to the break-in. When the two reporters asked Mitchell to comment on the pending story, Mitchell gave one of the more famous responses in modern journalism: "Katie Graham is going to get her tit caught in a big fat wringer if that's published." The owner of the *Post* was not deterred.

By early October, Woodward and Bernstein had reported that the Watergate break-in was part of a "massive campaign of political spying and sabotage on behalf of President Nixon's re-election and directed by officials of the White House."

As the two reporters worked the story, Mary sent a note to both: "I don't really know what you are doing, but I'm glad you are doing it." When she bumped into Bernstein, she was self-deprecating: "What a mistake you made. You've just gone on to achieve fame and fortune. You could have stayed with us and got our coffee and pencils for the rest of your life. You blew it."

Mary considered Watergate the greatest journalistic feat of modern times. "That story happened because a brilliant and bold editor, Ben Bradlee, took a chance on two guys under thirty and held them to high standards," she argued. "They showed you what journalism was all about: shoe leather and persistence, and will and determination, and knocking on doors and going back and knocking on doors again, and not being intimidated."

When the president expressed concern that the *Post* was running stories "based on hearsay, innuendo, guilt by association, and character assassination," Mary noted that this was a rather remarkable assertion for a politician who had built an entire career on exactly the same methods. Thanks in no small part to the general ineptitude of the McGovern campaign, Watergate was not a major issue in the 1972 campaign. A bloody Palestinian Liberation Organization terrorist attack on Israeli athletes at

Mary, with her father, mother, and brother, John, as a girl in Roslindale. She described her upbringing as equal parts romantic and puritanical.

A comic strip first piqued her interest in being a reporter. Mary as a young girl.

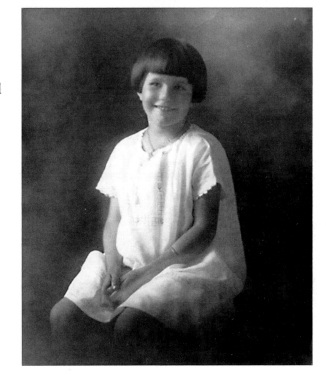

RIGHT: Newly elected as class treasurer, Mary as a college freshman.

EMMANUEL FROSH OFFICERS

Officers of the freshman class at Emmanuel College, elected yesterday are (left to right): Dorothy Noonan, Brighton, president; Mary Raftus, Dorchester, vice-president; Agnes Cox, Woburn, secretary; Mary McGrory, Roslindale, treasurer.

LEFT: On the eve of World War II, Mary's Emmanuel College yearbook photo.

Newby Noyes sits next to Mary in a staged editorial meeting photo while she was working as a book reviewer at the *Star* in the early 1950s.

Her parties became the stuff of Washington lore. Mary in 1950, when she was a book reviewer at the *Star*.

Washington Star staffers sing as Crosby Noyes plays the piano. Mary is second from left.

Joseph Welch, the army's lead counsel, walks up the steps of the Senate Office Building alongside Mary in 1954. Smitten with her, Welch inscribed the photo: "To the one I love."

Mary at the Army-McCarthy hearings.

A birthday party for the children from the St. Ann's orphanage. Mary was militant in enlisting others to also help out with the kids.

On the run near the White House.

Phoning in a story from the campaign trail.

Receiving the Washington Newspaper
Guild award in 1959 from editorial
cartoonist Herblock.

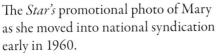

The *Star's* promotional photo of Mary
as she moved into national syndication
early in 1960.

Mary and her close friend and
confidante Liz Acosta outside her
apartment in the 1950s.

Mary and Eugene McCarthy compare notes on the floor of the 1960
Democratic convention that nominated JFK for president. McCarthy's
impassioned plea on behalf of Adlai Stevenson at the convention thrust him
into the national spotlight and badly alienated the Kennedys.

The disastrous
summit between
Kennedy and
Khruschev
quickly led to
sharply escalating
Cold War
tensions. Mary
looks on as the
two leaders meet
in Vienna during
1961.

The kids from St. Ann's with Mary at Bobby and Ethel Kennedy's home in McLean, Virginia, "Hickory Hill."

Mary with columnist Ralph McGill and President Lyndon Johnson at a State Department reception in 1965. Mary was an outspoken critic of LBJ's Vietnam policy.

Mary in her apartment in Northwest Washington, D.C.

LBJ and Mary in his "little office" just off the Oval Office in May 1965. The charm offensive he directed at Mary was equal parts political and romantic.

Bobby Kennedy signed this picture to Mary: "It looks like you are about to kiss me and that is why I look so excited. Love xxoo Bobby."

Mary enjoys a birthday celebration in her apartment, circa the mid-1960s.

Mary and Blair Clark at a
dinner party.

Mary with Bobby Kennedy
on his campaign plane in
1968.

Mary and Ethel Kennedy
chat, along with Bobby and
Jim and Blanche Whittaker,
probably during the 1968
Oregon primary.

As Bobby Kennedy once remarked, "Mary is so gentle—until she gets behind a typewriter."

ABOVE: Mary on a yacht off the coast of Greece with some of the *Star's* owners in the early 1970s.

Mary and Nixon when the president visited the *Star* for a stag luncheon in 1970. Mary's opinion of Nixon: "If he were a horse, I would not buy him."

Mary ponders Watergate testimony and later (below) holds court among reporters and observers at the hearings.

Robert Redford in Mary's office when he visited the *Star* to research his role in *All the President's Men*. He inscribed the photo: "Dear Mary, Boy can you draw a crowd—love and thanks."

Mary at the *Star*. She likened the pressure of producing columns to staying "one step ahead of the sheriff."

Mary and her first grandniece, Katie, on the porch of her beloved Maplehurst Inn in Antrim, New Hampshire, 1978.

President Ronald Reagan and Mary have lunch at the *Star* in August 1981—just days before the paper closed. Mary was no fan of Reagan, but she gave him great credit for visiting the *Star* in its dying days.

Mary insisted that she hated appearing on television, but she was a regular guest on *Meet the Press*, hosted by her friend Tim Russert. Lisa Myers is at the center.

President Clinton salutes Mary in 1995 as they board Air Force One after she received the Four Freedoms Award.

Mary's tombstone in Antrim, inscribed NEWSPAPER WOMAN AND VOLUNTEER.

the 1972 Olympic Games, in Munich, seemed to only reinforce the public's sense that they needed Nixon's steady internationalist hand at the helm.

In late October, Mary wrote a column reflecting a small burst of optimism for McGovern as she traveled with the candidate in Michigan. "If the same coalescence of grassroots organization, labor muscle, and heavy registration occur in other big industrial states, the mandate could be something less than the size of Mt. Rushmore on November 7." It was not a prediction of a McGovern upset and, as prognostication goes, it was very guarded.

Timothy Crouse's bestseller, *The Boys on the Bus*, gave on insider account of reporters covering the 1972 campaign and singled out Mary in highlighting the danger of reporters getting caught inside the bubble of campaigns. Crouse had seen Mary repeatedly express her admiration for McGovern and her acute distaste for Nixon on the trail.

He recalled an incident from one of the final nights of the campaign as reporters and staff disembarked from the McGovern campaign plane at the Little Rock airport. Mary was the only person to notice a small crowd of McGovern supporters gathered at the fence.

"Frank. Frank," Mary shouted as she ran after McGovern's campaign manager, Frank Mankiewicz. "Make him go over there! Christ, it's one-to-one and it won't take a moment," she said.

"So McGovern went to the fence and drank in the adoration of the blacks and college kids who had been waiting for hours to see him," Crouse wrote. "She watched them reaching for his hands and glowed with happiness."

While Crouse thought Mary was too biased, he also viewed her as a first-rate reporter, with her columns "full of facts and incidents that appeared nowhere else, the fruits of her hard digging." He also noted, "The men on the plane, who were not necessarily friends of the feminist movement, automatically treated her as an equal." Which brought Crouse to Mary's column about McGovern's improving chances in Michigan. "Privately, she went beyond this prediction; she was convinced that McGovern was going to win the election," he wrote. During a drive with the Nixon motorcade, Mary gleefully counted the McGovern signs they passed along the way. When they passed an auto dealership adorned with a large NIXON IN '72 sign, Mary's riposte was quick: "Used car place, figures."

Over the next two weeks, Mary became increasingly anxious about the Michigan column, even though her words had been artfully hedged. "I've taken more grief for that article than for almost anything I've ever written," Mary said. Crouse wrote that she "began to talk about it obsessively with her friends on the McGovern plane. During the last week, she phoned the *Star* from an airport press room in Corpus Christi, making monster faces throughout the conversation."

Mary's editors had said they had spoken with sources in Michigan who thought she had gotten it wrong. "If McGovern loses, I'm moving to Ottawa," Mary said. "I mean, I really went out on a limb and it could be very bad." Yet Mary survived McGovern's landslide loss to Nixon—who carried Michigan by fourteen percentage points—with little ill effect.

Crouse was damning in his assessment: "But the fact that these people thought McGovern had a chance to win showed the folly of trying to call an election from 30,000 feet in the air." One only had to look back on Mary's columns from the Eagleton affair to know that in her heart of hearts, she did not really think McGovern was going to win—but she wanted him to. The 1968 McCarthy insurgency in New Hampshire might have given her undue faith in electoral upsets and the hope that anything could happen.

Mary was chagrined by her treatment in the Crouse book. "I hit the pits in 1972," she wrote later. "A week before the election, I wrote that McGovern canvassing figures showed that he could take Hamtramck, a blue-collar suburb of Detroit. From that I skated off to a conclusion that he could win the election. I will never live it down." She was also frank about the pressure of producing four columns a week: "One day you make a complete idiot of yourself, get it all wrong, write something clumsy, inaccurate, stupid. The next day, maybe you get it right."

Certainly, Mary made more than her share of mistakes through the years. She confused the president of Cambodia with its prime minister. She mixed up a B-1 bomber with a B-2. She had Louis XIV's head chopped off rather than Louis XVI's. She put boxer Rubin "Hurricane" Carter on death row rather than giving him life without parole. One of her editors even noted that Mary had a less than salutary habit of simply making up people's middle initials when she was in doubt.

And like many writers, Mary had a tendency to make people and events more grandiose, not less. She told her version of the truth, and sometimes it was larger than life. But if the 1972 presidential race highlighted Mary's tendency to write with her heart rather than her head, Nixon's second term would illuminate her many gifts.

CHAPTER SEVEN

Enemy

Richard Nixon had reopened relations with China, he'd won the 1972 reelection in a landslide, and his Democratic opponents were in complete disarray. But in the U.S. District Court for the District of Columbia, Judge John Sirica presided over the 1973 trial of the Watergate burglars, and it became clear that federal prosecutors were eager to avoid any discussion of who had directed the men to break into the Democratic headquarters. Mary described the scene in the courtroom as a "curious spectacle of defense and prosecution in friendly competition to limit the scope of the inquiry."

With the burglars taking the fall for the break-in, Watergate might have died there, but one of the defendants wrote to Judge Sirica in March 1973 alleging that he had been pressured into perjury. It also came to light that White House counsel John Dean had been allowed to monitor FBI questioning of White House staff members. The scandal spread.

Mary had a field day. "The president knows that Watergate is the one confrontation that an inept and despised Congress might win," she wrote. "Yet he has chosen to fight it out the way he has fought all his other battles: with secrecy and defiance, with no quarter, no compromises, and no concessions." Mary scoffed at Nixon's claims that he had been too trusting of his underlings, saying that it was implausible for a man "whose whole career has been based on an unlimited suspicion of his fellow man."

As Watergate gained steam, so did the volume of Mary's hate mail. She was threatened by an anonymous caller to the *Star*: "If Nixon goes down, Mary McGrory goes too." One of the security guards at the *Star*, Clarence, took the threat as a personal affront and subsequently insisted on escorting Mary to her car nightly.

With a Senate Watergate Committee slated to begin hearings in May 1973, Nixon was forced to fire four trusted members of his team in an effort to cauterize the bleeding. Those let go included counselor John Ehrlichman, Chief of Staff H. R. Haldeman, White House Counsel John Dean, and Attorney General Richard Kleindienst.

With Dean's lengthy testimony before the Watergate Committee casting stark light on the Machiavellian dealings in the White House, Mary described the scheming as a curious mix of evil and ineptitude, a Marx Brothers movie as retold by the German General Staff. Mary called Nixon "a demented monarch, totally removed from reality, calling down vengeance upon his enemies, surrounded by imaginary foes, threatening to 'get' the press for publishing Watergate stories, complaining that the IRS was not sufficiently tormenting his tormentors."

Dean announced that he would release Nixon's enemies list, a compilation of key administration opponents who the president's aides felt should be targeted with dirty tricks. With word that the list was going to be released on June 27, Bernard Kalb, who was covering the hearings for the *Star*, contacted Dean's lawyer.

"I will never tell anybody where I got it," Kalb promised. "Have we got anybody on the list?"

The response: "Mary McGrory."

Mary's was the final name on the list of the president's twenty key enemies, her entry highlighted with two stars and an asterisk. The list singled her out for writing "daily hate Nixon articles." Other notables on the list included CBS reporter Daniel Schorr, actor Paul Newman, Congressman John Conyers, and the president of the United Auto Workers, Leonard Woodcock.

The enemies list was a remarkably formal plan by a sitting president to neutralize his opponents. Its language was a chilling mix of officiousness and macho bluster. "This memorandum addresses the matter of how we can maximize the fact of our incumbency in dealing with persons known to be active in their opposition to our administration. Stated a bit more bluntly—how we can use the available federal machinery to screw our political enemies." The memo detailed the tools at hand: IRS audits, litigation, denial of federal contracts, and even selective prosecutions.

Mary was delighted to discover that her name was on the enemies list, proclaiming it to be the nicest thing that had ever happened to her. When the news broke, her friend Art Buchwald insisted on taking Mary to celebrate with a meal at Sans Souci. As Mary walked into the restaurant, the patrons spontaneously rose and gave her a standing ovation under the restaurant's crystal chandelier.

Fan mail quickly overwhelmed Mary's hate mail. A policeman from New Jersey volunteered his services as a bodyguard. At a cocktail party in Denver, a woman shouldered up to Mary and insisted that she autograph her bus pass, saying, "We never get to shake hands with an enemy in Denver."

A friend expressed concern that Mary was not treating the situation with more gravity: "You know, you should be very indignant about this. This is a terrible reflection on democracy and freedom of expression."

"Yes, it is all that," Mary replied, "but we found out about it."

Privately, Mary was not so glib, writing to a reader, "I wondered why my tax returns were audited three years in a row; I often thought my phone was tapped. I never allowed myself to think about how far they were prepared to go. Had the Nixon staff plans been enforced—if there had been no Watergate disclosure—I am certain great efforts would have been made to silence me and other critics."

When Mary learned that former White House counselor Chuck Colson was writing notes of apology to those on the enemies list, Mary penned an open letter to him, saying that she had been "fooled completely" into thinking that the break-ins at her house had been the work of "honest thieves" and that the IRS had audited her out of conscientiousness. Mary insisted that Colson not apologize; the experience had been grand.

John McKelway, who wrote the Rambler column for the *Star*, penned an ode to Mary, "It Helps to Know Thine Enemy." It was one of Mary's favorite things ever written about her:

The Mary McGrory named on the White House list as an enemy is, as far as I can tell at this point in Watergate time, the same Mary McGrory who struggles a few feet away in this office.

One nice thought about the list, in her case at least, is that it does show someone at the White House could read . . .

Since those at the White House were deep in the business of listing people, what they should have done with this particular name was to have included a single sheet within that black collection under the heading: "And then there is Mary McGrory." That would have been the only way to handle the dark deed properly.

She comes into the office late in the afternoon.

She has spent long hours watching those in charge, feeling things, listening to her colleagues, probing here and there into the play of thought. She works very hard.

She is capable of a number of moods. One must wait to be on the safe side to see which way the wind is blowing.

Pretty and always well dressed, the disturber of the thoughts of men, she scowls at her mail box. She is on other lists not so public. She gets hate mail of the worst kind, complimentary notes written with care.

Mary McGrory hears the telephone ringing as one frequently does in a newspaper office. Mary McGrory says, "Is that my telephone?" It is a demanding question, and it is best for all concerned to get the matter settled before the next sounding of the bells.

Mary McGrory goes into her cubicle and begins to telephone, or answer calls, or nibble graham crackers. She doodles—many firm squares connected. As the evening closes in she tries to begin writing. The polishing will come later, later at night. The writing does not come easy, but she takes great pride in it. She has to do it.

Sometimes you will have an amusing anecdote to tell Mary McGrory. She may hear it; she may not. The eyes fall on what she is reading. She is elsewhere, quite far away.

But other times, she listens. The laughter comes rollicking out; she is doubled up by, say, the absurdity of it all. Her mind sparkles. She embellishes. She is funny. Her wit can demolish. . . .

Mary McGrory can be infuriating. She can be right, she can be wrong, but always she writes it so well. That is why she was listed. They could not take it.

Haynes Johnson reflected on Mary's inclusion on the enemies list. "That was typical of Nixon," he said. "He would talk about enemies, and she would be an enemy. That we have to destroy her, we have to mitigate her influence, crush her if possible, defame her. That would be Nixon. Absolutely Nixon."

Mary was a self-admitted Watergate junkie long before being named. Not only was Nixon, her least favorite politician, being slowly roasted alive, but the hearings offered a wonderful parade of personalities. Mary put Senator Sam Ervin, who chaired the hearings, front and center, calling him the rock that all the waves dashed against: "His bright eyes and quivering wattles suggest the rooster greeting the day, joyful and alert. At 76, he is doing what he was born to do—trying to find out if the Constitution, which is graven on his heart, is alive and well in high places." It was the best material from a hearing Mary had enjoyed since Joe McCarthy terrorized the U.S. Army.

But as spring faded into summer, it looked as though Nixon might actually survive. That is, until Alexander Butterfield testified before the committee on July 16, 1973, acknowledging under oath that Nixon recorded his own conversations with an Oval Office taping system. Suddenly a definitive answer could be found to the question "What did the president know and when did he know it?" Nixon insisted that he would not make any tapes available, touching off a legal battle in which the presidency hung in the balance.

Watergate was changing journalism in ways too numerous to count. Not only had the *Washington Post* gotten the scoop of the century; it had established itself as the second most important paper in America, behind only the *New York Times*. The *Star* lagged badly behind. Watergate also produced a new zeal for investigative journalism, pushing reporters and politicians into ever more wary and antagonistic relationships.

In the fall of 1973, a television crew filming a documentary on the media and Watergate caught up with Mary as she sat in the hearing room. The young interviewer asked why the reporters covering the hearings were not out scouring for new evidence and allegations.

"Yes, except that some of us can't do it," Mary explained. "It's a gift, investigative reporting, and a lot of people don't have it. They don't have the stomach for it; they don't have the brass that it takes to go up to a total stranger and take him by the lapels and say, 'Now you tell me.' I can't for instance."

The interviewer pressed on, hoping to embarrass Mary: "You're more comfortable in this situation?"

"Yes," Mary said. "It's all handed to me on a platter. I just have to sit here and take it all in. It's much easier than going around knocking on doors at midnight and meeting people in underground parking spaces in the dead of night, which is what, as you know, Woodward and Bernstein did."

"But you're going to say there's something of value in your being here, I hope," suggested the interviewer.

"It keeps me off the streets," observed a bemused Mary. She was far from an armchair pundit and sourced all of her material firsthand, unlike many of today's commentators. But at the same time, she never had any taste for relying on anonymously sourced quotes or tips. She did not engage in intrigue when it came to reporting.

Mary covered every single day of the hearings, and her work underscored her unique ability as a reporter and a writer to take events that we could see with our own eyes and layer in observations, emotion, and detail that provoked us to think again—and think differently—about what we had seen.

It is no coincidence that Mary's most famous columns—on the Army-McCarthy hearings, Nixon's "exit snarling" press conference, JFK's funeral, and the Watergate hearings—were all written about public events. She helped people make sense of public life. She humanized the players on the stage. She took what people knew and used it to help them understand how they felt. She looked at the world with eager, discerning eyes, even after decades in the business.

Mary did not sprinkle her column with anonymous background quotes from politicians and press secretaries. As much as she admired Woodward and Bernstein's approach, her style was simply different. The *Post* reporters had built Watergate on double-sourced anonymous tips, mainly from law enforcement officials and key contacts in the administration. The identity of their main source, "Deep Throat," was a matter of speculation for more than a quarter of a century. By contrast, Mary's work was transparent. She was not looking for book deals or speaker's fees, her quotes were on the record, and she thought what the man in the street had to say mattered.

Mary's style was perfectly suited for an era when television was making it harder and harder for newspapers to keep up. Because her columns were built on the strength of her observation and wit, it did not matter that readers had to wait until the next day to read them—indeed, they were usually an even better read if you were already keeping up with the story.

As prosecutors and Congress slowly pried out the White House tapes, Mary and other reporters got their first taste of the detailed conversations that had taken place in the Oval Office when the large blue book of tape transcripts arrived at the newspaper on April 30, 1974. "It was torn apart in big chunks like loaves of bread at the zoo," Mary recalled.

In July 1974, the Supreme Court ruled that the nation's constitutional form of government would be in serious jeopardy if Nixon were allowed to withhold tapes of his choosing. Sentiment was growing in Congress, including among Republicans, to impeach the president.

In early August, Mary headed to Antrim for vacation. Her editors had told her to take a break and prepare for the coming impeachment debate in the House of Representatives. On August 7, she was walking up the path from Gregg Lake, where she had been swimming, when she spied the owner of the Maplehurst Inn rushing down the trail. "Your office just called," he panted. "They think he is going." Nixon was going to resign. Mary's vacation had lasted twenty-three hours. One of her cousins drove her at breakneck speed back to Boston so she could fly home. By 8:45 P.M. Mary was in her office at the *Star*.

On August 8, President Nixon announced in a televised address to the nation that he was quitting the highest office in the land. Mary thought the speech was unmemorable and bereft of contrition, sounding "eerily like thousands of others he has given during the almost 40 years he has been seeking, gaining and losing public office." But, as Mary observed, "Richard Nixon's small store of pity had always been reserved for himself."

Nixon's resignation marked the end of an era for Mary. She had written about him more than anyone else during her career. Mary viewed Nixon's fall as a victory for a free press, and she felt no small measure of vindication. As she wrote to a Nixon defender shortly after he stepped down, "I realize he still has many friends, but I don't think history will be among them."

"He was a man who never should have been president of the United States, not even in politics as far as I was concerned, because he didn't like people," Mary maintained. But at the same time, she recognized that Nixon had given her endless fodder as an opinion writer. "He was really something. Divine. Really, divine. I miss him still."

On August 22, 1974 (her birthday), the House Judiciary Committee, under Representative Peter Rodino, passed a unanimous resolution, 38–0, praising Mary: "Resolved, that in her conduct of the office of the press, in her exercise of the constitutionally protected First Amendment right of freedom of speech, Ms. Mary McGrory has, to the best of her ability, preserved, protected and defended the people's right to have access to the truth from one who writes like the wind and speaks from the heart."

At the White House, the beleaguered staff tried to restore some measure of normalcy and calm as Gerald Ford became president. At the daily press briefing, the White House spokesman sonorously intoned to the gathered journalists, "This is not the time for partisan recriminations."

A slender hand rose firmly from within the overwhelmingly male sea of reporters pressing their questions. It was Mary.

"If now isn't the time for recriminations," Mary wondered, in her soft but direct voice, "when would be the time?"

The combination of Nixon and Vietnam had shifted Mary's worldview. She still had enormous faith in democracy, but, like many, she increasingly doubted that people in the government would do the right thing. Her writing became more personal and reflective. She became more willing to poke fun at herself in her columns, and her observations increasingly glided between the drama of politics and the travails of daily life. "She understood something that most of these Washington pundits and gasbags don't understand," explained her friend Phil Gailey. "You can write about the serious stuff day after day, but at some point you have to step back and give yourself and the readers a break."

There was no better example than Mary's annual garden column, which she started writing in 1975. Mary came from a family of gardeners, and she had always enjoyed puttering around in the small flower beds behind her corner apartment. In her columns, she transformed her slightly bedraggled garden plot into a place of tragedy and triumph. She endured raids by rapacious squirrels, and the rosebushes failed to produce a single bud. Mockingbirds dug up her seeds, and mourning doves flung themselves against her kitchen window. Only the ever faithful impatiens saved Mary from despair. "For many years, the surest sign of spring in Washington was not the flowering of cherry trees, or the blooming of azaleas," Todd Purdum of *Vanity Fair* wrote, "but the arrival of Mary McGrory's first gardening column of the season."

"I like February, because it is the month when my garden is at its peak, although—or, perhaps I should say, because—it is not yet planted," Mary wrote in her initial gardening column. The columns were love letters to spring, and they were fantastically popular. Her frequent complaints about squirrels—"four-footed tire-slashers, avid, shameless, persistent, bird-feeder raiders"—touched some kind of national pulse. "It's questionable advice to give to a young or aspiring journalist, but I have to tell you that if you really want to get the public going, you should write about squirrels," Mary observed.

Readers shared elaborate squirrel-proofing diagrams with Mary, featuring wire, brackets, and plastic tubing. One woman advocated installing a miniature electrified fence. Someone suggested greasing the bird feeder, and a reader from Michigan swore by balls of human hair hung in stockings.

Mary hung bars of Irish Spring soap from tree branches to deter deer. When she read that coyote urine repelled squirrels, she reasoned that an even more dominant predator would prove an even more powerful deterrent and enlisted National Security Adviser Anthony Lake to see if he could procure lion dung from the nearby National Zoo. Lake reported that since lions were on the endangered species list, it was against the law to remove their excrement.

"She had her scraggly little garden crumbling off a cliff into Rock Creek Park that only a Roslindale girl could love—with its mismatched collection of plantings and bars of soap hanging from trees for reasons that I could never understand," her cousin Brian McGrory recalled. "Yet, she looked at that patch of earth like the queen looks at the grounds of Buckingham Palace." The garden might not have been much, but for readers it was a welcoming place. "For us, there is always tomorrow," Mary comforted her fellow gardeners.

Mary had initially welcomed Gerald Ford's rise to the presidency as a breath of fresh air. Ford was jovial, collegial, and not consumed by the towering insecurities that had undermined Nixon and Johnson. That all changed for Mary when Ford pardoned Nixon, on September 8, 1974. Her response to what she called "a moral Pearl Harbor" was scathing.

Yet Mary substantially changed her view of Ford and the pardon over time and eventually printed a heartfelt mea culpa to Ford in 2001. "What seemed then to be cynicism now looks more like courage," she wrote. Ford wrote to Mary in response, "I understand your position in September 1974, although I obviously disagreed. I am very honored with your viewpoint in 2001 . . . our longstanding friendship has been wonderful."

Major change came to Washington with Nixon's departure, and a major shake-up soon hit the *Star* as well. The paper was facing mounting financial difficulties, losing more than $8 million in 1974 alone. The *Star*'s owning families began to court outside investors.

The paper soon found itself with an unlikely suitor: Joe Allbritton. Allbritton, a pint-sized Texan and self-made millionaire, had grown up in a hardscrabble background, with his father running a general store in a small Mississippi lumber town. After getting a law degree, Allbritton pushed into banking and insurance, before opening up a chain of successful mortuaries on the way to amassing his fortune. Having made his millions, he pursued more refined tastes, collecting racehorses and fine art.

Allbritton decided that he wanted to get into the newspaper business and made an initial investment of $5 million in the *Star*. When the *Star* continued to struggle, the owning families went back to him, hoping for another injection of cash. Allbritton offered to buy the paper outright. He knew almost nothing about the newspaper business, but he knew that owning the *Star* would give him an important entrée into Washington.

Mary thought that the fundamental foreignness of journalism was a big part of the allure for Allbritton. "He had made his money in mortuaries and banks, and he was just drawn to newspapers because he figured people with a fraction, a not even calculable fraction, of his income, were having much more fun than he was," she said. Allbritton also thought buying the *Star* made good business sense, because a local television studio was included in the purchase.

Mary had an unusually close relationship with Allbritton, and she made it her personal mission to woo him to the aid of the *Star*. In April 1974, she attended the annual Gridiron Club press dinner with Allbritton as talks between him and the owning families bogged down. Mary was at Allbritton's side all night long. The two of them sang "Wouldn't It Be Loverly" together.

Shortly after the dinner, Allbritton wrote to Mary: "The Gridiron dinner on Saturday last was not climaxed by Newby Noyes' magnificent performance, but the crescendo was our duet streaking through the men's dressing room to the sanitary facilities. I enjoyed meeting you so very much that I am going to a wee bit of difficulty so that I may perhaps have the opportunity of seeing you again and 'with a little bit of luck' it may come about. Now wouldn't that 'be loverly'?" Allbritton and the owners had resumed negotiations the day after the Gridiron.

Negotiations made progress until the owning families made an agreement with one of the *Star*'s unions when the sale was nearly complete. It was a reasonable deal, but Allbritton had explicitly warned against any new union contracts before the sale. Allbritton "went up like Mount Etna, which was, I might say, his custom," Mary recalled. She was alarmed that the entire deal might collapse and leave the *Star* bankrupt. She wrote to Allbritton: "Dear Joe, say it ain't so. Yours sincerely, Mary McGrory."

The next day, Mary was in her office, working on her column, when a delivery boy approached her desk, carrying fifty yellow roses. The card read, "It ain't so, Joe."

Mary proudly displayed the flowers on her cramped desk. As the afternoon wore on, people from all over the newspaper stuck their heads into her office to see them.

Eventually the owning families who had run the *Star* for more than a century agreed to sell for $35 million. Newby Noyes, who had meant so much to Mary as a mentor and a friend, retired to Sorrento, Maine. It was a bittersweet moment for Mary. She had helped convince Allbritton to buy the *Star*, but in doing so she closed an important chapter in her life.

Allbritton rapidly introduced austerity measures, cutting two hundred positions and instituting a salary freeze. "In 1974, when the angel of death hovered close, we were faced with a choice, take a 20 percent pay cut—euphemistically called a 'four-day week'—or let it die," Mary recalled. "I remember that black day in December. Young faces, with little children and big mortgages, came to my door." Mary helped convince her fellow staffers that there was no alternative.

But for all the financial peril, there was also a sense of renewed optimism at the paper. Allbritton "crashed into town like a tiny thunderbolt," said reporter Duncan Spencer. "He brought a new fresh spirit. He didn't come to be a loser." Mary was grateful to Allbritton. "Mary was really very excited and welcoming," Jack Germond said, "because it was a sign of somebody who wanted to get on board the sinking ship."

The *Star* enjoyed a remarkable infusion of new talent despite the hardships. Allbritton tapped Jim Bellows as the paper's editor in January 1975, an unusually savvy choice. Bellows lived and breathed news and had earned a reputation as a newspaper impresario, innovator, and oddball. He was a writer's editor, and his vision of where the newspaper business was headed was decades ahead of its time.

Bellows had a fantastic eye for good reporters, and reporters wanted to work with him because he was a free spirit and a very good editor. He hated the stuffy, moribund style of most papers and wanted copy that read like a daily magazine, rich with personality, color, and flair. Bellows knew that newspapers needed a dramatic remake if they wanted to compete with television. He was brash and willing to fail. He was an idea-a-minute guy, and while some of his plans were gimmicky, others were revolutionary.

Bellows knew that the *Star* needed hype and buzz to take on the richer and better-resourced *Washington Post*. He soon established a wildly successful gossip column, written by Diana McLellan, called the Ear, which regularly skewered Ben Bradlee and his eventual second wife, Sally Quinn, dubbing them the "fun couple." Under Bellows, the entire *Star* staff referred to the *Post* as the "O.P."—the other paper. Bradlee once made a request from the *Star* to reprint an article contingent upon Bellows's agreeing not to mention his name in the column for an entire month. (Bellows agreed, but made sure there was a piece on Bradlee the day after the agreement expired.)

Bellows made important editorial changes at the paper, and morale revived. He brought computers into the newsroom for the first time. Mary so resisted technology that eventually she had to be ordered to use a computer. "Oh, she was offended!" Jack Germond recalled. The *Star* was now Washington's upstart.

Bellows was legendary for his cryptic interpersonal style, and one pro-file observed that he communicated "with hand signals, nonsense syllabic jabbering in crumbling, mumbled sentences." Mary recalled Bellows tell-ing her how he wanted her to write by mimicking a boat tossing on the waves. "I don't know what that means," she said. But Mary and Bellows were a happy fit. He loved vibrant writing; she provided it in spades.

Ed Yoder, a well-regarded editor and columnist, also joined the *Star* under Bellows. When Yoder came aboard, Bellows made clear that two things would stay under his direct editorial control: Mary's column and Pat Oliphant's editorial cartoon.

"I have a rather vivid memory of my first encounter with Mary," Yoder shared. "She came into my office one day, the first week I was in Washing-ton. She mumbled something about coming to a dinner at her house for Mr. Somebody. I didn't catch the name. My family was still in Greens-boro, and I was still commuting on the weekends, so I welcomed the op-portunity to go to somebody's house. It turned out to be a lasagna party for Robert Redford," who was in town researching his role in *All the Pres-ident's Men*. Later, Redford fondly remembered how proud Mary had been to share her hate mail with him when he visited her at the paper.

In May 1975, Mary put her own stamp on the *Star*'s revival when she re-ceived a cable from William McGill, president of Columbia University: "You were awarded Pulitzer Prize for Commentary today. Congratulations." She was the first woman to win a Pulitzer for commentary. Mary was thrilled, and the fact that she had won for her coverage of Watergate only made the victory sweeter.

Mary informed Allbritton, and he called it the brightest day since he had purchased the paper. She made only one demand of him when they spoke on the phone: "If we do anything, can we do it for everybody?" Allbritton ordered cases of Moët & Chandon champagne and more yel-low roses to be delivered to the newsroom.

As soon as the champagne was uncorked, Mary hand-delivered a glass to Clarence, the security guard who had insisted on escorting her to her car nightly during the Watergate hearings. Mary was not one for false modesty when it came to journalism's highest award. "Who wants the Pulitzer Prize? The answer is that I do," Mary said. "I don't care if it drinks or beats its wife—I wanted it."

Mary smoked Marlboros, sipped champagne, ate cake, and held court in the newsroom, thanking everyone from Clarence to Allbritton. The Italian ambassador sent his chauffeur around with a bottle of champagne, and when the editor of the *St. Louis Post-Dispatch* tried to call Mary, he was told by the operator, "She's getting an award, and I think they are having a party."

Mary received an outpouring of congratulatory letters and cables. "First the enemies list and now the Pulitzer Prize," joked Art Buchwald. "Have you no shame?"

Jacqueline Onassis wrote, "You should win it every year."

Anchorman Tom Brokaw deserved high marks for creativity. "I was deep in the Yucatan when a small boy on a burro came through the jungle, shouting something in Spanish," he wrote. "The villagers cheered and began a three-day celebration with much drinking, dancing, and singing. Naturally, I joined in, participating to the point of exhaustion. As I was preparing to drag my limp body back to civilization I asked, 'What news did that small boy bring that inspired such joy?' and the village priest answered, 'Didn't you know? Mary McGrory won the Pulitzer.' Smiling wearily, I replied, 'Huzzah!' I return to Washington with fresh hope."

"As you know—I love you," author Teddy White shared. "And I hate the Pulitzer Prize people. The Pulitzer Prize should have been awarded to you at least as early as 1954; if not then, in 1960 and 1961; and then for the lead on the Kennedy funeral story in 1963; and then again, in any year from 1965 to 1970; and again in 1973–74. By my count there are four Pulitzer Prizes due to you."

President Ford personally congratulated Mary at a press conference, although in exchange he got a tough question about whether or not he would grant amnesty to Vietnam draft resisters. (To Mary's credit, even though she adamantly opposed the war, she also became one of the most important national champions of efforts to assist Vietnam veterans.)

Even Scotty Reston, the man who had once made a job offer contingent upon her answering the phones, weighed in with praise. "If you could have heard the comments of your colleagues on the Pulitzer jury and the board about your work, you would have felt that it was all worthwhile. Not only was the vote unanimous, even against so formidable a candidate as Russ Baker, but the emphasis was put, not mainly on last year's reporting but for the whole body of your writing on the *Star*."

The award triggered a spate of profiles on Mary by outlets like the *New York Post* and *Ms.* magazine, the best of which was written by her colleague Duncan Spencer at the *Star*:

> Into the newsroom of the *Star*, a place as romantic as a parking garage, as evocative as a hospital waiting room, marches Miss Mary McGrory, quick step. Mary is usually in tatters after a day on Capitol Hill. Her brow is furrowed with thought, her jaw working on a wad of gum, her hands shaking for a sit-down cigarette—her hands have been bothering her hair. But the step is quick and athletic, her legs carry her along a familiar route to a familiar corner. Her steps have taken her past sleepy building guards, into a metal box of an elevator that stinks of sour roto ink, along a tiled corridor as lonely and nameless as an empty mineshaft, to the lighted, noisy newsroom, the place of her struggle. . . . She will come out, agitated and tense, asking for a cigarette. Nothing ever seems to diminish the number of false starts or the quivering of hands, or the effort. By these rigorous means, she produces a prodigy of copy.

Mary reflected on the rigors of producing her column. "I think about it constantly, because there's never a moment when you can rest. I'm always one step ahead of the sheriff."

Her dedication to the St. Ann's orphanage remained constant. While St. Ann's had been populated by kids from lower-middle-class white families when Mary arrived in Washington, by the 1970s, when St. Ann's relocated to a low-slung brick building in nearby Hyattsville, Maryland, it largely served black kids from the slums of D.C.

Despite the public's perception of orphanages as grim, despairing places, Mary knew that St. Ann's was a refuge for a lot of kids. The short notes she sent out to her fellow volunteers before picnics and Christmas parties were wry, unblinking glimpses into life for the young and un-wanted in the nation's capital:

> Tarrone: He is five years old and totally traumatized. He saw his ten-month-old baby sister killed by her father, who was outraged that she and her twin had climbed up on a forbidden sofa. If Santa made reference to Tarrone's progress with the alphabet and his card-box, I think it might be well-received. He cries easily.... Dion, he is seven. He is an attractive and likable child, except when he goes to school, where he does really awful things and is thrown out. He says he is insulted by [a] bully, whose side is taken by [the] teacher. On the pos-itive side, he wants to be a fireman. Santa should know that Dion had a good talk about his problems with Chief Judge Rogers of D.C. Court.

Some of the children were so demoralized by their own lack of an edu-cation that they burst into tears at the very sight of the alphabet. When the kids went to school, many of them lashed out with anger and violence against their peers, ashamed that they could not read.

Mary invested time and money at St. Ann's. She bought the kids Christmas presents, paid private school tuition for some of the children, helped out some of the young mothers and staff at St. Ann's financially, and wrote checks to the orphanage when there were budget shortfalls.

She made a difference. One need only read the extraordinary letter Mary received from a St. Ann's graduate, Rita Markley, who had been at the orphanage in the late 1950s and early '60s (the same Rita who had so charmed Bobby Kennedy when he visited with the St. Ann's kids). The letter deserves to be quoted at some length:

I used to call you Mary Gloria when I was a little girl. I remembered this unexpectedly while I was at a party a few months ago.
Someone was holding forth about the plight of boarder babies and
unwanted children, the horrors of institutionalizing the young. I
usually ignore drunken sermons, and the loud prating bores so fond
of delivering them, but I found myself straining to hear all of it, even
though the speaker was clear across the room. He rambled on about
the lack of love and attention for institution children and portrayed
orphanages as little more than incubators for psychopaths. I wanted
to break his neck, but realized this would only confirm his view of
orphan alumni. . . .

I fumed silently and then remembered you so suddenly and clearly
that it made me laugh out loud. Not complete memories, but quick
images like slides or snapshots: you splashing in the pool with us at
Hickory Hill, scooping me up in your arms countless times when
that dog Brunus (Bruno?) came bounding too close; passing out
those peanut butter and jelly sandwich squares so emphatically that
no one ever dared refuse. One afternoon we rode all over the lawn in
a golf cart (was it a golf cart?). You helped me find my tennis shoe a
hundred times, always underneath that trampoline beside the pool. I
put it there deliberately more than once. And you took us to the best
Christmas parties in the world. I remember the Santa Claus who said
that he couldn't find a parking place for his reindeer, and how I
thought that was about the funniest thing I'd ever heard. . . .

I wondered if any of us ever thanked you. Or if you knew, directly,
how much we loved our Mary Gloria. I'm writing because I want you
to know. . . .

After I was adopted, it took me several years to adjust to my new
home. I missed everyone at St. Ann's terribly, especially at dinner
time. The concept of separate houses and yards, separate toys, separate lives was entirely foreign to me. I had to learn not to take the
roller skates from someone else's front steps, not to leave my bike outside for someone else to use when I was finished riding. At St. Ann's,
we all had equal claim to any toy in sight. The cardinal rule was to
share and the worst punishment was not for screaming or turning

over chairs but for being selfish. Even a crybaby or a tattletale was better than someone who didn't share. . . .

I do not advocate institutions for every child in a difficult home situation. And I can't presume to know what goes on in all orphanages. But I felt safe and very loved in mine. You had a lot to do with that. It's hard to believe that I would have had nearly as much fun in a foster home. I'm not even sure early adoption would have been so much better. This is not to say that I don't suffer from some institutional hangovers: I have a peculiar fondness for cafeteria food; an unbounded affection for the Daughters of Charity; about twice a week I still wake up with my thumb in my mouth. I also have a tendency to view complicated issues like poverty and illiteracy in very simple terms. There is no intellectual wavering, or posturing either. I think people don't share enough. This is not just a political conviction but an emotional one that goes straight back to the day room at St. Ann's. I know quite a few people who would have done well to spend some time there learning the cardinal rule. You are very much part of why my early memories are such happy ones. And why I felt so loved. I'm sorry it has taken me so long to thank you.

No one ever delivered a more eloquent encomium to Mary's work with kids. Mary was so delighted with Rita Markley's letter that she insisted that she join her for a visit back to Hickory Hill so she could swim in the pool one more time. Rita, upon seeing Mary for the first time in years, was struck by several things. Mary seemed younger than she imagined her to be, and she wore "amazing shoes." Markley marveled that Mary had kept up her work with disadvantaged kids for decades without ever becoming tedious or dull—"because that wasn't who she was." Markley, who went on to run a nonprofit that provides shelter for the homeless, credits Mary with helping her understand the difference that "one person seeing you can make in a life."

With President Ford having been appointed rather than elected, the 1976 presidential race promised to be an unusually open contest, and a striking contrast with Nixon's walkover win in 1972. The action was intense not just on the Democratic side; Ronald Reagan was making a conservative challenge to upend Ford in the Republican primary. In New Hampshire, Mary quickly realized that Ronald Reagan, whom many had dismissed as a lazy and ineffective campaigner, was energetic and gifted on the stump. She did not think he was a serious man, but she took him seriously as a candidate.

The Democratic contest included a record number of candidates and no clear favorite. Georgia governor Jimmy Carter gained momentum coming off a win in the Iowa caucus, but Mary's northern reserve and Catholicism clashed sharply with Carter's effusive southern evangelicalism. She did not like people who wore religion on their sleeve, and she thought Carter humorless. Mary's disdain for him was evident in her columns, although she described him as the craftiest and toughest of the Democratic candidates.

Many of Mary's readers wondered why she remained lukewarm toward Carter, accusing her of harboring an antisouthern bias. The charge had some merit, and Mary never took well to southern evangelicals, but she also pushed back against the notion that she should be easier on Carter just because he was a Democrat: "It is not my job to elect the man, but to observe him."

But for Mary and the *Star*, the 1976 race was most memorable not for Carter, Ford, or Reagan but for the first major crisis of the Joe Allbritton era, which began on the nation's bicentennial celebration.

The nation's two hundredth birthday started innocently enough for Mary, and she happily covered tall ships arriving to fanfare in New York Harbor and parades in Washington. After the upheaval of the Nixon years, the festivities on the National Mall—where police and young people intermingled with ease—felt like innocence restored.

Not far away, Joe Allbritton and his wife watched the Fourth of July fireworks from the Truman Balcony of the White House as special guests of President Gerald Ford. Allbritton felt like he had arrived.

Later that night, Allbritton hosted a barbecue for the *Star* staff and others at his house on N Street in Georgetown. He pulled aside Jim Bellows as the other guests laughed and chatted. He said that he had hatched a secret plan. Bellows blanched. "What plan?"

"I am not going to tell you," Allbritton replied, "because you would veto it."

Bellows mentioned the exchange to Ed Yoder, who was equally perplexed.

Later that night, Bellows got a panicked call from the paper's night editor. Allbritton had phoned in the text of an editorial that he had written himself, endorsing President Ford in the Republican primary, and said he wanted it to run on the paper's front page.

It was an almost unheard-of move, and all hell broke loose.

Bellows ordered the night editor to spike the piece, but when Allbritton learned he had been countermanded, he fired the night editor over the phone. The editorial in question was, if nothing else, colorful. It led with a classic story about a Texas railroad that had decided to get rid of two old trains by colliding them together on the same track as a publicity stunt. The event had generated so much attention, with some forty thousand people turning out to watch, that a small town sprung up on the site of the planned collision: Crush, Texas.

However, things ended badly when the trains' boilers exploded on impact, killing three. Allbritton used the story as a parable to argue against the continued infighting between Ford and Reagan in the Republican primary, and urged Reagan to quit the race.

Bellows called Yoder at 5:30 in the morning: "What do you know about this Ford editorial?"

Yoder replied, "This is news to me."

The two men went to Allbritton's townhouse in Georgetown at dawn, Yoder still wearing his pajamas beneath his pants. Bellows tried to keep his temper in check, but he was exasperated by the idea of a publisher ignoring his editors and using the front page for a political endorsement.

Allbritton bristled. He owned the *Star* and felt he had the right to say what he wanted. Bellows called a front-page endorsement "the nuclear

weapon of editorial journalism" and insisted that editors had to be consulted before taking such a bold step. Allbritton was puzzled, saying that
he hadn't wanted to bother Bellows or Yoder, since his endorsement
would not be on the editorial page.

Yoder tried a different tack: "Joe, it would be as if you loaned all the
money in your bank to one borrower."

"Ed, now you are speaking my language," Allbritton declared. The ten-
sion eased.

It was agreed that the endorsement would be rewritten and appear on
the editorial page several days later.

Allbritton was pleased that the endorsement got a warm reception at
the White House, and he showed Yoder a handwritten note of thanks
from President Ford, but he also harbored lingering resentment toward his
editors. One of Allbritton's aides told Yoder that even a small additional
incident might push the publisher to close the paper. With the *Star* in
seemingly perpetual financial difficulties, most of the staffers had gotten
used to feeling as if the rug might be pulled out from underneath them at
any moment. Allbritton, in particular, felt like an unstable molecule.

As a result of the dust-up over the editorial, staffers came to rely on Mary
as a liaison to Allbritton. "The one who could deal with him was McGrory,"
explained Lance Gay. "She would go up and hold his hand and tell him, 'Joe,
this is not really the way we do things at the newspaper.'" Mary told Bellows
that she believed in humoring Allbritton. "I'm an old maid, and we have to
humor people," she said. "We're in a very precarious situation."

Mary traveled to New York to cover the Democratic convention.
Democrats and the city of New York were in an unusually good mood.
The spirits of the city had been buoyed by the bicentennial, a visit from
Queen Elizabeth, and the convention itself. Democrats were enthusiastic
about the Carter nomination, and even Mary was warming toward the
Georgian. She was pleased that his acceptance speech emphasized Demo-
crats like FDR and John Kennedy more than saving souls.

The 1976 Republican convention, in Kansas City, was a throwback to
the era when conventions actually mattered, with the nomination poised

between Ford and Reagan. Conservatives tried to shout down the Ford supporters, saying that the president was soft on the Soviets and abortion (which had been legalized by the *Roe v. Wade* Supreme Court decision in 1973). Ford supporters insisted that Reagan was hopelessly hard-line and would prove an electoral debacle. Ultimately, Ford prevailed, but Reagan's electrifying concession speech left many wondering if they had picked the wrong man.

For Mary, the Republican convention and its passionate arguments were politics and journalism as they were supposed to be. And for the *Star*, it was a renaissance. The editorial changes that Jim Bellows had put in place made the paper feel like a guerrilla operation taking on the stodgy *Washington Post*.

"Our party after the close of the Republican convention in Kansas City was strictly a world-class blast that lasted till dawn and attracted fellow degenerates from nearly every other news organization there," recalled Mary's colleague James Dickenson. "The major attractions were the tangos and rumbas (or so we fancied them) that several of us danced, with long-stemmed roses in our teeth at the approach of dawn, with Mary McGrory, who epitomized the heart and soul and spirit of the *Star*. Once again, for a glorious, fleeting glimmer, we all were young and drunk and 21 and thought we were going to live forever." But such moments were short-lived, and the *Star* was headed for trouble.

Jimmy Carter went on to win the election, but Mary was not upbeat.

CHAPTER EIGHT

The Death of a Star

In February 1977, crisis again erupted at the *Star*. At 5:30 on a Monday morning, Joe Allbritton, who was traveling, phoned the night desk. He ordered the night editor to immediately remove his name as publisher from the paper's masthead.

The move sparked a frenzy of speculation as Allbritton remained out of sight. Was the owner angry with Bellows? Was the move a negotiating tactic aimed at the unions? Was Allbritton selling the newspaper? The development was all the more perplexing because no one at the paper knew what had precipitated it.

Jim Bellows visited Mary in her office, asking, "Do you know where he is?" Mary had no idea, but she concurred that Allbritton's move was a "serious explosion." Having the owner remove his name as publisher of the paper clearly indicated that something was seriously amiss.

Several hours later, Bellows returned. "Heard from Joe?" he asked. Mary had not.

Bellows came to Mary's office a third time. She still had not heard from Allbritton. "Listen, Jim," Mary said, "I think the relationship between the editor and the publisher is the most sacred relationship on a paper, and I would not dream of intervening for one split second, unless you tell me to. Would you like me to try to find him?"

"Yeah, why don't you," Bellows responded unenthusiastically. Mary phoned Allbritton's wife. After some gentle cajoling, she acknowledged that her husband was in Houston.

Mary knew that Allbritton's return was the only way to save the *Star*. She eventually located him, and the two engaged in a series of lengthy telephone conversations. "His lament," Mary shared, "was that nobody listened to him, which was quite true, and they didn't take his advice, which was quite true." It also turned out that Allbritton was offended that he had not been featured more prominently at the annual Gridiron dinner. After considerable persuading, Allbritton agreed to fly back to Washington to come to Mary's apartment for a meal and to further engage the *Star*'s unions. The future of the *Washington Star* appeared to hinge upon Mary's ability to talk Allbritton down over veal ragout and Székely cabbage.

The mealtime conversation between Allbritton, Yoder, and Mary was congenial. She let Allbritton vent at great length about Bellows, the *Star*, and Washington, which improved his mood. Allbritton saw himself as the *Star*'s savior but was frustrated by what he called "obtuse, ungrateful, nit-picking editors."

The trio had drinks and sang Baptist hymns after lunch. Mary seemed to have everything back on track.

It was four o'clock, so Mary had to finish her column for the next day. When she got to the paper, a reporter from the *Washington Post* called, knowing that Mary was close with Allbritton. Without thinking, she told the reporter, on the record, that she thought everything was going to be all right.

The *Post* printed Mary's comments. Allbritton hit the roof and quickly canceled his planned meetings with ten unions and a federal mediator. He was furious with Mary: "If I can't trust you, Mary, who can I trust?" The two spoke on the phone three or four times a day, and Mary described the back-and-forth: "Terrible reproaches and telephone calls, and how bad I had been, and what a disappointment, and how I had let him down, how I had betrayed him."

The *Star* had never gotten a handle on its unions and trucking fleet the way the *Washington Post* had, and it was bedeviled by snarled afternoon traffic, raw mismanagement, a bloated workforce, and changing tastes. All across America, afternoon newspapers were in trouble as people were turning to the evening news rather than the paper. The *Star* was losing seventy thousand dissatisfied customers a year, primarily because papers

were being delivered late or not at all. The paper had always been successful in getting new subscribers, but it wasn't enough to keep up with the
torrent of people fed up with not seeing their paper in the delivery box
when it was supposed to be. One senior editor was so frustrated that the
paper was not reaching his own house on time that he finally told his delivery boy he would "shoot him in the kneecap" if it did not start appearing
more promptly.

Mary hatched another plan. She was scheduled to appear at the
swearing-in of the new National Press Club president, and she remembered
that when Carter's vice president, Fritz Mondale, had gone to London at
the beginning of the year, he had ended up singing old Welsh and Scottish
songs with Prime Minister James Callaghan. Mary called the British ambassador, Sir Peter Ramsbotham, and asked if he would be willing to sing
with Mondale. He was. Mondale had cold feet, but one of his staffers told
Mary the best way to convince him: have the British ambassador call and
act as if everything had already been agreed. The strategy worked, and
Mary, the vice president, and the British ambassador ended up singing from
the podium. In a fortunate twist, CBS broadcast some of the performance,
and not only did Allbritton see it—he loved it. "It was just the kind of thing
that he thought he was in the newspaper business for," Mary said.

Allbritton agreed to put his name back on the paper's masthead, as
chairman. Mary's bad cooking and enthusiastic singing had saved the *Star*
from near calamity, but it was a brief reprieve.

Jim Bellows left the *Star* for the *Los Angeles Herald Examiner* nine
months later, in November 1977.

Concurrently, although the news was not immediately public, Joe Allbritton was essentially forced to sell the *Star* when the Federal Communications
Commission determined that he could not own both the paper and a local
television station. The TV station was profitable and likely to become more
so; the *Star* was a sinkhole. Allbritton quietly reached out to several potential
suitors for the *Star*. Time Inc. was first on the list.

Between September and December 1977, Allbritton met repeatedly
with James Shepley, the president of Time Inc. Shepley wanted to purchase

the *Star* and felt it would give Time an important voice in the nation's capital, parroting the symbiotic relationship between *Newsweek* and the *Washington Post*.

No one on the *Star*'s staff, not even Mary, knew that Allbritton had entered talks with Time. Ed Yoder observed that Allbritton's mood brightened with the news that Bellows was leaving the paper. "It seemed for a brief stretch," said Yoder, "as if some stability had crept into the operations."

As the *Star* dealt with its internal turmoil, Mary kept about her work. She tried to like President Carter but never succeeded. She was perplexed by his clumsy, tone-deaf relations with Congress, gaining much of her ammunition on this topic from her close relationship with the Democratic Speaker of the House, Tip O'Neill. O'Neill adored Mary, and this only gave her more influence on the Hill. Mary was voicing O'Neill's own frustrations when she described Carter as a "compulsive and pietistic Southerner, who understood nothing about tickets, perks, appointments and serving hard liquor at the White House."

But on balance, Mary's columns on Carter were not her best. They felt small. They were not illuminated by the magnificent anger she brought to Nixon or Vietnam, nor did they enjoy the pointed personal insight of her columns about Gene McCarthy, Lyndon Johnson, or the Kennedys.

On February 1, 1978, Joe Allbritton called James Shepley of Time. He was willing to sell the *Washington Star* for $20 million in cash. Shepley soon returned the call; Time's board approved the purchase. Allbritton might not have been the world's best newspaperman, but he was plenty savvy. The television station he'd purchased when he originally bought the *Star*, known as WJLA today, would end up being worth over a billion dollars. Allbritton was sad to sell the *Star*, with one associate saying he "was almost in grief over it," but the ruling from the FCC and the paper's poor financial position forced his hand.

On February 3, 1978, the deal was announced publicly—and it came on the same day that the *Chicago Daily News*—one of the best-known afternoon newspapers in the country—declared that it was going out of business. Shepley pronounced, "The *Star* has a bright future," and insisted that Time's vast resources and long track record of success in publishing would again push the *Star* to the top.

Mary was initially welcoming of Time's ownership. She shared her view of the company's arrival to her old friend William Shannon:

> The matter was of earthquake proportions. In the dark of night, the intrepid Mr. Allbritton slipped up to New York and made common cause with Mr. James Shepley. The last time I saw Mr. Shepley was during the Nixon campaign, when, as he reminded me today, when we met in a glow of mutual congratulation, we had some differences. Last Saturday night, for the first time I can remember, I went to a party where there were representatives from the Other Paper and no one asked me solicitously, "Is the *Star* going to make it, Mary?" It was rather delicious.

Time was convinced that, with some editorial changes, the *Star* would soon be profitable. Murray Gart was appointed as the *Star*'s editor and Shepley as chairman of the board. Neither had run a major newspaper before. Workmen installed a large marble-topped desk and a huge map of the world in Gart's office, a striking change from the austere environment favored by Bellows.

A Bostonian, Gart was a graduate of Boys' Latin School, and had served as Time's chief of correspondents. He traveled around town in a limousine, and he and Shepley became active on the Washington social scene, lunching with Henry Kissinger and other power players.

Gart was a driven corporate man, usually waking at five in the morning, with a penchant for micromanaging reporters and editors. At his first editorial meeting, he declared, "We have to decide whether we're going to be a daily magazine or a daily newspaper. I can tell you right now we're going to be a daily newspaper." He rejected Bellows's editorial approach, despite the fact that it had invigorated the *Star*'s copy. Gart did not want long features or pieces of analysis. He did not want color and personality. He wanted hard news and straight reporting. "Murray wanted to put his imprint on the paper," Jack Germond observed, "but he threw out everything, the baby with the bathwater, and some things Bellows had done were brilliant."

He also developed a morning edition designed to compete with the *Post*, and he wanted to abandon the afternoon entirely but was overruled by the rest of the management team, despite the widespread evidence that afternoon newspapers were dying, being squeezed by the evening news and by rush-hour traffic that made distribution increasingly difficult. The *Star* remained awkwardly in between, neither fully an afternoon nor a morning paper, unable to dent the *Post*'s commanding position.

Gart insisted that the paper prominently cover the doings of Time Inc. executives and board members. He called the desk every night to approve the stories that would appear on the front page the next day. "People here became aware that regardless of how many meetings they had during the day, there was only one meeting that mattered," Mary said, "and that was the meeting when Murray called the news desk at 11 at night and made up page one by phone."

Mary, widely viewed as one of the paper's important assets by rivals like the *Post*, thought Gart was too loyal to Time, too secretive, and prone to behaving like a "roman general in a province." Nothing did more to sour the relationship between Gart and Mary than his effort to push her column to the op-ed page. Gart, acknowledging in advance that Mary would "be deeply displeased," wrote to her: "I feel quite strongly that some columns must move, and, perhaps, be replaced by others. Yours is one I believe should move to the op-ed page. I completely suspect how deeply you feel about the matter, but I also trust that your readers will follow you wherever your column may appear." Mary was incensed. Her columns had always appeared inside the news pages, either on the front page or on page three. She viewed her column's placement as sacrosanct. There was certainly a case to be made that Mary's column belonged on the opinion pages, but with circulation and finances a mess, starting a turf war with one of the paper's most venerable staff members was a poor choice.

Mary, in a huff, announced that she would take a brief vacation, and she decided that she would go from writing four columns a week to three (still a prodigious output by today's standards). Mary was in her early sixties, and the demands of her work were considerable. However, Gart's unctuous response only irritated her further: he claimed that he had long worried about the pace being too much for Mary and suggested that she write a day in advance of publication, "so that some of those late nights can be eliminated." Mary's columns would appear on the op-ed page Tuesdays and Thursdays and on the first page of the opinion section on Sundays.

Mary seethed as her column not only was moved to the opinion pages but often appeared on different parts of the page. She was given varying word lengths with which to work, leading her to complain that she was being treated as if she were "just putty to fill up holes." She insisted that she could not work under such conditions. "The only thing that interests me is a return to the news section," a distraught Mary wrote to Gart. "You know how difficult it is to contemplate leaving this paper. Now I find it more difficult to contemplate staying on."

Gart eventually agreed to fix Mary's column in a regular position on the op-ed page, addressing at least part of her complaint, and he preemptively declared, "It is clear to me that we have at long last found the right location in the paper. Unless I hear otherwise from you, I will assume we are in agreement." Gart quickly heard from Mary. They were not in agreement. "I belong in the company of my peers in the news section."

Gart eventually acceded, and Mary's column was placed on page four of the first section of the paper. Mary's relationship with Gart and Time Inc., however, never recovered from the battle.

In early August 1978, Pope Paul VI died, and Mary was dispatched to Rome to cover the funeral and the selection of a new pontiff. Mary thought Paul VI's unwillingness to support the use of birth control had needlessly pushed millions away from the Church, and she quoted an Italian woman to make her case: "To be a Catholic doesn't mean to be an imbecile."

Mary's views on contraception and abortion said a great deal about the centrality of faith in her life. While she disagreed strongly with the pope's

positions on contraception and, later in her life and to a lesser degree, homosexuality, Mary was in strong agreement with many of the teachings of the
Church, including those on abortion. But she carefully steered clear of writing about abortion in her columns, and it was one of the only areas of political belief where Mary pulled her punches. She was a member of the
increasingly endangered minority of adamantly pro-life Democrats.

Mary did not like the fact that most pro-life groups had little interest
in encouraging adoption or implementing child-friendly public policies,
and she objected to the view within Democratic ranks "that every single
intelligent person is pro-abortion." Her own belief was that abortion ex-
tinguished a life: "You can phrase it a lot of different ways, but that's what
I think it comes down to."

Mary's faith was absent from her columns, but it shaped her far more
than most of her readers, and even many of her friends, appreciated. Her
faith was her moral center. "Mary was so wonderfully caustic and funny
about life that it probably didn't occur to most of us that she was deeply
religious," observed fellow columnist Anthony Lewis. "It was an anomaly
among that group of people."

Even the nuns at St. Ann's were surprised by the depth of Mary's devotion. Sister Josephine Murphy remembered visiting Mary's apartment and
seeing the centuries-old *The Following of Christ*, by Thomas à Kempis, on
her nightstand. When Josephine pointed out the book, Mary said simply,
"That is kind of what I try to live by."

Mary was reluctant to impose her view of religion on others. She
blended very traditional Catholicism with distinct strains of liberation
theology, the idea that social and polical change in support of the working
class was a natural extension of her faith. She prayed on her knees every
night before bed. She almost never missed a Sunday Mass. She felt that
the entire point of religion was to assist the oppressed and less fortunate—
something in which she thought the Church often fell criminally short.
Mary saw social justice as the cornerstone of responsible Catholicism and
believed in a God of love and compassion.

Her initially stern disapproval of homosexuality drove a wedge between her and several others in her circle. "When I came out of the closet in 1977, Mary was one of those who had a great deal of difficulty with it," her old friend David Mixner related. "Her working-class background and her devout Catholicism made it very difficult for her to understand or accept my sexuality."

Mary's view of homosexuality softened with time, and when Mixner wrote a memoir, she passed it on to a relative who was struggling with his own sexual identity, along with a simple inscription inside the front cover: "Here my darling, I think this will help you, from a person who I really love."

In Rome, Mary was very pleased with the rapid selection of Pope John Paul I as Paul VI's successor, but his reign was short, and John Paul died just thirty-three days after being selected. Mary was shocked when the cardinals selected someone who wasn't Italian, the first in centuries, to be the new pope: John Paul II.

During the funeral ceremonies for Pope Paul VI, Mary spent a good deal of time with Senator Ted Kennedy, whom President Carter had dispatched as his envoy to the ceremonies. Mary was eager for Kennedy to challenge Carter, whose approval ratings were in the mid-forties, in the 1980 Democratic primary. Kennedy made a September 1978 visit to New Hampshire to dip his toe in the presidential waters. However, Carter enjoyed a surge of popularity when he brokered a peace agreement between Menachem Begin of Israel and Anwar Sadat of Egypt, complete with a White House signing ceremony. Carter had no plans to go quietly, even if pushed by a Kennedy.

Mary knew from experience that Teddy was very different from his late brothers. He lacked Jack's regal cool and Bobby's raw intensity. He was more like everyone's favorite boisterous uncle, and Mary wondered whether Teddy had the fire for a competitive run.

Christmas 1978 was a gloomy one at the *Star* as the financial outlook turned bleak. The paper had lost $10 million in 1978 and was set to bleed even more red ink in 1979. Citing its troubled bottom line, Time threatened to walk away from the paper unless the *Star*'s unions renegotiated their contracts by midnight on New Year's Eve. Negotiations went to the deadline, leaving a nervous Murray Gart pacing the newsroom as the year drew near an end. The unions agreed to a new contract just before midnight. Gart was relieved, and he broke out a bottle of Scotch. The mood quickly dampened when James Shepley called, declaring that the paper would not publish the next day—Shepley wanted to see the agreement in writing. No true newspaperman would have ever made the decision not to publish with an agreement reached.

For one day, on January 1, 1979, there was no *Washington Star.*

Management tried to boost staff morale by holding a lavish, belated New Year's party at the Sheraton-Carlton Hotel. With bartenders wearing tuxedos and a giant ice sculpture gracing the center of the ballroom, *Star* staffers groused that such money would have been better spent on benefits. Still, in its lead editorial on January 2, the Time Inc. leadership declared, "We are here to stay," promising to pump an additional $60 million into the paper over the next five years.

There were hopeful signs. Circulation rose during 1979, and a number of offices were renovated within the *Star* building. Still, the staff greeted the layer of new editors imported from Time Inc. with a wariness that bordered on hostility, objecting to the idea of remaking the *Star* as a carbon copy of *Time.*

On March 29, 1979, a nuclear reactor at Three Mile Island, Pennsylvania, suffered a partial meltdown, and the entire nation was gripped with nuclear anxiety. Mary was not about to remain on the sidelines, and she headed to Pennsylvania with her friend and colleague Phil Gailey.

As Mary arrived for breakfast with Gailey and several other reporters at a Harrisburg hotel, she clutched a newspaper in her hand. She thrust it toward the group. There was a vivid picture on the front page of a terrified mother fleeing with her child, who was wrapped tightly in a blanket. The cooling towers of the power plant loomed in the background.

"I have to find that mother," Mary said.

One reporter suggested that she should find a different story—surely the woman had already left town. Mary responded with annoyance, "*This is the story.*"

Gailey quickly realized how his day would be spent, and he agreed to assist Mary in the search. They showed the photo to clerks, gas station attendants, and local reporters. They drove around neighborhoods near Three Mile Island, trying to re-create the photo's camera angle. After hours of fruitless searching, the landscape finally appeared to match the picture. They found the house.

No one was home. Mary stalked around the property, taking notes in shorthand. She assayed the flower boxes and toys scattered around the yard. She got the name MAYBERRY off the mailbox. After she chatted with a neighbor who thought the family had fled to an evacuation center, Mary and Gailey went to all of the evacuation centers, passing the increasingly dog-eared photo from hand to hand. No luck. They tried calling every person with the same last name in the telephone book. Finally they had luck: the woman in the picture was staying with relatives living seventy-five miles away.

Catherine Mayberry shared how she had escaped with her one-year-old daughter cradled in her arms, and her husband said that she was still so frightened that she sometimes trembled when holding their daughter. "I'm totally against nuclear power," Catherine declared. "I'd go back to candles rather than go through another week like this." For Gailey, the entire episode was a perfect example of Mary's dedication to following her gut instincts on a story and putting in the time to deliver a colorful story illuminated by real reporting.

Back in Washington, Mary continued to hammer away at Jimmy Carter. Disaffection with the president was widespread amid a growing energy crunch and a sharp spike in gas prices. Mary wrote to a reader, "I'm sorry to hear you think the press is crucifying the president. To be honest, I thought he was doing a pretty good job of it himself."

Mary was skeptical that Ted Kennedy would challenge Carter, knowing that his personal life was messy and that a presidential race would reopen all the old questions about his disturbing behavior during the accident at Chappaquiddick.

By the fall of 1979, it was clear that Kennedy was going to run. However, he stumbled from the start, including during an awkward interview with Roger Mudd of CBS News, when he struggled to explain why he was running. Mary shredded Kennedy's performance in the Mudd interview as "epic haplessness" and declared that he was "patently wretched" in trying to explain away Chappaquiddick. Like her columns on Bobby in 1968, Mary's take on Teddy felt brutal because of their friendship.

Although friends with Kennedy, Mary never approved of his lifestyle. She thought Chappaquiddick was a moral stain and frowned on his heavy drinking and well-known womanizing. Elizabeth Shannon, a close friend of Mary's, later dated Kennedy after her own husband had passed away and Kennedy was divorced. At one point Mary sniffed to Shannon about her relationship with Kennedy, "I thought you had better taste than that." Although she was disappointed by his personal failings, Kennedy remained an important source for Mary, and she was a regular attendee at after-hours, off-the-record discussions with Kennedy in his office over a bottle of Scotch.

The seizure of American hostages by Iranian revolutionaries in Tehran complicated the Democratic race, and the slow-moving drama became a defining episode for the already beleaguered President Carter. The public initially rallied around the president, and Kennedy's aura of inevitability evaporated.

Mary covered one of the signature moments in the Republican primary and one of the signature moments in the career of Ronald Reagan at a New Hampshire debate hosted by the *Nashua Telegraph*. During the contentious back-and-forth over who would actually participate in the debate, the *Telegraph* editor asked that Reagan's microphone be turned off. A visibly angry Reagan snapped, "I am paying for this microphone." Mary wrote that "Reagan was transformed into a party leader," while George Bush "looked like a studious patron of the public library who is determined not to be disturbed by the noisy boys at the magazine rack."

Mary might have objected to Reagan's worldview, which she called "making life more comfortable for the comfortable," but Carter left her cold. She described the likely clash between Carter and Reagan as "a choice between a Democrat who can't govern and a Republican who won't."

Ted Kennedy lost to Carter by double digits in New Hampshire. Although Kennedy managed to win a number of states, his campaign was ultimately embarrassing, and the race with Carter was bitter.

At the Republican convention, in Detroit, what should have been a relatively uneventful coronation for Ronald Reagan was made dramatic by an eleventh-hour suggestion from former president Gerald Ford that he would consider serving as Ronald Reagan's running mate. Speculation about the potential dream ticket swept the Joe Louis Arena as envoys from the Ford and Reagan camps engaged in frantic negotiations.

The talks eventually collapsed, and Reagan chose George Bush as his running mate. Mary likened the scene of Ronald and Nancy Reagan and George and Barbara Bush standing on the convention stage to "the parents of the bride and bridegroom who are determined to put a good face on a marriage of convenience."

The Democratic convention, in New York, became most famous for Kennedy's swan song, a rousing, nostalgic speech that left many delegates wondering where the real Ted Kennedy had been during the primaries. Kennedy finished his speech with his most famous words: "For me, a few hours ago, this campaign came to an end. For all those whose cares have been our concern, the work goes on, the cause endures, the hope still lives, and the dream shall never die." It was an unprecedented moment of defeat for a Kennedy, and, as Mary said, Teddy was desperate to show that Carter had not destroyed the Kennedy magic. It was a great speech, but Teddy had served his party's nominee poorly, and he said next to nothing about supporting Carter. The speech had given Kennedy his measure of revenge, and Mary said that Carter left the convention looking like an airline pilot "whose passengers have defected to the hijacker."

Mary recognized the enormity of the moment. The last of the Kennedy brothers had acknowledged on the grand national stage that his dreams of the presidency were finished. "Everything is a big deal for the Kennedys," she said, "and they have a very powerful sense of entitlement. And they are treated like royalty. . . . No matter what the tabloids say, no matter what happens, they are there, because the Kennedys are different from you and me."

When Carter stumbled in one of the presidential debates, saying that his young daughter, Amy, had told him that nuclear proliferation was the greatest issue facing the nation, Mary knew a Reagan win was almost inevitable. Carter's efforts to paint Reagan as a dangerous ideologue just did not mesh well with the former actor's affable image.

Reagan destroyed Carter in the election, carrying forty-four states as Republicans gained control of the Senate for the first time in a quarter-century. Mary wrote, "That was no election. That was Mt. St. Helens, pouring hot ash over the whole political landscape, burying a president and much of his party." The American hostages in Iran were released on Carter's final day in office, ending a personal and national humiliation and further boosting the sense of enthusiasm that had greeted the Reagan victory. A conservative tide had swept the country, and Mary's was suddenly a relatively lonely liberal voice in the wilderness. Lots of reporters were still liberals, but the opinion pages of America's newspapers were increasingly being dominated by ascendant right-wingers.

Mary's brother, John McGrory, died in the fall of 1980. She very much loved her brother, although his struggle with alcoholism had made it an often demanding and frustrating relationship. Mary no longer had any immediate family alive, and it seemed unlikely that she would ever wed. People across America read her words every day, and she had a wonderful circle of friends and relatives once removed, but Mary was a solitary figure in many ways.

Even after Mary's tough words for him in the primary, Ted Kennedy went out of his way to express his condolences. He wrote to Mary, "Having also known the blessing of a brother's love, and the grief of a brother's death, my heart goes out to you on the loss of your beloved brother John."

Mary thrived despite being at odds with the prevailing conservative national mood. The Reagan presidency reinvigorated Mary's column and provided her with a seemingly endless wellspring of new outrages. Indeed, she took strong exception to one of Reagan's very first acts as president. In the waning days of the Carter administration, a lawyer at the Energy Department had made the decision to transfer $1 million in penalties paid by major oil companies, for overcharging consumers, to four charities, including the Salvation Army. The Reagan administration immediately tried to reverse the decision and asked the charities to repay the funds, but they had already spent much of the money helping poor families with winter fuel bills.

Mary was at home watching her television and saw an interview with Colonel Ernie Miller of the Salvation Army. Miller, emerging from a frustrating meeting at the Energy Department, told a waiting camera crew that the Salvation Army would "put kettles on the streets to ask the public to help" if needed. Mary leapt into the fray, calling Miller for an interview.

Miller explained that he was under enormous pressure. His national commander was demanding an explanation, and advisory board members from across the country, many of whom were Republican, were screaming for his scalp. Mary liked Miller instantly; his pleasant baritone would become a fixture at her parties for years to come.

Mary's resulting columns blazed about "grim feds bursting into a hovel demanding from the resident widow the return of taxpayers' money for her belated winter fuel." She arranged for Miller to make a television appearance with Andrea Mitchell of NBC News, and Miller brought the camera crew to meet an out-of-work carpenter whom the Salvation Army had given $39.07 to help pay his heating bill.

By the time Mary arrived at her office the next morning, there was a message on her answering machine from White House press secretary Marlin Fitzwater. "The money is going to the charities." Mary and the Salvation Army had won in a rout. "With Mary McGrory's help and interpretation, we were able to turn the situation around," Ernie Miller recalled. "That was probably the first time the Reaganites reversed course—and it may have been nearly the last time."

On a rainy day in March 1981, Mary was scheduled to hear Reagan speak at a local hotel. She was running late and arrived at the Washington Hilton at around 2:30 as a light rain fell. The entrance to the hotel was complete chaos, with police shouting, a Marine band moving about in jumbled confusion, and photographers snapping pictures. Several people were receiving medical attention. Mary thought there had been an accident or someone had suffered a heart attack. She asked a bystander what was happening. "Someone shot at the president," was the reply. "But he's okay; he's gone back to the White House." Everyone Mary spoke with said that the president, who had been in office just seventy days, had not been hurt.

The people were wrong. The president was badly wounded by the assassin's bullet. Mary began an unsatisfying vigil in her office, watching updates on television and hoping that the president would survive.

The next night, one of her colleagues gave her a ride home. They passed the scene of the shooting, and Mary's friend wondered, "Can you imagine what it would have been like if that bullet had been a few inches closer?" Mary snapped in reply, "I don't have to imagine it. I was here for Kennedy's funeral."

Reagan responded to the near-death experience with humor and light. He joked with his doctors that he hoped they weren't Democrats, and waved sunnily to the public from his hospital window. It proved a turning point in his presidency. Mary shared the sentiment Tip O'Neill had expressed after visiting President Reagan in the hospital: "A beautiful person. I wish he agreed with me."

At the *Star*, circulation numbers brought a steady stream of bad news. By May 1981, the *Post* was selling more than 600,000 copies a day, the *Star* only 320,000.

The declining circulation fed a decline in advertising, a newspaper's lifeblood. The *Star* was poised to lose $20 million in 1981. While Murray Gart and the team from Time Inc. had revamped the paper's editorial content, they had not come to terms with the underlying management rot that was the *Star*'s real problem.

A long article in the *Washington Monthly* eviscerated Time Inc. for its management of the *Star*, airing complaints long heard in the newsroom about the move away from feature writing, Gart's aloofness, and Time's habit of using the paper to shill for its favorite causes. Newby Noyes wrote Mary not long after the story was published: "I can't help feeling that Time Inc. is bound to wake up and replace Gart if he really is that awful."

The news got worse. At a dude ranch in Encampment, Wyoming, the Time Inc. board of directors gathered for its annual meeting. Dressed in country casual attire, James Shepley detailed the *Star*'s grim vital statistics. Ads and circulation were plummeting, losses were mounting, and Time Inc. had spent $85 million on the *Star* in a little more than three years. The turnaround Shepley had confidently promised was nowhere to be seen.

On July 16, the Time board of directors met in more familiar environs, on the forty-seventh floor of the Time-Life Building, in New York. For close to four hours, they debated whether there were any remaining alternatives to save the *Star*. The ultimate decision: the paper had to be closed.

Staffers at the *Star* were unaware that their fate had been set even as construction crews completed one of the new offices just off the newsroom. On July 21, Gart traveled to New York on one of Time's private jets to meet with Shepley.

On July 22, Shepley's committee gathered for a half-hour meeting with Gart. Shortly after noon, they formally voted to close the *Star*. All present were instructed to keep the decision secret until eight the next morning, when it would be released to the newswires.

Back at the *Star*, rumors swirled. Many hoped that Gart's appearance in New York signaled his imminent ouster.

On July 23, the calls started before sunrise. Editors of the *Star* were informed that there would be an emergency meeting in Gart's office. "The news is not good." Sixteen grim-faced editors crowded into Gart's office promptly at seven, many of them disheveled from their rapid commute. Gart silently passed out the text of a Time press release announcing that the *Star* would close in two weeks.

As he stood in front of his map of the world, Gart insisted that he had fought hard for the paper, neglecting to mention that its fate had been decided before he was consulted. The press release would go out to the wire services within the hour.

The editors flinched. The *Star*'s employees would learn they were losing their jobs on the radio, scooped on their own demise. After some back-and-forth, Gart relented and said that editors could inform their own people.

Executive Managing Editor William F. McIlwain asked how much severance employees would receive and how long their benefits would remain in place.

Gart didn't know. He called Shepley, who didn't know, either. "Time will honor its contracts," Gart reassured McIlwain.

The normally soft-spoken McIlwain, who was on crutches following foot surgery, exploded. "What kind of shabby fucking talk is that? You mean the president of the company is going to go out and have a press conference of what's happening and you haven't bothered to find out the answer to the most important question for your people?" McIlwain's passion roiled the room.

The meeting was completed by 7:45, and at 8:00 A.M. the nation's capital woke up to the news that the *Washington Star* was ending its 128-year run. A few minutes after the press release hit, Mary's phone rang. It was one of the national editors. "Mary, I want to tell you something. Time is closing the *Star* in two weeks."

Mary's home would be no more. She rushed to the office, wading through a phalanx of camera crews and reporters who had taken up positions outside the paper's doors, fielding a few questions before saying that she had a column to finish.

At a press conference at the Madison Hotel in Washington, J. Richard Munro, president and chief executive officer of Time Inc., announced that the *Star* was hemorrhaging money. "We have no choice but to close it." It rankled Mary that Munro, a man she had never met, delivered the paper's obituary. The *Star* became the 316th afternoon newspaper in the United States to go out of business since 1970, a tidal wave that would leave no survivors. "I never believed they'd do it," said Mary in reaction. "The capital of the Western world with one newspaper."

Gart ventured around the newsroom. He offered little in the way of comfort but made calls to other papers trying to find landing spots for some of his top talent. He offered his hand to Mary. She refused to shake it. One thought burned in Mary's mind: "You were never part of this."

As the shock wore off, the anger mounted among the staff. Bill McIlwain fumed that Gart had still not spoken directly to the employees. "I can't believe it—the guy doesn't have the courage to face his staff."

McIlwain huddled with Mary, telling her, "I blame him for everything. I blame him for the weather. I blame him for my foot." McIlwain was already leaving the paper, having accepted a job with the *Arkansas Gazette*. His going-away party was scheduled for the same afternoon. Mary was not shy in expressing her own opinions. "I'm angry at the way they handled this," she said of Time, "angry at the town for not supporting us."

Reporters anxiously gazed at the bulletin board as openings at other papers were hastily tacked up. "Every time we were on the precipice in the past," observed Maureen Dowd, who had risen to be a feature writer at the paper, "there always seemed to be a Superman waiting to swoop down and save us. This time . . . there's no one out there."

McIlwain's farewell party became a very different kind of gathering, and by three o'clock the champagne, beer, and wine had begun to flow. The scene was a swirl. Reporters drank with grim zeal and sang. Others scrambled to update their résumés and placed long-distance calls. People shared war stories, laughed, hugged, and cried. Empty champagne bottles littered the file cabinets. Some reporters pecked away at their stories to meet deadlines—cold comfort in a disappearing routine.

At around five, Murray Gart finally addressed the newsroom. He was greeted by intermingled applause and muffled hisses. The room grew quiet. Gart said that he had spoken with Ben Bradlee, of the *Post*, and Mike O'Neill, of the *New York Daily News*, about finding placement for his reporters. Someone quipped: "A name-dropper to the last." Gart insisted he had done everything in his power to keep the paper alive. "Maybe a miracle will happen before August 7," he said. Gart's speech meandered until finally a compassionate deskman raised a glass and said, "Well, here's to you, Murray." The reporters desultorily raised their glasses.

Gart gestured across the room to the white-haired McIlwain, who awkwardly climbed atop a desk with his crutches to address the crowd. As he began to speak, the reporters broke out in applause, drowning out his words. The cheers and clapping grew louder; people stomped their feet. The whole room erupted in a cathartic cacophony, roaring as if one. The shouting went on for a full two minutes. McIlwain, moved nearly to tears, could only choke out, "I admire you all."

With the speeches done, the drinking intensified. Phil Gailey played his autoharp in the middle of the newsroom. A drunken Lance Gay head-butted a computer. Like a desperate Christmas party, the gathering involved much kissing and flirting among the tears.

In the *Star*'s final days, Mary received a surge of letters from friends and family. Acquaintances in New Hampshire, Massachusetts, Vermont, and Colorado offered their homes so Mary could come, rest, recuperate, and mourn. "People said it was like a death in the family, and it was: telephone calls, telegrams, flowers. But it was worse," Mary said. "It was the death of a family."

On Friday, the *Star* newsroom was somber as the shock wore off and reporters faced the grim work of trying to find new jobs. Time Inc. did little to burnish its image in the last days. Staff had their bags searched both as they entered and left. A memo from the executive editor was posted on the newsroom bulletin board, warning, NO LIQUOR MUST BE BROUGHT INTO THE BUILDING. Beneath the sign, a newsroom wag scribbled, ANYONE IGNORING THIS MEMO WILL BE FIRED.

Job security was not an issue for Mary. Meg Greenfield of the *Washington*

Post called her daily to offer her a position. "I don't want to talk about any of it until the *Star* is gone," Mary finally snapped in reply.

Mary's waning days at the *Star* were not without crisis. On Saturday around lunch, Mary got a call at home from the Sunday editor. He was apologetic, but he had been told that he had to spike Mary's column about the *Star*. Gart did not want any commentary about the paper's closure to appear in the *Star* until its last day, fearing that it might jeopardize any potential last-minute sale of the paper. Mary brooded. All through Vietnam, the tumult of 1968, and the Nixon years, her column had run as she had written it. She had never had a column spiked, although many of her opinions drove the *Star*'s conservative editors to distraction.

Mary called her old friend and former editor John Cassady, the steady hand who had guided thousands of her columns to publication. "Well, John, it's finally happened," she said. "My column will not run tomorrow." Mary declared that she would quit if she could not write about the biggest story in the city during her last two weeks.

"I'm with you one hundred percent," Cassady responded, "but you know you will lose your severance." Mary worried that she would look "vainglorious, walking out on a dying newspaper," but she thought that anything less would send the wrong message. Mary began composing her resignation letter in her head, but she knew that she first had to speak with Gart, who was at a wedding in New York.

Mary called and left a message. She waited two very long hours before Gart called back. He said that he did not want to jeopardize any possible deals for the paper. Mary said little. Eventually, she said that she did not want anyone to think that she "had collapsed under calamity," arguing that being professional meant writing about disasters as they unfolded.

There was a long silence. Gart, realizing that having his most famous columnist quit in protest during the final two weeks of publication would not help his battered reputation, declared that the column would run. Mary claimed it was the only argument she ever won with Gart.

On July 26, Mary's remembrance of the *Star* ran in the Sunday paper. She noted that she had gotten used to reporters from other papers addressing her as if she were the wife of a terminally ill husband—"How is the *Star*?" She aimed sharp words at Time, saying that the gulf between "the weekly and the daily, between structure and free form, between reverence and cheekiness" had never been never bridged.

President Ronald Reagan invited himself to a farewell lunch at the *Star*. Given that he was still recovering from his gunshot wound, Mary regarded it as an incredibly gracious gesture. Reagan, Mary, Murray Gart, White House counselor Ed Meese, Ed Yoder, and several others filled the head table.

Reagan, with great relish, discussed spaghetti Westerns and some of the memorably bad subtitles he had seen dubbed in foreign productions. While always resisting his policies, Mary liked Reagan. "He has cut food stamps, jobs training, projects that help orphans and widows," she said. "And he is a demonstrably nice man, capable of kind gestures like bending over a dying newspaper."

As most of America was still aglow from the grandeur of Prince Charles and Lady Diana's wedding in London, August 4 marked Mary's thirty-fourth anniversary at the *Star*. Phil Gailey and others presented her with thirty-five long-stemmed roses and champagne. The newsroom was nearly deserted, with only a skeleton crew still working. "I always dreamed that the best way to go would be to be carried out between editions," Mary said, smiling ruefully. She said that many people had asked why she had stayed at the *Star* for so many years. "One of the reasons I couldn't ever leave the *Star* was I couldn't imagine what the farewell party would be like." She added, "And now I don't have to. And isn't that nice?" and then she cried.

On August 6, the eve of closing day, the editorial staff debated the final headline. The first attempt, "Goodbye," seemed too informal. Gart suggested "Farewell." The editors eventually agreed on "The Final Edition." Mary worked on her last column, fondly remembering the characters who had filled the newsroom during her three and a half decades at the paper: Newby Noyes, Jim Bellows, Joe Allbritton, and others.

Mary saw Tom Kenworthy, a young reporter who had arrived at the

Star just three months before, looking forlorn. She sat next to him as they wrote their final stories. Many of the staffers wore small black buttons bearing the dates 1852–1981 as they cleaned the last detritus from their desks. Ed Yoder finished his column, packed the books from his shelf, and proofed the final editorial page. He walked down to Mary's small office. They hugged, not exchanging a word. There was nothing left to say.

She walked out with Phil Gailey. The lobby was jammed with people buying the final edition. Gailey scolded in their general direction, "Where were you when we needed you?" Mary held his hand. The two sang several verses of "Nearer, My God, to Thee" as they departed.

Mary and Gailey headed to the Jenkins Hill pub, on Capitol Hill, with the other members of the staff. The reporters sang and drank, and a few wore black armbands. Mary did not stay long. This was one wake at which she could not bear to linger.

CHAPTER NINE

Life at the *Post*

The day after the *Star* closed, Ben Bradlee of the *Washington Post* took Mary to lunch.

Over their meal, Bradlee, somewhat gingerly, inquired, "Now?"

"Yes," said Mary.

"How much?" Bradlee asked. Mary named a salary. It was more modest than Bradlee had imagined. The two shook hands. "And that was that," said Bradlee. Mary McGrory was a columnist for the *Post*.

Bradlee was gracious, telling Mary that during all the years she had been at the *Star*, he felt like he had not been doing his job. Bradlee was smart enough not to replicate Murray Gart's mistakes.

He knew that Mary was an institution, and sometimes difficult. The *Post* wanted Mary because she was a premier talent with a well-established readership. But at the same time, some at the *Post* worried that she might not fit in at a paper that she had always viewed as the enemy—despite being more in tune with the paper's political slant. Mary was in her sixties but had lost little of her drive. As Cokie Roberts recalled, "There was all sorts of *sturm und drang* about 'Oh God, what do we do with her?'"

Mary was given a nice outside office, next to Bob Woodward. She brought her assistant, Liz Acosta, with her, a luxury no other *Post* columnist enjoyed. Don Graham, who had become the *Post*'s publisher as his mother assumed the role of chairwoman of the board, noted that having an assistant created some tensions, "but not with anybody who understood the importance of having a Mary McGrory on the paper." Mary would write three columns a week, appearing on page two and on the front page of the Sunday Outlook section. Kay Graham informed Mary that her late husband, Phil, wherever he was, was pleased.

After a much deserved August holiday, Mary's first *Post* column appeared on September 8, 1981. There was no reference to switching papers, and Mary picked up where she had left off, skewering Republicans for worrying that Reagan appointees were working in insufficiently opulent offices.

The *Washington Post* had Mary's pen, but her heart remained at the *Star*. Mary highlighted the differences between the *Star* and the *Post* by comparing two European cities: "The *Star*, disheveled, disorganized, welcoming, mellow, and forgiving, was Rome. The *Post*, structured, disdainful, elegant, and demanding, was Paris."

The *Post* was bigger, better funded, and more impersonal than the *Star*. Because it was a morning newspaper, Mary's deadlines were earlier, and she was no longer able to labor on her columns deep into the night. The rest of her daily routine remained largely unchanged. She started her days in her bright apartment by turning on National Public Radio, preferring it to the labored enthusiasm of morning television. She read the *Post*, the *New York Times*, and the *Wall Street Journal*, looking for the big story of the day.

After breakfast, she would lay out her outfit for the day. Invariably, her clothes were well tailored and impeccable. She usually arrived at the office at around ten with a column in mind. After another cup of coffee, Mary slowly picked up speed, leafing through her letters and the inevitable stack of pitches from press secretaries hoping that she would write about their pet issues.

Marjorie Williams, who worked with Mary at the *Post*, described her at work. "While harried reporters bustled past her, Mary drifted from desk to desk in what seemed to be aimless, sociable circles," and yet Mary "always made you feel as if you were the one person she had been pining to discuss the topic with. But in the midst of this breeze-shooting you found yourself telling her about a lunch you'd had with a member of the relevant committee staff two weeks ago, or something you'd heard secondhand from someone you trusted in the White House, or the best idea you'd had in three weeks. She was completely competitive and extraordinarily kind."

Mary would then make a series of phone calls, or venture up to the Hill, still determined to do her own legwork. Back in the office by 3:30, she would start trying to put words on paper, perusing her notebooks full of shorthand. She would pester Liz Acosta for relevant articles from her voluminous subject files and pace the newsroom.

Back at her computer, Mary revised and revised again. Her colleagues knew to give a wide berth when she was concentrating. She had Acosta print out draft copies of her column, and she still tore off pieces of paper and rolled them into small balls as she smoked. She would fidget and tug at her hair as she read.

Eventually, Mary would relinquish her column to an editor, never fully pleased. She would then retire to her apartment, cooking a late dinner and unwinding with a drink and a good book or while watching one of her favorite television shows. She always had a soft spot for both *M*A*S*H* and *Cheers*.

Mary quickly discovered that the *Post* was "strictly temperance." No liquor was served at major celebrations. "Everything is celebrated with a cake: farewells, promotions, prizes. And they stick to it," lamented Mary. "Great emotion is celebrated in thick frosting." Mary was horrified that even when the paper won a trio of Pulitzers, no champagne was in sight.

She felt that the *Post* was terribly self-important. Since the paper attracted accomplished reporters and had found itself at the top of the industry after Watergate, it was less interested in nurturing young talent or taking chances than it had once been. Ben Bradlee was increasingly the paper's last bastion against stodginess.

Mary put the best face on her new circumstance. She lined the walls of her office with books of poetry and history, and she told an interviewer, "They have given me a lovely office and a kind editor and the freedom to write anything I want. I really could not ask for more." She said that she was "totally, happily, uninvolved" in the *Post*'s management and added that she was pleased to have more time to focus on her writing.

None of it was the least bit convincing.

Mary wrote to a friend, complaining of the *Post*, "We take ourselves very seriously, and are much too busy to say good morning even ten hours before deadline." Mary often felt slighted: "They never say whether they particularly like what I write," Mary said of the editors. "I don't appreciate power, and they certainly do."

"She quite frankly hated the *Post*," Lance Gay remembered, describing the paper as a "great aircraft carrier sort of a place. You look out there and there are all these desks, a sea of reporters, and she could not find anyone to have lunch with." Mary told Gay that she did not fit in well. "She had an office and a secretary and they treated her very well," he explained, "but she had no friends there, she was lonely. She was affected by the fact that she had no life beyond the column." Ben Bradlee fully acknowledged that the *Post* never replaced the *Star* in Mary's heart. "I understood it. Loyalty was written all over that big Irish face."

Mary was writing for one of the most important newspapers in the nation, and her column was widely syndicated. Yet for all of the acclaim, it felt to Mary as though the bad guys had won by 1981. Ronald Reagan was president, the country was tilting dramatically to the right, funding for schools and homeless shelters was being slashed, the *Star* was bankrupt, and Mary hung her hat in the newsroom of her once dreaded rival.

Mary found a measure of solace when she entered a romantic relationship with Bob Abernethy, an NBC reporter. She had gotten to know Abernethy and his wife, Jean, when Jean worked as a copy girl at the *Star* in the mid-1940s. Bob and Jean were married in 1955, but she had died in 1980.

Bob and Mary had known each other casually when Jean was alive and occasionally bumped into each other at events or on the campaign trail. Both Mary and Abernethy had been at Andrews Air Force Base when Kennedy's body arrived from Dallas in 1963. He was the first person to call Mary when the news of the *Star*'s closure was announced.

"We dated," Abernethy remembered. "And we went out to dinner together. She loved a place on Connecticut Avenue near where she lived: the

Roma. We would go there, have something to drink, and talk. I was very fond of her; she was very fond of me." Mary taught Abernethy her favorite Irish songs, and they made each other laugh.

"The public Mary was the Mary I saw at her parties," Abernethy recounted. "But to be with her in private was always fun and enlightening and warm. She was really wonderful." He was impressed by Mary's commitment to her friends and the way she reached out to people in times of sorrow. But he was also realistic about her as a person, saying, "She wasn't sweet; you couldn't describe her as sweet. She certainly liked to be the center of attention. She could be really tough."

Mary's romance with Abernethy was unusual in several respects. It was the first relationship in Mary's adult life about which she was reasonably open with her friends and family. Mary's niece Anne Beatty recalled flying down to Washington with her husband to visit Mary. Even though Beatty had not known Mary was dating, Bob Abernethy greeted her and her husband at the airport.

Mary did not bring many of her usual preoccupations to the table with Abernethy. She didn't push him to volunteer at St. Ann's and didn't engage with him much about her columns. For the first time, Mary allowed herself to relax and not be overwhelmed with the preoccupation of wondering what others might think. One friend recalled how girlish Mary seemed around Abernethy.

"Bob Abernethy was her last serious relationship," Phil Gailey commented. "Mary did not want to give up what she had going, even for marriage to a man she probably loved. . . . Mary was not easy to live around or be around. She did have an imperial-highness side. She required much."

The relationship fell apart after several years. "It did not blossom into something more than a very happy and fond time together," said Abernethy diplomatically. Per custom, after it ended, Mary never said a word about the relationship. "The next time we visited," said Anne Beatty, "there was nothing. He just wasn't there and there was no mention of it."

Mary's transition to the *Post* was made even more difficult when she ran into legal trouble as a result of one of her columns. After a visit to Northern Ireland in the fall of 1981, Mary sang the praises of Seán Donlon, the departing Irish ambassador to the United States, who had made a strong push against Northern Irish terrorism and congratulated him for taking on the Irish National Caucus, "providers of funds for the fray." The caucus, claiming that Mary's column had accused them of financing terrorism, announced its intention to sue Mary and the *Post* for a million dollars. Mary had been on the job less than a month. Ben Bradlee, no stranger to legal threats, just smiled. "It sounds like you're having fun," he said. "Don't worry about it." The suit was eventually dropped after the *Post* offered a minor clarification.

On January 19, 1982, Mary attended President Reagan's White House press conference marking his first year in office. Though she was usually relegated to the back of the room, one of her *Post* colleagues was stuck in traffic, and she got a front-row seat. Mary felt obligated to ask a question, something that she didn't do very often in large groups.

The press conference was nearing its end, and reporter Helen Thomas, who was usually given the last question, raised her hand.

"Helen," said President Reagan. "I think Mary got up before you did, Helen, so I'll take her question."

"Mr. President," inquired Mary, "in New York last week you called upon the rich to help the poor in this present economic difficulty. Are you planning to increase your own contributions to private charity to set an example to the rich people of this country to do more for the poor?"

Reagan grimaced and then, in an amiable stage whisper to Helen Thomas, declared, "Helen, I just want you to know whenever you speak from now on, I'm shutting up." Mary said that Reagan looked as if he had "just about swallowed his epiglottis."

"No, Mary, I tell you," Reagan said, "I realize that some had noticed what seemed to be a small percentage of deductions for worthwhile causes. And that is true. And I'm afraid it will be true this year, because I haven't changed my habits. But I also happen to be someone who believes in tithing—the giving of a tenth—but I have for a number of years done some of that giving in ways that are not tax deductible, with regard to individuals that are being helped."

Mary was not convinced, and she noted in her column that in 1980 Reagan had given only $3,089 in charitable contributions, out of his $227,968 in earnings. "Our millionaire president has cut the government's allowance to the unfortunate, the old, the cold, the young, the slow. But he cheerily informs us that any big holes in the safety net will be mended by volunteers from the ranks, apparently, of the deserving rich," she wrote. Mary also noted that Republicans had not batted an eye when Pentagon contractors absconded with tens of millions of dollars, "but the thought of a single peanut butter sandwich going down an undeserving throat gives them acute dyspepsia."

Mary would hound Reagan and the White House press secretary with this line of questioning for several years. In reward for her audacity, Reagan refused to call on her during White House press conferences for the next four years and five months. Mary noted that she had been placed "back with the lepers" on the White House seating chart.

The issue of charitable giving was a personal one for Mary. Although she was never a wealthy woman, she routinely gave away 20 percent of her salary to charity. She was old-fashioned when it came to money. She did not invest in stocks and, other than her annual trip to Rome and her taste in clothes, lived frugally.

The next year, 1982, marked the advent of one of Mary's most popular series of columns. She had received a letter from a friend, Ned Kenworthy, who had retired from the *New York Times*, saying, "There's not much to be said for retirement except that it gives you time for weeding and reading Jane Austen." Inspired, Mary went out and bought a copy of *Emma*. She whisked through the book in two days.

Mary wrote a column about Jane Austen, and—like her pieces on gardening and squirrels, which she maintained as regular staples when she moved over to the *Post*—it became a sensation. At a time when the city was hot and half deserted and the headlines were full of bad news, Mary championed Austen as a "great enemy of incivility and squalor."

Universally approving mail came in from all over the country. One day when Mary was on the Hill, Oklahoma congressman James Jones, the head of the Budget Committee, hurried down the hallway past her. The two had never spoken before. "Read all of Jane Austen," Jones exclaimed without breaking stride.

"The first time I wrote about Jane Austen, I was simply stunned," Mary recalled. The following year, she was invited to speak at a meeting of the Jane Austen Society, in Philadelphia. Mary was impressed by the devotion of the two hundred attendees. One man had read *Emma* fifty times. After writing a column about the experience, a clergyman in Ohio asked Mary to "examine her conscience" for not providing the society's address in her story.

Mary pondered why Austen was so enduring. "Maybe it is because she deals with one subject, what is called today, 'interpersonal relationships' and the eternal theme of young women in search of husbands," Mary wrote. "She also describes loneliness, mostly through her delineations of old maids (she was one herself) who must be ingratiating, obliging, never revealing their own feelings in order to be tolerated."

Two issues dominated Mary's columns in Reagan's first term—Cold War tensions in Central America and the burgeoning antinuclear movement.

She was outraged when the administration downplayed the murder of four American nuns by El Salvador's right-wing government. "In the ugliest moment so far," Mary observed, "former secretary of state Alexander M. Haig Jr. told a House committee that the victims probably got what they were asking for by running a roadblock and exchanging fire with Salvadoran security forces. Actually, they were shot in the back of the head, execution-style."

Mary also took congressional Democrats to task for failing to stand up to the president: "What congressmen want more than anything in the world is to be let off the hook when it comes to difficult choices." Republicans remained thirsty for a broader fight with Democrats on Central America policy, and Mary quoted Representative Dick Cheney of Wyoming as saying that the real lesson of Vietnam was that "we did not do enough."

The early Reagan years sparked a national conversation about nuclear arms and the possibility of a nuclear freeze. The administration went to ridiculous lengths to convince the public that it should learn to live with the bomb. After presidential counselor Ed Meese described nuclear war as "something that may not be desirable," Mary called it the ultimate in understatement.

It was natural that Mary was drawn to the nuclear freeze. It was a grassroots movement made up of scientists, church people, and housewives. After the shaggy rebellion of the Vietnam protests, the nuclear freeze felt distinctly highbrow. Mary was delighted when she heard Mozart playing in the background at one of the meetings. There were no flag burnings, and no one seized the dean's office.

Mary was smitten when a discussion of a nuclear freeze dominated a town hall meeting in her beloved Antrim, long a Republican stronghold. She brought a photographer from *Newsweek* to the debate, and the freeze was discussed just after a motion from an Antrim restaurant to build an entrance ramp.

By a two-to-one margin, the citizens of Antrim joined forty other towns in New Hampshire and voted for a bilateral nuclear freeze with the Soviets. Somewhat oddly, they also passed a motion at the same meeting in favor of establishing an official partnership with the USS *Antrim*, a nuclear missile cruiser. Mary called it the finest political gathering she had ever attended. Pictures of the debate appeared in *Newsweek* and were featured in a textbook discussing democracy in action. (Mary was, of course, already something of a local legend in Antrim, and townspeople still discussed the time she had asked the town clerk to join her for a baked bean dinner with Walter Cronkite.)

Mary, in full cheerleading mode, urged on the activists: "The public, after a 35-year sleep on the question, has suddenly sprung awake and demanded a halt to the arms race."

The Reagan administration and its allies pushed back hard against the freeze movement. The head of the National College Republicans, Jack Abramoff, told Mary that while not everyone involved in the freeze movement was a Communist, all were guilty of "supporting the Kremlin line."

Mary repeatedly circled back to Reagan's personality and easy political touch in explaining his enduring popularity. A September 25, 1983, column summed up her take on Reagan:

> What he has going for him more than anything else, though, is his seemingly indestructible nice guy image. As president, Reagan has instituted policies that are hard on people, that are even mean. He shamelessly chooses guns over butter. While ever striving to permit the rich to keep more of their money, he has tried to make sure that the poor don't get too much. . . . At Reagan's press conferences, he routinely makes gaffes and misstatements. He says things that are inconsistent or just plain wrong. His staff stoically cleans up after him. He doesn't seem bothered. He knows what happens to compulsively well-informed chief executives—like Jimmy Carter and Lyndon Johnson. He may know, from a source hidden from the rest of us, that the public is more at ease with a non-perfectionist, no-sweat, average-guy kind of presidency.

As Mary scanned the Democratic horizon for an alternative to Reagan, one politician in particular caught her attention: Governor Mario Cuomo of New York. There was much for Mary to like. Cuomo was religious, outspokenly compassionate, and a skilled orator. Mary loved it when Cuomo declared in his inaugural speech that government could both "pay the bills and still help people in wheelchairs."

When Cuomo sat down with Mary and the *Post* editorial board, the governor was asked his thoughts on the likely 1984 Democratic presidential nominee, former vice president Walter Mondale. "My mother thinks

Mondale is polenta," Cuomo said. Most of those in the room did not understand the reference. Cuomo elaborated: "You know polenta, it's quite bland." Mary went further, describing polenta to the gathered editors and writers as the Italian version of cream of wheat—"terribly good for one, but not much fun." After Mary ran a column that prominently mentioned the remark, Governor Cuomo sent Mary a note insisting, unconvincingly, that polenta was an underappreciated gem.

One of Mary's favorite encounters took place at a January 1984 going-away party for David Gergen, one of President Reagan's key political advisers. Richard Darman, another Reagan aide, was chatting with Mary, along with Ed Rollins, the White House political director. Darman was preening, eager to demonstrate to Rollins that he could handle Mary.

"You have no influence, you know," Darman asserted to Mary. "I read you. You write well, and it's logical. Aesthetically, it might be the best column of all. I read it. But it has no effect whatever because you are so predictable." Darman insisted that with conservatives in control of Washington, Mary's columns amounted to little more than left-wing entertainment.

She was used to this criticism from the Reagan White House. Republican operatives insisted that she was too liberal, out of touch, and over the hill. Mary had known Darman for some time, and she did not dislike him. As she weighed how best to respond, ABC correspondent Ann Compton joined the conversation.

Compton offered Mary effusive thanks: "I had the lead story on the evening news last night because of you."

"How interesting," Mary cooed, glancing at Darman.

Compton cited a column that Mary had written earlier in the week breaking the news that President Reagan was about to make a conciliatory speech on the Soviet Union and was trying to reach an arms agreement with Moscow.

"How did you approach the story?" Mary asked.

"I just took it right from your column and put it on the air," Compton said.

Mary turned to Darman. "No influence?" She smiled.

"Only with eighty million people," Darman said good-humoredly, and blushed. Mary was fond of recounting the incident, calling it a "very satisfactory moment." She might have been out of step with the conservative revolution, but the Reagan era cemented her role as one of the most important liberal voices in the country. She was still able to break news despite being at odds with the party in power, because she worked her sources so hard.

The exchange underscores some of Mary's more obvious contradictions. She expounded at great length about her lack of influence but delighted in stories that spoke to her clout. She described herself as an outsider but hosted parties attended by Supreme Court justices, senators, and the most powerful reporters in the country. Mary depicted herself as well-intentioned and a bit hapless, but most politicians and fellow reporters quickly learned that she was incredibly shrewd and purposeful in the ways of Washington.

Gloria Borger recalled covering politics with Mary on the Hill. "Mary allowed us all to shout out our weedy questions about the day's headlines. 'Do you think the highway bill will pass?' or 'What's the final defense spending number in the budget?' Then she would catch us all up short by asking, 'Senator, don't you think so-and-so behaved badly today?' or 'Can you tell us why the White House is asking you to do this?' It was usually a tough question, but always posed politely. Mary had a way: sounding as sweet as your grandmother while being as tough as Tony Soprano."

Mary could sit patiently for hours, covering the most mundane of hearings, but dismiss someone she considered a windbag with a wave of her hand. Shortly after John Kerry first won his seat as a junior senator from Massachusetts, he attended a party at a local hotel with Mary. She grabbed Kerry by the arm, eager to introduce him to someone at a different function taking place in another part of the hotel.

As Mary pulled Kerry through the crowd, they were stopped by John Volpe, who had served in Nixon's cabinet. Volpe droned on, missing the obvious body language saying that Mary wished to be elsewhere. "Hey,"

Mary finally interjected, "you were the secretary of transportation: where are the elevators?" Mary and the senator were off without another word.

The September 1984 *Vanity Fair* profiled what it considered to be the most influential and powerful opinion writers in the country. Mary was the only woman of the bunch, her column being carried in 187 papers around the country, which put her fifth highest on the list, behind James Kilpatrick, George Will, David Broder, and William F. Buckley Jr.—all conservatives. Mary's ability to crack this group as a woman and a liberal spoke volumes about the quality of her work, and success also said a great deal about the importance, particularly for a woman, of not watering down opinion with "he said, she said" constructions. It is no coincidence that the most successful female columnists to follow Mary—Molly Ivins, Maureen Dowd, and Gail Collins—all relied on a formula somewhat similar to Mary's, with their knockout punches usually wrapped in humor.

The Reagan years saw conservative pundits rise to new levels of importance. President Reagan carefully cultivated relationships with writers like George Will and conservative talking head John McLaughlin. Former Nixon speechwriter Pat Buchanan, who had turned news commentator after Nixon's resignation, returned to the White House as Reagan's communications director. Coming from Hollywood, Ronald Reagan implicitly understood the power of pundits in helping to set the national narrative. This, in turn, spurred more and more political hands to quickly recast themselves as commentators once they left their posts—despite having no real grounding in journalism.

Mary's friend Bob Healy of the *Boston Globe* suggested that Mary had become even more influential after moving to the *Post*. "She has a facility for drawing people out like I've never seen in our business. She gives someone that little-old-lady, I-can't-quite-hear-you routine, and then she's got the guy's balls on the floor." Her columns felt more personal than they had at the *Star*, and the *Post* was a more prominent perch. Columnist James Kilpatrick, who almost never agreed with Mary on substance, praised Mary's style for keeping his "adrenals pumping" and saluted her ability to throw in "off-beat pieces about her birds or her garden or whatever the hell she wants to write about."

On background, other columnists offered a mix of praise and exaspera-tion. One observer, most likely Jack Germond, complimented Mary for making the rounds every day on her "skinny little legs" but added, "She'll drive you goddamn bananas because she's become such a queen." Germond was not alone in thinking that Mary could be a pain in the ass, but it is equally true that few wallflowers make it to the top rung of opinion writing.

It was widely recognized that any Democrat faced a tough campaign against President Reagan as he ran for reelection. With Walter Mondale the front-runner in a weak Democratic field, Mary feared the "inevitable encounter between him and Reagan will be as predictable as the contest between Christians and lions."

Mondale's fortunes appeared even rockier after an upset loss to Sena-tor Gary Hart in the New Hampshire primary. The former vice president simply did not generate much passion, and many Democrats hedged their support with qualifiers—"Mondale, I guess." Mary liked Mondale, but he was too much of a committee thinker for her taste, someone who would not say that the sky was blue without a focus group. Mondale ultimately prevailed in the primaries and, although it was an unconvincing perfor-mance, his selection of Congresswoman Geraldine Ferraro as his running mate electrified the convention, in San Francisco. "The excitement in that hall was indescribable," Mary wrote. "I remember an older black woman standing on her chair with tears pouring down her cheeks just outside of herself with joy and happiness and hope."

Not only was Ferraro the first woman on a major-party ticket, but the bold choice helped challenge the notion that Mondale was hopelessly cau-tious. Mary, sounding more like her male colleagues than she might have liked, approved of Ferraro, and compared her to "the president of a good department store." But she also had her concerns: "Her voice is flat, she talks too fast, and she swallows the ends of her best lines."

Mary was elated by Mario Cuomo's keynote speech at the convention, and she wished he, rather than Mondale, had been delivering the acceptance speech. "The Republicans have nobody like Cuomo, an intellectual with street smarts, a first-generation American who is crazy about words and ideas." Cuomo talked about his immigrant father's calloused hands and his personal belief that Democrats would rather have laws written by Saint Francis of Assisi than Charles Darwin. It was Mary's kind of speech.

As exuberant Democrats departed San Francisco, Mary talked with her aunt Kate to see what she thought of the Ferraro selection. Never particularly interested in politics, Kate was a lifelong Republican and wary of feminism. Kate had watched, and loved, most of the convention and was convinced that Ferraro could run the country. Mary pointed out that Mondale was the head of the ticket, not Ferraro. "Oh," Kate replied with some impatience, "he wouldn't dare do anything without consulting her."

It did not take long for the bloom to go off the rose as questions cropped up about the Ferraro family tax returns and the failure of Ferraro's husband, John Zaccaro, to disclose his wealth. Democrats remained seemingly incapable of vetting vice presidential candidates. "It may be the paramount irony of 1984," Mary observed, "that the first female candidate was judged not for herself but for her husband."

With Reagan enjoying a large and growing lead in the polls, the Republican convention, in Dallas, felt to Mary like a gaudy bout of triumphalism. Not even a classic Reagan gaffe just a week before the convention—when he joked into an open microphone about bombing Russia—could slow his momentum. America's conservative fringe had become its center. In private correspondence, Mary's frustration with Reagan bubbled over as she despaired of "that mean, dumb man."

Mary was torn from the campaign trail when Aunt Kate suffered a heart attack and died on September 2, 1984, at the age of ninety. Mary delivered Kate's eulogy, and it was heartfelt. Without Kate's willingness to look after Mary's mother, Mary would never have left Boston and probably would never have been a national columnist.

Taking a few days off the campaign trail, Mary sorted through Kate's old stacks of letters and belongings, reading the letters she had written to Kate after first moving to Washington: updates about finding an apartment, worrying about the cost of a couch, and her date with a young Jack Kennedy. She leafed through pictures of her father at the cabin in Antrim. Although the Beatty family was on hand to help Mary sift through Kate's belongings and offer their support, Mary had no husband or children to ease her grief. Holding the faded black-and-white photos in hand, Mary must have pondered the cost of her choices.

Back on the campaign trail, Democratic operatives had reverted to gloom, spending much of their time picking apart Mondale's flaws: his lack of charisma, poor television performances, and forced smile. "The good news for Democrats is that Walter F. Mondale does, after all, have an instinct for the jugular," Mary declared. "The bad news is that it seems to be for his own."

Mondale got a brief bounce after Reagan struggled in their initial debate, fueling speculation that the president was starting to lose his edge mentally. However, Reagan dazzled in the debate rematch. "He looked rosy and rested; he blithely strewed errors, indiscretions, and zany ideas and liberally passed the buck for foreign-policy mishaps and disasters," Mary observed. "But he was also dispensing quips and quotes and one-liners and crisp comebacks." Reagan brought down the house when he joked that he would not take advantage of Mondale's relative youth and inexperience.

Aunt Kate's death and Mondale's tepid performance made the 1984 campaign one of the least engaging of Mary's career. The results at the ballot box were as one-sided as they were predictable: Reagan swept forty-nine states and set a record with 525 electoral votes. It was a complete wipeout. Some 55 percent of women voted for Reagan despite Ferraro's presence on the Democratic ticket.

In 1985, Mary became particularly struck by the ascension of Soviet premier Mikhail Gorbachev and his very public embrace of reform. When Gorbachev announced that Moscow would suspend nuclear testing for five months, and even longer if joined by the United States, Mary said the Reagan administration had responded as if Gorbachev had engaged in "something between a social error and an act of terrorism." She took her fellow journalists to task for dismissing the offer as traditional Soviet propaganda, arguing that broader changes were afoot in Moscow.

Mary became part of the story in September 1985 when Gorbachev sat down for an interview with *Time* magazine. Gorbachev said that he was disappointed with the tone of many of Reagan's speeches but was still looking forward to an upcoming summit meeting. "We agreed to the Geneva meeting because we thought we could do a lot by trying to meet each other halfway," Gorbachev said. "So we see that there are some who want to generate a situation to persuade the U.S. and the American public that, as Mary McGrory put it, even if the only thing to come out of the summit was an agreement to exchange ballet troupes, then even so, people would be gleeful and happy."

Mary joined a congressional delegation headed to Moscow several weeks later. While Gorbachev was driving reform, most of the officials the delegation met with were not. When the Americans raised the issue of human rights, Soviet officials countered with well-rehearsed examples of American injustices and repression. During a discussion of Soviet dissident Andrei Sakharov, a Soviet official burst out, "What about in your own country? A female from Woodside, California, the mother of seven, imprisoned for eighteen years for damaging a Minuteman missile concrete? Nobody speaks about it." Mary had no idea what the man was talking about, but she passingly referred to the discussion in a subsequent column.

Not long after returning, she received a letter from Helen Woodson, the woman mentioned by the Soviets. "Yes, Mary, there is 'a female, the mother of seven' (actually it's 11, with seven still at home) who was imprisoned for 18 years, after being accused of touching (attempted disarmament) of a Minuteman missile. The event took place in Kansas City, not Woodside, California, but the 'stony-faced Soviet' can be forgiven that slight error."

Woodson said that Mary should visit her in prison if she wanted to learn more. Mary was intrigued. Woodson, along with two Roman Catholic priests, had tried to symbolically damage a nuclear missile site near Kansas City with a jackhammer in November 1984, and she was sentenced to eighteen years in prison.

Mary wrote to Woodson saying that she was deeply interested and that the press—including herself—was deserving of reproach for not knowing more about the case. Mary said that she would visit Alderson Federal Prison Camp if the warden would permit it.

Woodson developed cold feet and told Mary that she would discuss her antinuclear activities but not her personal life. (Woodson had one natural son, now grown; three autistic foster children who had been reassigned to other families because of her civil disobedience; and seven adopted, developmentally challenged children at home, including one with brain damage, being cared for by friends.)

Mary's response to Woodson was artfully manipulative. "I understand and sympathize with your desire to preserve your privacy. As you have learned, this is a difficult thing to do when you have committed a public act. My experience has been that it is the person rather than the issue which often moves people," Mary wrote. "But activist resistance is something they turn away from. All I am saying is that when they know a little about the human being who makes a sacrifice such as yours, they have to think about the commitment and then about the cause." She reiterated that she was willing to visit the prison to meet with Woodson but added, "If you think that something I would write from such a meeting would be intrusive, I would respect your wishes and forget about it."

Woodson agreed to the interview. Mary's column on Woodson reflected real admiration for her commitment to the antinuclear cause, but her unease with Woodson's decision to essentially abandon her foster children because of her activism was palpable. Mary might also have been contemplating her own decision never to have children in service of her career.

In the fall of 1985, Mary was given the Elijah Parish Lovejoy Award, one of the more important laurels in journalism. Ben Bradlee could not have been kinder when he wrote to the awards committee praising Mary: "She has an angel's eyes, all-seeing and compassionate. Hers has been a constant voice, unswayed by the moment. She has consistently shown the courage to stand against the wind."

While pleased with the honor, Mary was anxious because she had to deliver a speech. Mary being Mary, she polled her friends and associates about fitting potential topics. Her former editor from the *Star*, Jim Bellows, came up with the winning entry: "Where has all the passion gone? Why are newspapers, TV, etc. so dull? Why no campus demonstrations?"

Mary's speech, at Colby College, in Maine, was sharply critical of both journalists and the general public. She noted that the previous recipients of the award had all been elder media statesmen—what she called "forest people," in that they shared a commanding view of public life. "I am strictly trees," Mary demurred. "I have spent my working years examining the underbrush, the saplings, and the occasional tall pine. The long view, the big picture, are beyond me." Grand introspection, she insisted, was not a luxury in which she indulged.

That said, she went directly to her central concern:

> There has been a sharp fall-off in the kind of impassioned mail that came my way when such enormous events as the Vietnam War and Watergate were unfolding. I have begun to wonder what people care about, or if they care at all. . . . I don't know what it is, if the public is sublimely content—that could be that Ronald Reagan has restored a sense of public happiness to the republic; if people have decided the issues are too complex and have retreated into comfortable assumptions that the poor get what they deserve, that industrial pollution is inevitable, [and] that politicians are always corrupt. . . . I tell you all this not as a way of taking the discussion from the shortcomings of the press. We can always do it better. Chaucer was right when he lamented "the lyfe so shorte, the crafte so long to lerne." Maybe it's our fault. Maybe we spent so many years telling people what officials were doing wrong that they hated to see us coming.

Congressman Tip O'Neill's last year in office was 1986, a sad chang-ing of the guard for Mary. O'Neill was rumpled and sounded like a Bos-ton ward politician. He liked whiskey and jousting with reporters. He took constituent services seriously. He was not a modern man, and Mary loved him for it.

Mary was misty-eyed at O'Neill's farewell, but when he decided to do several American Express commercials after he retired, Mary described her horror upon seeing O'Neill pop out of a suitcase in an ad, like "some elderly, white-thatched cobra."

"Tip O'Neill got very, very mad at me, not-speaking mad, because I criticized him for doing that American Express ad," Mary recalled. When the two met at a party, O'Neill refused to even acknowledge her—he "just cut me dead," observed Mary.

But after more time passed, the two met at a dinner. O'Neill came up behind Mary and put his arm around her waist. "Hello, darling."

Mary looked up in surprise at the bearlike former Speaker. "I thought you were mad at me?"

"I was mad," O'Neill said in his soothing baritone, "but now I'm not mad anymore."

President Reagan's grip on events became an increasingly pressing is-sue with the emergence of the Iran-contra scandal. By August 1985, Mary and others had flagged the role of Marine Lieutenant Colonel Oliver L. North in orchestrating aid to the Nicaraguan contras from the White House, despite legislation banning such assistance. When Mary pointed out that North was funneling private funds to the contras, Reagan vaguely and falsely asserted that no laws had been broken. Other than a masterful handling of the space shuttle *Challenger* disaster in January 1986—and his remembrance of its crew, who had "slipped the surly bonds of earth to touch the face of God"—Reagan was increasingly off-kilter, what would later be revealed as the onset of Alzheimer's Disease. His public appear-ances, always a strength, were becoming liabilities.

When a plane full of weapons for the contras was shot down, Mary argued, in October 1986, that the "crooked trail" led straight to the National Security Council. A new and sensational angle to the scandal soon emerged: the White House had provided weapons to Iran in exchange for the release of American hostages held in Lebanon—and then used the proceeds from the arms sales to finance the contras. It was Rube Goldberg diplomacy of the highest order. "Yes, Ronald Reagan, at one remove, shook hands with the Devil," Mary penned.

After the news broke that Oliver North had directly engineered both the arms sales and the diversion of profits to the contras, it looked for a time as though the scandal might bring down the president. Mary pounced: "It is the wedding of policies that were made for each other: two slimy, misbegotten ventures that Reagan carried on in contempt of the law and the Congress." Reagan was forced to fire North and National Security Adviser John Poindexter.

The president reluctantly agreed to the appointment of an independent counsel, and Oliver North took the Fifth Amendment forty times in an initial appearance before the Senate Intelligence Committee.

Mary had high hopes for the congressional Iran-contra hearings. It was a good cast of characters, skullduggery had taken place at the highest levels of government, and the scandal pitted Congress against the executive branch. But covering the hearings was difficult, since a foot operation had left Mary tottering across the unforgiving marble floors of Congress on crutches. David Corn observed, "She had trouble walking, but she managed to maneuver herself through narrow rows and find a place at the front of the press table. When the hearing was over, she hobbled up to the dais to ask senators why their questions had not been more penetrating."

One of Mary's fellow reporters noticed that all of the best seats in the press section were reserved with large placards noting names of papers, like WASHINGTON POST and NEW YORK TIMES. Only one seat was different; it bore a placard that simply read, MARY MCGRORY.

In her many years covering hearings, Mary had never seen a single witness shift events as profoundly as Oliver North did during his star turn as a patriotic "vulnerable scamp" before the committee. North's testimony transformed him from the shadowy figure in the center of a terrible scandal to someone many viewed as a national hero. Mary was not buying what the colonel was selling, but she knew North was winning the public relations battle in a rout. North proudly displayed stacks of telegrams from admirers all around the country. Mary described the Senate Caucus Room as "a smoking ruin" as members were reduced to giving inane speeches defending their own patriotism.

President Reagan had dodged the most serious threat to his presidency, but it was a story that Mary would later return to with devastating effect.

Mary's longtime assistant and close friend Liz Acosta suffered a stroke in 1987. Mary hired a replacement only reluctantly, bringing Tina Toll onto the staff when it became clear that Acosta could not return to work. It was a job that took some getting used to. One minute Tina was expected to get the Senate majority leader on the phone, the next she was calling nuns to ensure that they would be at Sunday dinner.

With the Reagan era petering to a conclusion, all eyes turned to the 1988 presidential contest. Mary yearned for a Mario Cuomo candidacy, but after having watched him perform for several years, her opinion was less adulatory: "His recent campaign for re-election fortified some doubts about his ability to stand the gaff of a national race. He takes things personally, lets nothing go by, and does not hesitate to engage in noisy public quarrels with archbishops and reporters who say or do things that are displeasing to him." Cuomo stated publicly that he was not inclined to run but also suggested that he might be persuaded otherwise.

One of the other likely Democratic contenders, Michael Dukakis, hailed from Massachusetts. Dukakis had a solid reputation as a skilled technocrat in the Bay State, but Mary thought he lacked both charisma and a sense of humor to a disqualifying degree.

As the primaries heated up, Democrats suffered a series of embarrassments. Senator Joe Biden's campaign collapsed under plagiarism charges. Senator Gary Hart flamed out after being caught red-handed in an extramarital affair. As Mary complained, "Dumbness has been the element that binds the Democratic disasters together."

On the Republican side, Vice President George Bush, Senator Bob Dole, and televangelist Pat Robertson all hoped to succeed Reagan, and Mary argued that they were "somehow more authentic human beings, more grown up than their Democratic counterparts, and with much stronger conviction."

However, Mary was incensed that Bush had avoided any culpability for the Iran-contra mess. While campaigning in Iowa in January 1988, Bush had challenged reporters to collectively submit their questions about Iran-contra so that he could respond to them. Reporters largely balked, but Mary accepted the challenge in her own way, dedicating an entire column to questions she hoped Bush would answer.

In fairly short order, the vice president's office hand-delivered a four-page letter to Mary answering all seventeen questions she had posed in her column, and Mary duly printed the responses in her follow-up.

Bush denied being at a key National Security Council meeting when serious objections to the plan were raised and insisted that he had not asked Secretary of State George Shultz or Secretary of Defense Caspar Weinberger, both of whom were against the arms-for-hostages plan, their views. He said that he did not recall anyone expressing major problems with the deal. George Bush, the consummate insider, argued that he was out of the loop. A number of the vice president's claims were untrue, but it would take time for those chickens to come home to roost, and for the time being no one had concrete evidence to the contrary.

After finishing third in the Iowa caucus, behind both Dole and Robertson, Bush limped into New Hampshire. The vice president quickly retooled his image. Although Mary found Bush's effort to portray himself as a "truck-driving, burger-chomping, back-slapping New Englander" implausible, it was enough for him to carry the Granite State. Mary was less than enchanted with the choices on the Democratic side. Dukakis's earnestness and rectitude reminded her of Jimmy Carter—no compliment—and she quoted party insiders as saying the governor had "a tin ear and a leaden touch."

Privately, she pined for Cuomo, telling friends that she viewed him as a man among boys, a rare public figure willing to take a moral stand on hard issues. It was this kind of flattery that led many of Mary's critics, and no small number of her friends, to suggest that throughout her career Mary fell in love with charismatic politicians—Adlai Stevenson, Jack and Bobby Kennedy, Gene McCarthy, Mario Cuomo—and promoted them overenthusiastically.

But as all of those politicians could attest, Mary still had a sharp pen even with her favorite sons. In April 1988, she wrote a column asking of Cuomo, "Did he really not want to be president, or did he just not want to go through the indignities of the primaries?" Cuomo wrote to Mary after the column ran: "I didn't miss the bus: I wasn't going anywhere." The governor was surprisingly thin-skinned for a New York politician. He wanted to charm Mary, but he had a hard time resisting the urge to argue with reporters over every line of their stories.

With Bush and Dukakis likely to face off in the general election, Bush wasted little time in launching blistering negative attacks on Dukakis, leading Mary to lament that "the fall campaign could bring us a new low in mindlessness." Dukakis was oblivious to his peril, assuring reporters that voters were "smarter than that."

Dukakis had a good convention and appeared to emerge in a strong position. His choice of the relatively conservative Senator Lloyd Bentsen of Texas as his running mate looked like the sort of crass electoral politics that actually helps win elections. Dukakis briefly managed to shed his image as a pedestrian technocrat at the convention, and his new-found self-confidence helped push him out to a seventeen-point lead in the presidential polls. The race looked like it was his to lose.

Mary tartly observed that many of the attendees at the Republican convention, in New Orleans, looked like fish out of water in such colorful surroundings, "a little inclined to go out and look for the U.S. Embassy." Bush misstepped early with his selection of Indiana senator Dan Quayle as his vice presidential nominee. Republicans appreciated Quayle's hard-line stance on foreign policy and economics, but, as Mary observed, "It's a little hard to see what J. Danforth Quayle III, blond, rich and 41, does for the Republican ticket." One delegate complained to Mary that Quayle looked more like a mascot than a vice president.

But Bush delivered a strong acceptance speech at the convention, speaking of a "kinder, gentler nation." It was George Bush as his own man, and Bush's strong convention performance, along with a renewed assault of negative advertising, put Dukakis in a tailspin. "The campaign is unfolding before their eyes like some ghastly fairy tale for cynics," Mary wrote of the Dukakis team. Making matters worse, Dukakis had reverted to his plodding preconvention self on the stump.

One of the highlights of the campaign for Mary came when Senator Bentsen deconstructed Dan Quayle in the vice presidential debate. When Quayle likened his congressional experience to that of Jack Kennedy, Bentsen was ready. "Senator," Bentsen said, "I knew Jack Kennedy. I served with him. He was my friend. Senator, you are no Jack Kennedy." After a moment of stunned silence, the hall erupted in both applause and catcalls. A flushed Quayle tried to recover from the blow, but Bentsen noted later, in a delicious bit of understatement, "I did not think the comparison was well taken."

But vice presidential debates don't determine elections, and Dukakis fared very poorly in the second presidential debate, in Los Angeles. The very first question from moderator Bernard Shaw was a macabre hypothetical: "If Kitty Dukakis were raped and murdered," Shaw asked, would Governor Dukakis change his opinion on the death penalty? Dukakis should have denounced the question. Instead he gave a technocrat's answer about the ineffectiveness of the death penalty. Mary pinpointed his emotionless answer as the exact moment when he lost the election.

George Bush was no longer in Reagan's shadow, and he coasted to an easy electoral win. Mary reflected on the race: "Bush's campaign was cheap and divisive, a cynical exercise in know-nothingism and intolerance." Yet Mary also understood that citizens would not vote for a candidate unwilling to defend himself.

As Christmas 1988 approached, Mary interviewed Dukakis under the gold dome of the Massachusetts State House. With the presidency no longer in the balance, Mary wrote of Dukakis in kinder terms: "The campaign did not change him. He is still a man who is crazy about public service and thinks that politics is about government programs and believes, although perhaps a little less surely, that everyone is as rational as he is."

Mary asked Dukakis why his race had been unsuccessful. He answered with a succinctness and candor that would have served him well in the preceding months. "I lost," Dukakis admitted, "because I ran a lousy campaign."

CHAPTER TEN

Gentleman George

Early in President George H. W. Bush's first term, Mary once again locked horns with the Gridiron Club. Gridiron president Larry O'Rourke announced to members that the executive board had decided to invite all of the living former presidents, including Richard Nixon, to the spring dinner. Mary, who never sang or danced at the festivities and usually had little to say at the few organizing meetings she attended, objected.

"I felt I had standing in this issue because I was on Nixon's enemies list," Mary said. She asked O'Rourke, in tones dripping with contempt, why Nixon was invited. O'Rourke noted that the board had discussed the issue, including Nixon's use of wiretaps and IRS audits against the press, but still wanted him there.

Mary, along with journalists Cheryl Arvidson and Joan McKinney, forwarded a motion to disinvite Nixon. The men in the room objected, insisting that since Ronald Reagan wanted to attend, they needed to be fair and invite all of the former presidents. Mary pointed out that Nixon had waged an all-out assault on both the media and the Constitution while in office. "But he has received the blessing of celebrity," she complained. "If you are famous, you are forgiven."

Mary pushed the debate into the public eye with a January 1989 column that exposed the behind-the-scenes debate at the Gridiron, calling it another reminder that many reporters "think they are part of the government establishment and feel called upon to protect and defend anyone who reaches high office no matter what." Reporters were publicly split about Nixon's potential attendance.

O'Rourke, who was furious with Mary for exposing the controversial decision, invited Nixon as a personal guest, but Nixon declined.

"We started bringing women into the Gridiron Club, and she was one of the first ones elected," Jack Germond observed. "But she would not participate, and she would not go to the meetings—let alone take part in the program." Eventually the board passed a rule that if members did not attend at least three meetings each year, they would not receive a ticket to the dinner. It was quickly dubbed the McGrory Rule.

Mary liked President Bush better than she liked candidate Bush, saying, "After eight years of a reclusive, programmed and scripted presidency, he seems wonderfully spontaneous." She also noted with relief that, unlike Reagan, Bush did not rely on index cards when he met with congressional leaders.

In February 1989, Mary decided to give up smoking for Lent. As someone who had smoked a pack a day for years, it was not easy. Mary succeeded in quitting, although her friends and colleagues walked on eggshells, given her irritability. "I feel fine, thank you, except that I gained 22 pounds," Mary wrote to a friend. "Everyone told me I was going to feel marvelous. They lied."

Mary closely chronicled the rise of an ambitious Republican House member, Newt Gingrich of Georgia, during this period. Gingrich approached politics as war, and his hyperbolic style was crudely effective.

Gingrich scored his most important early victory in 1989 by leading the charge to bring down Democratic Speaker of the House Jim Wright when Wright became embroiled in a petty scandal related to bulk purchases of his autobiography. Wright had brought the scandal upon himself, but Gingrich's tactics ushered in an era that viewed bipartisanship as treachery. The old habit of Democrats and Republicans disagreeing during the day, drinking together at night, and ultimately getting deals done was over. It was a new age of party-driven implacability.

"In the little private dining room where members of both parties used to eat cafeteria-style, sitting wherever there was room, there is now a Democratic table and a Republican table and not much friendly banter between them," Mary observed. Democrats continued to make Gingrich's work easy, as several congressmen faced ethics charges resulting from sex scandals. The Democratic-run House felt broken.

While Congress was mired in pettiness and muck, global events moved with a far grander sweep. In July 1989, Mary traveled with President Bush across Poland, Hungary, and Czechoslovakia as pro-democracy protests bubbled up all across the Eastern Bloc. Bush received a rapturous welcome.

The momentous change that was sweeping Europe was greeted with suspicion by many in Washington, and Bush administration officials scoffed at the audacity of Poland's Lech Walesa when he asked for $10 billion in assistance over three years. But as Mary pointed out, the administration had no qualms about requesting $10 billion a year for construction of the B-2 bomber. "Poland is a much better investment," she insisted.

Many of the pundits in Washington refused to believe that change in the Communist world was genuine. On November 9, 1989, conservative columnist George Will predicted that "the Wall will stay." The Berlin Wall fell later that day.

Mary was not impressed with Bush's initial reaction: "Why did the leader of the western world look as though he had lost his last friend the day they brought him the news of the fall of the Berlin Wall?" Mary's criticism stung. When President Bush and Ben Bradlee had lunch a short time later, Bush plaintively inquired, "How can I get through to Mary McGrory?" Bradlee suggested that not much could be done. When he related the conversation to Mary, she was pleased. "So they do read me. That is all I want."

Whatever his hesitancy meant, President Bush benefited politically from the enormous tide of change, and he handled his international role well after the early uncertainty. His approval rating moved above the 80 percent mark.

The late 1980s and early '90s were particularly hard times at Mary's beloved orphanage. The crack cocaine epidemic, coupled with the rise of HIV/AIDS, decimated American inner cities, and few more so than Washington. More and more children fled deeply dysfunctional home lives, sparking a vituperative national debate about how best to protect them. Most courts still preferred to return children to their natural parents—no matter how derelict those parents might have been. Mary and the sisters at St. Ann's fumed about arbitrary court decisions that sent children back into dangerous environments where further abuse seemed inevitable.

Mary continued to volunteer at St. Ann's during the 1980s and '90s. Tom Noyes, the longtime Santa for the Christmas parties, suffered a heart attack and relinquished his role. Even Mary was willing to accept, albeit reluctantly, a quadruple bypass as a legitimate alibi. Mary's fellow columnist Mark Shields stepped in as his able successor. Mary had also helped engineer a visit from Nancy Reagan to St. Ann's when she was first lady, further proof that politics stopped at the orphanage door for Mary.

The focus of much of her ire was the Family Reunification Act, a federal proposal to expedite the return of children caught up in the social welfare system to their birth families, which made the continued existence of institutions like St. Ann's difficult. Sister Josephine Murphy spoke with Mary about the act. "Mary, you need to take a stand, and you have to write an article," she urged. "If you don't, nobody is going to do anything about it."

Mary said that she needed to ask some questions on the Hill and see if it made sense.

"But, Mary, you know you love kids. It is the only way to go." The two went back and forth. A short time later, Mary called Josephine back: "I am going to do it."

Mary knew that taking on the idea of family reunification was controversial. Almost everyone instinctively believes that children should be reunited with their families as quickly as possible. Reality was more complex. With drugs, AIDS, and the city's foster care program in disarray, it was clear that putting a child's interest first sometimes meant *not* speeding them back into home life. "The Family Reunification Act," argued Mary in her column, "is predicated on the gooey notion that every woman who gives birth is by definition a mother."

Mary described the travails of one boy at St. Ann's as he was buffeted by the local court system:

When we went swimming in the summer, the boy avoided the water. He made a wide circle around the pool. One of the child-care workers said he didn't like water. Someone remembered that he had come to St. Ann's at the age of 18 months, with two-thirds of his body burned. The judge sent him home with his mother. She said she had forgotten the hot water was running. Standing beside the pool, the boy gradually decided to risk it and was soon splashing and shrieking with the rest of the children. Later, there had been an episode involving a haircut undertaken with a razor. The judge sent him back home again, with a fatherly lecture to his mother about going to the barber next time.

Mary argued that places like St. Ann's were a reasonable alternative until parents could get their act together or a foster family could be found. She called Sister Josephine shortly after her column ran. There was no preamble. "Sister Josephine, I want to tell you one thing. In all my years of writing for newspapers, I have never gotten as much hate mail as I have for that article on the Family Reunification Act."

"That's good," Josephine argued. "That means people are reading it."

The issue of parents' rights versus those of their children continued to roil Washington for much of the 1990s after a series of spectacular abuses and shocking judicial decisions, including the return of two children to a mother who had suffocated her six-week-old, stuffed the body in a dumpster, and then attended a barbecue with her boyfriend.

Mary's time at St. Ann's pushed her to get personally involved in a number of cases involving kids and the D.C. courts, including intervening to get one young boy whom she had helped for years released from Washington's St. Elizabeths psychiatric facility.

The boy's mother so resented Mary's continuing involvement that she got a court order to prevent Mary from visiting the boy at school and the boy from going on St. Ann's outings. A second judge lifted the ban after Mary wrote to the court explaining her activities. Mary's work with St. Ann's was not an abstraction. It was the grindingly hard work of trying to make a difference in an indifferent system with families teetering on the edge. It meant working with families who sometimes viewed her efforts to move a child to foster care or an orphanage as hostile, destructive, or racist. "She was probably these kids' greatest defender," Sister Josephine maintained. "Who but Mary could have done the things that Mary got done?"

Some of the more problematic elements of the Family Reunification Act were indeed altered over time, and there was a growing recognition in both law and practice that sending children back into a clearly abusive environment was inhumane.

The positive national mood spurred by the fall of the Berlin Wall took a sharp negative turn with Iraq's invasion of Kuwait in August 1990. Mary was no hawk, but she acknowledged that Iraqi president Saddam Hussein had crossed a line that America could not tolerate, writing, "Bombs, blockades, whatever—Saddam has asked for it."

Bush's resolute performance in planning a response to the invasion of Kuwait highlighted an important dichotomy for Mary. "It is increasingly plain that in George Bush, the American people got two presidents for the price of one," she wrote. "Each of the chief executives comes equipped with a totally different personality, so that it is easy to tell them apart. The foreign policy president is cool, measured, tough, coping. The domestic policy man is strident, petulant, self-pitying."

Everything seemed to break right for President Bush as the war commenced, although Mary was uneasy with the conflict's slick packaging. "So far, President Bush has given the country the war it said it wanted in the polls: a war almost free of casualties, or at least many that we can see. Moreover, Operation Desert Storm is a telegenic combination of air show and arms bazaar, with marvelous weapons for every contingency being uncovered precisely when needed." Small wonder, then, that potential Democratic presidential contenders stayed on the sidelines. Bush was so popular that a challenge seemed foolhardy. As Bush delivered his State of the Union address in January 1991, Mary remarked that Congress had been reduced to the status of an American Legion post, "required only to shout and cheer, and leap to its feet at every mention of our warriors."

Some 86 percent of the public approved of Bush and his handling of the war. In less than a month and a half, coalition forces defeated Iraq's forces and Saddam Hussein ordered a hasty retreat from Kuwait, but Mary expressed growing queasiness with the way the administration airbrushed the conflict.

Mary's prickly attitude toward the Gulf War and President Bush sparked considerable backlash from readers. "My patriotism is often questioned by readers," Mary explained. "I come down to saying that I think it is possible to love my country without loving its wars. That's pretty defensive, but if you saw my mail, you would know why."

President Bush had some fun with Mary's fierce position on the war. At the March 1991 White House Correspondents' Dinner, an annual dinner much like the Gridiron event, spirits were high in the wake of the Gulf War triumph. General Colin Powell was mobbed by reporters and well-wishers. The black-tie-and-gown crowd took in a lighthearted speech by President Bush.

"Bill Dickinson of the Armed Services Committee was there," said President Bush of the Gulf War, "and he reminded us of some events that all of you are familiar with, how several hundred Iraqis surrendered to a helicopter. We remember that one, and I think Tom briefed on it. Several more surrendered—and this is a true story—to a drone that was going by. And get this one: others surrendered to an Italian photographer—I can't imagine surrendering to the press. To Mary McGrory, I say, 'Never! Come and get me. I'll never surrender!'" The crowd erupted in laughter and applause, Mary included.

Len Downie became the *Post*'s chief editor in 1991, and Mary was increasingly at odds with the paper's management. Downie was more cautious than Bradlee and never had easy relations with female staffers. Downie objected to Mary's column appearing on the news pages instead of with the op-ed columns, and Mary was filled with sour memories of her tussles with Murray Gart at the *Star* on the same subject. "I didn't have any great trouble getting him to understand that Mary was a special case," explained Don Graham about the paper's ultimate decision not to move the column. "She wound up on the front page of Outlook on Sunday and the inside pages the other days. She was treated as a special case, and should have been." Mary won the battle, but she and Downie engaged in a reluctant détente.

Mary treated most editors with a "good help is hard to get" attitude. Bill Hamilton, one of her editors at the *Post*, was fond of saying that when Mary introduced him as her editor, "it was clear who was working for whom." Mary liked Hamilton and Ken Ikenberry, but she had increasingly scratchy relations with her other editors at the *Post*, who she thought were picky and prone to micromanagement, leaving her to tell one in exasperation, "Well, you know, *my* name's on it."

Her relationship with her peers and editors became more challenging as she got older. "She became more imperious, more regal, I think, as the Mary McGrory persona took hold," said her former colleague Haynes Johnson. Don Graham, the publisher of the *Post*, would send Mary nice handwritten notes when he particularly enjoyed a column. "We became sort of partisans of each other," said Graham. "She would use me to score points against the editor."

Mary's assistant, Tina Toll, was blunter about the level of respect Mary was accorded by the paper's management and staff. "Everybody deferred to Mary McGrory; it was a little bit of a fear," said Toll. "They would stand there like puppy dogs."

After Bush's wartime triumphs, the nomination of Judge Clarence Thomas to the U.S. Supreme Court brought domestic issues back to the forefront in the fall of 1991. By nominating an extremely conservative African American nominee with a rags-to-riches backstory and a short paper trail, President Bush knew he was putting Democrats in a bind.

Mary wanted to ensure that she had a good seat for the hearings and was, unsurprisingly, irritated when one of the *Post*'s editors told her that he did not have an extra pass for her to attend. Yet when the editor turned on his television to watch the hearings, he saw Mary being escorted to her front-row seat by the Judiciary Committee chairman, Senator Joe Biden.

The already high-profile Thomas hearings turned into a national sensation when Anita Hill, a former colleague of the judge, accused him of sexual harassment. She was hastily scheduled to speak before the committee and a riveted national audience. Mary remembered the scene:

> I went to the Senate Caucus Room, where so many years before, I had seen Joseph R. McCarthy—who was to be much invoked again—for the first time. In those days the press tables were drawn right up beside the witnesses, and we could see the whites of their eyes and almost their tonsils. Through the years, we of what is called redundantly the "writing press" have been gradually moved back so that we only see the backs of their heads. It was all the way it had been when someone is about to lose or gain a reputation, and some tale of betrayal, chicanery, larceny or dirty pool was about to be revealed.

For Mary, conservative in all things sexual, Hill's allegations were as damning as they were shocking. "It was as if a river of raw sewage had suddenly been unleashed in the marble chamber." Mary thought Hill could not have been more credible: "Hill defended herself with poise and dignity. She walked proudly through the mire."

In the middle of the hearings, Mary was scheduled to fly to Maine to spend the weekend with Newby Noyes to mark the tenth anniversary of the closing of the *Washington Star*. The clashing schedule was ironic given that it was Newby who had dispatched Mary to cover the Army-McCarthy hearings forty years before.

Mary decided that she would still leave. Surely President Bush would withdraw Thomas's name as a result of Hill's devastating testimony. Mary worked and reworked her Sunday column on the flight to Maine. Newby greeted Mary at the Bangor airport, saying, "I didn't think you'd come." If it had been anyone other than Newby, Mary probably wouldn't have. Newby, his wife, Beppie, and Mary took a long walk by Frenchman's Bay, reveling in the late-autumn colors and crisp air. As they stopped at a store, Mary noticed that virtually every car in the parking lot was listening to the hearings.

When the White House decided to forge ahead with Thomas's nomination, Mary found herself watching his testimony on television. Thomas was aggressive, declaring that God, not the Senate, was his judge. Mary and Newby agreed that the swipe would play well with a public that never thought much of Congress. Thomas claimed that Hill was lying and that the Senate was conducting "a high-tech lynching." It was clear that Democrats had little stomach for the fight, although the evidence suggested that Thomas had indeed harassed a number of women and not just Hill.

Mary, panicked that the hearings would drag on for days, booked an emergency flight back to Washington. She need not have bothered. Thomas had won the showdown. Mary graded the Democrats dismally: "a collection of damaged souls and swollen egos, who have found no cause larger than their next election." She argued that it was also a powerful demonstration of why Republicans won elections: "The old CIA motto, 'whatever is necessary,' guides them. The Republican members of the Judiciary Committee got their marching orders and their script from the White House for the ferocious counterattack.... The Democrats never even caucused."

Mary singled out Ted Kennedy for his ineffectiveness. She pointed out that his long history of women problems—drunken carousing, the long shadow of Chappaquiddick, and the events of the previous spring, when Kennedy had been out drinking with a nephew who would later be charged with rape—all combined to silence the man best suited to challenge Thomas. Mary's grim postmortem for the Massachusetts senator: "Kennedy, gravely wounded in the dirty war, cannot escape the limits of his usefulness."

The 1992 presidential campaign got off to an unusually late start, and Mary teased New York governor Mario Cuomo for his extended anguish about whether to mount a bid: "Nobody knows what Cuomo is waiting for as he issues daily bulletins from somewhere deep inside his psyche. In his latest soliloquy, divertingly recounted in the *New York Times* by Maureen Dowd, he blames God for his dilemma. The Almighty has not obliged him with a shaft of lightning such as was visited on Saul of Tarsus on the road to Damascus."

After reading the column, Maureen Dowd dropped Mary a note, saying that she had come up in her conversation with Cuomo. "I'm not discussing anything I said to Mary," insisted Cuomo, "because I'm not myself when I'm with McGrory. She's crazy. She can get anything she wants from me. She is magnificent. Not only is she smart, gracious, nice. She's also human. She's got enough of the devil in her, you know, so that you know she's real and beautiful. If she didn't have a little bit of the Irish in her, and a little bit of Boston and a little bit of the old stories, she'd be too perfect."

Mary still tried to goad Cuomo into running. Her next column was in verse, again following a biblical theme: "How odd of God, says Mario C. Not doing for me the same as he did for Saul of T." Minutes after reading Mary's column, Cuomo called and left a voice-mail message on Mary's answering machine. "How odd of Mary to do this to me, to mock my tormented musings. My frantic, fumbling efforts first to forge political fusings. Doesn't she know I need to think, to ponder and to ruminate? Doesn't she know that otherwise I will not be able persuasively to fulminate?" For Mary, the literate sparring must have felt like shades of her old relationship with Adlai Stevenson or Gene McCarthy.

"I am convinced that Mario Cuomo will run," Mary wrote to a friend in November 1991. "It better be soon, or somebody will lynch him."

Just before Christmas, Cuomo announced that he would not run, and Mary called it "coal in the Christmas stocking of the Democratic Party." Mary finally had hit her breaking point, telling a friend in Antrim, "I'm sick and tired of Mario Cuomo and his peekaboo."

The great irony of the 1992 race was that while many Democrats stayed away from the race because of Bush's enormous popularity, there were growing signs of his weakness as the campaign began. Most ominously for Bush, the economy was dipping just as firebrand television commentator Pat Buchanan geared up for a Republican primary challenge against him.

Mary painted a bleak picture as President Bush courted Granite State voters: "New Hampshire, site of the first presidential primary, is afflicted with massive unemployment, foreclosures, bank failures, and plant closings, and George Bush was wary when he took its hand." She spoke with many Republicans who planned to vote for Buchanan simply to send a message about the economy, and it seemed safe to do so, since the Democratic field looked weak. Buchanan appealed to voters as if he were leading an angry mob toward Frankenstein's castle.

On the Democratic side, Mary devoted a good amount of coverage to the rising Democratic contender Bill Clinton. She nicely captured the Arkansas governor, "a tall, square-shouldered, pumpkin-faced extrovert, bowls people over with his charm. Color him effervescent. . . . With little children, with old ladies, he is magic." While Clinton exuded southern charm, he was free of Jimmy Carter's rectitude. Carter told New Hampshire voters he loved them; Clinton told them they deserved to be the first presidential primary state because they were so demanding.

In mid-January, Mary noted that reports of womanizing could prove an Achilles' heel for Clinton in New Hampshire, saying that his rivals knew "that the hint of scandal may be the only way of stopping the radiant, ruddy stranger who seems to have captured New Hampshire's stony heart." When Bill and Hillary Clinton went on *60 Minutes* to fend off charges of his philandering, they saved the campaign. Ever prudish, Mary found the spectacle of politicians and their wives talking so publicly about the pain of infidelity undignified. "I was extremely critical of Governor Clinton's treatment of his wife," Mary wrote to a friend. "I thought it so unattractive that he would never be nominated." Yet Mary was quick to learn that Clinton had what she called "truly awesome recuperative powers."

But Mary kept her harshest judgments of Clinton out of print, recognizing that some of her complaints sounded old-fashioned, and her language describing Clinton was more playful than condemnatory: "He is like Tom Jones, the hero of a picaresque 18th-century novel that was made into a riotous movie—a big, good-looking, good-hearted, lusty, scrape-prone lad."

Even at seventy-three, Mary traveled gamely across New Hampshire as if she were herself a candidate. In mid-February, with the temperature eight degrees above zero, she trudged with a campaign volunteer through the streets of Ward 7 in Manchester, convinced it was still the best way to read the tea leaves of the electorate.

Mary enjoyed close relationships with a number of Clinton's key advisers, particularly George Stephanopoulos, whom she had gotten to know when he was working as an aide to Congressman Dick Gephardt. "One of my boss's constituents was a young man named Steven McKenna, who was born deformed by thalidomide that had been given to his mom by a government doctor," explained Stephanopoulos. "The Justice Department was stopping him from suing for damages. Exactly the kind of case Mary adopted as her own. She wrote the column, Steve got his day in court. I made a friend."

Stephanopoulos helped Mary in her garden, volunteered with the kids from St. Ann's, and tended bar at Mary's parties. In the run-up to the campaign, Mary and several other friends tried to dissuade Stephanopoulos from going to work for Clinton, insisting he was a long shot. Stephanopoulos sensibly ignored the collective wisdom and signed on as Clinton's communications director.

When Stephanopoulos's career skyrocketed and he became one of President Clinton's closest advisers at the age of thirty-four, *Washington Post* reporter Al Kamen and his wife saw him on television one evening. His wife turned to him and asked, "Isn't that the guy who used to serve us at Mary's?"

The campaign was a stern test of friendship for Stephanopoulos and Mary. Clinton exploded at Stephanopoulos when he read critical columns from Mary. Mary would pester Stephanopoulos when he was slow to respond to her inquiries. "Dear George," she wrote him at one point. "Ever since I began writing about the Clintons, you have stopped returning my calls. What kind of a message is that?"

Although Bill Clinton finished second to Paul Tsongas in the New Hampshire primary, he sold his performance as that of the "comeback kid." On the Republican side, President Bush turned back the effort by Buchanan, but voters were uneasy.

This restlessness found a standard-bearer with the entry of Texas billionaire Ross Perot into the presidential race as an independent. The plainspoken Texan offered blunt assessments of the ills of government in terms that were colorful and easy to understand. The initial public response was electric.

In early May 1992, Mary had a lengthy interview with Perot, and she liked him. He funded programs for inner-city schoolkids out of his own pocket and was animated in a way that reminded her of Joe Allbritton. Mary loved the fact that Perot was bringing new people into the political process and turning out volunteers in droves. It was significant praise that she called his campaign the most "exhilarating adventure" in American politics since Gene McCarthy's New Hampshire insurgency. But Mary also spotted storm clouds on the horizon: "It is hard to see him keeping cool during a presidential debate when a rival charges him with being all wet." For a period before the conventions, Ross Perot led in the polls in a three-way contest with Clinton and Bush.

Len Downie noted that it was Mary who had asked Hillary Clinton the now famous question about the balance between being a professional woman and a mother. Clinton's response to Mary was, "I suppose I could have stayed home and baked cookies and had teas, but what I decided to do was to fulfill my profession, which I entered before my husband was in public life." Clinton's answer quickly became campaign fodder, with critics saying that she was a radical feminist demeaning stay-at-home moms. The fact that Clinton's response came to a question from Mary, a woman who had never baked cookies or raised a child, was no small irony.

Clinton announced the selection of Tennessee senator Al Gore as his running mate in advance of the convention in New York. Gore was more conservative than Mary would have liked, but she knew that Gore's service in Vietnam, environmental credentials, and solid family life provided Clinton with what she called a "character graft."

The gathering in New York took on new import as Ross Perot made the dramatic announcement that he was dropping out of the race. Mary had been unsparing toward Perot even before the announcement, given his increasingly strange behavior on the campaign trail. "This is the scary Perot," she said, "the raging paranoid who far from being the Trumanesque figure of earlier impressions, combines the worst features of Richard Nixon and Lyndon Johnson." Perot's announcement meant that millions of votes were suddenly up for grabs. Mary saw his withdrawal as a particularly grave sin, because he had gotten so many Americans excited about the political process for the first time and then abandoned them out of pique.

When Mary was in New York, she learned that Gore was holding a fundraiser at a local law firm, Cravath, Swaine & Moore. When Mary arrived, she was told it was a private event. "Closed to the public?" stormed Mary. "What are you talking about? Is this man running to be a partner in Cravath, Swain and Moore, or is he running for the vice presidency of the United States?" Mary, the only reporter present, was given a front-row seat. "You have to keep a sense of outrage and indignation, and you get very cross with people who are trying to keep you from doing what you are supposed to," Mary explained.

On the convention floor, both Clinton and Gore delivered intensely personal acceptance speeches. "These were probably the most intimate acceptance speeches in the history of the art, and real weepers," observed Mary. "They had to be, say the handlers, because people don't know Gore and don't trust Clinton. By the time the delegates departed with their Clinton pennants, they were sure their Dixie duo would do just fine."

From New York, Mary headed to the Republican convention, in Houston. Although a speech by former president Ronald Reagan was received blissfully, the convention became most famous for a fiery oration by Pat Buchanan that called America to a "cultural war" against radical feminists, homosexuals, environmentalists, and other "malcontents." When he spoke of a "block-by-block" effort to retake America's cities, using force if necessary, the crowd in the hall gushed. The audience at home winced.

Mary wrote, "The Republican assembly was not a joyous gathering of like-minded people. It was more of a putative expedition against people the Christian Right considers reprehensible, a fairly sizable number, which includes gays, reporters, the "gridlocked Democratic Congress," single mothers, women who have abortions, and above all, Hillary Clinton.... The pillars of faith, hope, and charity came in for little attention."

In October, Ross Perot jumped back into the presidential race, despite his deeply wounded image. The race was down to Bush and Clinton, and Bush was gaining steady ground on Clinton through a drumbeat of attacks on his character and lack of experience.

But then came an October surprise: special prosecutor Lawrence Walsh, who had been investigating the Iran-contra scandal for years, dropped a bombshell: Vice President Bush had lied about his role in the arms-for-hostages saga. Walsh not only indicted former defense secretary Caspar Weinberger for lying to Congress, but released key information just four days before the election that made clear that Bush had also lied about his part in the scandal.

Mary's earlier open questions to Bush about Iran-contra were central to Walsh's findings. The day after Bush's open letter to Mary had appeared in the *Post* in 1987, Weinberger and Secretary of State George Shultz had spoken on the phone. Weinberger complained angrily to Shultz about Bush's assertion to Mary that he would have taken a different view of arms sales to Iran if he had known there was opposition in the cabinet. Unfortunately for Bush, an aide to Shultz took detailed notes of the conversation between Weinberger and the secretary of state. Weinberger told Shultz that Bush's answers were "terrible" and that the vice president had clearly known that both Weinberger and Shultz vehemently objected to the arms deal. Weinberger wondered, "Why did he say that?"

Once again a politician had hung himself on what he thought were relatively softball questions from Mary. Walsh had effectively destroyed Bush's campaign in the eleventh hour with a very rough form of justice.

With Ross Perot managing to take close to 20 percent of the popular vote, Bill Clinton became the forty-second president of the United States.

Mary continued to weigh on President Bush's mind even after the election. Jim Baker, who had served as Bush's secretary of state, had become embroiled in a minor brouhaha over whether Republican political appointees had accessed Bill Clinton's passport file in an effort to gather compromising information.

Shortly before Christmas 1992, Mary wrote of Baker, "The man who served as secretary of state for four years, who was considered the ablest man in two Republican administrations, the slick and ferocious campaign manager who made Democrats tremble, has vanished. His disappearance is the talk of the town's Christmas parties. No Republican wishes to be quoted—Baker is much feared and respected—but the general feeling is that he has suffered grave damage to his reputation and his quest for the presidency."

After reading Mary's column, President Bush wrote in his diary, "An ugly editorial by Mary McGrory . . . and it will have Jim Baker climbing the wall. . . . I feel sorry for Jim Baker. Mary McGrory tries to act like Barbara and I are opposed to him in some way—the meanest, nastiest, ugliest column. She has destroyed me over and over again, and Jim is so sensitive about his own coverage that he will be really upset."

For her part, Mary was looking forward. She sent a fax to George Stephanopoulos letting her old friend know that they had served lasagna at the Christmas party. There were leftovers available if he was interested.

CHAPTER ELEVEN

The Grande Dame

Arriving along with the Clinton administration was a great tidbit of gossip. When a staffer at the U.S. embassy in Rome was asked who he thought was in the running for the plum post of ambassador to Italy, he reeled off the names of several people he thought it would be fun to work for, and Mary's name was high on the list.

The day after Clinton was sworn in, Mary's friend Al Kamen noted in his *Washington Post* column that the Italian press was speculating that Mary was under consideration. Not long after, Mary attended a dinner at the Italian ambassador's residence in Washington, and the ambassador made a great fuss over her, telling his guests with a broad smile, "You see, Mary and I are not just friends anymore. We are colleagues." Mary reveled in the attention. "It has all been great fun, and I don't tell everyone it is just that."

Mary reached out to George Stephanopoulos frequently in the early days of the administration. In January 1993, she asked his help in getting on the inaugural bus to Monticello, invited him to a pesto dinner with Phil Gailey, complained that Clinton adviser Paul Begala was not returning her calls, and berated the transition team for considering a former Oliver North protégé for a job.

Mark Gearan, who went to work in the administration as the deputy chief of staff at the White House, knew that managing a relationship with Mary was not easy. Gearan recalled President Clinton reacting like a "hurricane" to one of Mary's columns. Gearan, Stephanopoulos, and others were repeatedly directed by the president to deal with the "Mary problem." But they had no more luck than the many previous denizens of the White House in getting Mary to soften her line.

In April 1993, Bill Clinton marked his first hundred days in office. At a White House press conference, Mary put her question to the commander in chief directly: "Mr. President, would you care to make your assessment of the first hundred days before we make one for you?" Clinton and the press corps laughed, and the president defended his record, arguing with some foresight that a hard-fought win on a budget resolution would make real progress in dealing with the deficit.

But early stumbles gave Mary plenty of material. Dubbing him "William the Procrastinator," she painted the picture of "a president who hates to make up his mind, an eternal campaigner who can't stand giving up on any constituency and who believes he can please all." She compared Clinton to a difficult adolescent who left his parents unsure whether he would win a merit scholarship or total the family car.

Mary wrote to one of her readers, "Like you, I want President Clinton to succeed. Unlike you, I have less hope now. I think he is doing badly for the same faults demonstrated in the campaign, self-indulgence, lack of focus and self-discipline." She described his first year in office as "a blur of blunders: exploding nominations, gays in the military, a haircut on the runway, and bone-crunching confrontations with Congress." Yet Mary also sensed real endurance in Clinton.

She had not given up on the president, and the Clinton White House had not given up on trying to bring Mary around. In June 1993, she attended a small White House dinner. Mary and first lady Hillary Clinton discussed clothes and innovative ways to assist families needing drug treatment as a pleasant evening breeze wafted through the room.

The president shepherded Mary and others through several rooms, sharing his newfound knowledge of the White House. He pointed out that Andrew Jackson, Theodore Roosevelt, and Harry Truman had all renovated, whereas FDR had done little because of the war.

As they sat down for a dinner of Atlantic salmon and pan-seared lamb, Mary was surprised to be seated between President Clinton and Ted Kennedy. Clinton waxed on at length about his sports heroes: Muhammad Ali, Arnold Palmer, and Ted Williams. Mary was never much for sports, although she did coin a classic quote about America and sports: "Baseball is what we were; football is what we have become."

Clinton talked about the many people who had given him advice upon taking office, saying that some of the best insights had come from author and historian David McCullough. As they were talking about Mc-Cullough, Kennedy noted how sad it was that Mrs. Truman had always left her husband alone every summer at the White House. "I would be a basket case," Clinton insisted at the idea of spending the summer without Hillary. Mary noticed that Clinton ate everything on his plate.

The Marine Band played softly in the background. Toward the end of the dinner, Kennedy scooped up the cardboard name placards in front of their settings, telling Mary that he was going to ask the president to autograph them. Mary said that it seemed "terminally tacky" to do so, and then promptly did the same.

After dinner, Mary watched as Bill and Hillary danced. "It was a stupendous evening, and I have never been more pleasantly shocked than to be seated next to the president," Mary observed. Even after decades covering presidents, the White House still held magic for Mary.

The White House charm offensive made some inroads, and Mary gave Hillary Clinton high marks for her appearance before Congress advocating for health care reform. "The first First Lady to lead the charge for a major program that she herself crafted showed such skill and strength that she set a new standard for presidential and other political wives, for White House witnesses, and perhaps for women in general," she wrote. "It's a long way to Tipperary on getting health care through Congress. But Mrs. Clinton has made a brilliant beginning." But Mary also recognized that Hillary's star turn had sparked considerable resentment in Congress.

When Mary attended a 1993 Christmas party for reporters at the White House, she painted a portrait of a president growing in his role. "He ostentatiously waved away a luscious torte with ginger sauce, displaying a self-discipline not seen on yesterday's romps through McDonald's. He showed off an enormous amount of information without seeming to show off."

The new year began on a down note for Mary with the death of Tip O'Neill early in 1994. For her it was both the loss of a friend and the passing of an era. Mary recalled the last time she had seen O'Neill alive—at a reception for his successor as Speaker, Jim Wright. "He was walking with a cane, his great white-thatched head was bent, and his voice, soft as rain in his prime, was almost inaudible." After a warm hug, Tip confided to Mary, "'I'm fallin' apart, darlin'—arthritis, diabetes."

Mary said of O'Neill's very Irish funeral, "I don't think I have ever been at a funeral where there was more love." O'Neill's son Thomas drew wicked grins when he reminded the crowd that whenever his father had spoken of Ronald Reagan's ancestral birthplace in Ireland, Ballyporeen, he always noted that it meant "valley of small potatoes."

"Every single politician in that church had the same thought running through their head during that funeral," Congressmen Ed Markey confided to Mary over drinks afterwards: "'My funeral won't be this good.'"

One of President Clinton's signature achievements was his assistance to the Northern Ireland peace process. Mary was initially skeptical, and many Irish American politicians, not to mention the British government, were alarmed when Clinton granted a visa to Sinn Féin spokesman Gerry Adams in February 1994. But Ted Kennedy gave Clinton important political cover when he said that Adams, although controversial, had a role in the peace process.

Mary sat next to Adams at a private dinner during his first trip to Washington. After politely listening to him speak, she leaned in and asked Adams about the Irish Republican Army. "Was it really necessary to shoot all those fathers in front of their children?"

Adams was taken aback. This was not the question he had been expecting from the genteel gray-haired reporter. After a moment he replied, "No, it wasn't, and I regret that." Mary was unimpressed when Adams claimed that nonviolence had failed to produce results.

Mary panned the visit. "Adams came for 48 hours, was given star treatment and puffball questions from the U.S. press, smiled his tight and ominous smile, failed to renounce terrorism, encouraged all the wrong people in the United States and Ireland. . . . The cause of peace in Northern Ireland was not advanced by a centimeter."

But even if it did not bear immediate fruit, Clinton's attention to the Irish American community got noticed. At a 1994 White House Saint Patrick's Day celebration, a crowd of four hundred Irish and Irish Americans gave Clinton a thunderous standing ovation. While it had been a long time since Irish Americans had been a marginalized political class, Clinton made them feel more loved than ever before.

Many viewed Mary as the embodiment of pure Irish Americanism. If she had avoided talking about her half-German heritage as a youth because of unease with her identity, she did so as an adult because it would have deconstructed a carefully cultivated image.

When Adams returned to Washington, Mary pressed him at a private dinner about why the IRA was unwilling to accept a permanent cease-fire. Adams tried to deflect the question. Mary asked again. Adams detailed the intricacies of the outstanding issues. Mary repeated her question. Finally, Adams laughed aloud and said, "Permanent, permanent, permanent."

Later, when a breakthrough in peace talks led to a cease-fire, and President Clinton made a triumphal visit to Ireland, Mary ate her crow as graciously as possible. "If President Clinton had listened to the likes of me, he never would have had his Irish triumph. I was one of those who thought he was mad to let in Gerry Adams, the IRA propagandist. But he paid no attention to us, Adams was the key, and last week, Clinton brought genuine joy to Belfast." For Mary, Clinton's Irish success was a powerful reminder of how much a president could achieve with political courage, helping end a war and reaping tremendous domestic political benefit as a result. When Clinton was feted and named "Irish-American of the Year," the master of ceremonies spoke of Clinton's daring, steadfastness, and resolve. Mary dryly noted that those were virtues that had "sometimes gone unremarked elsewhere."

The president's annual Saint Patrick's Day party became *the* event on the Irish American social calendar. Clinton, a collection of Kennedys, the president of Ireland, senior members of the cabinet, Mary, and Hollywood heavyweights like Liam Neeson and Paul Newman delighted in the wearing of the green at the White House.

In 1998, a referendum was to be held on the historic Good Friday peace agreement. Mary called her old friend and fellow columnist Maureen Dowd and suggested that they travel to Ireland for the event: "It will be fun, a girl's bonding trip."

"There was no chance to bond, of course," Dowd explained. "On the train from Dublin to Belfast, after staying up all night on the plane, Mary interviewed everyone at the station, everyone on the train, including the lame woman whom she got to carry her bags, the cabdriver on the way to the hotel, the waitress at the hotel coffee shop, the room-service waiter carrying our tea, and the priest at Sunday Mass." (Mary insisted that, although she always relied on bearers, this time she had turned down the offer from the lame woman to help with her bag.)

A broad array of American journalists were on hand for the referendum. Mary dined with Dowd, Mike Barnicle of the *Boston Globe*, Chris Matthews, and Richard Berke of the *New York Times*. When Christiane Amanpour, a very accomplished journalist, approached the table, Dowd introduced her. Mary blurted out, "I know you, you are Jamie's girl"—a reference to Amanpour's fiancé, State Department spokesman Jamie Rubin. Mary's ability to strategically deflate others remain unrivaled. The Good Friday peace plan passed by an enormous margin.

But for all of his success with Northern Ireland, President Bill Clinton remained dogged by problems at home, primarily the Whitewater scandal. Although Whitewater began as an investigation of the president and first lady's links to a failed land deal in Arkansas, his Republican opponents had broadened the investigation to include everything, including extramarital affairs.

Mary believed that the original events at the heart of Whitewater were relatively inconsequential but that the Republican obsession with bringing down the president, coupled with Clinton's tendency to behave as if he were "generically guilty," made the scandal self-perpetuating. In Mary's theatrical terms: "a strong cast of wayward Arkansans, but a weak plot." Mary reasoned that the Republicans' ferocious focus on White-water would eventually backfire, saying that the public "knew they were not electing a role model when they elected Bill Clinton."

As the Clinton administration tried to push through universal health care, the president came under daily assault from right-wing radio—a growing force in the country. Mary had little but contempt for talk show gasbags like Rush Limbaugh, but she worried that Clinton was inclined to wallow in self-pity when under fire. She made her case directly to the president in an August 1994 White House press conference: "Mr. President, would you tell us why you hold so few solo press conferences? This is only your third, and you have been heard to complain that the lords of the right-wing radio have uninterrupted communication with the American people, and you have the same chance but don't take it. Could you tell us why?" Clinton smiled in response, saying, "I think it's a mistake, and I intend to do more on a more regular basis." Reporters laughed in disbelief.

Mary had particularly tough words for the congressional Whitewater hearings that summer. "If the Whitewater hearings were a series, it would have been canceled, if a show, closed, and if a horse, shot." Mary—and most of America—were appalled as congressional Republicans repeatedly insinuated that the suicide of White House counsel Vince Foster had been the result of foul play, charges she called "scummy and out of bounds."

Clinton's halting performance during his first two years in office led to miserable results for Democrats in the 1994 midterm elections, and they lost control of both the House and the Senate. Mary described the president after the election: "He was pretty much in the Ancient Mariner mode, haunted and babbling. He couldn't stop talking about the ship-wreck that had just occurred, but he couldn't think of anything to say, either."

Power in Washington had shifted dramatically, and the new Speaker of the House, Newt Gingrich, was determined to stand the Capitol on its head. Mary's columns on Gingrich moved with easy verve. "The newly designated House speaker, with his gray thatch and X-ray eyes, is tearing around town these days, spewing directives, reading lists, edicts, advice and predictions," she wrote. "He swims in a sea of approval. To young House members, he is a legend, a combination of Robert Bruce and Knute Rockne."

Gingrich was a consummate showman. He arranged for circus elephants to march around the Capitol as his colleagues voted on a Republican tax plan. His every move was followed by scores of reporters as he took aim at everything from the school lunch program to foreign aid.

One of Gingrich's early gaffes propelled Mary and the Speaker into an interesting conversation. When Gingrich suggested that children from poor mothers might be better off in orphanages, Democrats unloosed howls of protest about Republican hard-heartedness. Hillary Clinton called Gingrich's plan "absurd," and the president suggested that Gingrich was trying to uproot loving families.

Mary, shaped by her experience with St. Ann's, was one of the few Democrats to speak out in Gingrich's defense. "Nobody is saying that an institution is better than a home," she wrote. "But what he and others are saying is that an institution is better than a crack house or a life on the street."

She wrote to a friend in Antrim, "Right now Newt is a lot of fun, or good copy anyway. It's a thrill a day, one loony idea after another. Strangely enough, I think he wants to help poor children." Clinton, on the other hand, she found to be "at the bottom of the Slough of Despond."

Mary and Gingrich exchanged a series of thoughtful letters on children and volunteerism. As she noted in one of the letters, "One of the things I feel most deeply is that what makes poverty and squalor even more unbearable is the feeling that no one knows about your suffering, and no one cares." It was not the company that most fans of either McGrory or Gingrich expected them to keep, but Mary was never less partisan than when it came to kids. However, Gingrich's penchant for slashing social programs soon brought them to loggerheads.

In April 1995, Mary was awarded the Franklin Delano Roosevelt Four Freedoms Award for freedom of speech and also presented with the first Robert F. Kennedy Lifetime Achievement Award in Journalism. The Four Freedoms Award was a considerable honor, and President Clinton presented Mary and the other honorees their awards at a ceremony in Warm Springs, Georgia, at the same site to which FDR had regularly decamped for healing spa treatments. The award came exactly fifty years to the day after Roosevelt had suffered a cerebral hemorrhage and died at the "Little White House" in Warm Springs.

For Democrats wounded by their congressional losses, the awards ceremony, on the porch of the Little White House, under a canopy of chestnut trees, was a balm. The *Atlanta Journal-Constitution* called the gathering "the most talented group of speakers probably ever assembled" in the state of Georgia.

Forty members of the Morehouse College choir sang a full-throated version of the spiritual "Ain'a That Good News" as President Clinton and the others walked up the dirt path to the podium. Anna Eleanor Roosevelt Seagraves, the granddaughter of Franklin and Eleanor, wowed the crowd when she argued that FDR's 1944 "Economic Bill of Rights" speech—which maintained that Americans had a right to education, decent wages, and health care—was not a "Contract with America, but a ringing articulation of America's contract with ourselves."

Mary's speech, which she had fretted over at great length, was warm and sharp. Even as she insisted that she was not worthy of the award, she asked forgiveness from those in the audience who might think that she was "vulgar" for being proud of her place on Nixon's enemies list.

She talked far more about FDR than about herself. "He had almost every newspaper publisher in this country grinding his teeth editorializing against 'that man in the White House.' But twice a week (that's twice a week!) the reporters trooped into the Oval Office, so the publishers got nowhere with their demonizing." She gave President Clinton a pointed glance and continued. "He understood instinctively that the way to lead was through constant communication with the people," she said. "I regret to say that—present company, of course, excepted—that the presidents who succeeded him did not wholly share his benign and wholesome view of the press."

In his remarks, President Clinton noted that FDR "never meant for anybody—anybody—to become totally dependent on the government when they can do things for themselves. But should we abandon the notion that everybody counts, that we're going up or down together?" At the end of his speech, Clinton joined the crowd and chorus in clapping his hands and singing "The Battle Hymn of the Republic." It was a great moment for Mary, made all the better when she was able to hop a ride back to Washington aboard Air Force One with the president.

Just days after the Four Freedoms ceremony, right-wing militia members bombed the Federal Building in Oklahoma City, killing 168, including 19 small children, and wounding close to 700. President Clinton was perhaps at his best in the days that followed, urging restraint, consoling families and loved ones, and calling for more tempered and reasoned debate. He singled out the rhetoric of right-wing radio as fueling anger against the government, although he did not point to any commentator by name.

Mary marched right into the debate: "People say the president should not have spoken out against intemperate talk show hosts. But if not he, who? That's what presidents are supposed to do." She took particular aim at Rush Limbaugh. "His offense is tastelessness. He burps on his show while his doting fans giggle at his devilishness; he suggested that the First Lady's problem during the health care debate had been that she was menopausal. No wonder he felt threatened when Clinton appealed for more civility."

Limbaugh took exception to Mary's comments, even as his response validated them. On the air, Limbaugh insisted that his belch had been accidental and claimed, "Now, as for the first lady in menopause, sorry again, Ms. McGrory, but you've got the wrong show. It never happened. My discussion about the health care debate concerned the substance of the administration's proposals and the credibility of those who are offering them. Menopause is not one of my many areas of expertise. I mean, I will leave menopause to others who know about it and leave them to discuss that subject. Ms. McGrory, do you have any suggestions, maybe?" On another show, Limbaugh suggested that "the men in little white coats" were soon going to take Mary from her office.

For Mary and others, Oklahoma City marked a watershed in Clinton's presidency. He became more self-assured and presidential. "Bill Clinton has made a remarkable discovery," Mary shared. "He has found out that he is president, and that if he tells people what's what, they don't mind. They even like it."

It quickly became evident that with relentless budget cuts targeted at the poor and the ongoing obsession with Whitewater, Gingrich and the Republicans were overreaching. Mary wrote, "The Republican attitude is exemplified by House Speaker Newt Gingrich, who, faced with a choice of heartlessness or tastelessness, often chooses both." Mary told one of her friends that it was a wonderful time to be a columnist. "I am kicking subjects away. Some days you think when Republicans try to pollute the air and water that parody can go no further, and then Clinton ups and delivers a knockout blow to himself."

When Newt Gingrich threw a tantrum about President Clinton allegedly snubbing him on the Air Force One flight back from Yitzhak Rabin's funeral in Israel, and subsequently forced a temporary government shutdown, the White House released a photo of Clinton and Gingrich chatting amiably on the plane. The *New York Daily News* then featured a front-page cartoon depicting Gingrich as a bawling baby in diapers.

Mary described Gingrich's almost Shakespearean fall in a speech at Georgetown University. "The Republicans are, as far as I know, not being paid by the Democrats, but they should be. Can you imagine, in your wildest dreams, a House speaker, Republican, who closes down the government because he was asked to leave a plane by the back door? No mortal hand could have devised that succession of events. It is beyond belief to me that he could have gotten off the plane by the back door, the servants' entrance, and that he should, within two days, close down the government."

Mary was also able to goad both Bill and Hillary Clinton into helping out at St. Ann's, and she arranged for Hillary to visit St. Ann's at Christmas in 1995. She held her breath as she watched the interaction between Sister Josephine and the first lady. Yet, as Mary observed, "The meeting between the ultra-contemporary first lady and the sisters of the ancient order of the Sisters of Charity, who have run the home for homeless children for over 100 years, was unexpectedly cordial." The two found common ground in talking about the shortcomings of the Family Reunification Act, and Hillary noted that she had been roundly criticized in the press for saying that "it takes a village" to raise a child. It was a position with which the sisters instantly sympathized.

The kids had diligently learned a new Christmas song and were singing it for the first lady when Tim Russert appeared, dressed as Santa. (Mary had told Russert that playing Santa for the kids was much like his role as host of *Meet the Press*: "They know they are going to get questions on which they would love to take the fifth. They will deny that they ever fight or hit each other while in the act of doing so.") The kids abandoned Clinton and flocked to Santa. One child stayed behind, hugging Hillary's leg and reassuring her, "It's okay, I'll stay here with you." Not surprisingly, given his day job, Russert was a more interrogatory Father Christmas than his predecessors. He quizzed the children in some detail about their lapses—"Did you bite? Did you fight?"—and delivered a lecture on the importance of responsibility. One of the children leaned over and asked Mary, "Is he ever going to give us presents?"

Several years later, Mary would manage to have the kids invited to the White House for Christmas. The children were enthralled by the Marine helicopter on the lawn and by the president's dog, Buddy. A young boy, Sherman, dashed over and thrust out his hand to President Clinton in greeting. "How do you do, Mr. President? I'm glad to see you." Clinton smiled broadly at the effusive welcome and smiled infectiously as he had his picture taken with the four nuns who accompanied Mary and the kids.

One day in 1995, Sister Josephine vented that most teachers did not bother to take a little extra time with the kids from St. Ann's. Mary agreed. She recalled the case of a boy named Dale, who was pleasant and social at St. Ann's but had been sent home several times for hitting other kids at school. "This was completely out of character and the reason was not hard to find," Mary observed. "He was striking out at those who were humiliating him." When Dale started getting tutoring, his problems at school vanished.

Mary had a plan in mind and offered to make an initial donation of $25,000, in addition to her already considerable regular support, to establish the "Mary Gloria Room," a space at St. Ann's where the kids could receive regular tutoring. She would pay to refurbish and furnish the room and help underwrite a tutor in residence. "Many fail not because they lack intelligence or willingness to learn," she explained, but because they "have never in their short, troubled lives been talked to, read to, sung to or had anything explained to them by an affectionate adult." Mary's charitable giving remained prodigious. During much of the late 1990s, she averaged well over $50,000 a year in charitable donations—more than a quarter of her annual salary, spread across some seventy organizations.

The Mary Gloria Room officially opened on Valentine's Day 2000, and it was as well equipped as any private school. Mary made brief remarks at the ribbon cutting. She confessed that she routinely lied when filling out her taxes, since the IRS required that she must have received "nothing of value" in return for her donations for them to be deductible. "That's not true. I have received great treasures," Mary shared. "I have learned about the infinite resilience, courage, intelligence, and kindness of these children. Some of them have told me about the violence they have witnessed, and even endured: knifings, shootings, and other things that shouldn't have happened. They bear their burdens with great valor. They are responsive and funny. If they just can weather the first grade, and understand that we believe in them and their potential, they'll do just fine."

In her later years, Mary became even more intent on using her perch as a writer to make a personal difference. She got to know a group of activists running a civil disobedience campaign against the School of the Americas, a Pentagon training facility notorious for its links to Latin American military officers with checkered human rights records. Mary learned that one of the key organizers of the protests, Father Roy Bourgeois, a Navy Vietnam vet and a Maryknoll missionary, had been arrested for picketing the school in Fort Benning, Georgia. Mary tried to contact Father Bourgeois in prison but was thwarted by prison administrators.

Mary called Congressman Joe Kennedy's press secretary, Brian O'Connor, and he followed up with the Bureau of Prisons. Mary was finally allowed to speak to Bourgeois. He was relatively upbeat. "Look, I don't mind this, Mary. This is all degradation and humility, but I don't mind because I think we will stir the conscience of America."

"You hope," Mary said.

"What I mind," continued Bourgeois, "is that Bill Corrigan, who is a 74-year-old World War II veteran, is being given a bad time by the guards. He has to pick up cigarette butts in the prison yard, and he is not allowed to call his wife, Lil. He can't call her up because the guard in charge won't approve his telephone list. He doesn't like him. He's military, and Bill's war record doesn't count. He's not a veteran; he's a troublemaker." Corrigan and his wife had been married for forty years and had hardly spent a day apart.

"You know, Father," Mary said, "I think I will put that in the paper. That does seem like petty tyranny to me."

Mary highlighted Corrigan's plight in a column that, most fittingly, ran on the Fourth of July, pointing out that Father Bourgeois and his fellow protestors had served more jail time than the Salvadoran military officers who had famously assassinated Archbishop Oscar Romero.

Bill Corrigan was allowed to speak with his wife the next day and was no longer forced to pick up cigarette butts. "I only have small victories," Mary reflected on the incident. "Other people can bring down presidents and change policies; this is what I have to settle for. And it is okay."

Mary dove into the 1996 presidential race, even as life on the campaign trail was becoming difficult. She was seventy-eight, and this would be her eleventh presidential campaign.

Although Senator Bob Dole was the presumptive Republican nominee, New Hampshire could not resist mischief and awarded a primary win to fire-breathing pundit Pat Buchanan. "A disaster with a crowbar has happened to Republican politics," Mary commented. "The know-nothings who have ever idolized Buchanan have been augmented by middle-American converts who have long suspected that their troubles are not of their own making."

In Appleton, Wisconsin, the Dole campaign was briefly grounded after a flight attendant took ill. As they killed time on the tarmac, one of the other attendants served beverages. Mary asked for Scotch. "Sorry, no Scotch," she was told. "Only wine and beer." Mary was appalled. "What kind of campaign plane doesn't have Scotch?" As one of her fellow reporters mused, "And what kind of campaign doesn't have Mary McGrory to keep them honest?"

But as the primaries ground on, Mary experienced a sharp uptick in her cholesterol levels, leading to a strict order from her doctor to cut back on fatty foods. "I've decided, with the help of a doctor, to slow down. I want to go to two columns a week," she told her agent. "I'll finish out the campaign on my regular schedule, take two weeks' vacation when it's over in November, and start the new regimen."

Mary also got into a spat with the editors at the *Boston Globe* because they were not running her pieces as frequently as she liked, primarily because of space considerations. Her cousin Brian McGrory, who worked at the *Globe*, was pulled into the matter, and he drafted a long e-mail to the *Globe* editors about why they should continue to run her column. Brian called Mary and read her the e-mail over the phone. When he finished reading, there was a long pause. "You save that," she finally said to Brian, "and you read it at my funeral."

Mary explored moving her column to the *Globe*'s rival, the *Boston Herald*. The *Herald* editors jumped at the chance and quickly prepared a contract for Mary's signature.

Ben Taylor, the *Globe*'s publisher, intervened to keep Mary from leaving, guaranteeing that at least one of her columns would appear in the paper every week. He wrote to Mary, "The last thing I wanted in my first months as publisher was to wake up one morning and read your column in the *Herald*." Mary stressed how important it was to reach people in her former hometown, "who love to think I've retired or died."

Mary tagged along as the Clinton-Gore campaign began a multistate train trip that would bring both men from West Virginia to the Democratic convention, in Chicago. The trip brought back fond memories of barnstorming around the country with Estes Kefauver and Blair Clark.

Mary had unexpected company for the journey: her cousin Brian, who had risen from covering local Boston crime stories to becoming a national reporter. He had moved to Washington in 1996 to cover the White House and the campaign for the *Globe*, and he often joined Mary for dinner on weekends. "I would go up to her house for Saturday afternoons, supposedly to garden, but she knew I hated it," Brian explained. "I would bring my dog, Harry, up, and he would lay in the flowers." Mary, never one to pass up a good dog story, featured Harry in several columns.

Brian had not realized that Mary was making the train trip with Clinton. "I remember being on the train in West Virginia and looking out the window and seeing Mary fumbling with her bags like John Candy in *Planes, Trains and Automobiles*. The thought just struck me at that moment: for the next week I am going to be her porter." He was.

As Mary and Brian worked their way through the Upper Midwest, Mary was touched by the public's reaction to Clinton. She later recalled to Tim Russert:

I hear about the cynicism and apathy and indifference. I didn't see it. I saw people standing along the road there the whole way, everywhere. I saw people outside Bowling Green, Ohio, five miles from the speech site. There were ten thousand people holding little lights, cheering the train as it went by. I saw people holding huge flags that they'd obviously got down from their attics, all yellow and frayed. And I saw people standing at attention as the train went by. And I saw a man standing up in a rowboat with his hand over his heart. That's not cynicism. They love presidents. I think they love their country, and I think they realize we have a perfectly wonderful system.

After all the years and all the campaigns, Mary still believed.

Mary was less thrilled with the convention. "They were trying to pretend they weren't politicians, which makes you think that they don't think it's a very high calling," she complained. When Clinton rattled off a long list of small-bore policy goals in his acceptance speech, Mary harrumphed that it sounded like he was running for "concierge rather than president."

"I cannot believe that you have now been at the *Washington Post* for fifteen years," Don Graham wrote Mary shortly after the convention. "Your unique method of covering political campaigns consistently teaches me things about the candidates I learn from no one else. You go out with them consistently. You listen and watch. You write about what they say, how people react, and how it all feels. How simple; but how uniquely powerful when it is so well done."

The 1996 race was largely drama-free. Clinton ran a calculated campaign, and Republicans were weighted down with the baggage of Newt Gingrich's government shutdown. The president was reelected by a comfortable margin.

At the end of 1996, Mary's friend George Stephanopoulos left the

White House. Her recollections as he left his post were fond, but thorny: "George tried to be funny about the hazards of being friends with certain people. He told about those mornings when the unhappy *Washington Post* reader in the Oval Office would haul him in and demand to know 'what's wrong with her today?' 'Her' was me. George began to fade from the Sunday night scene."

One night over dinner, Mary complained to the Italian ambassador. "Don't you understand?" he retorted to Mary. "He is blamed for every bad story you write." Mary later asked Stephanopoulos if that was indeed the case. He sighed, "I carried you on my back as long as I could." When you pen unvarnished political opinion for a living, friendships are a fragile thing.

American politics veered into a remarkable period of turbulence during President Clinton's second term. In the summer of 1997, with shades of Julius Caesar, Republican House members plotted unsuccessfully to overthrow Newt Gingrich as Speaker, and Mary described the atmosphere within Republican ranks as "thick with charges of vile treason."

Against that backdrop, independent counsel Kenneth Starr continued his Whitewater investigation. Mary was aghast that Starr was on an open-ended hunt for Clinton's sexual escapades, complaining in June 1997, "They shoot mad dogs. Mad-dog prosecutors are a different story." The Starr investigation, combined with an ongoing lawsuit by former alleged Clinton paramour Paula Jones, led to a media frenzy focused on the president's sex life.

When rumors surfaced that the president's genitalia had certain "distinguishing characteristics," Mary threw up her arms at the wall-to-wall coverage. At a cocktail party, she ran into Arthur Ochs Sulzberger Jr., the publisher of the *New York Times*. Mary noted that the *Times* had avoided printing a detailed discussion of the ins and outs of the president's private parts. She asked if it was a result of a *Times* policy on such matters. An uncomfortable Sulzberger could only say, "We try not to be tacky."

Any hopes of avoiding epic tawdriness were dashed with the January

1998 accusation that President Clinton had sex in the Oval Office with a twenty-four-year old intern, Monica Lewinsky. Making matters far worse for Clinton, a confidante of Lewinsky's, Linda Tripp, had recorded her conversations with Lewinsky about the affair. Mary wondered if the president would survive lying under oath. "Morally, he is in mud. Legally, he's in worse trouble.... We are talking about an impeachable offense." Both Clinton and Lewinsky denied the relationship, but unconvincingly so.

Mary was outraged by the president's behavior, dubbing him a "Dog-patch Don Giovanni" and adding, "If Clinton had any shame, he would have long since expired of it." But she was also horrified by the great roar of innuendo stoked by a whole new source: Internet blogs like the right-wing *Drudge Report*.

Mary had never been a fan of opinion delivered without actual reporting, and suddenly the Internet offered a Pandora's box of insta-punditry that was uncouth, unkind, and often uninformed. Mary loved the idea of citizen journalism, but much of what she saw on the Web simply felt like shouting. For someone who slaved over every word after hours of legwork, the idea that Matt Drudge was shaping the national debate with anonymous rumors seemed like a throwback to the dingy days of McCarthyism. "We have fallen into a dim age," Russell Baker wrote to Mary. "Not for the first time I suppose, but the press-public slobbering brought on by Monica has surely never been equaled in the squalor department."

Certainly the Internet alone was not to blame. The creation of twenty-four-hour cable news stations like CNN, Fox News, and MSNBC during the 1990s meant that there was a limitless maw of programming that needed to be met, and pontificating pundits provided a cheap way to fill airtime. If ratings were good, it didn't matter if anyone actually did any reporting or knew what they were talking about. As author David Foster Wallace once complained, talk radio, the Internet, and cable news "enjoy the authority and influence of journalism without the stodgy constraints of fairness, objectivity, and responsibility that make trying to tell the truth such a drag for everyone involved." Mary had harsh words for the media's approach. "The press, terrified of being scooped, poured on poorly sourced or even dead wrong details to feed the public a story nobody wanted to read, foisting sensational disclosures on a Congress that was cowering under its desk."

Republicans assumed that the damning revelations doomed Clinton. They were in for a rude shock—polls showed Clinton at an all-time high in approval ratings. "The country was awed," said Republican congressman Chris Shays of Connecticut. "It was like seeing Houdini in action. They saw him put in the box, chained and padlocked, and thrown overboard. And the next minute they saw him not just out, but steering the ship." Impeachment was starting to look more dangerous for Republicans than for Clinton.

Washington was gripped by a seemingly endless series of allegations, revelations, and shocks. By March 1998 Mary was pleading for relief. "We can't go on this way. It has to stop," she wrote. "We've been on a diet of gossip that is the functional equivalent of *foie gras* and brandy three times a day. We can expect nothing but gout and hardening of the arteries unless we quit."

In April, Mary attended the White House Correspondents' Dinner. She wrote to a friend, that she went to the "dinner which was full of ladies wearing too much or too little and men who think they own the world. I was kissed by Sam Donaldson, Peter Jennings, and Warren Beatty. Had long conversations with the president's lawyer. He says they do not worry about the report coming from Kenneth Starr. Hoping for a one day wonder."

Mary was vacationing in Italy, on an island near Mount Vesuvius, when the Starr Report was released. She tried to read the first excerpts in the newspaper *Corriere della Sera*. "It wasn't easy. My dictionary did not have all the words, and I hesitated to ask the bar staff." Mary was worried that other lounge patrons would think she was reading pornography.

The Italians at her hotel were puzzled by the scandal. "*Signora*," the hotel manager gravely told Mary, "I am praying your country will come to its senses and let your president continue to govern for the good of the whole world." Over dinner, a jeweler from Nettuno could barely contain his anger with the scandal. "Why? Why? He is a good president, Wall Street likes him, the world loves him. He has reduced unemployment. People are happy."

Mary asked how Italians would feel if it were revealed that their prime minister was "having a disgusting affair."

"We would say 'Bravo,'" he replied.

An interesting dispute erupted when author Gay Talese accused prominent Irish Catholics in the media—including Mary, Maureen Dowd, Tim Russert, and Pat Buchanan—of "high-minded pontificating" when it came to the scandal. "The Irish media want the president to climb up the hill on bloody knees like the Stations of the Cross," Talese wrote. Others picked up on Talese's charge, with Irish American reporter William Powers accusing the Irish American media of behaving like a "Roman Legion." Most of them shrugged off the complaints, but they were a close-knit group, and Mary was among those who often gathered to chat politics after they attended Mass in Georgetown. While calling the group a "mafia" was excessive, Irish American journalists and politicians in Washington often did function as a clan, one of the many powerful circles of friends and associates who operate just beneath the surface in Washington.

In October 1998, the House of Representatives voted 258–176 to begin an impeachment inquiry, despite its public unpopularity. In the 1998 off-year elections, Democrats actually picked up five seats in the House. As Mary said of Clinton after the election, "Millstone? No, he's Moses."

Angry Republicans again blamed Newt Gingrich for the strategic blunder of pursuing the Lewinsky scandal and pushed him out of his post not long after the election. Gingrich huffed that he was not willing to preside over "cannibals" and quit Congress.

The seismic shocks continued. After Republicans elected longtime Louisiana congressman Bob Livingston to replace Gingrich as Speaker, it was revealed that Livingston had also been engaged in an extramarital

affair. He resigned. For Republicans, it was exploding cigar after exploding cigar. At least four other senior Republicans admitted to extramarital
affairs, and one member of the leadership confessed to fathering a child
out of wedlock. "The Republicans are beyond reason," Mary lamented.
"They are like people on New Year's Eve determined to have a wild time,
no matter the cost."

Clinton was ultimately impeached by the House, on a largely party-
line vote, in December 1998. He was then acquitted by the Senate in February 1999, having achieved one of the great escape acts in American
political history.

Amid the political upheavals, Mary was honored with the Fourth Estate Award at the National Press Club. It was one of the few times that
Mary allowed a big deal to be made for her, and Walter Cronkite, Kay
Graham, Gene McCarthy, and a host of other luminaries attended the
televised event.

Roger Mudd led off by praising Mary's work and he read John McKelway's column from when Mary had been included on the Nixon White
House enemies list. Ted Kennedy was next to take the podium. The senator looked tired, and his prepared remarks were oddly stilted. But Kennedy's praise was heartfelt when he declared Mary the "poet laureate of
American journalism" and added, "Nothing compares to four extraordinary columns and the editorial she wrote for the *Washington Star* thirty-
five years ago this month, when we lost Jack. They are some of the most
beautiful words ever written about my brother, and they helped immensely to ease the pain. We love you, Mary, and always will."

Kennedy then broke into song: "Every word's a perfect pearl, and all of
us are here to tell you, dear, you're a grand old girl." The crowd ate up the
performance.

Maureen Dowd gently lampooned Mary:

> I have modeled my career on hers. Not the writing, of course, be-
> cause no one writes like Mary McGrory. I have emulated her other
> talents. Her uncanny ability, even in remote parts of New Hampshire

or Ireland, to find some sucker to carry her bags or to drive her car. The way she nobly resists this passing fad called technology. The way she uses the imperative tense in the style that Old West gunslingers used to shoot at people's feet to make them dance. The way she acts helpless like a barracuda. From Joe McCarthy to Henry Kissinger to Robert McNamara to Murray Gart to Gerry Adams, every public figure she has elegantly sautéed has learned to beware when Mary sounds confused and begins asking seemingly innocent questions—you are about to enter the McGrory House of Pain.

Calling Mary "the most luminous writer and clearest thinker in the business," Dowd, to much laughter, praised Mary for her rebellious streak. "She insists on continuing to act like a beat reporter and continuing to leave her office and grill politicians and see events in person—which is, like, way unnecessary if you ask me." Dowd closed by saying, "She is, as her beloved Italians put it, our *bella figura*. But never, ever eat her Jello Surprise." Mary was pleased.

Russell Baker followed, saying that he had stiff competition, between Dowd's wit and Kennedy's turn as "the Irish Pavarotti." Baker pointed out to the audience that when Mary had first worked as a reporter, she could be admitted to the room in which they were gathered only if she sat in the balcony. "Congratulations, Mary: you have come a long way."

Perhaps the evening's most poignant remarks came from Kay Graham, who said she felt like "one legend talking to another" and slyly admitted to being jealous of Mary. "I work very hard," she said, "to collect the right people, seat them carefully, make the table pretty, and ensure the food is delicious. Mary collects as good, or better, guests, but she gets them to do the work."

Graham shared another reason she was jealous of Mary: "She has very clear and high standards of what matters and what doesn't and how people should behave. . . . She is a courageous and real liberal at a time when the rest of the country has retreated to the bland center."

The former *Post* publisher also bittersweetly observed that her own paper had never won Mary's heart. She explained how her late husband had tried again and again to persuade Mary to leave the *Star*. "She kept saying no, even when it became clear that the *Star* wasn't going to be viable," she said. "Sadly, after all these years, Mary is still loyal to the *Star*. She would still pick the *Star* over the *Post*, and Newby Noyes is still her first love," Graham said of Mary's former editor, who had died two years before. "Mary, I understand that—Newby was wonderful. Maybe someday, after we are all gone, you will love us as much."

Graham and Mary hugged warmly after Graham presented her with the Fourth Estate award. Mary was delighted that Graham had paid her "the high compliment of speaking her mind." In a telling postscript, Graham wrote Mary a long, angst-riven letter full of apologies and worries that she had overstepped her bounds. "Self-doubt was back," Mary observed. "It was, as ever, out of place."

In her acceptance speech, she noted that Maureen Dowd's writing was so sharp-tongued that it made readers view her own work as kindhearted, lauded Kennedy for his golden pipes, and thanked Graham for putting up with her. She said that she had initially been inclined to turn down the award because she worried that afterwards she would have no choice but to either "die or retire—and neither option appeals to me."

Mary spoke to her place as a columnist in Washington. "No great men ever call me. You want to know who calls me? Losers. I am their mark. If you want to abolish land mines. If you want to reform campaign spending," Mary said. "If you want to reduce nuclear weapons, if you want to eliminate them, if you want to save children from abuse, or stupid laws, or thickheaded judges, you have my telephone number."

But Mary made clear that she would not have it any other way. "I never wanted to be anything but a newspaperwoman, and I still don't want to be, and that word is going to go on my gravestone. Because I think it is a very proud and wonderful thing to do. But I should confess, although I probably shouldn't, that I have always felt a little sorry for people who didn't work for newspapers."

The luster of the award and the thrall of the incredible political happenings in Washington were dimmed, to a degree, by the illness of one of Mary's closest friends, Gertrude Cleary.

A short time later, Brian McGrory was promoted from the White House beat to his own column back in Boston with the *Globe*. Mary greeted the news morosely: "Everybody important in my life is either leaving or dead."

CHAPTER TWELVE

The Last Hurrah

The rhythm of the seasons was a constant for Mary.

Spring was the budding of slender bulbs in her scraggly garden on the slopes of Rock Creek. Early summer was the riotous sounds of orphans from St. Ann's splashing in the pool at Ethel Kennedy's home at Hickory Hill. August was the Plaza in Rome and the splendor of people watching from a small café near the Spanish Steps. Labor Day was her beloved Antrim and the restorative waters of Gregg Lake.

Autumn brought the rigors of the campaign trail: debates, town hall meetings, indifferent chicken suppers, and political promises proffered with abandon. Christmas was Santa Claus fast asleep on the couch waiting for the children from St. Ann's, scrod at the Ritz-Carlton in Boston, shared laughter, and a Scotch at the Parker House Hotel.

And from all this, the lovingly crafted words came and came. Mary stalked the newsroom, testing out her next lead and trying to capture the perfect turn of phrase. She dressed down press secretaries and buttonholed senators in the long marble hallways of Congress. It was as if she might obtain grace through the patient repetition of the things she loved the most.

Her production was staggering. During her career, Mary wrote more than eight thousand columns. Although she often waited until the last minute, she missed her deadline only once during her entire career—because she was stuck on a plane. Mary said that the constant pressure of producing columns sometimes made her feel like a hitched horse walking circles at a mill, but it was a discipline that she welcomed.

But the years had also taken their toll, and the indignities of age mounted. Mary's fallen arches made it difficult to stand at parties. Her blood pressure was high, and cutting back on rich food was a struggle. She missed smoking cigarettes, and still enjoyed drinking. Her penchant for losing keys, purses, and other belongings only accelerated. (She had lost an entire rental car during the 1984 primary in New Hampshire.) Her driving skills, awful to begin with, only deteriorated further. Her Mercedes was constantly in and out of the shop with minor damages, and Tina Toll was kept busy paying a small stack of parking tickets.

One of Mary's relatives observed, "You would see her cook a dinner or just do any daily task and you would think, 'My God, this woman should not live alone.' Then she would have people over and she would start talking about politics, and what was going on in the White House, and you would think, 'My God, where did you come from?' The light switched, and she was on."

At eighty-one, Mary had reached the point in life when going to the funerals of friends becomes depressingly common, and her gifts as a writer were frequently employed writing eulogies. Meg Greenfield, Newby Noyes, John McKelway, and several others close to Mary all passed away in the closing years of the century. At the memorial service for Noyes, she scrawled two notes to herself on the program: a lyric from a hymn—"Publish Glad Tidings"—and the words "inscription on gravestone." Mary not only was pondering her own mortality; she was planning for it.

Her great love, Blair Clark, died in 2000, at the age of eighty-two. He was survived by his widow, Joanna.

Mary was candid about her regrets late in her life, telling more than one interviewer that she wished she had gotten married and confiding to relatives that she wished she'd had children. These reflections did not define Mary, yet it was impossible to elude a sense of lingering sadness in her twilight years. For a woman who delighted in the heroines of Jane Austen and the lovely lilt of poetry, her own story of romance did not enjoy a happy ending.

While Mary told a fellow reporter, "We could be here all night talking about what I would do differently," she did not wallow in sentimentality, as a wonderful exchange with Tim Russert made plain.

Mary, who had always insisted that she hated going on television, started to appear regularly on *Meet the Press*, hosted by Russert. She was never the most natural guest, and her observational style was ill-suited to the staccato pace of Sunday talk shows, but Russert liked having her on, and the two became good friends. Mary, despite her feigned protestations, loved going on the show.

During a broadcast, Russert asked her how the country and politics had changed during her long decades of writing. Mary demurred, as she often did, saying that it was her job to look at the trees, not the forest. She allowed that being one of the few women when she first started covering campaigns was not the worst thing in the world, although she knew that some saw such a view as "very retrograde."

"Those were the good old days?" Russert queried.

"No, of course not," Mary responded.

"But were people kinder to one another then? Were they more respectful, more gentle with one another in terms of their political opinions?"

Mary put Russert in his place. "Joe McCarthy, you're thinking of? Chuck Colson, perhaps?" Mary was under no illusion that the 1950s, '60s, or '70s had been easier days.

Mary was the grande dame of Washington reporters. After observing her being feted at an awards ceremony, former *New Yorker* editor Tina Brown proclaimed that she wanted to age like Mary had—as a "sparky old broad," an unapologetic liberal with "spectacular balls." Her friend Phil Gailey observed that Mary had acquired the manner of an aging countess. Marjorie Williams of the *Post* remembered Mary in her later years as the Katharine Hepburn of journalism, sweeping into the newsroom in a wide-brimmed black hat and a wool cape. Mary demanded respect, and she had sharp words for those who challenged her authority. "She would arrive at a press conference called for ten o'clock," Jack Germond recalled. "She would get there at 10:05. She would march down to the front row, and somebody would always go ahead and give her a seat. It was never me, because I thought it was insulting."

In many ways, Mary was as much an anomaly at the end of her career as she was at its beginning. When she broke through, during the Army-McCarthy hearings, she was the lone female reporter in the room. On the campaign trail, she was the one woman surrounded by a hundred men. By the end of her career, she was working in an environment where there were more and more women, most female reporters were married, and employers like the *Post* provided maternity leave and benefits. To this new generation of women, Mary was a throwback: the woman who took on McCarthy and Nixon; the pioneer who was forced to decide between career and love; a beloved relic from an earlier era who drank with the Kennedys and crafted handwritten thank-you notes. Mary had gone an entire career without ever being the norm.

Mary's family and friends cautiously broached the idea of retirement from time to time, but she was not interested. She needed the camaraderie of the newsroom and could not conceive of life without reporting. When asked publicly about it, she was categorical that she would not stop: "I am going to die in the newsroom—it's like oxygen to me."

There were whispers that Mary's finest work was in the rearview mirror. "Did Mary hold on too long? I don't want to say it, but sure," said Ben Bradlee. Mary was a step slower, and she no longer had the same twinkle in her eye.

But every editor and fellow reporter marveled at one inescapable fact: Mary kept legging out stories.

In January 2000, Mary headed to New Hampshire for the presidential primary on her twelfth presidential campaign. A birthday party for Jack Germond held at the Wayfarer Inn bar in mid-January underscored how much the business of covering campaigns had changed. The Wayfarer was still popular with old pros like Mary and Germond, but a new Holiday Inn in downtown Manchester was increasingly the preferred base, because it had a better Internet connection.

The constant demands of reporting in the digital age had turned even the most thoughtful journalists into wire service reporters expected to constantly be on e-mail, updating blogs, and sending in revisions. Journalism had always been competitive, but now newsroom budgets were constantly shrinking, demands for content were ever growing, and the camaraderie of earlier years seemed to be fading. Tom Brokaw, who threw the party for Germond at the Wayfarer, recalled, "We were watching the Super Bowl on the one hand, talking politics on the other, and celebrating Jack. Jack threw his arm around me and said, 'Brokaw, these kids today are going to the gym and drinking Perrier water at the end of the day. I've got to get out of this business.'"

At one point, Mary canvassed some of her *Post* colleagues about how print media could even justify its existence in the television age. An assistant national editor, Phil Bennett, chipped in, "We begin where they leave off. They show you the bombs falling. We tell you what happened after the bombs fell, why they were loosed, and what the future may hold." Mary's favorite answer came from Bob Barnes, the *Post*'s assistant metro editor: "People like to read. They like to read about what they have seen. They like to read about a game they have been to. They like to read about an opera or a play. They like to share the experience. It is a kind of validation." Mary added her own two cents: "I hope they like to read. It is going to be awkward for me if they don't."

A short time later, Mary and Jack Germond appeared on CNN together to discuss the changing nature of campaigns. "Oh, it's a lot less fun," complained Germond.

"Technology is eating up our business the way it is everyone else's," said Mary. "People used to talk about horses and jockeys and strategy and victories and losses, and they used to write songs. No more. It is all about floppy disks and modems and the near-death experience with a pay phone that stopped mid-transmission. I find it very boring."

And by God, Mary did love politics. For all the nonsense, she loved elections and the idea that we could better govern ourselves. In 2000, Anne and Tom Beatty took Mary to New Hampshire to watch one of the primary debates, shortly after a blizzard had swept across the state. "We drove her up. There was so much snow," recalled Tom. To get in the hall,

Tom and Anne had to help catapult Mary over a snowbank. Mary was thrilled. New Hampshire. Snow. Presidential politics. Even in the era of television, citizens of the state still demanded that politicians woo them in coffee shops, high school gyms, and living rooms.

Brian McGrory remembered traveling to New Hampshire to cover the primary in 2000 for the *Boston Globe*. After a long day on the trail, he and Mary retired to the Wayfarer Inn. It was well after midnight. "Someone had just sent over a bowl of raspberries, and she was drinking her fifth Campari and was ready to go," said Brian. Finally, he surrendered: "Mary, I can't do it anymore. I have to go to bed."

When George W. Bush's parents, the former president and first lady, rushed to New Hampshire to bolster their son's chances against John McCain in the Republican primary, Mary compared George W. Bush to a distressed boy writing a letter home from summer camp: "The water is very cold and nobody here likes me." When asked about Mary's column, former first lady Barbara Bush sarcastically sniffed, "She's always loved us." McCain beat Bush in New Hampshire by double digits.

The freewheeling McCain campaign ground to a halt after he lost the South Carolina primary amid a flurry of negative attacks from the Bush campaign. Al Gore and George W. Bush would face each other in the general election. Mary did not love the choices. She recoiled at Bush's antipathy for intellectualism and education, referring to him in private correspondence as a "dim-witted frat boy." She thought Al Gore was undercut by a tendency to "lecture audiences as if they were enrolled in an English-as-a-second-language class."

Mary took a brief break from the presidential campaign trail to cover Hillary Clinton's Senate bid in New York. Author Beth Harpaz marveled that, although Mary was old enough to be her grandmother, her writing and reporting were still sharp. It was hard for Mary to get in and out of the campaign vans, and other reporters had to assist her. "This would be utterly humiliating for anyone else, but for McGrory, it's just another reason to respect her," Harpaz wrote.

Harpaz was not the only one to notice Mary's increasing infirmity on

the campaign trail. After a presidential debate in Boston, reporter David
Corn encountered Mary walking away from the John F. Kennedy Library
alone in the dark. She was trying to find the bus that would take her back
to the hotel. "But the scene was a bit chaotic," remembered Corn, "and she
appeared unsure where to head." Corn offered to help Mary find a taxi or
accompany her. Mary politely pushed Corn aside. "Need I remind you
that we're in Boston?" With that, Mary turned and walked off into the
night.

In early August, she traveled to Philadelphia for the Republican convention. When Bush selected Dick Cheney as his running mate, Mary
was convinced that Bush thought he had won the race. "He's already in
the Oval Office," she wrote, "and has his camp counselor by his side whis-
pering sagely in his ear."

Mary viewed the Republican convention, with its emphasis on "compassionate conservatism," as preposterous but effective. "There were more
gospel choirs than you would expect to hear at a gathering of the NAACP,"
she wrote. She shared the opinion of a delegate who said he preferred the
old conventions, "where people got up and argued about stuff."

Mary's views on Al Gore briefly improved with his solid performance
at the Democratic convention, in Los Angeles. She thought the selection of
Joe Lieberman, the first Jewish candidate ever selected for a national ticket,
suggested that Gore might be emerging from his long-running identity crisis. Although she noted that some Democratic pros thought Lieberman
was a "sanctimonious backstabber," she was pleased by Gore's boldness.

Yet it did not take long for the candidates to again wear on Mary. As
Election Day approached, she described the race as a "battle between the
unlikable and the unprepared." America was just as torn about its choices,
and Mary was soon reporting on an election for the ages, a virtual tie. On
Election Night, Gore was declared the winner by the networks, then Bush
was declared the winner; Gore made a concession call to Bush; Gore re-
tracted his concession; and then the whole process descended into acrimony and endless debates about the returns in Florida.

Mary's coverage of Florida and its aftermath was notable for its sense of calm. At a time when the media was hyperventilating, Mary brought a welcome sense of perspective. "Life goes on," she wrote. "There are no tanks in the streets and the telephones are working while the country learns the hard way that every vote counts." Mary took her colleague and fellow columnist David Broder to task for his melodramatic claim that having an election still unsettled at Thanksgiving made for the saddest day for the nation since the Kennedy assassination. "He is all wet," Mary declared.

That said, Mary did not think much of the Supreme Court verdict that finally awarded the presidency to George W. Bush. "The best that can be said about it is that it might be marginally better for them to have the last word than for the panting Florida Legislature or the possessed House of Representatives."

Mary was at a Christmas party hosted by former Nevada senator Paul Laxalt when Gore delivered his reaction to the Supreme Court decision. Laxalt was a conservative Republican, but he and Mary had long been friends. A who's who of senior Republicans and luminaries were at the party, including Vice President–elect Dick Cheney and Supreme Court justices Antonin Scalia and Anthony Kennedy. Mary noticed that many of the Republicans at the party were preemptively prepared to take umbrage with Gore. Yet Gore was gracious and to the point: "Just moments ago, I spoke with George W. Bush and congratulated him on becoming the forty-third president of the United States, and I promised him that I wouldn't call him back this time." Laxalt's Christmas party erupted in cheers. Mary wished that Gore had acted so naturally on the campaign trail.

Not long after, Mary sent a note to President Clinton's national security adviser, Sandy Berger, expressing appreciation for her treatment on the campaign trail with Gore: "Thanks for the ride—the last of my lifetime." It was an unusually blunt admission by Mary that she was getting too old to do the work she loved.

Mary's enthusiasm for writing was increasingly dimmed by a long-running battle with one of her editors, Steve Luxenberg, who managed Mary's copy for the Sunday Outlook section. The situation came to a head in the summer of 2001. As fellow *Post* editor Ken Ikenberry observed of Luxenberg, "He is a good guy, but he is a very fussy editor." Mary and Luxenberg argued about everything from style to word choice, and she lacerated him in a private note for what she called his "leaden touch" and "predilection for the cliché in thought and expression."

When Luxenberg made a number of changes to one of Mary's columns, she hit the roof. "When I looked at the Sunday paper, I found more maddening evidence of your gratuitous meddling with my copy," Mary complained, "once again displaying your strongest suit as an editor, which is to make copy as lumpy and stuffy as possible." Mary's bottom line: "Unless I receive assurances that the manhandling and bullying will stop, I will not write for Outlook again." Luxenberg's reply: "It would be a shame if you stopped writing for Outlook. Please don't."

When Mary's old friend Kay Graham died in July 2001, it was another sharp reminder of mortality. Graham's funeral, held at the National Cathedral, would have befitted a head of state. Former president Bill Clinton and Vice President Cheney shared a pew. Cellist Yo-Yo Ma played Bach. Henry Kissinger and Arthur Schlesinger offered eulogies.

Shortly after the service, Mary wrote a seven-page letter dictating her own funeral arrangements in meticulous detail. "The letter actually referenced Kay's funeral," Brian McGrory recalled, "and she thought it was too grand for her. She wanted a plain gray casket." Mary's letter to her lawyer indicated not only the church where her funeral should take place (the Shrine of the Most Blessed Sacrament), the type of ceremony ("a low Mass please"), and who should officiate, but also the time of day, the number of speakers, the number of minutes they were allowed to speak (not a second over seven minutes), and the lettering to be used in the program (Celtic). Front-row seats were to be reserved for old colleagues from the *Star*, and all the eulogists were men, as were the pallbearers. Both of her hymn choices referenced her life in the newspaper business: "O Zion, Haste," with its refrain of "Publish Glad Tidings," and "I'll Meet You in the Morning." After the funeral, a reception for close friends was to be held in her apartment, the last gathering of the Lower Macomb Street Choral Society.

Mark Gearan remembered getting a call from Mary. He asked her what she had done with her weekend. "It was gloomy and rainy and I wrote my funeral," she responded. "Ernie Miller is singing and you are playing." Gearan had not played the organ since high school, but he was not about to say no. "We just had to do what we were told—which I've been doing for twenty years," Gearan said.

Phil Gailey remembered a similar conversation. After several brandies, Mary informed him that he would be one of her eulogists, along with Brian McGrory and Bill Hamilton of the *Post*. Although uncomfortable with the topic, Gailey agreed. "Good," said Mary. "Now here are your instructions—be brief, talk about why the *Washington Star* was such a special place for us, and don't go blubbery on me the way you do when you read a dog story with a sad ending."

The turn of the century had brought monumental news stories: the impeachment of a president, the downfall of a series of House Speakers, and a presidential election decided by a mere 537 votes in Florida. But if Mary was thinking about the end of her career and the end of her life, there was more wrenching drama to come.

After her usual Italian vacation in August, Mary returned to work in early September 2001. On the morning of September 11, a beautiful blue-sky day in Washington, she attended an unremarkable press breakfast hosted by several Democratic strategists. A flurry of cell phone calls disrupted the meeting. Sara Fritz of the *St. Petersburg Times* told Mary that a plane had crashed into the World Trade Center.

Mary rushed back to her office. She and her colleagues watched the slow-motion footage of the collapsing towers again and again. They heard the reports of the dead and wounded at the Pentagon, which had also been struck by a hijacked plane, and they responded with alarm to rumors that a car bomb had gone off at the State Department. They watched in amazement as every single airport in the country was closed.

Mary's column on September 13 stands out as one of the most important of her career, not necessarily for what she wrote, but for the public's reaction. Mary led with the shock of the day, the "blank misery" and "an ocean of tears to be shed."

She praised New York mayor Rudy Giuliani for his heroic and reassuring performance from Ground Zero on September 11 as the nation came to grips with the loss of three thousand people. "The mayor spoke forcefully, as New Yorkers are wont to do," Mary wrote. "He promised that the city would regroup and go on. No one watching those around him could doubt it."

She had less kind words for President George W. Bush, who had been visiting an elementary school in Florida and was then flown to secure air bases in Louisiana and Nebraska after the attacks. "George W. Bush could not find the beat," wrote Mary. She disliked the way the president had jarringly referred to the terrorists as "folks" in his initial comments, and thought his stops at the air bases before returning to Washington late in the day made him look like a fugitive, "more apprehensive than resolute." She declared that Bush had failed the first great test of his leadership.

With the distance of time, Mary's column does not seem controversial. President Bush *was* hesitant and disjointed in the hours following the attacks. Mayor Giuliani did a far better job mastering the details of the situation in real time and laying a soothing hand on a frightened city and a grieving nation. Bush was not a great leader, and his presidency subsequently offered ample examples of that fact.

Mary received hundreds and hundreds of scathing letters and e-mails written in the coarsest and most vulgar terms imaginable. It was a torrent unlike anything she had ever seen, including during the Watergate and McCarthy eras.

"You are a shameful and disgusting journalist."

"People such as yourself are even worse than the terrorists who attacked our country."

"You are a disease upon the body of this last great free society."

Compounding matters, right-wing radios hosts singled Mary out for criticism, and even more letters cascaded into her office. Mary, ever conscientious, composed a form response letter of what she called "laborious civility," pointing out that she and the letter writers still lived in America and that the right to have different opinions was as American as apple pie. After receiving her letter, one reader sent her a brief note: "You may have lost your marbles, but you have kept your manners."

The day after her column ran, the *Post*'s ombudsman, Mike Getler, sent an e-mail to the paper's staff:

> There was a large, and angry, response to me, and others, concerning Mary McGrory's Thursday column. In times of real, national tension such as this one, that can be expected and, of course, Mary can say whatever she likes and undoubtedly many others agree with her views. But it does raise an issue for the paper because Mary's opinion column, during the week, appears uniquely at the start of the main news section. . . . But the paper probably pays something of a price for this in terms of coloring the views of some readers about whether the *Post* shares her views at times such as these. Maybe everybody understands that this is the place the column has always been. But maybe it could also go on a list of things that somehow can be explained to readers.

Getler's e-mail was hardly a ringing defense of the importance of informed dissent in a time of crisis. It felt as though the paper were distancing itself from Mary. Her placement in the paper was an issue that had been revisited periodically throughout the years, and rightfully so, but to bring it up in response to a flood of hate mail looked weak. Mary had been at the *Post* for twenty years, and she was disappointed in the lack of resolve from a paper that had achieved fame by taking on Nixon.

Jim Lehrer of PBS put the situation in perspective: "An emotional event triggers emotional responses. My guess is that it had less to do with Mary than the event itself. People were just very upset. It was understandable that anything that walked on the upsetness, which Mary was doing, would get a vehement response."

Mary wrote to a friend: "Politics as we knew it has disappeared. We have a president who has a 90 percent approval rating, which means you can't say a syllable against him. I thought he was pretty feeble in his darting about to airbases on the 11th—and said so—and was inundated in the worst, most corrosive criticism in my long life."

Mary recognized the surge of public support for President Bush in the wake of September 11, but she had been around long enough to understand that it also brought perils. She noted that many Democrats had come to regret granting President Lyndon Johnson sweeping powers in the wake of the Gulf of Tonkin incident during the Vietnam War, but that few Democrats (and no Republicans) were of a mind to even politely question President Bush as he pushed through the Patriot Act, which granted law enforcement broad, and largely unchecked, new authority. Mary also objected to Attorney General John Ashcroft's willingness to jettison attorney-client privilege for terror suspects as the nation established emergency military courts. "And don't think you need to put out more flags," wrote Mary in her column. "Patriotism can be quiet, too. And you might point out that there are several ideas behind the flag, like, for instance, the Constitution." She argued that it was not treason to suggest that the president was less than perfect, and she worried about the early signs that the administration was preparing for war not only in Afghanistan but in Iraq as well.

In November 2001, the *Washington Post* presented Mary with the Eugene Meyer Award, its highest honor. It was a bittersweet moment for Mary. She appreciated the recognition, but she still simmered about what she saw as a lack of support after September 11. Inevitably, it was also a moment for her to contrast life at the *Post* with the *Star*.

"You know, I'm old and tired, and I have just been through the worst clobbering in my life," Mary said when accepting the award. "I wrote that the commander in chief was AWOL for several hours on the worst day of our lives, September 11. The roof fell in. I was called a traitor to my country, a disgrace to my profession. The telephone rang with canceled subscriptions and calls for my head. A seven-inch stack of e-mails and letters called me names I can't repeat." She said that by giving her the award, the *Post* was in essence saying, "'Hell no, she won't go. She is one of us.'"

But Mary's comments were also barbed. She noted that with regard to her move over from the *Star*, "Some of you thought I should have come over sooner, and thought I was spoiled and overrated, which I probably was—and am to this day. You thought I was given to gab and levity; I thought you took yourselves too seriously and found saying 'Good morning' an unconscionable intrusion on your thoughts." Mary again compared the difference between the *Star* and the *Post* to that between Rome and Paris: the atmosphere at the *Post*, "businesslike, professional, and calm," was only occasionally broken by "bursts of laughter from the financial section."

"It has crossed my mind a time or two to retire," continued Mary, but she declared that she simply could not face the idea of a retirement ceremony with only cake. She expressed her gratitude to Ben Bradlee (although she twitted him for being a slightly reluctant bearer) and Don Graham. In closing, Mary declared, "When I die, I want just one word on my tombstone: 'newspaperwoman.' If anyone asks for credentials, I will show them the Eugene Meyer."

The stress following September 11 was only compounded by another blowup with Steve Luxenberg in January 2002. After a particularly intense argument on a Friday afternoon, Mary not only lost her voice, but had trouble even forming words. When the situation did not improve, she was rushed to George Washington University Hospital.

Brian McGrory remembers visiting Mary at the hospital. She described the incredible volume of hate mail she had received after September 11. The reaction was so vitriolic that she was stunned. Mary feared that she had lost her handle on the public and wondered if it was time to retire. When the *Post*'s executive editor, Len Downie, visited the next day, Mary offered to resign. He told her that he would not accept her resignation. "She was beyond thrilled," Brian recalled. "It was a very important moment for her."

Mary had suffered a small stroke. After a battery of tests, she was put on blood thinners and told to monitor her blood pressure. The incident convinced Mary that she could not work with Luxenberg as an editor, and she wrote to Fred Hiatt, "Do you have space for me on your op-ed page? The sooner the better. I have reached the end of the road with Outlook and the prosecuting attorney style of editing. I regret to say that I blew a fuse in the last dreadful encounter last Friday. It literally made me sick."

It says a great deal about Mary's exasperation with Luxenberg that she was willing to move her columns rather than be under his hand. "I prized my perch in the A-section," Mary wrote to Hiatt. "But it's time to move."

In January 2002, her columns started appearing not on page two but on the op-ed page. Whereas Mary had been livid with the move when it had happened under Murray Gart at the *Star*, this time she was resigned and wounded. That sting was not lessened when one of her friends wrote to her about how galling it must be for her to be in the company of the "pygmies" on the *Post*'s editorial pages.

With the United States already having invaded Afghanistan, the Bush administration moved toward military action against Iraq, and by October 2002, congressional Democrats had joined Republicans in backing President Bush's request for authority to use force against Baghdad. Mary was convinced that Democrats were more concerned about their own electoral prospects than the dangers that would accompany an ill-advised war in Iraq. "Sheepish Democrats continue to show the electorate that when it comes to the fateful business of sending young Americans into battle," wrote Mary, "they are at one with the Republicans." When Democrats fared poorly in the 2002 midterm elections, Mary saw it as no surprise. "They emitted a bleat, and mistook it for a message."

Mary was unconvinced that war with Iraq made sense. The *Post* editorial page, far more conservative than it had been in earlier years, was distressingly uniform in its support for the Iraq War. Mary railed against the casualness with which the potential for "collateral damage" was dismissed by armchair generals, forgetting that it meant "children with big dark eyes who will die for reasons not entirely clear to everybody."

Her position on the war veered sharply after Secretary of State Colin Powell's dramatic February 2003 presentation to the United Nations Security Council, making the case that Saddam Hussein possessed weapons of mass destruction. Mary had long liked and respected Powell, and she saw him as a voice of reason within the administration.

Mary's column the day after Powell's presentation was titled simply, "I'm Persuaded." "I don't know how the United Nations felt about Colin Powell's *J'accuse* speech against Saddam Hussein," Mary wrote. "I can only say that he persuaded me." Mary noted that she was not a pacifist, but that she truly thought that war should be a last resort. "I have resisted the push to war against Iraq because I thought George W. Bush was trying to pick a fight for all the wrong reasons—big oil, the far right—against the wrong enemy."

But Powell had changed her mind. "He made his case without histrionics of any kind, with no verbal embellishments." Mary did not buy the effort to tie Iraq to Al Qaeda, but she said of Powell's speech, "I'm not ready for war yet. But Colin Powell has convinced me that it might be the only way to stop a fiend, and that if we do go, there is reason."

Mary's conversion was news. White House spokesman Ari Fleischer cited Mary as an example of how public sentiment was shifting in favor of war. Television entertainer and outspoken liberal Phil Donahue lamented that Mary's column amounted to a "valentine for the president and his plans." Oliver North, the disgraced colonel of the Iran-contra scandal, who had been reborn as a conservative talk show host, said that Mary sounded as if she was ready to volunteer for the Marines. Mary was chagrined when several congressmen informed her that her column had "liberated" them to support the war.

Bob Woodward argued that Powell's speech and Mary's column

represented something of a turning point: "When Mary McGrory, who—a relentless Bush critic—said she believed Powell on this, that probably turned many minds. She had the ability to do that." Powell's speech was persuasive by almost any measure, and in a poll after the speech, some 66 percent of viewers said they found his case convincing.

Mary quickly had second thoughts about her column, and her second thoughts were spurred in no small part by a flood of reaction from upset liberals. One writer asked, "How could you? Truly, how could you?"

If Mary found any comfort in the stream of letters, it was that liberals were considerably more polite in their reproaches than were the conservatives who wrote after September 11.

"If there was one column that I know of that she might have regretted, it was the Colin Powell speech at the UN," said her colleague Al Kamen. The lacerating criticism from the right on her September 11 column, and from the left on her Powell column, introduced an element that had always been absent in Mary's work: uncertainty.

On March 6, 2003, she penned an open letter to her readers: "We have been through a great deal together—the Kennedy assassination, Vietnam, El Salvador, Grenada, Lebanon, and Florida. For the first time I can remember, we are estranged. That is, you have been since I wrote a column Feb. 6 about Colin Powell's U.N. indictment of Saddam Hussein. You have declared yourselves to be shocked, appalled, startled, puzzled, and above all disappointed by what you thought was a defection to the hawk side."

Mary insisted that her words had been poorly written (a rare and painful admission for her). She maintained that while she believed what Colin Powell had said at the UN, she was still "not convinced that war was the answer." She cited the deluge of comments from her longtime supporters, claiming that she had done something that President Bush never did: "I offended my base." Mary closed her column with a heartfelt plea: "You see how sorry I am. I hope now that all is forgiven and that I can come home again. Yours, The Unintentional Wanderer."

Most of Mary's readers and friends were willing to give her the benefit of the doubt, feeling that her long career had earned her that privilege. However, one reader argued that he could not "imagine a more invalidating moment for a columnist than the admission that she must follow her base." But Mary was genuinely wary of the Iraq invasion. As she wrote to one of her readers, "So mighty, so rich, so strong and we can't think of anything else but to go to war. The Founders would weep."

On Friday, March 14, 2003, Mary bustled about. She was hosting her Saint Patrick's Day party the next day and had to make sure all of the preparations were in place. She also had a column to finish that drew a contrast between spring's arrival in Washington and the coming Iraq invasion:

> The slopes off Rock Creek Parkway will soon be carpeted with daffodils. The crocuses and hyacinths will perfume the air. Wait until the stand of azaleas starts blazing along Klingle Road. Spring really is inevitable. Mother Nature has her calendar. Rainy season, dry, it's all the same to her. She has everything lined up, ready to go in sequence. Forsythias first, showering gold on every street corner, dandelions fiercely pushing up through cracks in the sidewalk, violets shyly venturing forward. Mother Nature is like the Pentagon in one respect. She likes everything in profusion. We have about 210,000 U.S. troops in Kuwait, for the invasion offensive; she's got an abundance of beauty in reserve.

Mary's assistant, Tina Toll, heard a sudden disturbance and rushed into Mary's office. She was at her desk and could not speak properly; her only words came out in a frustrated jumble. "I called 911, and I knew something was very, very wrong," Toll said. "And then we waited and waited and waited for what seemed like forever for help to come." It was clear that she was seriously ill. After Mary was taken away by ambulance, editor Ken Ikenberry put the finishing touches on her column. He knew that Mary would not want to miss a deadline.

Mary was rushed to George Washington University Hospital. The prognosis was grim. She had suffered a major stroke and had a severe case of aphasia. The consequence could not have been crueler: Mary had been robbed her of her ability to communicate. Although she understood what people were saying, she could no longer speak or write coherently, and she could no longer read.

On Saturday, her friends and family rushed to deal with the situation. Toll had let everyone know that Mary's party was canceled. But one guest did not get the message, and one of Mary's friends was surprised to find Gene McCarthy sitting on the stoop of Mary's apartment building, waiting for the festivities to begin.

"I flew down there on a Saturday morning," Brian McGrory remembered. "It was awful; just terrible. The vicious irony of a person who made their living with words being unable to express themselves was just beyond painful."

Mary's nephew, Ted McGrory, and her niece Anne Beatty, who had always seen it as their duty to look after Mary, flew down from Boston to help take care of her. After just a few days, Mary was desperate to get out of the hospital. She had been unable to sleep at all and was distraught. Family members arranged for home care at Mary's apartment, and she was eventually released from the hospital.

After the short car ride home, Mary walked into her apartment and headed straight down the hallway into her living room. She made an unsteady beeline for her window seat, where she curled up in a fetal position and immediately fell into a sound sleep. Mary was home.

She soon received stacks of correspondence and cards wishing her a speedy recovery. Many fans apologized for taking the liberty of addressing her with the more familiar "Mary," rather than "Ms. McGrory," and almost always cited the same justification for doing so: They had read her for so long that she felt like an old friend. Said one, "Get well damn it. The world needs you."

With the Iraq invasion in full force, Mary's friends let her know that her voice was missed. "They tell me you've been under the weather,"

Russell Baker wrote. "I am sorry to hear it, but don't dawdle about getting back into action. Our country is being hijacked." Phil Gailey wrote, "With you out of commission temporarily, the president no doubt decided this was the time to strike," and he insisted that Mary needed to be ready by autumn to serve as his translator in Rome. George McGovern shared with Mary that he, his wife, and several friends had sung "Shall We Gather at the River?" in Mary's honor as they dined at a local restaurant—much "to the amusement of the people in nearby booths."

Mary consulted a wide range of neurological experts and underwent intensive therapy to treat the aphasia in an attempt to rehabilitate her language skills. Her notebooks from after the stroke were filled with page after page of pinched and almost illegible writing as she tried to reteach her shaky hands to shape letters.

"It was one of the weirdest things I have encountered," said her friend Lance Gay. "You could talk to her, and she could understand you. She would then respond, but she could not make a coherent English sentence. It was all gibberish."

"Mary continued to call me after she had a stroke in March 2003," Maureen Dowd shared. "You could understand a bit here or there—'casserole' or 'Cheney.' It broke my heart to hear the words coming out so jumbled from lips that never uttered a less than perfect sentence."

Mary was galled by her lack of progress as spring stretched into summer and then fall. Awkward scene followed awkward scene as she realized that her friends and family could rarely understand her attempts at speech no matter how Herculean her effort. During one of her conversations with Phil Gailey, Mary managed to croak out the phrase "worse than death." Gailey was sure it probably was. When one of Mary's friends told her, "We miss your words," Mary mustered the reply, "So do I."

Mary was far from a model patient, and she often lashed out at the nurses attending to her in the apartment. Her friend Lee Cohn remembered visiting one day when Mary got a wine glass down from the shelf and poured herself a hefty draft of Irish whiskey. Cohn asked the nurse with some concern, "Is that all right?"

"If you find someone who can tell her what to do," sighed the exasperated nurse, "you let me know."

Mary's friends and colleagues came out in force to show their support. Ted Kennedy and his wife brought covered dinners. Senator Chris Dodd called frequently. "We knew she would still want gossip," Gloria Borger said of visiting Mary. "We went out on the back deck with her nurse, and we brought chocolates and had a glass of wine." Mary nodded, sometimes trying to comment, and chuckled in between the silences. For Borger, Mary's decline seemed to be the final act for the *Washington Star*.

When it was time to leave, Mary's nurse asked Borger if she and Mary could be dropped at five o'clock Mass. Borger was happy to help. Mary walked up the slight hill on Macomb Street, and climbed into the front seat of Borger's car.

"Which church are you going to?"

"I don't know," the nurse responded. "Mary always picks different ones."

"Then, without missing a beat," Borger shared, "Mary proceeded to direct us to the church, like a traffic cop giving directions." Borger was amazed.

Al Kamen was as frustrated as anyone by his interactions with her: "She would write things, scratch things—two parallel lines—and show it to me. This was supposed to mean something. What did these lines mean? You couldn't respond." He hit on an idea for a better way to spend time together.

Kamen began taking Mary for rides in his convertible Mazda Miata with the top down and opera music playing. They would drive down Rock Creek Parkway, along the river, and past the Kennedy Center. Although getting Mary into the small convertible was a bit of a process, she enjoyed the sun and the wind in her hair. It was a triumph of nonverbal communication.

Mary often arranged to be taken into the *Post* newsroom. "One day I went over to her apartment," remembered Lee Cohn, "and she was sitting there with her press pass on a chain around her neck, waiting for someone from the *Post* to pick her up." Len Downie had to be diplomatic as Mary asked, in barely intelligible words, when she could resume her column. The pathos was suffocating. Eventually, Mary agreed to retire from the *Post*, realizing that she would never author another column.

Mary received a number of tributes during her illness. One of those that touched her most deeply was a November 2003 column by Brian Mc-Grory singing her praises in the *Boston Globe*. Begging forgiveness for "the boorish act of bragging about a relative," Brian acknowledged that eight months after her stroke, it was clear that Mary was unlikely to fully recover, "ending one of the most important, colorful, and enduring newspaper careers that the American public has had the pleasure to read."

On November 12, 2003, Mary was feted during a black-tie dinner at the Pierre Hotel, in New York, as she received the John Chancellor Award for Excellence in Journalism. Mark Shields offered a wonderful piece of commentary in his remarks:

> When I think of Mary McGrory I think of the table. The table is where people come together for food and companionship. For many, there is not enough food, and for some, there is no table at all. The table is where people come to make decisions in their neighborhoods, in their families and even their nations. Too many people have no place at that table. Their voices are not heard, their needs are often unaddressed. Mary McGrory's magnificent life work has been to remind all of us that all of God's children deserve a place at our table.

Phil Gailey, Maureen Dowd, David Halberstam, Anna Quindlen, and others turned out to pay tribute to Mary. "If the evening had any excess," Gailey recalled, "it was at the bar and not at the speaker's lectern."

Mary's condition seemed to stabilize, but gains in her language rehabilitation remained elusive. In March 2004, she was again honored, this time at the American Ireland Fund's 12th National Gala, on the eve of

Saint Patrick's Day. Harps and Celtic songs played in the background as laughter and tall tales were the order of the evening. British prime minister Tony Blair, Mary, and Representative Peter King were honorees. A number of speakers marveled at the progress of the peace process in Northern Ireland, and the Irish prime minister, Bertie Ahern, personally thanked Mary for all she had done for the cause of peace. "Here in Washington, you may like to think of her as one of your own," said Ahern, "but we know her as Mary from the shores of Lough Swilly, who is not only a great friend of many years' standing, but a very dear member of our extended family as well."

After Ahern's remarks, and to everyone's amazement, Mary offered three or four perfect sentences of thanks. "It was amazing," said Phil Gailey, and surely it had required a monumental effort on Mary's part.

Mary's aphasia kept her away from St. Ann's for longer than she would have liked. Not being able to read to the children was simply too painful. "After Mary had her stroke, she did not come here for a while," said Sister Josephine Murphy. "I was very upset about that, because our children understand people's problems." But the sisters from St. Ann's made regular visits to Mary and joined her in prayer in her living room, and Josephine eventually convinced her to pay a visit to St. Ann's.

Sister Josephine carefully briefed the children in advance. She told them that Mary was going to come but that she was sick and would not be able to talk the way she had before. "They just accepted her," said Josephine, "and she just accepted them."

Before her stroke, Mary had made a particular impression on one of the boys who struggled with a speech impediment. Mary had singled him out for special attention, reading to him for hours.

During the visit, Josephine poked her head in to see how Mary was doing with the children. The boy, who had overcome his speech impediment, was sitting on Mary's lap. He glanced up at Josephine.

"When I couldn't read and I needed help, Mary Gloria was here for me," the boy explained. "She helped me. Now Mary Gloria can't read too good and needs help, and I am reading to her."

On April 16, 2004, Mary's appendix burst and she was rushed to George Washington University Hospital for surgery. On April 21, 2004, Mary Dorothy McGrory died at the age of eighty-five, following complications from surgery.

On a spring day in Washington, dappled with sun and rain, her funeral was conducted just as she had directed.

Mary was laid to rest at Maplewood Cemetery, in Antrim, New Hampshire. Her headstone is modest. It is inscribed: MARY MCGRORY: NEWSPAPER WOMAN AND VOLUNTEER. The words, of course, are her own.

Acknowledgments

This book would have been impossible without the support, insight, and assistance of a long line of people. First and foremost, my appreciation to my wife, Brenda, for her patience and putting up with me when I would disappear into archives on Saturday afternoons. Thanks also to my children—Ian, Eliza, and Phoebe—for much needed daily doses of inspiration and laughter, and to all of the extended Norris and Bradberry clans for being such good readers.

Special thanks go to Mary's most immediate surviving family members: Anne and Tom Beatty, Ted McGrory, and Polly McGrory. They have all been fantastically supportive through the long trek of writing this book, from gauzy concept to final product. Getting to know all of them has been a lasting pleasure. Thanks also to Brian McGrory for his considerable assistance and unique insight into Mary as both a person and a journalist.

I also want to single out the small circle of friends whom I rather cruelly subjected to early and very unfinished versions of this book: Mike Petrosillo, Robert Templer, and John Raho. All did me the favor of providing honest feedback, and the text is much better for it as a result. Greg Pollock, Jason Forrester, Matt Berzok, Charles Kenny, and Mark Joyce also deserve many thanks for their long-standing and unflagging support of my efforts to write and tell a compelling story.

I can't say thank you often enough, or in enough different ways, to Mary's good friend, John O'Brien, who appeared like an angel to help me find such a fine home for this book at the eleventh hour.

Special thanks also to Gail Ross, my agent, who has been such a good, resolute partner in this endeavor and so supportive of my work.

I consider myself incredibly fortunate to have worked with Wendy Wolf as my editor on this book. Few authors are lucky enough to work with someone doubly blessed with such good nature and such a graceful pen. I owe a considerable debt of gratitude to both Wendy and Kathryn Court for believing in this book and embracing it. Thanks to you both. I also owe special gratitude to the editorial team at Viking for first-rate work in copy editing, fact-checking, and design.

Many thanks also to Susan Glasser and her team at *Politico*, who did such a nice job in shaping the first article I published on Mary.

I also want to offer special recognition and credit to the scores of Mary's friends, colleagues, peers, and associates who agreed to be interviewed as part of my research on this book and have wanted it to succeed every step of the way. Getting to talk at length to such a fascinating group of people has been an abiding pleasure. Mary was blessed with a great circle of friends.

I also want to say a special thanks to the staffs at not only the Library of Congress, but the many archives and presidential libraries whose resources I frequently called upon while writing this book. Even when my research requests verged on looking for a needle in a haystack, these professional librarians and archivists were friendly, encouraging, and stubbornly persistent. They are a deeply underappreciated wonder.

Many thanks to my friend and colleague Annie Malknecht for her gracious assistance in wrestling stubborn photos and PDFs into shape. I also want to acknowledge the fine genealogical sleuthing of Brent Bradberry that was so helpful in reconstructing Mary's roots, and to thank Kai Bird for his initial introduction to Gail Ross.

Lastly, and while realizing I am surely missing others who deserve kudos, I want to thank Mary McGrory—not only for leading a splendid, interesting life, but for launching me on such an intriguing pilgrimage.

Notes

All endnotes citing "Mary McGrory Papers" refer to the Mary McGrory Papers, housed in the Manuscript Division at the Library of Congress, in Washington, D.C. The 184-box collection was invaluable to my research.

All mentions of "McGrory family correspondence" refer to additional letters, not housed in the Library of Congress collection, to which I was allowed access by Mary's nephew, Ted McGrory, and her nieces, Anne Beatty and Polly McGrory.

All references to "Clark family papers" pertain to correspondence made available by Blair Clark's widow, Joanna, for purposes of my research.

All dates given for Mary McGrory's columns reflect the date they were originally published in the *Washington Star* or the *Washington Post*, as reflected in the hard copies of these columns filed with her papers in the Library of Congress collection.

Throughout the text, I interchangeably refer to either the *"Washington Star"* or the *"Washington Evening Star"* for ease of use. The paper went through a series of name changes during the period covered by this book, which included, among other iterations, the *Washington Star*, the *Washington Evening Star*, and the *Washington Star News*.

Chapter One: A Boston Girl from Out of the Blue

1 **"Say, Mary, aren't you":** Mary McGrory, interview by Kathleen Currie, Women in Journalism Oral History Project, Washington Press Club Foundation, August 4, 1991, and July 26, 1992; Winzola McLendon and Scottie Smith, *Don't Quote Me: Washington Newswomen and the Power Society* (Boston: E. P. Dutton and Co., 1970), 30–39; "A Writer's Life," event of Washington Independent Writers, C-SPAN, Washington, DC, November 21, 1997; Barbara Belford, *Brilliant Bylines: A Biographical Anthology of Notable Newspaperwomen in America* (New York: Columbia University Press, 1986), 270–78; Amelia Young, "Mary

McGrory—Washington's Top Woman Reporter," *Information: The Catholic Church in American Life*, January 1961, 12–19; David Von Drehle, "Columnist Illuminated Half-Century of Washington," *Washington Post*, April 22, 2004; Duncan Spencer, "A Reporter at Her Primitive Best," *Washington Star*, May 6, 1975.

2 **Noyes offered Mary McGrory:** *Fox Special Report with Brit Hume*, Fox News Network, June 16, 1998.

2 **McGrory entered the Senate hearings:** Maria Braden, *She Said What? Interviews with Women Newspaper Columnists* (Lexington: University Press of Kentucky, 1993), 24–34.

2 **Suddenly a friendly face:** Maureen Dowd, "A *Star* Columnist," *New York Times*, December 26, 2004 (correction appended); Maureen Dowd, *Are Men Necessary?* (New York: Berkley Books, 2005), 130–34.

2 **"He was an Irish bully boy":** McLendon and Smith, *Don't Quote Me*, 30–39.

3 **After six hours:** Young, "Mary McGrory—Washington's Top Woman Reporter."

4 **"There were 36 anguishes":** Von Drehle, "Columnist Illuminated."

4 **She described Welch:** Mary McGrory, column, May 12, 1954.

5 **As Mary recalled, "All of a sudden":** "Queen of the Corps," *Time*, November, 10, 1958, 71–72.

5 **"So you have joined":** Mary McGrory Papers, container 10.

5 **Readers asked Mary the color:** Young, "Mary McGrory—Washington's Top Woman Reporter."

5 **A caller to the *Star*'s switchboard:** Mary McGrory Papers, container 10, May 24, 1955.

5 **The cartoonist Herbert Block:** Herbert Block, *A Cartoonist's Life* (New York: Three Rivers Press, 1998), 342.

5 **Longtime CBS news anchor:** Roger Mudd, interview by author, December 8, 2009.

5 **Howard Shuman, a longtime:** Howard E. Shuman, interview by Donald Ritchie, July 22, 1987, Senate Oral History Project, Senate Historical Office, Washington DC.

6 **Mary not only emulated:** Belford, *Brilliant Bylines*, 270–78; McGrory, interview by Currie; Mary McGrory, column, August 2, 1970.

6 **As the buzz around:** Von Drehle, "Columnist Illuminated."

6 **The hearings degenerated:** Mary McGrory, column, June 9, 1954.

7 **"It also brought forth":** Mary McGrory, column, June 10, 1954.

7 **Tom Oliphant, who was:** Thomas Oliphant, "A Journalist's Truth and Beauty," *Boston Globe*, April 25, 2004.

8 **Mary was fond of describing:** Sara Sanborn, "Byline Mary McGrory: Choice Words for Bullies, Fatheads, and Self-Righteous Rouges," *Ms.*, May 1975, 59–61, 74–75.

8 **According to Mary, her father:** Mary McGrory Papers, containers 139 and 165; "National Press Club Fourth Estate Award," C-SPAN, Washington, DC, November 5, 1998.

8 **By Mary's own account:** "National Press Club Fourth Estate Award."

8 **If Mary's father brought:** Mary McGrory, interview by John Arnold Schmalzbauer, Washington, DC, 1994, transcript made available by Schmalzbauer.

8 **"She was not a laughing Colleen":** Mark Shields, interview by author, March 13, 2010.

9 **"I only heard her speak":** Elizabeth Shannon, interview by author, December 21, 2009.

9 **Irish Catholic priests threatened:** Tom O'Conner, interview by author, April 21, 2010.

9 **The McGrory half:** Brent Bradberry, of Moscow, Idaho, was of great assistance in helping research the genealogy of the McGrory and Jacobs families, as was family correspondence shared by the Beatty and McGrory families.

10 **The school, located on:** Gloria Negri, "Recalling Latin Roots; Girls' Class of '35 Delights in Annual Reunion," *Boston Globe,* June 8, 1995.

10 **As seventh graders:** Mary McGrory, columns, July 17, 1983, and September 14, 1975; Von Drehle, "Columnist Illuminated."

10 **The years at Girls':** Mary McGrory, column, August 20, 1995.

11 **Mary had her heart set:** Helen Dudar, "A Pulitzer Prize," *New York Post,* May 10, 1975.

11 **"With the passing of the years":** Mary McGrory Papers, container 165.

11 **It was a dark time:** Mary McGrory Papers, container 165, journal entry of September 2, 1939.

11 **Her mood rebounded considerably:** Braden, *She Said What?* 24–34; Von Drehle, "Columnist Illuminated."

12 **She had been attracted:** Braden, *She Said What?* 24–34; McGrory, interview by Currie.

12 **As author and media historian:** Eric Alterman, *Sound and Fury: The Making of the Punditocracy* (Ithaca, NY: Cornell University Press, 1999), 22.

12 **Mary longed to work:** McGrory, interview by Currie; Von Drehle, "Columnist Illuminated"; Sanborn, "Byline Mary McGrory."

12 **Frustrated, Mary appealed directly:** "Lady with a Needle," *Newsweek,* March 21, 1960, 114–15; McLendon and Smith, *Don't Quote Me,* 30–39.

12 **In March 1946:** Sanborn, "Byline Mary McGrory."

12 **Her story about Mac:** Mary McGrory, column, March 7, 1946.

13 **In 1946, the *Times*:** Arthur Gelb, interview by author, October 14, 2010.

13 **She finally had freedom:** Mary McGrory Papers, container 165.

13 **More important, "in Boston":** McLendon and Smith, *Don't Quote Me,* 30–39.

14 **"It was heaven":** Colman McCarthy, "Mary McGrory, *Post* Columnist, Dies; Appreciation," *National Catholic Reporter*, May 7, 2004.

14 **"Newsrooms are large places":** Mary McGrory, column, April 8, 1977.

15 **Not long after settling:** Mary McGrory Papers, containers 168, 128, and 139, 1949, including draft of George Kennedy article; "Memories of Mary McGrory," *Washington Post*, April 27, 2004; Young, "Mary McGrory—Washington's Top Woman Reporter"; Mary Bader, interview by author, January 7, 2010; Mary McGrory, column, December 23, 1961; Gordon Brown, "Bobby: My Moral Beacon," *New Statesman*, April 30, 2007.

16 **Back at the *Star*:** Gale Reference Team, "Biography—McGrory, Mary (1918–2004)," in *Contemporary Authors* (Farmington Hills, MI: Gale Publishing, 2005).

16 **She described Senator Alexander:** Mary McGrory, column, March 22, 1953.

17 **But Mary was not cowed:** Mary McGrory, column, February 22, 1953.

17 **Johnson liked the quote:** Mary McGrory Papers, container 139.

17 **After the piece ran:** Mary McGrory Papers, container 5, Senator Lyndon Johnson letter of March 20, 1953.

17 **"Some old hands took":** McLendon and Smith, *Don't Quote Me,* 30–39.

18 **He told Mary that:** John Stacks, *Scotty: James B. Reston and the Rise and Fall of American Journalism* (Omaha, NB: Bison Press, 2003), 171–72.

18 **"The paper was very antsy":** Anthony Lewis, interview by author, March 9, 2010.

18 **Arthur Gelb concurred:** Arthur Gelb interview.

18 **"It's quite remarkable that":** Braden, *She Said What?* 24–34.

18 **Phil and Katharine Graham:** McGrory, interview by Currie.

19 **On her trips, she:** Mary McGrory Papers, container 169.

19 **"It didn't matter where":** Gerry Kirby, interview by author, September 1, 2010.

Chapter Two: Arrived

22 **Joining a small corps:** Mary McGrory, column, January 18, 1966.

22 **"Unlike Mr. Stevenson":** Mary McGrory, column, September 17, 1956.

23 **Mary was proud:** McGrory, interview by Currie; Mary McGrory, column, May 24, 1992.

23 **Mary's cousin Brian McGrory:** Brian McGrory, "Simply the Best," *Boston Globe*, November 11, 2003.

23 **Mary acknowledged that many feminists:** Mary McGrory, column, July 21, 1985.

23 **"Not a gentle world":** Dan Rather, interview by author, March 1, 2010.

24 **They are always communicative:** McLendon and Smith, *Don't Quote Me,* 30–39.

24 **David Broder noted that:** *Morning Edition*, National Public Radio, April 22, 2004.

24 **"It seemed to me"**: Jack Germond, interview by author, October 15, 2009.

24 **Noting that Noyes had:** Mary McGrory Papers, container 62, telegrams of September 18, 20, and 21, 1956.

25 **"Much as we deplore"**: Mary McGrory Papers, container 62.

25 **After visiting Sidney, Montana:** Mary McGrory Papers, container 139.

25 **Kefauver, the would-be vice president:** Blair Clark, unpublished autobiography, courtesy of the Clark family.

26 **They were all mock missives:** Mary McGrory Papers, container 62.

26 **Mary had first laid eyes:** Mary McGrory, column, November 24, 1963; John F. Kennedy Presidential Library and Museum, Press Panel Oral History Interview with White House Correspondents George Herman, Peter Lisagor, and Mary McGrory, John F. Kennedy Oral History Collection, August 4, 1964.

27 **JFK then asked her out:** McGrory family correspondence.

28 **As Mary later recounted:** JFK Library Press Panel.

28 **During the debate:** Mary McGrory, column, November 24, 1963.

28 **"Here was this handsome"**: JFK Library Press Panel.

28 **It is no wonder:** Thomas Maier, *The Kennedys: America's Emerald Kings* (New York: Basic Books, 2003), 246.

28 **JFK began trying the hats:** JFK Library Press Panel.

29 **Where Kefauver delivered a standard:** Mary McGrory Papers, container 62.

30 **Stevenson was a gifted speaker:** Mary McGrory, column, October 27, 1954.

30 **"For want of a better term"**: Al Spivak, interview by author, February 22, 2010.

30 **"She periodically shouted back"**: Herbert Klein, *Making It Perfectly Clear* (New York: Doubleday, 1980), 68.

31 **A pair of members:** Mary McGrory, column, July 23, 1965.

31 **One editor joked that:** Mary McGrory Papers, container 163.

31 **A number of congressional graybeards:** "National Press Club Fourth Estate Award"; Russell Baker, interview by author, March 17, 2010.

31 **"She was absolutely loyal"**: Roger Mudd interview.

31 **"Men naturally like to explain"**: McLendon and Smith, *Don't Quote Me,* 30–39.

32 **Mary complained halfheartedly:** McLendon and Smith, *Don't Quote Me,* 30–39; Mary McGrory Papers, container 125, Mary McGrory speech at the Omaha Press Association, April 17, 1982.

32 **"The fact that I don't raise"**: Braden, *She Said What?* 24–34.

32 **Mary would dance:** Belford, *Brilliant Bylines,* 270–78.

33 **Supreme Court Justice Arthur Goldberg:** Mary McGrory Papers, container 5.

33 **"Is the *Star* really like this"**: Mary McGrory Papers, container 1.

33 **Mark Shields appeared to be:** Mark Shields interview.

33 **"She loved music"**: Don Graham, interview by author, December 1, 2009.

33 **Hosting also allowed Mary:** McLendon and Smith, *Don't Quote Me,* 30–39.

34 **But while Mary was:** Federal News Service, National Press Club Luncheon Address with Helen Thomas, May 16, 1996.

34 **They could not ask:** Nan Robertson, *The Girls in the Balcony* (New York: Random House, 1992), 100–3.

34 **Reporter Haynes Johnson concurred:** Haynes Johnson, interview by author, November 12, 2009.

34 **Mary bitterly resented it:** Mary McGrory, column, July 21, 1985; Braden, *She Said What?* 24–34.

34 **In September 1957, George Minot:** Mary McGrory Papers, container 1.

36 **"Why don't we hire her?":** Mary McGrory Papers, container 139.

36 **"She writes swiftly and well":** "Queen of the Corps."

36 **"I have not forgotten":** Mary McGrory Papers, container 139, 1958.

36 **"The world is yours":** Mary McGrory Papers, container 1.

36 **On a single day:** Mary McGrory Papers, container 139, Pyke Johnson letter of November 7, 1958, Wayne Andrews letter of November 7, 1958, Edward Kuhn letter of November 7, 1958, and Henry Robbins letter of November 7, 1958.

36 **"When are you going to write":** Mary McGrory Papers, container 1, Stewart Alsop letter of November 14, 1958.

37 **Mary joked to one:** Mary McGrory, *The Best of Mary McGrory: A Half Century of Washington Commentary*, ed. Phil Gailey (Kansas City, MO: McMeel, 2006), xii–xviii.

37 **In January 1959:** James Butler, "Mary McGrory," *Editor & Publisher*, January 17, 1959, 48–49.

37 *Newsweek* **ran its own:** "Lady with a Needle."

37 **The** *Globe* **was one:** Mary McGrory Papers, container 128, editor's note above McGrory *Boston Globe* column of February 3, 1960.

37 **Mary felt strongly about:** Belford, *Brilliant Bylines*, 270–78.

38 **"Mary did something remarkable":** Russell Baker interview.

38 **Within a year of syndication:** Haynes Johnson interview.

38 **Baker, his wife, Drury:** Russell Baker interview.

38 **Both Mary and Baker:** Mary McGrory, review of *Advise and Consent*, by Allen Drury, January 25, 1959.

39 **The country was still:** Michael O'Brien, *John F. Kennedy: A Biography* (New York: Thomas Dunne Press, 2005), 424.

39 **Senators Hubert Humphrey:** Mary McGrory, column, July 21, 1959.

39 **"The sun-tanned senator":** Mary McGrory, column, May 3, 1959.

40 **Mary added a comment:** Mary McGrory, column, May 4, 1959.

40 **As Mary put it:** JFK Library Press Panel.

40 **"He loved it":** Mary McGrory Papers, container 162.

40 **Years later, when she was asked:** JFK Library Press Panel.

40 **She argued that JFK's:** Mary McGrory, column, January 3, 1960.

40 **But behind the scenes:** Mary McGrory Papers, container 7.

41 **With a challenge from:** Mary McGrory, column, February 21, 1960.

41 **She thought he was awkward:** Ibid.

41 **Mary and Blair were:** Blair Clark autobiography; Anthony Summer and Robbyn Swan, *Sinatra: The Life* (New York: Vintage, 2006), 263.

42 **"She is kindly and stolid":** Mary McGrory, column, March 30, 1960.

42 **Mary's editors, delighted with:** Mary McGrory Papers, container 63, cable of March 29, 1960.

42 **Yet despite his charisma:** David Broder, "Consummate Politician," *Washington Post*, November 17, 1993.

42 **"I had been with Hubert Humphrey":** JFK Library Press Panel.

43 **"They have withstood gnawing winds":** Mary McGrory, column, April 4, 1960.

44 **"There is a wounded rhinoceros":** Mary McGrory Papers, container 1, Mary McGrory letter to Liz Acosta, May 6, 1960.

44 **Mary watched as a misty-eyed:** Mary McGrory Papers, container 128.

45 **"I don't mind campaigning":** JFK Library Press Panel.

45 **As Mary's colleague Duncan Spencer:** Spencer, "A Reporter at Her Primitive Best."

45 **While they both practiced:** Mary McGrory, column, August 20, 1978.

46 **"They screamed 'we want Kennedy'":** Mary McGrory, column, July 10, 1960.

46 **McCarthy was no fan:** "Unforeseen Eugene," *Time*, March 22, 1968, 30.

46 **Hailing from the small town:** Dominic Sandbrook, *Eugene McCarthy and the Rise and Fall of Postwar American Liberalism* (New York: Anchor Press, 2005), 3.

47 **Mary was stirred:** Mary McGrory, column, July 24, 1960.

47 **"Thus ended a tentative":** Mary McGrory, column, July 14, 1960.

48 **"I never would do that":** McGrory family correspondence.

48 **"Two weeks ago":** Mary McGrory, column, July 24, 1960.

48 **"When Mr. Nixon presides":** Mary McGrory, column, August 11, 1960.

49 **She described Johnson playing to:** Mary McGrory, column, October 13, 1960.

49 **His own partisans feared that:** Mary McGrory, column, October 6, 1960.

50 **"There is so much immediacy":** "A Writer's Life."

50 **Mary couldn't help but notice:** Mary McGrory, column, September 28, 1962.

50 **While she disliked Nixon:** Mary McGrory, column, October 8, 1960.

50 **"But the Senator has learned":** Mary McGrory, column, October 19, 1960.

51 **"I have followed you for four years":** JFK Library Press Panel.

51 **"As he arrived in Hyannis Port":** Theodore H. White, *The Making of the President 1960* (New York: Atheneum, 1961), 15.

51 **When he called out:** JFK Library Press Panel.

51 **With some satisfaction, Mary noted:** Mary McGrory Papers, container 10.

52 **JFK's father, Joseph Kennedy:** Mary McGrory Papers, container 7.

52 **With some amusement, Mary watched:** Mary McGrory, column, November 10, 1960.

52 **"Hard-hearted Jack with tears":** Sally Bedell Smith, *Grace and Power: The Private World of the Kennedy White House* (New York: Random House, 2005), 6.

Chapter Three: He Would Have Liked It

53 **"A sharp wind knifed":** Mary McGrory, column, January 14, 2001.

53 **The official program:** Todd Purdum, "From That Day Forth," *Vanity Fair*, February 2011, http://www.vanityfair.com/society/features/2011/02/kennedy-201102.

54 **Mary was suddenly hit:** JFK Library Press Panel.

54 **Clark had just been promoted:** David Halberstam, *The Powers That Be* (Champaign: University of Illinois Press, 2000), 384; Gary Paul Gates, *Air Time: The Inside Story of CBS News* (Berkeley, CA: Berkley Publishing Group, 1979), 108.

55 **"There was something of the Irish mother":** John Seigenthaler, interview by author, March 24, 2010.

55 **"When he was in the White House":** Mary McGrory Papers, container 8.

55 **"We knew that before Sy Hersh":** Mary McGrory Papers, container 9.

56 **"As his father before him":** Mary McGrory, column, December 7, 1997.

56 **As a frustrated Stevenson:** Mary McGrory Papers, container 128.

56 **"It was as if, discouraged":** Mary McGrory, column, May 6, 1961.

56 **"But Kennedy would:** Mary McGrory Papers, containers 128, 96, and 8; Richard Reeves, *President Kennedy: Profile of Power* (New York: Simon and Schuster, 1994), 153–54; Mary McGrory, columns, May 26 and 31, 1961, June 1, 2, 4, 5, and 6, 1961, and November 24, 1963; JFK Library Press Panel.

58 **Irritated by Clark's continued:** Clark family papers, Blair Clark letter to Mary McGrory, June 12, 1961.

58 **"How fierce I think we would have been":** Ibid.

59 **Mary was uneasy about:** Mary McGrory, column, November 22, 1968.

60 **Haynes Johnson, a close friend:** Haynes Johnson interview.

60 **"Bobby tried to teach me":** Mary McGrory Papers, container 7.

60 **As Mary confided to a fellow visitor:** Fred Harris, *Does People Do It? A Memoir* (Norman: University of Oklahoma Press, 2008), 154.

60 **Racing back down the street:** Mary McGrory, column, November 22, 1968.

61 **He invited all of the Catholics:** Mary McGrory, column, June 4, 1963.

61 **It struck Mary that:** Mary McGrory, column, July 26, 1961.

62 **With Kennedy approaching the end:** Mary McGrory Papers, containers 128 and 7; Mary McGrory, column, January 16, 1962; McGrory, interview by

Currie; Kevin Hamilton, "Books; Understanding JFK—Two Detailed Studies of His Life, Death," *Seattle Times*, October 31, 1993; JFK Library Press Panel; Roberta Wyper, "Mary McGrory: Tiger in the Typewriter," *W*, October 28–November 4, 1977, 20–21.

64 **She had once written:** Mary McGrory Papers, container 2.

64 **"It is merely the one":** Mary McGrory, column, October 12, 1962.

64 **"At 1:50, the atmosphere":** Mary McGrory, column, November 7, 1962.

65 **"For Richard M. Nixon":** Mary McGrory, column, November 8, 1962.

66 **"I have been a reader":** Mary McGrory Papers, container 10.

66 **Ben Bradlee and:** Mary McGrory Papers, container 5, cable of November 8, 1962.

66 **"Four of us read 78 entries":** Mary McGrory Papers, container 1, W. P. Hobby letter to Mary McGrory, March 11, 1963.

67 **"It would have been hard to say":** JFK Library Press Panel.

67 **Perhaps Mary's only regret:** Debra Gersh Hernandez, "Nixon and the Press; There Were a Handful of Journalists that the Late President Didn't Hate, but Most Were Viewed as Ideological Enemies," *Editor & Publisher*, June 25, 1994, 82–91.

67 **Mary enlisted the Kennedys:** Mary McGrory, column, March 28, 1976.

68 **At the *Star*, Newby Noyes:** "Catch a Falling *Star*," *Time*, April 19, 1963, 108.

68 **Mary swam in the bracing lake:** Mary McGrory Papers, container 165.

69 **"Death came to Pope John XXIII":** Mary McGrory, column, June 4, 1963.

69 **When someone suggested that:** Mary McGrory Papers, container 67, Daniel Patrick Moynihan letter to Mary McGrory, June 27, 1963.

70 **"It was interesting that":** JFK Library Press Panel.

70 **They were just twenty feet away:** Louis Harris, interview by Vicki Daitch, April 12–13, 2005, John F. Kennedy Oral History Program.

70 **"Dynamite has become":** Mary McGrory, column, September 19, 1963.

71 **On a plane ride back:** Mary McGrory Papers, container 162.

71 **"It is not my responsibility":** McGrory, interview by Schmalzbauer.

71 **Mary thought of herself:** Dudar, "A Pulitzer Prize."

71 **"Her role was to influence":** Haynes Johnson interview.

71 **But Barry Goldwater:** Mary McGrory, column, September 18, 1963.

71 **Mary wrote that when Goldwater's:** Mary McGrory, column, November 1, 1963.

72 **"This most rational man refused":** Mary McGrory, column, November 24, 1963.

72 **Calm and deliberate:** Lance Gay, interview by author, May 9, 2007.

73 **"The men picked up":** Mary McGrory, column, November 23, 1963.

73 **They headed back to:** Clark family papers, Mary McGrory letter to Blair Clark, n.d.

73 **As he stood over her:** Belford, *Brilliant Bylines*, 270–78.

73 **The news story came:** McGrory, interview by Currie.

74 **"He brought gaiety":** Mary McGrory, editorial, November 23, 1963.

74 **"She wrote that column":** Lance Gay interview.

74 **The staff was replacing:** *Tim Russert*, CNBC News Transcripts, December 16, 2000.

74 **"Heavens, Mary," Moynihan replied:** Mary McGrory Papers, container 7.

74 **"I don't think there's any point":** Martin Nolan, "Across America, a Loss of Youth and Promise," *Boston Globe*, July 23, 1999.

75 **"When he came to the White House":** Mary McGrory, column, November 24, 1963.

76 **"No, I can do it":** "A Writer's Life."

76 **During the ceremony:** Ephraim Hardcastle, *Daily Mail* (London), January 1, 1999.

76 **After the funeral, Mary walked:** McGrory, interview by Currie; *Tim Russert*, CNBC News Transcripts, March 9, 1997; Phil Gailey, "Words That Emblazoned History," *St. Petersburg Times*, October 26, 2006; "A Writer's Life"; "Longtime Washington *Star* Editor John Cassady," *Washington Post*, August 2, 2003; "National Press Club Fourth Estate Award."

77 **Mary's column on Kennedy's funeral:** Mary McGrory, column, November 26, 1963.

79 **Jackie Kennedy wrote to Mary:** McGrory family papers, Jackie Kennedy letter to Mary McGrory, December 20, 1963.

79 **"He invaded Cuba":** Mary McGrory, column, November 20, 1983.

79 **He did his best:** Walter Sheridan, interview by Roberta W. Greene, June 12, 1970, John F. Kennedy Library Oral History Program.

79 **Mary coaxed Bobby:** Charles Kaiser, *1968 in America: Music, Politics, Chaos, Counterculture, and the Shaping of a Generation* (New York: Grove Press, 1988), 10; Mary McGrory Papers, container 139; Arthur Schlesinger, *Robert Kennedy and His Times* (Boston: Mariner Press, 2002), 613.

Chapter Four: Picking Up the Pieces

81 **"Miss Mary McGrory, passenger":** Mary McGrory Papers, container 5, cable of January 10, 1964.

81 **"For millions of Americans":** "L.B.J.: Naked to His Enemies," *Time*, April 19, 1976, 36.

81 **"The moment that would provide":** Mary McGrory, column, March 1, 1964.

82 **"When I sat down":** Gloria Cooper, "Hey, Hey, LBJ: How Many Journalists Did You Tape Today?" *Columbia Journalism Review*, May/June 1998, 71.

82 **Johnson also complained:** William Miller, *Fishbait: The Memoirs of the Congressional Doorkeeper* (Englewood Cliffs, NJ: Prentice-Hall, 1977), 173.

82 **Johnson warned that Mary:** Lyndon B. Johnson, conversation with Senator Mike Mansfield, August 18, 1964, Presidential Recordings Program, Miller Center, University of Virginia, http://millercenter.org/presidentialrecordings.

82 **"You learn that Stewart Alsop":** "L.B.J.: Naked to His Enemies."

83 **With a bracing chill:** Maier, *The Kennedys*, 486.

83 **"Oh," interjected John Jr.:** *Weekend All Things Considered*, National Public Radio, July 18, 1999.

83 **Despite the light moment:** Maier, *The Kennedys*, 486.

83 **But with the television lights:** Mary McGrory, column, November 21, 1965.

83 **He sobbed in response:** Mary McGrory, column, June 9, 1968.

84 **Mary knew that many angry:** Mary McGrory, column, March 17, 1964.

84 **Nothing in life made Mary:** Robin Toner, "Mary McGrory, 85, Longtime Washington Columnist, Dies," *New York Times*, April 23, 2004.

84 **The Wayfarer also offered:** Jules Witcover, interview by author, September 8, 2010.

85 **"The Senator, handsome":** Mary McGrory, column, September 20, 1964.

85 **"The Senator is not a bloodthirsty man":** Mary McGrory, column, May 27, 1964.

85 **With Goldwater stumbling:** Mary McGrory, column, June 22, 1964.

86 **She described McCarthy as:** Mary McGrory, column, December 29, 1963.

86 **The Kennedy family still fumed:** Maier, *The Kennedys*, 509.

86 **"Gene's mother was German":** Martin Nolan, "The Baffling Gene McCarthy," *Boston Globe*, December 12, 2005.

86 **"Gene really felt terrible":** Kaiser, *1968 in America*, 7–8.

87 **This led LBJ to grumble:** Michael Beschloss, *Taking Charge: The Johnson White House Tapes, 1963–1964* (New York: Simon and Schuster, 1997), 489.

87 **In Mary's words:** Mary McGrory, column, August 28, 1964.

87 **Gene McCarthy, an assiduous:** Sandbrook, *Eugene McCarthy*, 115–16.

88 **When Mary wrote:** John Skipper, *Showdown at the 1964 Democratic Convention* (Jefferson, NC: McFarland, 2012), 153; Mary McGrory, column, August 28, 1964.

88 **While he had a knack:** Gates, *Air Time*, 108–9.

88 **He then became the associate:** Marilyn Nissenson, *The Lady Upstairs: Dorothy Schiff and the New York Post* (New York: St. Martin's Press, 2007), 295–98.

88 **Mary told Blair:** Clark family papers, Mary McGrory letter to Blair Clark, August 16, 1964.

89 **"She always downplayed herself":** Anthony Lewis interview.

89 **Crowds often booed:** Mary McGrory, column, October 23, 1964.

89 **Mary called it "the most moving":** Mary McGrory, column, October 11, 1964.

90 **The next day, Johnson:** Beschloss, *Reaching for Glory*, 51.

91 **As she confided to Blair:** Clark family papers, Mary McGrory letter to Blair Clark, September 1960.

91 **Mary's friend Elizabeth Shannon:** Elizabeth Shannon interview.

92 **"It wasn't so much him":** Maureen Dowd, interview by author, February 2, 2010.

92 **"He assumed, I guess":** Phil Gailey, interview by author, April 12, 2010.

92 **Perhaps it was no coincidence:** Mary McGrory, column, January 20, 1965.

93 **Watergate co-conspirator John Ehrlichman:** Henry Mitchell, "Ehrlichman's View; His Adventures in the Flag Lapel Pin Years," *Washington Post*, February 1, 1982.

93 **As the workers jostled:** Mary McGrory, column, November 4, 1964.

93 **As Tommy Noyes recalled:** Thomas Noyes, "Washington *Star* Memories; Newsroom Nostalgia and Legends of the *Washington Star*; Celebrity Lunch Circuit," *Washington Post*, August 7, 1981.

94 **Still, the *Star* continued:** Howard Kurtz, "A *Star* Is Mourned; 10 Years after the Newspaper's Demise, Reporters Recall Its Headline Days," *Washington Post*, August 6, 1991.

94 **Indeed, Mary once bragged:** Belford, *Brilliant Bylines*, 270–78.

95 **"She held grudges":** Haynes Johnson interview.

95 **By 1966 she embraced:** Mary McGrory, column, February 6, 1966.

95 **Some readers resented Mary's:** Sanborn, "Byline Mary McGrory."

96 **Mary dubbed Vietnam:** Mary McGrory, column, November 22, 1966.

96 **By mid-1966 Mary was advocating:** Mary McGrory, column, July 31, 1966.

96 **Mary noticed that the BOBBY IN '68 signs:** McGrory, interview by Currie.

96 **For Mary, the intense:** Mary McGrory, column, October 25, 1966.

97 **After they had dined:** Nissenson, *The Lady Upstairs*, 297.

97 **Some thought that her admiration:** Belford, *Brilliant Bylines*, 270–78.

98 **"I didn't think she was a very sexual":** Ben Bradlee, interview by author, November 19, 2009.

98 **"I think for a woman":** Cokie Roberts, interview by author, January 15, 2010.

98 **When several dates between:** Clark family papers, Mary McGrory letter to Blair Clark, April 4, 1967.

98 **"Sweet Mary, we had such fun":** McGrory family correspondence.

98 **"By now you will have guessed":** Ibid.

99 **Mary and Joanna would meet:** Joanna Rostropowicz, interview by author, January 19, 2012.

99 **"Don't let your career":** Laura Gross, interview by author, June 11, 2012.

100 **That October, Mary:** McLendon and Smith, *Don't Quote Me,* 30–39.

100 **The intense and uncomfortable:** Mary McGrory Papers, containers 62 and 7, including Mary McGrory interview notes with Robert F. Kennedy, November 16, 1967; Mary McGrory, columns, November 26, 1967, and June 9, 1968;

McGrory, interview by Currie; "1968: The Year and the Campaign," C-SPAN, Washington, DC, September 7, 1993; Kaiser, *1968 in America*, 34.

103 **"The sudden, startling emergence":** Mary McGrory, column, November 17, 1967.

103 **Mary asked Seigenthaler why:** John Seigenthaler interview.

104 **Mary covered Gene McCarthy's:** Mary McGrory, column, November 19, 1967.

104 **Anything below that 29,000-vote:** Mary McGrory Papers, container 62, Mary McGrory notes from meeting with Bill Dunfey, November 21, 1967.

104 **O'Donnell had a bleak view:** Mary McGrory Papers, container 62, Mary McGrory notes from conversation with Kenneth O'Donnell, November 26, 1967.

105 **Mary's conversations led her:** Mary McGrory, interview by Dominic Sandbrook, October 17, 1999.

105 **When a reporter asked:** Martin Nolan, "The Baffling Gene McCarthy," *Boston Globe*, December 12, 2005.

105 **"His skilled and spirited":** Mary McGrory, column, December 1, 1967.

105 **Both McCarthy and Noyes:** Mary McGrory, column, October 31, 1989.

106 **Johnson said the lunch:** Haynes Johnson interview.

106 **She was particularly eager:** Blair Clark, interview by Dominic Sandbrook, April 18, 2000.

106 **Shortly before McCarthy announced:** Ibid.

106 **"Fine," McCarthy responded:** Ibid.

107 **Clark quickly learned:** Ibid.

Chapter Five: Splendid, Doomed Lives

108 **By early January 1968:** Mary McGrory, column, January 14, 1968.

109 **Mary was enraged:** Peter Edelman, interview by author, February 3, 2012.

109 **Journalist Rowland Evans remembered:** Rowland Evans, interview by Roberta W. Greene, July 30, 1970, John F. Kennedy Library Oral History Program.

110 **While Mary never relented:** Mary McGrory, column, March 6, 1968.

110 **"It was in the back":** Kaiser, *1968 in America*, 89.

110 **As Mary said, it was as if:** "1968: The Year and the Campaign."

110 **Mary helped the "kids":** Mary McGrory, column, March 12, 1968.

110 **Blair Clark argued that:** Blair Clark autobiography.

111 **In an oral history:** McGrory, interview by Currie.

111 **Mary noted that she had written:** Mary McGrory Papers, container 99.

112 **"You've seen Gene a lot":** Blair Clark, interview by Sandbrook.

112 **His speeches tended to:** Ibid.

112 **Once, in the middle:** "Unforeseen Eugene."

112 **Flying back up to:** Kaiser, *1968 in America*, 90.

112 **"You fight from a low crouch":** Mary McGrory, column, March 13, 1968.

112 **"McCarthy, one of the senate's":** Mary McGrory, column, February 5, 1968.

113 **The headline announced:** "1968: The Year and the Campaign."

113 **The news only further:** "Unforeseen Eugene."

113 **Most pollsters thought McCarthy:** William L. Dunfey, interview by Larry J. Hackman, March 23, 1972, John F. Kennedy Library Oral History Program.

113 **"I think I can get the nomination":** "1968: The Year and the Campaign."

113 **McCarthy then reiterated:** Mary McGrory, column, October 31, 1989.

114 **"Kennedy thinks that American youth":** Mary McGrory, column, March 15, 1968.

114 **Ted Sorensen, Jack Kennedy's:** Ted Sorensen, interview by author, March 8, 2010.

115 **Mary described McCarthy as:** Mary McGrory, column, March 24, 1968.

115 **"There in the savage orange":** Mary McGrory Papers, container 62.

115 **Mary's column the next day:** Mary McGrory, column, March 29, 1968.

116 **"I think it's very plausible":** Dominic Sandbrook, interview by author, November, 24, 2010.

116 **Gwen Gibson, a female reporter:** Gwen Gibson, interview by author, April 1, 2010.

116 **But Bradlee did not:** Ben Bradlee interview.

116 **Student leader David Mixner:** David Mixner, interview by author, February 2, 2012.

116 **In February 1968:** Blair Clark, interview by Sandbrook.

117 **Haynes Johnson remembered chatting:** Haynes Johnson interview.

117 **"And you'll find out":** Robert Dallek, *Flawed Giant: Lyndon Johnson and His Times, 1961–1973* (Oxford, UK: Oxford University Press, 1999), 530.

118 **On April 4, Mary:** Mary McGrory, column, April 7, 1968.

118 **"In the church":** Mary McGrory, column, April 30, 1994.

118 **"You know, he kind of brought":** Blair Clark, interview by Sandbrook.

118 **"She had the notion that Gene":** Jack Germond interview.

119 **Asked on *The Tonight Show*:** Mary McGrory Papers, container 62.

119 **As Blair Clark complained:** Blair Clark, interview by Sandbrook.

119 **As Mary lamented:** "1968: The Year and the Campaign."

119 **For Mary, the great drama:** Mary McGrory, column, May 12, 1968.

119 **"Kennedy has spent most of his time":** Mary McGrory, column, May 22, 1968.

120 **"He just didn't think McCarthy":** Peter Edelman interview.

120 **The senator said he did not:** Blair Clark autobiography.

122 **"It was the ghastly finale":** Mary McGrory, column, June 5, 1968.

122 **David Mixner, who remained:** David Mixner interview.

122 **On June 7, Mary received:** Mary McGrory Papers, container 96.

122 **"Bobby was a Celt":** Mary McGrory, column, June 9, 1968.

123 **Her parting words for Bobby:** Ibid.

123 *Time* **magazine declared:** "Second Thoughts on Bobby," *Time*, June 21, 1968, 58.

123 **"She just exploded":** John Seigenthaler interview.

123 **On the train, there was discussion:** Mary McGrory, column, June 11, 1968.

123 **"Maybe Bobby had gone too far":** Frank Mankiewicz, interview by author, October 6, 2009.

124 **"You would have been hard put":** David Mixner interview.

124 **Mary's faith in him:** Mary McGrory Papers, container 62.

124 **People might have viewed Nixon:** Mary McGrory, column, August 4, 1968.

124 **"The Republican convention was":** Mary McGrory, column, August 11, 1968.

125 **There were policeman posted:** Mary McGrory, column, August 18, 1996.

126 **Mary had described the New Hampshire primary:** Mary McGrory, interview by Sandbrook.

126 **"You would see friends":** "Recent Democratic National Conventions," C-SPAN, Washington, DC, July 12, 1992.

126 **Mary joined McCarthy:** Mary McGrory, column, August 29, 1968.

127 **Mary described the convention:** Mary McGrory, interview by Sandbrook.

127 **He was asked to:** Mary McGrory Papers, container 111.

128 **As a** *Star* **reader complained:** Mary McGrory, column, September 8, 1968.

128 **The two finished lunch:** Al Spivak interview.

128 **"Many Democrats feel remorse":** Mary McGrory, column, December 5, 1977.

128 **"They quit in the most meaningful":** "1968: The Year and the Campaign."

129 **Mary wrote that many:** Mary McGrory, column, December 1, 1968.

129 **Neither effort was particularly:** Mary McGrory, interview by Sandbrook.

129 **"Someday someone will figure out":** Mary McGrory Papers, container 8.

129 **Sister Editha sharply disapproved:** McGrory family correspondence.

129 **"You are not helping Mary":** Ibid.

130 **"I breathe better there":** Wyper, "Mary McGrory: Tiger."

130 **When Mary was asked:** Spencer, "A Reporter at Her Primitive Best."

130 **"She had a great life":** Phil Gailey interview.

Chapter Six: Nixon

131 **"Please come by my place":** Mary McGrory, column, January 26, 1969.

131 **"I had read Mary McGrory's":** Klein, *Making It Perfectly Clear*, 68–69.

131 **The** *Star* **made the most:** Mary McGrory Papers, container 139.

132 **For the first time since:** Mary McGrory, column, December 14, 1969.

132 **With her column appearing:** Lance Gay interview.

133 **He was also struck:** John Ehrlichman, *Witness to Power: The Nixon Years* (New York: Simon and Schuster, 1982), 244–45.

134 **"And for that I cut my hair?":** David Mixner, *Stranger Among Friends* (New York: Bantam Books, 1996); David Mixner interview; Ehrlichman, *Witness to Power*, 244–45.

134 **She had brought:** David Mixner interview; Mixner, *Stranger Among Friends*, 93–94.

135 **In late 1969, Mary:** McGrory, interview by Currie; Mary McGrory, columns, April 18, 1975, and December 7, 1969; Von Drehle, "Columnist Illuminated."

137 **Kissinger, "with the wise look":** Mixner, *Stranger Among Friends*, 110–11.

138 **Mary, who had downed** Henry Catto, *Ambassadors at Sea: The High and Low Adventures of a Diplomat* (Austin: University of Texas Press, 2010), 32.

138 **"Mary was very upset":** Belford, *Brilliant Bylines*, 270–78.

138 **Newby replied to her:** McGrory, interview by Currie.

138 **"I think it was always understood":** Ibid.

138 **"I love her but":** Mary McGrory Papers, container 162, commentary by Edward P. Morgan of ABC News, May 7, 1975.

138 **"Many of the letters":** Mary McGrory Papers, container 1.

139 **"All the cute guy reporters":** "National Press Club Fourth Estate Award."

139 **Gene McCarthy delivered:** Mary McGrory Papers, container 105; Mary McGrory, column, August 2, 1970.

139 **"You know all they":** Susan Brophy, interview by author, May 16, 2014.

140 **"She did have a temper":** Phil Gailey interview.

141 **If everything about Antrim:** "Nixon to Attend Stag Lunch," *Washington Star*, July 23, 1970; "President Attends Stag Luncheon," *Washington Star*, July 24, 1970; Mary McGrory Papers, container 1.

142 **"The question arises":** Mary McGrory, column, March 15, 1971.

142 **One policeman wondered:** Elizabeth Kastor, "The Grand Old Gridiron; the Club for Press and Political Play Marks Its 100th Year of Follies," *Washington Post*, March 23, 1985.

142 **The first woman:** Mary McGrory, column, March 18, 1973.

143 **In 1971, Bella Abzug:** McGrory, interview by Currie; Mary McGrory, column, July 21, 1985.

143 **Writing jobs were for men:** Braden, *She Said What?* 24–34.

143 **Stahl, who had gotten:** Lesley Stahl, *Reporting Live* (New York: Simon and Schuster, 2000), 25.

143 **"She definitely fit in":** Phil Gailey interview.

144 **"Mary was not of the women's":** Jack Germond interview.

144 **Elizabeth Shannon remembers:** Elizabeth Shannon interview.

145 **Journalist Marjorie Williams noted:** Marjorie Williams, "A Woman Who Knew Her Due," *Washington Post*, April 25, 2004.

145 **Mary would send nice handwritten:** Williams, "A Woman Who Knew."

145 **Williams also received:** Marc Fisher, "Honored to Have Known Mary McGrory," *Washington Post*, April 27, 2004.

145 **"Mentoring, in today's parlance":** Gloria Borger, "An Inspiration Named Mary," *U.S. News & World Report*, May 3, 2004; *Capital Report*, CNBC News Transcripts, April 22, 2004, 28.

145 **"Mary was very much":** Cokie Roberts interview.

146 **Yet within the halls:** Hernandez, "Nixon and the Press"; Mary McGrory Papers, container 102; Mary McGrory, columns, May 16 and September 18, 1971, and February 27, 1997; *Tim Russert*, CNBC News Transcripts, March 9, 1997; Brian McGrory, "Simply the Best," *Boston Globe*, November 11, 2003; Lance Gay interview.

147 **Ironically, Mary eventually received:** Mary McGrory Papers, container 165.

148 **"Intellectually, Nixon saw her":** Frank Mankiewicz interview.

148 **"The New Hampshire primary is":** Mary McGrory, column, February 25, 1972.

148 **Mary noted in her:** Mary McGrory, column, February 29, 1972.

149 **As the convention played out:** Mary McGrory, columns, July 10, 13, and 14, 1972.

149 **As Mary jested, McGovern:** Mary McGrory, column, August 4, 1972.

149 **When Senator Eagleton read:** Joe McGinniss, "I'll Tell You Who Is Bitter, My Aunt Hazel," *Life*, August 18, 1972, 30–31.

150 **"What a mistake you made":** "A Writer's Life."

150 **"That story happened because":** "A Writer's Life"; "National Press Club Fourth Estate Award."

150 **When the president expressed:** Mary McGrory, column, October 17, 1972.

151 **"If the same coalescence":** Mary McGrory, column, October 22, 1972.

151 **Crouse had seen Mary:** Timothy Crouse, *The Boys on the Bus* (New York: Random House, 2003), 342–46.

152 **"I hit the pits":** Mary McGrory, column, September 23, 1979.

152 **"One day you make a complete":** Linda Daily, "McGrory Pursues Politics in Iowa," *Quad-City Times*, January 11, 1980.

Chapter Seven: Enemy

154 **Mary described the scene:** Mary McGrory, column, February 26, 1973.

154 **"The president knows":** Mary McGrory, column, April 15, 1973.

154 **Mary scoffed at Nixon's:** Mary McGrory, column, April 23, 1973.

154 **One of the security guards:** McGrory, interview by Currie.

155 **With Dean's lengthy testimony:** Mary McGrory, column, April 20, 1980.

155 **Mary called Nixon:** Mary McGrory, column, June 26, 1973.

155 **The response: "Mary McGrory":** McGrory, interview by Currie.

156 **Mary was delighted:** Gale Reference Team, "Biography."

156 **As Mary walked into the restaurant:** Von Drehle, "Columnist Illuminated."

156 **"I wondered why my tax returns":** Mary McGrory Papers, container 12.

156 **When Mary learned that:** McGrory, interview by Currie.

156 **Mary insisted that Colson:** Mary McGrory, column, March 31, 1974.

157 **"The Mary McGrory named":** "National Press Club Fourth Estate Award."

158 **"That was typical of Nixon":** Haynes Johnson interview.

158 **"His bright eyes":** Mary McGrory, column, July 22, 1973.

159 **In the fall of 1973:** Sanborn, "Byline Mary McGrory."

160 **"It was torn apart":** Mary McGrory, column, July 24, 1974.

160 **Her editors had told her:** Mary McGrory, columns, September 11, 1994, and October 1, 1995.

161 **On August 8:** Mary McGrory, columns, August 6 and 8, 1974; Sanborn, "Byline Mary McGrory."

161 **As she wrote to a Nixon defender:** Mary McGrory Papers, container 11.

161 **"He was a man":** Daily, "McGrory Pursues Politics."

161 **But at the same time:** Mark Perry, "The McGrory Story," *Washington City Paper*, May 20, 1982.

161 **On August 22, 1974:** Mary McGrory Papers, container 161.

162 **"She understood something":** Gailey interview.

162 **She endured raids:** Mary McGrory, column, February 18, 1975.

162 **Mockingbirds dug up:** Mary McGrory, columns, August 29, 1982, and June 26, 1983.

162 **"For many years, the surest":** Todd Purdum, "Spring Hatches in Washington," *Vanity Fair*, April 27, 2009, http://www.vanityfair.com/online/daily/2009/04/spring-hatches-in-washington.

162 **Her frequent complaints about squirrels:** Mary McGrory, columns, June 2, 1985, May 22, 1988, August 27, 1995, July 13, 1997, August 5, 2001, and September 10, 2002; Braden, *She Said What?* 24–34; Mary McGrory Papers, container 117.

163 **"She had her scraggly":** "She Loved, She Loathed and Oh, How She Lived," *Washington Post*, May 2, 2004.

163 **Her response to what she called:** Mary McGrory, column, September 9, 1974.

163 **Ford wrote to Mary:** Mary McGrory Papers, container 7.

164 **Major change came to Washington:** Dale Russakoff, Ron Shaffer, and Ben Weiser, "The Death of the *Washington Star*: Time Inc. Had a Vision of Reviving a Great D.C. Newspaper," *Washington Post*, August 16, 1981; Dale Russakoff, Ron Shaffer, and Ben Weiser, "The Death of the *Washington Star*: Bitter Feud Erupted at Times *Star*; Bitterness on Bridge of Sinking Ship; Church and State Dissolved in Acrimony," *Washington Post*, August 17, 1981; Dale Russakoff, Ron Shaffer, and Ben Weiser, "The Death of the *Washington Star*: Downward Spiral Wouldn't Stop; Slick Promotion Failed to Shore Up Reader,

Advertiser Losses; Problem Was Getting Paper to Readers; No More Rabbits Left in the Hat," *Washington Post*, August 18, 1981; J. Y. Smith, "*Washington Star* Editor Newbold Noyes Dies," *Washington Post*, April 10, 1974; Mary McGrory Papers, container 5; David Montgomery, "The Bank of Dad; Interest Is High as Robert Allbritton Weighs the Future of the Washington Institution Acquired by His Father," *Washington Post*, June 23, 2004; Lance Gay interview; Edwin Yoder, interview by author, July 28, 2010; McGrory, interview by Currie; Mary McGrory Papers, container 111; Jack Germond interview; Edwin Yoder, *Telling Others What to Think* (Baton Rouge: Louisiana State University Press, 2004), 124–29; Carl Stepp, "The Peripatetic Jim Bellows," *American Journalism Review*, April, 2002, 65; Allan Jalon, "The 'Lion' in Winter: At 79, a Former Newspaper Editor Pitches a Quirky Story—His Own," *New York Times*, April 14, 2002; Larry Kramer and Art Harris, "*Star* Editor Bellows Quits for Calif. Job," *Washington Post*, November 16, 1977; Kurtz, "A *Star* Is Mourned"; Mary McGrory, column, July 26, 1981; Curtis Wilkie, "Opining for the Past," *Washington Post*, September 14, 2004.

166   **"Oh, she was offended!":** Jack Germond interview.

167   **In May 1975:** Mary McGrory Papers, containers 161, 162, and 163; McGrory, interview by Schmalzbauer; Russakoff, Shaffer, and Weiser, "Time Inc. Had a Vision"; Gale Reference Team, "Biography"; Von Drehle, "Columnist Illuminated"; Wyper, "Mary McGrory: Tiger"; Spencer, "A Reporter at Her Primitive Best"; McGrory, interview by Currie; Sanborn, "Byline Mary McGrory"; Dudar, "A Pulitzer Prize."

169   **Her dedication to:** Mary McGrory Papers, container 168.

172   **Mary was so delighted:** Rita Markley, interview by author, December 9, 2014.

173   **The charge had some merit:** Mary McGrory Papers, container 7.

173   **But for Mary and the *Star*:** Mary McGrory, column, July 6, 1976; Edwin Yoder interview; Montgomery, "The Bank of Dad"; McGrory, interview by Currie; Lance Gay interview; Ed Yoder, "Personal Encounters," *Washington Times*, June 9, 2004; Yoder, *Telling Others,* 128–31.

176   **"Our party after the close":** James Dickenson, "*Washington Star* Memories," *Washington Post*, August 7, 1981.

Chapter Eight: The Death of a Star

177   **In February 1977:** Mary McGrory Papers, container 55; Yoder, *Telling Others*, 132–36; Edwin Yoder interview; Stepp, "The Peripatetic Jim Bellows"; Stephen Klaidman and Douglas Watson, "*Star* Actions Spur Paper Sale Rumors," *Washington Post*, February 11, 1977; McGrory, interview by Currie; McGrory family correspondence; "Allbritton's Name Is Back on the *Washington Star* but as Chairman Now," *New York Times*, February 20, 1977.

180 **"It seemed for a brief stretch":** Edwin Yoder interview.

181 **"The matter was of earthquake proportions":** Mary McGrory Papers, container 5.

182 **"I feel quite strongly":** Mary McGrory Papers, container 110.

182 **There was certainly a case:** Mary McGrory Papers, containers 110, 2, and 1.

183 **In early August 1978:** Mary McGrory, column, May 18, 1981.

184 **Mary did not like:** McGrory, interview by Schmalzbauer.

184 **Her own belief was:** Ibid.

184 **"Mary was so wonderfully":** Anthony Lewis interview.

185 **"When I came out":** Mixner interview.

186 **Mary was not about to remain:** Belford, *Brilliant Bylines*, 270–78.

187 **"I'm totally against nuclear power":** Mary McGrory, column, April 3, 1979.

187 **Mary wrote to a reader:** Mary McGrory Papers, container 7.

188 **Mary shredded Kennedy's performance:** Mary McGrory, columns, November 5, 1979, and January 22, 1980.

188 **At one point Mary:** Elizabeth Shannon interview.

188 **Although she was disappointed:** Lance Gay interview.

188 **Mary wrote that "Reagan was":** Mary McGrory, column, March 2, 1980.

189 **She described the likely clash:** Mary McGrory, column, April 14, 1980.

189 **Mary likened the scene:** Mary McGrory, column, July 18, 1980.

189 **The Democratic convention:** Mary McGrory, column, August 13, 1980.

189 **The speech had given Kennedy:** Mary McGrory, column, August 19, 1980.

190 **"Everything is a big deal":** *Hardball with Chris Matthews*, CNBC News Transcripts, November 24, 1999.

190 **"That was no election":** Mary McGrory, column, November 7, 1980.

190 **He wrote to Mary:** McGrory family correspondence.

191 **Indeed, she took strong exception:** Fisher, "Honored to Have Known"; "National Press Club Fourth Estate Award"; Mary McGrory Papers, container 7; McGrory family correspondence; Mary McGrory, columns, March 17, 1981, February 17, 1981, and July 15, 1986; Mary McGrory Papers, container 115.

192 **On a rainy day:** Mary McGrory, column, April 5, 1981.

192 **Mary shared the sentiment:** Mary McGrory, column, April 12, 1981.

192 **At the *Star*, circulation:** Russakoff, Shaffer, and Weiser, "Downward Spiral Wouldn't Stop"; Margot Slade and Eva Hoffman, "Time and Money Are Not Enough to Save the *Star*," *New York Times*, July 26, 1981; Gregg Easterbrook, "Who Will Catch the Falling *Star*?" *Washington Monthly*, May 1, 1981, 13–26; Mary McGrory Papers, container 2; B. Drummond Ayres, "*Washington Star* Is to Shut Down after 128 years," *New York Times*, July 24, 1981; Neil Henry, "A Hell of a Loss to This Town: Employees, Readers Feel Shock, Loss and Outrage," *Washington Post*, July 24, 1981; Lynn Rosellini, "A Bitter and Angry News Staff Mourns Its Fallen *Star*," *New York Times*, July 24, 1981; Julia Malone, "Business Ups and

Downs: A Newspaper Demise, TV Gold Mine, Chrysler Outlook; In the Nation's Capital: A *Star* Falls," *Christian Science Monitor*, July 24, 1981; "Death in the Afternoon," *New York Times*, July 25, 1981; McGrory, interview by Currie; Haynes Johnson interview; "*Star* Follows Long Trend of Declining Evening Papers," *Washington Post*, July 24, 1981; Mary McGrory Papers, containers 1, 5, 19, and 139; Mary McGrory, columns, July 26, 1981, and May 24, 1992; Dowd, "A *Star* Columnist"; Dowd, *Are Men Necessary?* 130–34; Lynn Rosellini, "*Star* Employees Put Last Issue to Bed," *New York Times*, August 7, 1981; Yoder, "Personal Encounters"; Christian Williams, "Unhappy Hour; the *Star*'s Final Fling," *Washington Post*, August 8, 1981; *World News Tonight with Peter Jennings*, ABC News Transcripts, April 22, 2004; Von Drehle, "Columnist Illuminated"; Mark Feeney, "Mary McGrory, 85, Columnist with Poet's Gift, Eye for Detail," *Boston Globe*, April 23, 2004; Yoder, *Telling Others* 141–44; Stepp, "The Peripatetic Jim Bellows"; Kurtz, "A *Star* Is Mourned"; Kramer and Harris, "*Star* Editor Bellows Quits"; Montgomery, "The Bank of Dad"; "Murray Gart, Time Writer, Last *Star* Editor," Associated Press, April 5, 2004; Garrett Graff, "See Howie Run," *Washingtonian*, July 1, 2005.

Chapter Nine: Life at the *Post*

200 **Mary McGrory was a columnist:** Ben Bradlee, *A Good Life: Newspapering and Other Adventures* (New York: Simon and Schuster, 1995), 452; Ben Bradlee interview; Cokie Roberts interview; "A Writer's Life"; Mary McGrory Papers, container 164; "F.Y.I.," *Washington Post*, August 9, 1981; Don Graham interview; Mary McGrory Papers, container 9; Phil Gailey interview; Lance Gay interview; McGrory, *The Best of Mary McGrory*, xii–xviii; Gale Reference Team, "Biography"; Braden, *She Said What?* 24–34; McCarthy, "Mary McGrory, *Post* Columnist, Dies"; "National Press Club Fourth Estate Award"; Perry, "The McGrory Story"; Kurtz, "A *Star* Is Mourned"; McGrory, interview by Currie; Mary McGrory Papers, container 8; Belford, *Brilliant Bylines*, 270–78; Mary McGrory Papers, container 2; Bob Woodward, interview by Larry King, *Larry King Live*, CNN, April 23, 2004; Eric Alterman, interview by author, March 11, 2010.

203 **"We dated," Abernethy remembered:** Bob Abernethy, interview by author, April 28, 2010.

204 **"Bob Abernethy was her last":** Phil Gailey interview.

204 **Mary's transition to the *Post*:** Mary McGrory, columns, May 24, 28, and 31, 1981, October 22, 1981, October 3, 1995; Elizabeth Shannon interview; Mary McGrory Papers, container 2; "Clarification," *Washington Post*, November 18, 1982.

205 **On January 19, 1982:** Mary McGrory, columns, June 22, 1986, and January 24, 1982; *The MacNeil/Lehrer Report*, PBS, January 19, 1982; Ronald Reagan

Press Conference, Washington, DC, January 19, 1983, http://www.reagan .utexas.edu/archives/speeches/1982/11982b.htm; Federal News Service, "National Press Club Luncheon with Longtime White House Reporter Helen Thomas," Washington, DC, July 13, 2000.

206 **Mary also noted that Republicans:** Mary McGrory, columns, December 15, 1983, and July 30, 1987.

206 **She had received a letter:** Perry, "The McGrory Story"; Mary McGrory, columns, December 16, 1984, November 28, 1993, and December 19, 1995; Kim Masters, "Revering the Irreverent; the Jane Austen Society, Celebrating Her Timeless Sensibilities," *Washington Post*, October 8, 1990; Mary McGrory Papers, container 125; Mary McGrory and Linda Wertheimer, discussion about Jane Austen, Woman's National Democratic Club, Washington, DC, January 19, 2002; "Most of Jane Austen's Texts Are Being Made into Movies," *All Things Considered*, National Public Radio, November 15, 1995.

207 **"In the ugliest moment":** Mary McGrory, column, July 13, 1982.

208 **Republicans remained thirsty:** Mary McGrory, column, July 26, 1983.

208 **After presidential counselor Ed Meese:** Mary McGrory, column, March 2, 1982.

208 **Mary was delighted:** Perry, "The McGrory Story."

208 **Mary was smitten:** Mary McGrory Papers, container 65; Mary McGrory, column, March 16, 1982.

209 **Mary, in full cheerleading mode:** Mary McGrory, column, May 11, 1982.

209 **The head of the National:** Mary McGrory, column, April 8, 1982.

209 **"What he has going for him":** Mary McGrory, column, September 25, 1983.

209 **When Cuomo sat down:** Mary McGrory, column, December 11, 1983; Mary McGrory Papers, container 6.

210 **One of Mary's favorite:** James Clarity and Warren Weaver, "Briefing," *New York Times*, January 19, 1984; Cameron Barr, "Mary McGrory's Liberal Voice," *Christian Science Monitor,* March 7, 1991; Alterman, *Sound and Fury*, 151.

211 **"Mary allowed us all to shout":** Borger, "An Inspiration Named Mary."

211 **Mary could sit patiently:** "She Loved, She Loathed"; Dowd, "A *Star* Columnist"; Dowd, *Are Men Necessary?* 130–34.

212 **The September 1984 *Vanity Fair*:** Robert Yoakum, "The Op-Ed Set," *Vanity Fair*, September 1984, accessed in Mary McGrory Papers, container 163.

213 **With Walter Mondale:** Mary McGrory, column, February 19, 1984.

213 **Mary liked Mondale, but:** Mary McGrory, column, March 4, 1984.

213 **"The excitement in that hall":** "Recent Democratic National Conventions."

213 **But she also had:** Mary McGrory, column, June 28, 1984.

214 **Mary was elated by:** Mary McGrory, column, July 18, 1984.

214 **Never particularly interested:** Mary McGrory, column, July 29, 1984.

214 **In private correspondence:** Mary McGrory Papers, container 8.

214 **Mary was torn from:** Mary McGrory Papers, container 165; Mary McGrory, column, December 2, 1984.

215 **"The good news for":** Mary McGrory, column, October 4, 1984.

215 **Reagan brought down the house:** Mary McGrory, column, October 23, 1984.

215 **In 1985, Mary became:** Mary McGrory, column, March 14, 1985.

216 **She took her fellow journalists:** Christopher Reed, "Obituary: Mary McGrory: Astute Reporter of American Power and Politics," *The Guardian*, April 24, 2004.

216 **Mary became part:** Gary Lee, "Gorbachev Building a Forceful Image," *Washington Post*, September 3, 1985.

216 **Mary joined a congressional delegation:** Mary McGrory Papers, container 121; Mary McGrory, column, October 1, 1985.

216 **While Gorbachev was driving:** Mary McGrory, column, November 17, 1985.

216 **Mary had no idea:** Mary McGrory Papers, container 124.

216 **Not long after returning:** Mary McGrory Papers, container 124; Mary McGrory, column, April 15, 1986.

218 **"She has an angel's eyes":** Mary McGrory Papers, container 163.

218 **"Where has all the passion gone?":** Mary McGrory Papers, container 163.

219 **Congressman Tip O'Neill's last year:** Mary McGrory, columns, October 19, 1986, December 14, 1986, October 12, 1989, January 8, 1994, and November 2, 1989; McGrory, interview by Currie.

219 **President Reagan's grip:** Mary McGrory, columns, August 13, 1985, October 14, 1986, November 11 and 27, 1986, December 4, 1986, March 15, 1987, May 5 and 12, 1987, June 7, 9, 11, 14, and 18, 1987, July 9, 14, 16, and 23, 1987, and November 18, 1987; Mary McGrory Papers, container 7; Borger, "An Inspiration Named Mary."

220 **"She had trouble walking":** David Corn, "The Death of Mary McGrory," *The Nation*, April 23, 2004, http://www.thenation.com/blog/156084/death -mary-mcgrory.

221 **As Mary complained:** Mary McGrory, column, October 4, 1987.

222 **On the Republican side:** Mary McGrory, column, November 1, 1987.

222 **However, Mary was incensed:** Gerald Boyd, "Bush Recalls No Strong Dissent on Arms to Iran," *New York Times*, January 14, 1988; Mary McGrory, columns, January 12 and 28, 1988, February 4, 1988, and April 14, 1988; "There Never Was a Formal NSC Meeting on Iran Initiative," *Washington Post*, January 14, 1988; David Hoffman, "Bush Asserts Wider Doubts on Iran; Vice President Says He Voiced Concern on Sales in Others' Presence," *Washington Post*, January 14, 1988; Gailey, "Words That Emblazoned"; "Bush Getting in a Deeper Iran-Contra Hole," *St. Petersburg Times*, January 15, 1988; George Lardner Jr. and Walter Pincus, "Phone Note Puts Bush Claim on Iran-Contra into Dispute," *Washington Post*, August 26, 1992; "Editorial; Come Clean on Iran-contra," *Atlanta Journal and Constitution*, October 24, 1992; Lionel Barber, "TV Anchorman Who Lost His Grip Lets Bush Off the Hook," *Financial Times*, January 30, 1988.

222 **Although Mary found Bush's:** Mary McGrory, column, February 18, 1988.
222 **Dukakis's earnestness and rectitude:** Mary McGrory, column, April 21, 1988.
223 **In April 1988:** Mary McGrory, column, April 24, 1988.
223 **He wanted to charm Mary:** Mary McGrory Papers, container 76.
223 **With Bush and Dukakis:** Mary McGrory, column, July 7, 1988.
223 **His choice of the relatively:** Mary McGrory, column, July 17, 1988.
223 **Mary tartly observed:** Mary McGrory, column, August 16, 1988.
223 **Republicans appreciated Quayle's:** Mary McGrory, columns, August 18 and 19, 1988.
224 **"The campaign is unfolding":** Mary McGrory, column, September 11, 1988.
224 **A flushed Quayle tried:** Mary McGrory, column, October 9, 1988.
225 **"I lost," Dukakis admitted:** Mary McGrory, columns, December 27, 1988, and December 30, 2001.

Chapter Ten: Gentleman George

226 **Early in President George H. W. Bush's:** David Nyhan, "The Grid-Irony of a Membership Invitation," *Boston Globe*, January 11, 1989; Marianne Means, "Why We Invited Richard Nixon to Dinner," *Washington Post*, January 14, 1989; Mary McGrory, column, January 8, 1989; Jack Germond interview.
227 **Mary liked President Bush:** Mary McGrory, column, January 24, 1989.
227 **In February 1989:** Mary McGrory Papers, container 156.
227 **"I feel fine, thank you":** Mary McGrory Papers, container 8.
227 **Mary closely chronicled:** Mary McGrory, columns, March 16 and 23, 1989, June 8 and 25, 1989.
228 **Bush received a rapturous:** Mary McGrory, column, July 13, 1989.
228 **The Berlin Wall fell:** Alterman, *Sound and Fury*, 223.
228 **"Why did the leader":** Mary McGrory, column, November 14, 1989.
228 **When President Bush and Ben Bradlee:** Mary McGrory Papers, container 8; Alterman, source materials for *Sound and Fury*.
228 **The late 1980s:** Mary McGrory, columns, July 19, 1990, and April 4, 1993.
229 **Mary continued to volunteer:** Mary McGrory, columns, December 25, 1983, and March 19, 1981; Francis X. Clines, "Faith and Fatalism Mix in Security-Wary Capital," *New York Times*, December 20, 1983; Donnie Radcliffe, "Fostering a Favorite; First Lady Tots It Up," *Washington Post*, March 19, 1981; Josephine Murphy, interview by author, January 19, 2010; Mary McGrory, columns, December 22, 1991, September 22, 1994, February 9, 1997, January 8, 1998, February 21, 1999, and December 16, 1999; Mary McGrory Papers, containers 2, 9, 10.
231 **"It is increasingly plain":** Mary McGrory, column, August 16, 1990.
231 **"So far, President Bush":** Mary McGrory, column, January 22, 1991.

232 **As Bush delivered his:** Mary McGrory, column, January 31, 1991.

232 **Some 86 percent:** Mary McGrory, column, February 21, 1991.

232 **"My patriotism is often":** Mary McGrory, "Patriotism," *The Nation*, July 15, 1991, http://www.thenation.com/article/what-patriotism.

232 **General Colin Powell was:** Jacqueline Trescott, "The Postwar Media-Military Mingle," *Washington Post*, March 20, 1991; President George Bush, "Remarks at the Radio-TV Correspondents Association Dinner," March 23, 1991, http://bush41library.tamu.edu/archives/public-papers/2823; John Aloysius Farrell, "Glitz Is Masculine at Reporters' Dinner," *Boston Globe*, May 1, 1991.

232 **"I didn't have any great trouble":** Don Graham interview.

233 **Mary liked Hamilton:** McGrory, interview by Currie; Dowd, "A *Star* Columnist"; Dowd, *Are Men Necessary?* 130–34.

233 **"She became more imperious":** Haynes Johnson interview.

233 **"We became sort of partisans":** Don Graham interview.

233 **"Everybody deferred to Mary":** Tina Toll, interview by author, July 26, 2010.

233 **Yet when the editor:** Dowd, "A *Star* Columnist"; Dowd, *Are Men Necessary?* 130–34.

234 **"Hill defended herself":** Mary McGrory, columns, October 8 and 20, 1991.

235 **"Nobody knows what Cuomo":** Mary McGrory, column, November 5, 1991.

236 **"I'm not discussing anything":** Mary McGrory Papers, container 2.

236 **"Doesn't she know that":** Maralee Schwartz and Christopher B. Daly, "Politics, 'Tormented Musings,'" *Washington Post*, November 12, 1991.

236 **"I am convinced that":** Mary McGrory Papers, container 8.

236 **Just before Christmas:** Mary McGrory, column, December 26, 1991.

237 **"a tall, square-shouldered":** Mary McGrory, column, February 18, 1992.

237 **Carter told New Hampshire:** Mary McGrory, column, January 26, 1992.

237 **In mid-January:** Mary McGrory, column, January 21, 1992.

237 **"I was extremely critical":** Mary McGrory Papers, container 8.

237 **Yet Mary was quick:** Mary McGrory, column, March 17, 1992.

237 **But Mary kept her:** Mary McGrory, column, March 31, 1992.

238 **"One of my boss's constituents":** *This Week with George Stephanopoulos*, ABC News Transcripts, April 25, 2004.

238 **When Stephanopoulos's career:** Al Kamen, interview by author, January 22, 2010.

238 **"Dear George," she wrote him:** Mary McGrory Papers, container 6.

239 **It was significant praise:** Mary McGrory, column, June 7, 1992.

239 **But Mary also spotted:** Mary McGrory, column, May 7, 1992.

240 **Gore was more conservative:** Mary McGrory, column, July 12, 1992.

240 **Mary had been unsparing:** Mary McGrory, column, June 28, 1992.

240 **Perot's announcement meant:** Mary McGrory, column, July 17, 1992.

240 **"Closed to the public?":** Dowd, "A *Star* Columnist"; Dowd, *Are Men Necessary?* 130–34.

240 **By the time the delegates:** Mary McGrory, column, July 19, 1992.

241 **"The Republican assembly was not":** Mary McGrory, "A Grip on the Party: Republicans Lean to the Christian Right," *Sojourners*, November 14, 1992, 13–14.

242 **"The man who served":** Mary McGrory, column, December 22, 1992.

242 **"An ugly editorial":** Bob Woodward, "Hammered," *Washington Post*, June 20, 1999.

242 **There were leftovers available:** Mary McGrory Papers, container 6.

Chapter Eleven: The Grande Dame

243 **Arriving along with the Clinton administration:** Al Kamen, "Now the Job Quest Begins in Earnest," *Washington Post*, January 21, 1993; Conor O'Clery, "Neo-conservatives on the Defensive over Iraq," *Irish Times*, April 24, 2004; Mary McGrory Papers, container 8.

243 **In January 1993:** Mary McGrory Papers, container 6.

243 **Gearan recalled President Clinton:** Mark Gearan, interview by author, November 17, 2009.

244 **Clinton and the press corps:** President Bill Clinton, press conference, *CBS News Special Report*, CBS News Transcripts, April 23, 1993.

244 **Dubbing him "William":** Mary McGrory, column, May 20, 1993.

244 **She compared Clinton:** Mary McGrory, columns, June 1 and 17, 1993.

244 **"I think he is":** Mary McGrory Papers, container 8.

244 **She described his first year:** Mary McGrory, column, January 20, 1997.

245 **"It was a stupendous evening":** Mary McGrory Papers, container 165.

245 **"The first First Lady":** Mary McGrory, column, October 2, 1993.

245 **"He ostentatiously waved":** Mary McGrory, column, December 9, 1993.

246 **After a warm hug:** Mary McGrory, column, January 8, 1994.

246 **Mary said of O'Neill's:** Mary McGrory Papers, container 9.

246 **O'Neill's son Thomas:** Mary McGrory, column, January 11, 1994.

246 **After a moment he replied:** "Columnist with a Laser Eye and a Rapier Pen," *Irish Times*, May 1, 2004.

246 **"Adams came for 48 hours":** Mary McGrory, column, February 24, 1994.

247 **Mary repeated her question:** Conor O'Clery, "Breaking Down the Barriers," *Irish Times*, May 18, 1996.

247 **"But he paid no":** Mary McGrory, column, December 5, 1995.

248 **Mary called her old friend:** "National Press Club Fourth Estate Award."

248 **"There was no chance":** Dowd, "A *Star* Columnist"; Dowd, *Are Men Necessary?* 130–34.

248 **Mary insisted that:** "National Press Club Fourth Estate Award."

248 **Mary blurted out:** "Names & Faces," *Washington Post*, June 6, 1998.

249 **In Mary's theatrical terms:** Mary McGrory, column, April 17, 1994.

249 **Mary reasoned that:** "Whitewater and the Media," C-SPAN, Washington, DC, April 19, 1994.

249 **Reporters laughed in disbelief:** President Bill Clinton, news conference (part 2), *News*, CNN, August 3, 1994.

249 **"If the Whitewater hearings":** Mary McGrory, column, August 4, 1994.

249 **Mary—and most of America:** Mary McGrory, column, August 2, 1994.

249 **"He was pretty much":** Mary McGrory, column, November 10, 1994.

250 **"The newly designated House speaker":** Mary McGrory, column, December 10, 1994.

250 **"Nobody is saying that":** Mary McGrory, column, December 13, 1994.

250 **Clinton, on the other hand:** Mary McGrory Papers, container 9.

250 **It was not the company:** Mary McGrory Papers, container 110.

251 **In April 1995:** Mary McGrory Papers, containers 6 and 115; "Post's McGrory, Dash Win RFK Journalism Awards," *Washington Post*, April 13, 1995; Susan Bickelhaupt and Ellen O'Brien, "Friday Celebrity," *Boston Herald*, April 14, 1995; John Harris, "Among New Deal Believers, Clinton Has His Skeptics; Comparisons Intrude upon FDR Ceremony," *Washington Post*, April 13, 1995; David Dahl, "Luminaries Celebrate FDR and His Accomplishments," *St. Petersburg Times*, April 13, 1995; Celestine Sibley, "FDR in Warm Springs: 50 Years Later," *Atlanta Journal and Constitution*, April 13, 1995.

252 **"His offense is tastelessness":** Mary McGrory, column, April 27, 1995.

253 **"Now, as for the first lady":** Rush Limbaugh, May 1, 1995, *The Rush Limbaugh Show*, 11:15 A.M. broadcast.

253 **On another show, Limbaugh:** Rush Limbaugh, July 6, 1995, *The Rush Limbaugh Show*, 11:15 A.M. broadcast.

253 **"Bill Clinton has made":** Mary McGrory, column, August 15, 1995.

253 **Mary wrote, "The Republican attitude":** Mary McGrory, column, July 27, 1995.

253 **"I am kicking subjects away":** Mary McGrory Papers, container 9.

253 **"The Republicans are":** Mary McGrory Papers, container 9, McGrory prepared remarks for speech at Georgetown University's Woodstock Theological Center, October 1996.

254 **Mary was also able:** Mary McGrory, columns, December 24, 1995, and January 10, 2002; Mary McGrory Papers, container 10.

254 **Mary had told Russert:** Mary McGrory Papers, container 110.

255 **One day in 1995:** Josephine Murphy interview; Mary McGrory Papers, containers 165 and 168.

256 **In her later years:** "A Writer's Life"; Mary McGrory, columns, September 26, 1996, July 4, 1996, and July 14, 1996.

257 **"A disaster with a crowbar":** Mary McGrory, column, February 22, 1996.

257 **As one of her fellow reporters:** Mary McGrory Papers, container 139.

257 **But as the primaries:** Mary McGrory Papers, container 9.

257 **"I've decided, with the help":** Mary McGrory Papers, container 164.

258 **When he finished reading:** Brian McGrory, interview by author, April 24, 2010.

258 **He wrote to Mary:** Mary McGrory Papers, container 109.

258 **Mary stressed how important:** Dan Kennedy, "Globe Nearly Loses Mc-Grory to the Herald," *Boston Phoenix*, June 20, 1997.

258 **"I would go up":** Brian McGrory interview.

259 **"I hear about the cynicism":** *Tim Russert*, CNBC News Transcripts, March 9, 1997.

259 **"They were trying to pretend":** Ibid.

259 **When Clinton rattled off:** Mary McGrory, column, September 7, 1996.

259 **"I cannot believe that you have":** Mary McGrory Papers, container 6.

260 **"George tried to be funny":** Mary McGrory, column, October 18, 1997.

260 **In the summer of 1997:** Mary McGrory, column, July 24, 1997.

260 **Mary was aghast:** Mary McGrory, column, June 28, 1997.

261 **"Morally, he is":** Mary McGrory, column, January 22, 1998.

261 **Mary was outraged:** Mary McGrory, columns, May 3, 1997, and August 2, 1998.

261 **"We have fallen into a dim age":** Mary McGrory Papers, container 109.

261 **As author David Foster Wallace:** David Foster Wallace, "Host," *The Atlantic*, April 2005, http://www.theatlantic.com/magazine/archive/2005/04/host/303812.

262 **"The press, terrified":** Mary McGrory, column, June 18, 1998.

262 **"It was like seeing Houdini":** Mary McGrory, column, February 5, 1998.

262 **"We can't go on this way":** Mary McGrory, column, March 5, 1998.

262 **"He says they do":** Mary McGrory Papers, container 9.

262 **Mary was vacationing in Italy:** Mary McGrory, column, September 19, 1998.

263 **Others picked up on:** Joe Carroll, "Irish Media in US Come Out Swinging at Talese," *Irish Times*, October 17, 1998; Mollie Dickenson, "Letter from Washington, Aging Hormones," *Salon.com*, August 5, 1998.

263 **"Millstone? No, he's Moses":** Mary McGrory, column, November 5, 1998.

264 **"The Republicans are beyond":** Mary McGrory, column, December 17, 1998.

265 **Dowd closed by saying:** "National Press Club Fourth Estate Award."

266 **"I never wanted to be anything":** "National Press Club Fourth Estate Award"; Mary McGrory, column, July 19, 2001.

267 **Mary greeted the news:** Brian McGrory interview.

Chapter Twelve: The Last Hurrah

268 **Mary said that the constant pressure:** Dowd, "A *Star* Columnist"; Dowd, *Are Men Necessary?* 130–34.

269 **"You would see her cook":** Ted McGrory, interview by author, April 22, 2010.

269 **At the memorial service:** McGrory family correspondence. Ted McGrory interview.

269 **Mary was candid about:** Von Drehle, "Columnist Illuminated."

270 **Mary was under no:** *Tim Russert,* CNBC News Transcripts, March 9, 1997.

270 **After observing her being feted:** Mark Feeney, Mary McGrory Papers, container 164.

270 **Her friend Phil Gailey:** Toner, "Mary McGrory, 85."

270 **Marjorie Williams of the *Post*:** Williams, "A Woman Who Knew."

270 **"She would arrive":** Jack Germond interview.

271 **When asked publicly:** Belford, *Brilliant Bylines,* 270–278.

271 **"Did Mary hold on":** Bradlee interview.

272 **"We were watching the Super Bowl":** Gay Jervey, "Every Four Years, a *Star* Is Reborn," *New York Times,* January 23, 2004.

272 **"I hope they like to read":** "A Writer's Life."

272 **"Technology is eating up":** "Relationship Between Hillary Clinton and New York Media Goes Sour; How Does Media Factor in on Campaign Trail?" *Reliable Sources,* CNN, January 22, 2000; "A Writer's Life."

273 **Finally, he surrendered:** Brian McGrory interview.

273 **When George W. Bush's parents:** Mary McGrory, column, February 3, 2000.

273 **When asked about Mary's:** *Late Edition with Wolf Blitzer,* CNN, February 13, 2000.

273 **She recoiled at:** Mary McGrory Papers, container 10.

273 **She thought Al Gore:** Mary McGrory, column, February 27, 2000.

273 **"This would be utterly":** Beth Harpaz, *The Girls in the Van: A Reporter's Diary of the Campaign Trail* (New York: St. Martin's Press, 2002), 84–85.

274 **With that, Mary turned:** Corn, "The Death of Mary McGrory."

274 **When Bush selected Dick Cheney:** Mary McGrory, column, July 27, 2000.

274 **She shared the opinion:** Mary McGrory, column, August 3, 2000.

274 **As Election Day approached:** Mary McGrory, column, November 2, 2000.

275 **"Life goes on":** Mary McGrory, column, November 12, 2000.

275 **"He is all wet":** Mary McGrory, column, November 23, 2000.

275 **"The best that can be said":** Mary McGrory, column, December 14, 2000.

275 **Mary wished that Gore:** Mary McGrory, column, December 17, 2000.

275 **Not long after, Mary:** Mary McGrory Papers, container 7, McGrory note to Sandy Berger, December 28, 2000.

276 **As fellow *Post* editor:** Ken Ikenberry, interview by author, March 18, 2010.

276 **Mary's bottom line:** Mary McGrory Papers, container 110.

276 **"She wanted a plain":** Brian McGrory interview.

276 **Mary's letter to her lawyer:** Mary McGrory Papers, container 165.

277 **"It was gloomy and rainy":** Mark Gearan interview.

277 **Gearan had not played:** Fisher, "Honored to Have Known."

277 **"We just had to do":** Joel Achenbach, "Columnist Mary McGrory, Having Her Final Say," *Washington Post,* April 27, 2004.

277 **"Good," said Mary:** Gailey, "Words That Emblazoned"; "Saying Farewell to Two Best Friends," *St. Petersburg Times,* May 2, 2004.

278 **She declared that Bush:** Mary McGrory, column, September 13, 2001.

278 **"You are a shameful":** Mary McGrory Papers, container 119; Mary McGrory, column, October 28, 2001.

279 **"But maybe it could":** Mary McGrory Papers, container 119.

281 **"If anyone asks for credentials":** Mary McGrory Papers, container 164.

282 **"She was beyond thrilled":** Brian McGrory interview.

282 **After a battery:** Mary McGrory Papers, container 155.

282 **"Sheepish Democrats continue":** Mary McGrory, column, October 17, 2002.

282 **"They emitted a bleat":** Mary McGrory, column, November 10, 2002.

283 **Mary railed against:** Mary McGrory, column, January 30, 2003.

283 **Mary's column the day after:** Mary McGrory, column, February 6, 2003.

283 **Oliver North, the disgraced:** *Donahue*, MSNBC, February 6, 2003; *Hannity & Colmes*, Fox News Network, February 7, 2003.

284 **"When Mary McGrory":** Bob Woodward, *Larry King Live.*

284 **"If there was one column":** Al Kamen interview.

284 **"We have been through a great deal":** Mary McGrory, column, March 6, 2003.

285 **As she wrote to one of:** Mary McGrory Papers, container 10.

285 **"The slopes off Rock Creek":** Mary McGrory, column, March 16, 2003.

285 **It was clear that:** Tina Toll interview.

286 **"Get well damn it":** Mary McGrory Papers, containers 5 and 3.

287 **"It was one of the weirdest":** Lance Gay interview.

287 **"Mary continued to call me":** Dowd, "A *Star* Columnist"; Dowd, *Are Men Necessary?* 130–34.

287 **During one of her conversations:** McGrory, *The Best of Mary McGrory*, xii–xviii.

288 **"If you find someone":** Lee Cohn, interview by author, September 1, 2010.

288 **"We knew she would still":** Borger, "An Inspiration Named Mary"; Gloria Borger, interview by author, March 17, 2010.

288 **"She would write things":** Al Kamen interview.

288 **"One day I went":** Lee Cohn interview.

289 **Begging forgiveness for:** Brian McGrory interview.

289 **"When I think of Mary":** Mary McGrory Papers, container 164.

289 **"If the evening had any excess":** Gailey, "Words That Emblazoned"; "Mary Gloria McGrory Still Follows Her Star," *St. Petersburg Times*, November 16, 2003.

290 **"It was amazing":** Mary McGrory Papers, container 165; Sean O'Driscoll, "Washington Goes Green...If You're Irish Come Down to the White House," *Belfast Telegraph*, March 12, 2004; Nora Boustany, "On a Festive Day, Irish Speak of Spain and Peace," *Washington Post*, March 19, 2004.

290 **"When I couldn't read":** Josephine Murphy interview.

Selected Bibliography

"1968: The Year and the Campaign." C-SPAN. Washington, DC, September 7, 1993.

"A Writer's Life." Event of the Washington Independent Writers. C-SPAN. Washington, DC, November 21, 1997.

Alterman, Eric. *Sound and Fury: The Making of the Punditocracy.* Ithaca, NY: Cornell University Press, 1999.

Beatty, Jack. *The Rascal King: The Life and Times of James Michael Curley, 1874–1958.* Cambridge, MA: Da Capo Press, 2000.

Belford, Barbara. *Brilliant Bylines: A Biographical Anthology of Notable Newspaperwomen in America.* New York: Columbia University Press, 1986.

Bellows, Jim. *The Last Editor.* Kansas City, MO: McMeel, 2002.

Beschloss, Michael. *Reaching for Glory: Lyndon Johnson's Secret White House Tapes, 1964–1965.* New York: Simon and Schuster, 2002.

———. *Taking Charge: The Johnson White House Tapes, 1963–1964.* New York: Simon and Schuster, 1997.

Block, Herbert. *A Cartoonist's Life.* New York: Three Rivers Press, 1998.

Braden, Maria. *She Said What? Interviews with Women Newspaper Columnists.* Lexington, KY: University Press of Kentucky, 1993.

Bradlee, Ben. *A Good Life: Newspapering and Other Adventures.* New York: Simon and Schuster, 1995.

Brinkley, Douglas and Luke Nichter. *The Nixon Tapes: 1971–1972.* New York: Houghton Mifflin, 2014.

Butler, James. "Accuracy and Agony Make Sparkling Copy." *Editor and Publisher,* January 17, 1959.

Caro, Robert. *The Passage of Power: The Years of Lyndon Johnson, Vol. IV.* New York: Vintage, 2013.

Crouse, Timothy. *The Boys on the Bus.* New York: Random House, 2003.

Dallek, Robert. *Flawed Giant: Lyndon Johnson and His Times, 1961–1973.* Oxford, UK: Oxford University Press, 1999.

Dowd, Maureen. "A *Star* Columnist." *New York Times,* December 26, 2004.

———. *Are Men Necessary?* New York: Berkley Books, 2005.

Easterbrook, Gregg. "Who Will Catch the Falling *Star?*" *Washington Monthly,* May 1, 1981.

Ehrlichman, John. *Witness to Power: The Nixon Years.* New York: Simon and Schuster, 1982.

Filene, Catherine. *Careers for Women.* Boston: Houghton Mifflin, 1920.

Gale Reference Team. "Biography—McGrory, Mary (1918–2004)." In *Contemporary Authors.* Farmington Hills, MI: Gale, 2005.

Gates, Gary Paul. *Air Time: The Inside Story of CBS News*. Berkeley, CA: Berkeley Publishing Group, 1979.

Gelb, Arthur. *City Room*. New York: G.P. Putnam's Sons, 2003.

Germond, Jack. *Fat Man in a Middle Seat: Forty Years of Covering Politics*. New York: Random House, 2002.

Graham, Katharine. *Personal History*. New York: Vintage, 1998.

Halberstam, David. *The Powers That Be*. Champaign: University of Illinois Press, 2000.

Harpaz, Beth. *The Girls in the Van: A Reporter's Diary of the Campaign Trail*. New York: St. Martin's Press, 2002.

Harris, Fred. *Does People Do It? A Memoir*. Norman: University of Oklahoma Press, 2008.

Hoerle, Helen Christene, and Florence B. Saltzberg. *The Girl and the Job*. New York: H. Holt, 1919.

John F. Kennedy Presidential Library and Museum. Press Panel Oral History Interview with White House Correspondents George Herman, Peter Lisagor, and Mary McGrory. John F. Kennedy Oral History Collection. August 4, 1964.

Kaiser, Charles. *1968 in America: Music, Politics, Chaos, Counterculture, and the Shaping of a Generation*. New York: Grove Press, 1988.

Klein, Herbert. *Making It Perfectly Clear*. New York: Doubleday, 1980.

———. "Lady With a Needle." *Newsweek*, March 21, 1960.

Maier, Thomas. *The Kennedys: America's Emerald Kings*. New York: Basic Books, 2003.

Mary McGrory Papers, Manuscript Division, Library of Congress, Washington, DC.

McGinniss, Joe. *The Selling of the President*. New York: Simon and Schuster, 1969.

McGrory, Brian. "Simply the Best." *Boston Globe*, November 11, 2003.

McGrory, Mary. Interview by Kathleen Currie. "Women in Journalism Oral History Project." Washington Press Club Foundation, Washington, DC, August 4, 1991, and July 26, 1992.

McGrory, Mary. *The Best of Mary McGrory: A Half Century of Washington Commentary*. Edited by Phil Gailey. Kansas City, MO: McMeel, 2006.

McLendon, Winzola, and Scottie Smith. *Don't Quote Me: Washington Newswomen and the Power Society*. Boston: E.P. Dutton and Co., 1970.

Miller, William. *Fishbait: The Memoirs of the Congressional Doorkeeper*. Englewood Cliffs, NJ: Prentice-Hall, 1977.

Mixner, David. *Stranger Among Friends*. New York: Bantam Books, 1996.

"National Press Club Fourth Estate Award." C-SPAN. Washington, DC, November 5, 1998.

Newfield, Jack. *RFK: A Memoir*. Washington, DC: Nation Books, 2003.

Nissenson, Marilyn. *The Lady Upstairs: Dorothy Schiff and the New York Post*. New York: St. Martin's Press, 2007.

O'Brien, Michael. *John F. Kennedy: A Biography*. New York: St. Martin's Press, 2006.

Oshinsky, David. *A Conspiracy So Immense: The World of Joe McCarthy*. Oxford, UK: Oxford University Press, 2005.

"Queen of the Corps." *Time*, November, 10, 1958.

Presidential Recordings Program, Miller Center, University of Virginia, http://miller-center.org/presidentialrecordings.

"Recent Democratic National Conventions." C-SPAN. Washington, DC, July 12, 1992.

Reeves, Richard. *President Kennedy: Profile of Power*. New York: Simon and Schuster, 1994.

Robertson, Nan. *The Girls in the Balcony*. New York: Random House, 1992.

Russakoff, Dale, Ron Shaffer, and Ben Weiser. "The Death of the Washington *Star*: Time Inc. Had a Vision of Reviving a Great D.C. Newspaper." *Washington Post*, August 16, 1981.

———. "The Death of the Washington *Star*: Bitter Feud Erupted at Times *Star*; Bitterness on Bridge of Sinking Ship; Church and State Dissolved in Acrimony." *Washington Post*, August 17, 1981.

———. "The Death of the Washington *Star*: Downward Spiral Wouldn't Stop; Slick Promotion Failed to Shore Up Reader, Advertiser Losses; Problem Was Getting Paper to Readers; No More Rabbits Left in the Hat." *Washington Post*, August 18, 1981.

Sanborn, Sara. "Byline Mary McGrory: Choice Words for Bullies, Fatheads, and Self-Righteous Rouges." *Ms.*, May 1975.

Sandbrook, Dominic. *Eugene McCarthy and the Rise and Fall of Postwar American Liberalism*. New York: Anchor Press, 2005.

Schlesinger, Arthur. *Robert Kennedy and His Times*. Boston: Mariner Press, 2002.

Sevareid, Eric, ed. *Candidates 1960*. New York: Basic Books, 1960.

Smith, Sally Bedell. *Grace and Power: The Private World of the Kennedy White House*. New York: Random House, 2005.

Spencer, Duncan. "A Reporter at Her Primitive Best." *Washington Star*, May 6, 1975.

Stahl, Lesley. *Reporting Live*. New York: Simon and Schuster, 2000.

Thomas, Evan. *Robert Kennedy: His Life*. New York: Simon and Schuster, 2002.

Von Drehle, David. "Columnist Illuminated Half-Century of Washington." *Washington Post*, April 22, 2004.

White, Theodore H. *The Making of the President 1960*. New York: Atheneum, 1961.

Woodward, Bob, and Carl Bernstein. *All the President's Men*. New York: Simon and Schuster, 1974.

Wyper, Roberta. "Mary McGrory: Tiger in the Typewriter." *W*, October 28–November 4, 1977.

Yoakum, Robert. "The Op-Ed Set." *Vanity Fair*, September 1984.

Yoder, Edwin. *Telling Others What to Think*. Baton Rouge: Louisiana State University Press, 2004.

Young, Amelia. "Mary McGrory—Washington's Top Woman Reporter." *Information: The Catholic Church in American Life*, January 1961.

Index